Payola in the Music Industry

PAYOLA
IN THE MUSIC INDUSTRY

A History, 1880–1991

by KERRY SEGRAVE

McFarland & Company, Inc., Publishers
Jefferson, North Carolina, and London

British Library Cataloguing-in-Publication data are available

Library of Congress Cataloguing-in-Publication Data

Segrave, Kerry, 1944–
    Payola in the music business : a history, 1880–1991 / by Kerry
Segrave.
        p.   cm.
    Includes bibliographical references and index.
    ISBN 0-89950-882-0 (lib. bdg. : 50# alk. paper) ∞
    1. Music trade — United States — Corrupt practices.   I. Title.
ML 3790.S385   1994
364.1′68 — dc20   92-56691
                                                              CIP
                                                              MN

Manufactured in the United States of America

McFarland & Company, Inc., Publishers
    Box 611, Jefferson, North Carolina 28640

CONTENTS

PREFACE

This book traces the history of a common practice in the music industry, that of giving money or some other consideration to someone in the expectation that the recipient will in return give more exposure, such as extra plays on a radio station, to the payola giver's musical creation. The development of payola and its various forms in the American music business over the period 1880 to the beginning of the 1990s is covered in detail, and a small amount of material on payola in the United Kingdom from 1880 to the early 1990s is also included.

Research was conducted at the UCLA libraries and the Los Angeles Public Library System. For the early years the most important sources were the backfiles of *Variety* magazine, biographies or autobiographies of singers such as Rudy Vallee and bandleaders such as Guy Lombardo, historical material on vaudeville, and memoirs of early music publishers and song pluggers.

For the more modern period *Variety* remained a major source of material. Biographies of music industry figures and periodical indexes covering general interest magazines and music periodicals provided further valuable information.

INTRODUCTION

Today the word "payola" is sometimes used to describe bribery or corrupt practices in almost any industry, evidence perhaps of the widespread use and acceptance of the word. Yet as recently as the late 1950s the term was so unusual it was often defined and explained to readers when it turned up in articles in the mass media. Originally coined over half a century ago, payola is a term used to describe the music industry practice of paying people a sum of money to promote a particular piece of music — with the expectation that the song would be heard by a wider audience, which, it was hoped, would lead to increased sales and profits. Payola is simply another word for bribery. Its occasional use in a wider and more general sense is little more than ten or fifteen years old.

While the practice of payola has never been absent from the music business it has only sometimes been subject to widespread media coverage. At other times it has been an issue limited to industry-related media, mostly absent from the general public arena. Almost universally, payola has been condemned as an unacceptable practice, as evil and immoral. Perhaps this is so because it flies in the face of traditional American ideas that talent, hard work, merit and perseverance lead to success. Under payola, success could come merely if enough money was expended; no other inputs were required.

Curiously, payola has never been and is not now illegal. Laws passed against payola in the early 1960s didn't make the practice illegal but made only the failure to report payola illegal. Perhaps this is so because of another article of faith in the free enterprise system, which encompasses the right to promote and sell products in any fashion. Today a disk jockey can accept a sum of money from a promoter, play that person's music exclusively on his program, and be completely legitimate — providing his station knows of the arrangement and that an announcement of the arrangement is made on the show. That announcement can be something as innocuous as "music supplied by John Doe Promotions." The exact necessary format and frequency of the announcement have never been specified by regulatory officials. The few attempts at regulation in the past never got off the ground. Of course, payola continues on as always, under the table. Perhaps this is due to the negative image payola certainly has —

that of a corrupt and sleazy practice. That which is payola in the music
business is just advertising in many other industries. Supermarkets accept
new product fees from producers, giving in exchange prime display space
to new items seeking a market. Companies pay film producers a fee to have
a product prominently displayed in a film. Both of those are standard
advertising techniques, yet similar transactions in the music industry are
deemed scandalous and labeled as payola.

Recipients of payola have always been the gatekeepers: those people
who stand between the music producers and the public; those people with
the power to introduce one to the other, the power to influence sales.
Changing times and technology have meant a changing group of gatekeepers over the decades. From 1880 through the first couple of decades
of the 20th century, payola was usually money paid directly to singers and
others who used incidental music in their acts. Those passing out the
money were song pluggers buying plugs. Pluggers worked full time for
music publishers. Both parties in the transaction complained. Singers complained of being besieged by the pluggers, that their artistic integrity was
being assailed. Mostly, however, it was the publishers who complained.
According to them, singers refused to consider performing a song unless
payola was forthcoming. In addition, many of these singers were said to
take payola, then refuse to perform the songs contracted for. At one point,
a group of publishers seriously considered bringing legal action against
singers for this very reason. As radio and big bands came to dominate the
music scene during the 1920s to mid–1940s, vocalists faded away as payola
targets since they had lost so much of their gatekeeping function. Bandleaders became the prime payola recipients, with many of them charging
fees for special "arrangements" of a publisher's song before they would
play it. Bandsmen also got themselves cut in on a song as a writer, even
though they hadn't penned so much as one note or one word. This ensured
that royalties would flow their way indefinitely, provided the tune sold
well.

At the end of World War II big bands faded away. They were replaced
as the prime gatekeeper in the popular music field by the radio disk jockey.
Money and cut-ins came the jockeys' way as parts of the industry howled.
Popular music changed as rock replaced crooning. The industry split into
two camps, making war upon each other through the two major music
licensing groups, ASCAP and BMI. Representing the old, established
music business, with money invested in long-term contracts to crooners,
ASCAP tried to brand BMI as purveyors of bad music, rock, and traders
in payola. For years ASCAP refused to produce most rock music, leaving
the field wide open to BMI, which watched its revenues soar at ASCAP's
expense.

All of this led to the most famous public airing of payola in the late

1950s, which tried—largely successfully—to portray the practice as something new and dealt out only by rockers because it was the only way music as bad as rock could get on the air. In other words, rock and roll caused payola.

By the 1980s and 1990s the song pluggers were long gone, having been replaced by the independent record promoter ("indie") who freelanced by taking on contracts with a record label to promote a song for a certain fee. This was convenient for the record labels since they distanced themselves from the promotion aspects. If an indie was charged with payola, the label could claim it knew nothing about the matter. Key radio stations reported their playlists to trade publications, which published the results. Other stations not polled used these lists to determine their own playlists. Thus what was important to a record was airplay at those relatively few key stations, or not even that, for just getting on the list was sufficient. In the 1980s this became known as "paper adds," whereby an indie promoter might give money to a key station program director to list the tune on his playlist, even though it hadn't aired even once.

Over the past century payola has remained as constant as the music industry itself. Frequent cries for government investigations have sometimes been answered—usually when reasons over and above an abhorrence of payola per se have been present. In the late 1980s Al Gore, as a senator from Tennessee, expressed his outrage at the existence of payola. Concurrently his wife, Tipper, was busy campaigning against certain types of rock lyrics, culminating in the current practice of labeling offending material with a warning sticker. Despite assurances he would investigate the payola matter, Gore quickly dropped the issue permanently to pursue an unsuccessful bid for the 1988 Democratic presidential nomination. On many, many occasions over the decades someone has announced the death of payola. In every case it was premature.

While payola was present before 1909, that year's compulsory licensing feature of the copyright law revision likely led to a greater degree of payola over the years. Under compulsory licensing, once a songwriter has contracted with a publisher to produce his work any other publisher can produce it without the songwriter's permission, but the writer does, however, receive a standard royalty. This has meant in practice that several versions of a song can hit the stores around the same time. A small company may release a new tune with a new and unknown singer only to have a large, major record label release its own version of the song— perhaps with a major singer—within weeks of the small company's original, and possibly killing the former's sales. This puts greater pressure on the small company to do everything in its power to get satiation airplay everywhere it can in short order.

Music companies themselves have been ambivalent about payola.

They favor a strict ban since that might prevent new companies from entering the industry. Once payola is banned, those then in the industry favor violating the ban since it would give them an advantage over competitors. When all the companies are engaged in widespread payola they oppose it, since they feel they gain no advantage and are paying recipients so their products will not fall into the "not played at all" category. Not surprisingly, these companies have joined together sometimes to fight payola and sometimes to support the practice; at other times they have attacked each other over payola.

While payola has changed in format over time, and while it undoubtedly has waxed and waned, it has remained a part of the music business. The pressure that fueled it in 1880 remains the same today: more songs are produced than can be heard by the public. Only a small portion of those heard can be hits. Intensified by other forces, such as compulsory licensing, payola is a logical result. While most products, be they cars, beverages, or motion pictures, advertise extensively in various media, such ads are rare for songs. The popular music industry relies mainly on airplay to get its message out; a combination of entertainment and advertisement. A song that fails to get airplay can't compensate by running ads in magazines or on billboards. A song that fails to get airplay, fails.

Kerry Segrave
Fall 1993

1 Not Enough Singers to Go Around, 1880–1899

The term payola did not become part of the American vernacular until the late 1950s when a pay-for-play scandal of the time received major news coverage. The term was first coined by the trade publication *Variety* in 1938. Some think it was a combination of the words "pay" and "Victrola." More likely it evolved from adding the ending "ola" to the word "pay." Well known for its penchant for generating new and slangy vocabulary, *Variety* was quite taken at that time with the ending "ola." For example, rather than write "on the cuff" *Variety* would style it "cuffola." A successful act was a "boff click" or "boffola."[1] According to the *Oxford English Dictionary*, payola means "A secret or indirect payment or bribe to a person to use his position, influence, etc., to promote a commercial product, service, etc., spec. such a payment to a disc-jockey for 'plugging' a record or song."[2] The practice of payola existed long before the term to describe it developed. It has been a pervasive part of the music industry since the inception of that business, and it has not been limited just to the United States.

William Boosey of the English music publishing firm Boosey and Company recalled the scene in 1880s England when he wrote:

> In the old days the leading singers also received a royalty for the term of years upon all new songs introduced by them. Antoinette Sterling, for instance, would have a royalty on "the Lost Chord" of Sullivan's, "The Better Land" of Cowen's, "Darby and Joan" and "Love's Old Sweet Song" both by Molloy. There was a special reason for giving the leading singers royalties, because if a leading soprano, contralto, tenor, or baritone introduced a new song at the ballad concerts, all the smaller singers, according to their voices, would take up the ballads made popular by star artists. Then a new publisher, W. M. Hutchinson, arrived on the scene to find he couldn't get his songs promoted that way as all the leading singers were tied up with other companies. Therefore, he approached all the lesser known singers paying them so much a time for so many concerts provided they sang the numbers he was pushing.

1

Boosey related, "I was the first of the leading publishers to understand immediately that this new system was going to deal a severe blow to our old system, so, although we still paid the big singers royalties, I set to work at once subsidizing the small singers in the same way that Hutchinson did."[3]

Also in Victorian England a young composer by the name of Arthur Sullivan, before he teamed up with William Gilbert, wrote a song called "Thou'rt Passing Hence." He got it performed publicly by paying a share of the royalties to a leading baritone of the day, Charles Santley. This singer was still collecting royalties on the tune when Sullivan died.[4]

During the 1880s in the United States life was difficult for songwriters. As often as not publishers took advantage of writers' financial need by buying songs from them outright for a small, fixed amount, thus denying them any royalties, no matter how big a hit a song became. This practice would be common again in the 1950s when firms bought rock songs outright from impoverished black writers. Joseph P. Skelly (melody), George Cooper (lyricist), and Charles Pratt (arranger) sold "Is Mother Thinking of Her Boy?" to the music publishing firm M. Witmark and Sons for $15, "then a high price for a song," recalled Isidore Witmark. At the time all three men were well-known and respected songsmiths. Publisher Frank Harding said of the barroom writers who worked for him in the 1880s, "They loved to write. But it was no use giving them more than ten dollars at a time. I used to buy beautiful songs from J. P. Skelly, six for twenty-five dollars." Prior to establishing his music publishing firm in 1894, Edward B. Marks tried his hand at songwriting. However, he "decided it was nice to write hits, but more profitable to publish them."[5]

At least one songwriter got a small measure of revenge in that era. James Thornton sold the song "When You Were Sweet Sixteen" to M. Witmark and Sons outright. As demand built up, the company "lined up professional singers for a heavy campaign." In the midst of this they were sued by the publishing firm of Joseph Stern who claimed to own the song. Thornton had sold it to both companies. Witmark ascribed this behavior to Thornton being drunk.[6]

The formation of the Witmark company in 1886 came about at least partly due to a payola promise that was not kept . In 1885 Julius Witmark, singer and brother of Isidore, was promised an interest in the song "Always Take Mother's Advice" by publisher Willis Woodward if he would push it that year. At the end of the season he found it hard to collect on Woodward's promise. Witmark said, "for his share in making a song the song of a nation he was patted on the back and presented with a twenty-dollar gold piece as a bonus." So angered was he by this injustice that Isidore and his brothers established their own publishing firm the following year. At that time there were only a few publishers involved in pushing popular songs, notably Woodward and T. B. Harms. They pushed such songs, said

Isidore, "by their primitive method of introducing and plugging songs that showed any signs of life. In fact, they . . . had the call on all the public singers and minstrels as introducers of their respective numbers."[7]

As the number of music publishers increased competition intensified. In those days, of course, it was the sale of sheet music that was the sole source of income for the companies. If a song could be performed it had a chance to become a hit. If it became a hit it would sell hundreds of thousands of copies or more of sheet music. Records would not become a major factor for several more decades. In the period around 1900 a piano was almost as common in the home as the record player was destined to become. In 1930 writer Isaac Goldberg remembered the music publishing scene of 1890:

> Competition was keen. Singers were hardly safe along the Song Market, where the publishers lay in ambush for strolling performers. . . . There were, in the first days, not enough singers to go around. Every effort was made to switch the allegiance of a headliner from this firm to that. The successful actor's hotel or boarding house was unceremoniously invaded by the publisher or his representative; he had about as much privacy as, to-day, a radio-orchestra leader. Pay his board bill. Buy him a suit of clothes. . . . Promise her a glittering stone. . . . Present him with a trunk. . . . Subsidize his act with a weekly pourboire. The performer heard but one refrain: "Sing our song."[8]

By the end of that decade little had changed for "It was dog eat dog. Music publishers were hardly on speaking terms. They were out to steal singers, songmakers and songs from one another, and devil take the hindmost." Where singers had previously often paid for their music, Witmark and other publishers issued professional copies free, teaching the singers in the bargain, thus creating the modern professional department. In addition, they furnished free orchestrations to go along with vocal arrangements. "They haunted the theaters, at rehearsals and at performances, seeking to cajole the artists into singing the biggest find of the year."[9]

Even when a songwriter retained his copyright, royalties were often uncertain. One well-known publisher once employed a bookkeeper named Anderson. Every time he submitted a royalty statement to a writer the joke was, "Another one of Anderson's fairy tales." It caused many a writer to set up his own publishing company — much easier to do in the old days than it would be now.

Harry von Tilzer sold "My Old New Hampshire Home" for $15 to publisher W. C. Dunn. Publisher Shapiro and Bernstein took it over and built it into a hit. Lottie Gilson sang that company's songs all over the country. At the end of the season Shapiro and Bernstein presented her with a diamond ring worth $500. From the beginning the policy of that company was "to go after the singing stars by the wholesale. Every publisher was being compelled, if he would make his pieces known, to effect a tie-up with a prominent vocalist who, in more senses than one, would 'sell' the song to the public."[10]

Charles Harris had a big hit, "After the Ball," in the early 1890s. On March 10, 1893, Harris wrote to L. E. Behymer, treasurer of the Los Angeles Theater. His letter read, "On March 23 to 25 the Primrose & West Minstrel Co. will play your theater. A young American tenor, Evan Williams, will sing my new song 'After the Ball.' I am enclosing my check for $10.00. If Mr. Williams sings it all four times you are to give him the $10.00. If he sings it only three times you are to deduct $2.50. In fact, deduct $2.50 for each omission and return the money to me." A leading baritone of the day, J. Aldrich Libbey, was also in on this song, and others, for he freely admitted he was to blame for "inflicting such songs on the public as 'After the Ball,' 'Kiss and Let's Make Up,' and 'Two Little Girls in Blue.'" For pushing "After the Ball" Libbey said he was paid $500 and a percentage of the sales. He estimated that not more than one published song in 200 paid a large profit to the publisher.[11]

Around the middle 1890s payola was so widespread that the publishers, in self-protection, banded together and agreed to give up the practice of buying singers to promote their tunes. It didn't last for the publishers quickly began to make secret arrangements with performers. This duplicity soon came to light. When he found out what was happening, Leo Feist, of the publishing firm of the same name, exclaimed, "If it's spending money, I'll show them how to spend it. I'll give them the bellyache."[12] All the publishers reverted to their old ways. This was the first time that music publishers banded together to stop payola. It would not be the last.

Sometimes the publishers found themselves squeezed. At the same time as they were banding together some complained they were "forced" to permit songs to be reproduced in their entirety in the supplements of the Sunday papers. This meant giving away a piece of music for nothing that could retail for up to 50 cents. When newspapers wanted a song from a theatrical or musical production they would exert pressure through the theatrical producer by holding out the bait of one- and two-page spreads of press matter, complete with pictures, advertising the show in which the number was sung. Pressed by the producer the publisher would agree to publication of the song fearing that if he didn't he might not get the publishing rights for the next production. Matters got so bad that publishers united with songwriters in refusing to release their best numbers to the newspapers. Eventually, a compromise was reached whereby newspapers would get a moderately good song to reproduce, instead of the featured hits.[13]

Song arrangements, which would normally be an expense borne by the performer, were more and more frequently supplied free to performers, if they would do the song. In its earliest days Witmark paid arrangers about $1 for ten parts. A top piano arranger such as Charles Pratt could command $3 for an arrangement. Later composers worked freelance; some were salaried employees of firms. Into the 1900s arrangements went for up to $15, with David Kaplan commanding as high as $35 for his dance arrangements. In the second decade of this century arrangements cost up to $75. Shapiro and Bernstein hired Arthur Lange exclusively for $18,000 per year to do two dance arrangements per week.[14]

Men who worked for the music publishing firms promoting their songs were called song pluggers. As firms grew larger they played a more important role. All of them were employed directly by the publishers. There were no independent freelance promoters. More than just a salesman, the plugger was also usually a singer and a musician, for he had to constantly demonstrate his product by singing and playing in front of performers or the general public. So professional were some of these pluggers in their promotion work that they moved on to become vaudeville performers. Commonly, these pluggers appeared in department stores and other retail outlets that sold sheet music to give live demonstrations of their music house's offerings. Will Rossiter founded a publishing house in Chicago in 1900. He is credited as the first to sing his own songs in the retail stores.[15] Some of these men were inside pluggers who worked solely in their employers' offices. Performers were brought to the offices where publishers would try to sell them on their material. If successful, the inside plugger would teach the performer how to do the song. Many worked both inside and outside.

During the last couple of decades of the 1800s the major agencies for promoting popular songs to the public were burlesque, variety, and minstrel shows, with vaudeville becoming the major agency in the first couple of decades of the 1900s. New York City was the center of the music industry with virtually all songs first breaking there before spreading around the country. Depending on who was singing a particular number and his own booking schedule, it could literally take years for the song to make its way to, for example, Chicago, and become a hit there. Minstrel show tours were the only agency considered well enough organized and pervasive enough to give a song the chance of becoming a nationwide hit within one year or season.

A song plugger in the 1890s might hit 40 to 60 cafés, beer halls, and the like in the course of a week. Often he would give each patron a slip of paper containing the words to the chorus of the song he was pushing so that everyone could sing along with the orchestra. If a real singer happened to be in the audience the plugger would try to coax him into singing a solo chorus.[16]

Before establishing his own business, Edward Marks worked for another publisher. One of his duties was to supervise a squad of boys, in the lobby after minstrel shows, in selling "all the hits of the show." Marks urged the show's musical director to sell his music on commission in towns on the road during the tour." Naturally I knew that if the director peddled our songs, he would play them in the show," explained Edward. Marks hit many a tenderloin dive and cheap saloon in his plugging days. Before handing out the chorus slips to patrons, Marks had either treated the piano player to a couple of drinks or paid a cash donation to the leader of the small band, to ensure his song was played. On occasion he also paid a professional to sing or whistle the number in the saloon since whistling was very popular then. Hounding the backstage area of variety venues such as Tony Pastor's in order to induce entertainers to perform his songs was another of his duties. Usually he bribed the doorman to gain entry. Payola was often given not in cash to performers but in the form of free publicity. The cover of the sheet music copy might read, "Dedicated by the composer to" or the cover might carry the performer's photo and read "Popularized by." This type of publicity was considered to be very valuable at the time. Having a song played on the burlesque circuit could also be profitable for a publisher — so remunerative in fact that publishers would pay for the costuming and staging of an entire production number just to feature a single song.[17]

As a teenager Gus Edwards, later a songwriter and theatrical manager, started his career with the Witmark company for $5 a week in 1896. Over the next couple of years Edwards could be found in the audience at various variety venues such as Pastor's. When a singer was doing a Witmark tune Edwards "just joined in from the gallery without being asked." So many people did the same thing for so many publishers that a burlesque performer came up with a spoof number, "The Song in the Gallery." Others were employed by Witmark and other publishers in those places as "water boys" at the same salary. They wandered through the audience, ostensibly to serve water to patrons but really to join in the choruses of the singer performing on the stage.[18]

At the end of the 1890s New York City had hundreds and hundreds of organ grinders out working the streets. Even these people were not forgotten by the music men. Only a few people controlled all of these instruments, leasing them out to others to actually play. Publishers and organ grinder owners enjoyed what was described as a mutually beneficial arrangement.[19]

A songwriter at that time got a negotiable royalty on the sheet music sales; however, 4 percent of the net price was a common amount. The initial copies of a song were printed without a trade cover and on the cheapest, thinnest paper possible. These were professional copies for free distribution among the singing profession onstage.[20] Only a few years earlier with the adoption of the International Copyright Law of 1891 was a writer afforded international copyright protection for his work. Before that companies in a country such as England could and did reproduce American material, and vice versa, with no need to obtain license from the copyright holder or pay royalties to anyone.

2 The Payment Evil Runs Wild, 1900–1929

Several other famous music men got their start in the business at the turn of the century by being involved in song plugging. Publisher Harry von Tilzer was another who paid singers to perform his numbers on the stage. In 1902-03 he employed the teenaged Irving Berlin for $5 per week to join in "spontaneously" from the audience and sing the same song as the performer at Pastor's Music Hall. Around the same time the teenaged Jerome Kern was paid $7 a week as a song plugger by Edward Marks's jobbing plant, Lyceum. Kern was assigned to Wanamaker's department store.[1]

Al Jolson got songbooks from the Charles K. Harris firm for 1 cent each. On the road during the 1903-04 season, he sold them between acts to patrons for 10 cents to supplement his income. Profits were split evenly between Jolson and the company. What helped boost sales of these books to burlesque patrons was the free picture of Little Egypt given away with each copy. Printed on thin, wavy paper, Little Egypt appeared to do a hooch dance when a lighted match was rotated behind the picture. In one Pennsylvania town Al was arrested for tampering with the morals of the community. The fine was paid and he toured on.[2]

Getting a song inserted into a musical production could be an expensive proposition. When Lew Fields put on the hit show *The Girl Behind the Counter* in 1905 he decided that one of the bits in the show wasn't working very well. Marks suggested Fields insert his song "Glow Worm" which had then been around for a time and had achieved popular success. Fields said to Marks, "Will you pay me $1,000 to put it in the piece?" The publisher declined but promised to pay that amount if "Glow Worm" was inserted and didn't become the hit song of the show. It was inserted and did indeed become the show's hit. So in this case the publisher didn't pay, but the incident indicated the existence of the practice.[3]

One turn-of-the-century plugger was Ray Walker, who started plugging in 1898 for New York's Willis Woodward Company. "Hot Time in the Old Town Tonight" was the first song he promoted. Walker was paid $3 a week. After more than 50 years in the business Ray recalled those early years. His experiences and way of doing business were perhaps typical of many pluggers in the first couple of decades of this century. Ray moved continuously, working for one music publisher then going to another. All of the major houses were in New York City, with most located in the famous Tin Pan Alley. Among his employers Walker numbered William Randolph Hearst, who had the American Advance Company in 1904, as well as future movie moguls Carl Laemmle and William Fox, who had separate music publishing concerns which employed Ray in 1904 and 1912, respectively. Walker was skilled enough to be offered a series of vaudeville dates, along with two others, when the trio dressed in messenger boy uniforms to publicize "I'm the Messenger Boy in Demand" in 1901. Ray declined the offer but the other two accepted, so the third spot was filled with yet another plugger.

For Walker and his peers a typical working day had them plugging their material from 7 to 10 P.M. in film theaters where they sang, accompanied by slides. After 10 P.M. they hit the cafés. Many of these places, such as Maxim's, the Abbey, and the Pre-Catalan, had a rule that the pluggers couldn't sing standing up. They were allowed to promote only while seated at their table. The pluggers also often worked all day from 10 A.M. onward demonstrating the songs in the 5-and-10-cent stores, where the public made most of their sheet music purchases. With any time that was left they would hound vaudeville theaters, doggedly trying to get performers to use their material. So great a nuisance did they sometimes become that United Booking Office, a major vaudeville booking agency, issued an order in 1915 barring all music publishing house representatives from the stage area of all the Keith circuit New York and Brooklyn venues.

Working the dime stores was one way of bringing a new song directly to the attention of the public. Another way was through stunts, which abounded. While employed by the Broadway Music Corporation in 1914, Walker and fellow company plugger Will Hart promoted "At the Hoboes' Ball" at a nudist colony on Long Island. In keeping with the male audience, the men were required to perform nude. Ray did keep his shoes on in deference to the piano pedals he had to pump as they delivered the song. The pair changed the words slightly to "At the Nudists' Ball." A few years later, plugging for Thomas and Walker, Ray promoted "There'll Never Be a League of Nations Without Ireland." Walker hired a truck, had four singers on board vocalizing through megaphones while he played the piano, and joined that year's St. Patrick's Day parade on Fifth Avenue.

The Stern company promoted "Sweet Adair" in 1916 by having several pluggers whistle the tune during the lunch hour at a busy New York automat restaurant. The group was promptly ejected bodily from the premises. Mastermind of that stunt was a Stern professional manager, Wolfe Gilbert. A week later Gilbert sent a wire to Grand Central Station addressed to Miss Adair, who was supposedly arriving on an incoming train. Wolfe also phoned the station to request his fictitious woman be paged and called to the phone. As a result a telephone page and the wire messenger were both wandering around the station yelling "Miss Adair" as loudly as they could.[4]

Leo Feist secured excellent plugs for some of his songs in the *Sunday American* newspaper. The material, in reality an ad, was written up as a news story with the song title mentioned conspicuously a number of times. Some years before that the Feist house got illustrations of songs on the magazine page of the *Journal* as well as getting song titles in several of the Hearst syndicated cartoon strips, having the chorus of the lyric printed with editorial comment and getting feature articles written up by Hearst staff reporters. "For this," wrote *Variety*, "the Hearst organization received a royalty bit. Later one or two other publishers replaced Feist in this arrangement, but in time it was dropped entirely.[5]

The pluggers did more than just pass songs along to performers. Often they coached them, taught them the material, and even played for them when they broke in their new acts. In 1910 Walker's employer sent him to play piano for Sophie Tucker when she broke in her first vaudeville act. Referring to the period 1900–1917 Walker said, "Most music publishers in those days, before the Music Publishers Protective Association theoretically curbed it, paid performers to use their songs, also loaned piano players to acts."[6]

Joe "Banjo" Santly started work for Witmark in 1900 at age 13 when he dressed up as a page boy and strolled up and down the aisles of Proctor's Fifth Avenue Theater during intermission singing his employer's numbers. A few years later he was employed as a pianist and song demonstrator for publisher Helf and Hager. During the day he taught songs to vaudeville, cabaret, and burlesque singers, while at night he had to cover eight to ten nickelodeons and small movie houses with micro slides. Employed by the Irving Berlin firm in 1911, Santly's duties included night work covering movie houses, dance halls, and any place of amusement that seated 50 or more people. In the daytime he taught entertainers songs from one of Berlin's 10 piano rooms. During the war years Santly's employer was Leo Feist. One of this company's plugging stunts involved hiring big trucks upon which Feist placed one of its four sets of singers, pianists, and pianos. By day the trucks roamed Fifth Avenue, by night it was Broadway. Through megaphones they helped sell millions of dollars worth of Liberty Bonds and millions of copies of sheet music. Between sessions as a plugger, Santly was a vaudeville performer with Jack Norton, an act billed as Santly and Norton. As a plugger at Remick's in 1924 Santly coached the new singer Helen Morgan and was her accompanist on opening night at Billy Rose's club.[7]

At the turn of the century, after a song was printed a plugger would go to the largest retail music counter in New York, then the Siegel-Cooper store at Eighteenth Street and Sixth Avenue, taking with him several thousand copies of sheet music of the song being plugged and left them at the counter on consignment. A time would be arranged for each publisher's demonstrator, the plugger himself, or a hired singer. During the allotted time the demonstrator would sing the songs while selling and wrapping copies for customers. Over time the same songs might be sung 100 times or more. Generally these tunes sold for 10 cents a copy, with customers often buying five or six copies for their friends.[8]

By 1910 payola was well entrenched in vaudeville with the singer selecting the song he wanted then blithely asking the publisher for a weekly salary to sing it. Most paid the price. An account noted that,

> To hold singers, publishers advanced the "plugging scale" somewhat — gave more money, little presents; in short, agreed to almost anything the singer demanded or asked. Then, another kind of money-paying publisher appeared. He offered to make the "production" plunging heavily on gowns for "women singles," supplied "special drops," did almost everything possible. The "act-making" publisher says he doesn't pay money, but that statement is accepted doubtfully. The extraordinary outlay for an act is supposed to hold it in line for the certain publisher's songs.[9]

A few years later an unnamed man representing Wall Street interests approached the largest music publishers, proposing they form a combine to protect their interests. On paper this man's plan was said to outline how the publishers could save over $1 million in the first year of the proposed combine through the "abolishment of weekly payments to singers, orchestra leaders and others who are and have been for a long time making great inroads upon the profits of the publishing houses." Nothing came of this idea. However, at the start of 1914 the publishers held secret conferences among themselves with a view to combining to eliminate payola. One of them estimated it then cost around $20,000 to "exploit" a new song, with no guarantee it would be turned into a hit.[10]

As discussions among the publishing firms continued it was revealed that more than $250,000 had been paid out by them in the preceding theatrical season in payola to singers. Payola was rife in vaudeville and "Musical comedies, burlesque and in fact all attractions employing popular songs exact tribute one way or another." One worry was that if payola was discontinued singers would demand salary increases to match their lost incomes, with possibly ruinous consequences for vaudeville. Publishers were also angry with the singers about being double-crossed and "overexacting." In other words, entertainers demanded too much money and often didn't sing the songs as per the agreements. *Variety* reported the situation by stating,

> Years ago a singer here and there would ask a publisher for a suit of
> clothes now and then, or the loan of $50, and be tickled to have the re-
> quest granted. Now they tell the publishers what they want to sing, how
> much a week they must have for singing the song or songs, and if not
> receiving a stipulated weekly "salary," think nothing of asking for an ad-
> vance. Every singer or published song is not on a music publisher's pay-
> roll, but there is hardly a singer who doesn't receive remuneration of
> some sort, for it has grown to be the custom, so much so that publishers
> who held out against the practice to the very last had to succumb.[11]

In the summer of 1914, 15 of the major music publishers came together
to form the Music Publishers' Board of Trade. This organization contained
most of the important publishing houses. Its sole aim was the elimination
of the practice of paying singers directly or indirectly to sing their songs.
A $5,000 fine could be levied against violators. With the formation of this
organization in July payola was to have "automatically ceased" among the
Board of Trade members. One holdout was the Leo Feist company, which
didn't join the combine arguing that since it was the last firm to engage in
payola it should be the last one to stop. It was hoped that with the "end"
of payola the public would be exposed to "good" music, since all too often
songs pushed were not popular with listeners but just with the singers and
the publishers.[12]

The Board of Trade estimated it would save its members a minimum
of $400,000 in "salaries" to stage singers within the following year. About
this organization *Variety* noted, "Its sole aims are to correct the impending
evils of the music publishing trade, evils that if allowed to endure will surely
decay and kill off one of the most important of the theatrical profession's
allied trades. . . . The very publishers who make up the Board of Trade
were the originators of the system and cheerfully admit that no one but
themselves were to blame for conditions reached. The singers were solicited and innocently made victims of the plague."[13] This group was dead
within a year or two.

Booking agents were also involved in early payola. During 1915 it was
brought to the attention of Joseph M. Schenck, the general booking
manager of the Loew vaudeville circuit, that an agent booking through the
Loew circuit was obliging his acts to sing only songs of the Leo Feist
publishing house. Schenck insisted he wouldn't stand for any agent interfering with Loew acts and hoped that any act ordered by an agent to
sing the songs of a particular publisher would immediately report the matter to him. The agent told his acts that if they didn't comply with his request they would not be booked onto the Loew circuit in the future. This
agent denied the allegations but admitted he felt himself under obligation
to the Feist company for furnishing so much material to the acts he
handled.

A method of paying performers indirectly was also in place by 1915. A two man singing act played vaudeville where they earned $150 per week. In addition, both men were listed as on the professional staff of the Feist organization for which they received a second weekly salary. Major music publishing concerns all had many full-time writers on staff. It was not uncommon for performers, as in this example, to be so listed. They were writers who never had to report to the office and who never wrote anything.[14]

By this time vaudeville was in its heyday. It was a national industry that required publishers to hire large staffs of pluggers to form contacts with the acts and train them in the singing of numbers. One observer noted that "vaudeville singers of good drawing power have received anything from five to a hundred dollars per week for carrying a song in their repertoire over the Keith and Proctor, Pantages, Sullivan and Considine circuit." Many vaudeville singers were on publishers' payrolls, openly carrying the dual function of song plugger and performer. So prevalent was payola that the Monday morning check system for rehearsals was instituted in vaudeville. It came about when, one evening before the audience, the opening act did its stuff to "I Didn't Raise My Boy to Be a Soldier." Second on the bill was a dance act which did "Soldier." Later in the bill a male quartet did the same number while the headliner of the night also featured "Soldier." Because of this the check rehearsal was begun under which "first come did its stuff and no song could be repeated on the same bill to the irritation of the audience." Some of the vaudeville circuits of the time, particularly the Keith booking office, when they heard of the payola transactions demanded the acts tell them how much money they received. Once uncovered these amounts were then deducted from the vaudeville salaries of the acts thus relieving the vaudeville circuits from some of their expenses.[15]

If a singer couldn't be convinced to perform a certain song then a publisher might, instead of offering cash, fix up the performer's act for him. Some of the firms had people on their staffs who would write a good comedy introduction for the act for free — if the entertainer featured the song being pushed. The Remick firm had over half a dozen staffers including Gus Kahn, Egbert Van Alstyne, and Dick Whiting willing and able to "fix up your opening." Once that was done other Remick pluggers would show the performer how to finesse the song in question into prominent usage.[16]

At cinemas or nickelodeons the most important person was the piano player who played up to ten hours a day. Pluggers appeared at these places to put over a song before the show or between or after the movies. Illustrated songs were popular. The projectionist was in his booth and the plugger would slip him a "set of slides and two bits" which ensured the song's going on the screen at the first open interval. When slides were not used chorus slips were handed out to the audience. A busy plugger could work six to eight film houses a night in this way.[17]

So rampant was payola in 1915 and so much of a drain was it on company funds that publishers began to think about taking action. What finally pushed the publishers into a response was the realization that they were sometimes ripped off. There was an unnamed male singer who sang five songs during each of his vaudeville turns. He made deals with three separate publishers to take three songs from each house. The publishers paid him weekly in advance, believing he was singing all their numbers at every performance, but when his scheme was discovered his three checks quickly stopped coming. On the vaudeville circuit the singer earned $60 a week but he was quoted as saying he "would gladly work gratis if he could arrange to change his turn once more weekly and thus be in a position to do business with at least one more publisher." By rotating his material the singer did use all nine songs but not as often as the publishers thought they had contracted for. Music publishers were well aware of the difficulty in checking on compliance with such deals, especially since the performers were paid in advance and were often on the road touring. Some of the publishers tried to check on compliance by corresponding with various out-of-town people but it was a method that didn't work. None devised any workable system. They were forced to rely "on the honor of the singer." When this case came to light their worst fears were realized — that singers took their money but didn't perform their songs.

Two or three of the leading publishers, after consulting with their lawyers, toyed with the idea of making complaints to the federal authorities with a view to prosecuting a number of singers who were not honoring the deals. A federal prosecution was thought to be the best way to proceed since most of the negotiations were conducted by mail. Therefore, it was believed by the publishers that mail fraud, a federal offense, had taken place. Any nonfederal prosecution would involve extradition of a singer from wherever he happened to be at the time. Nothing came of this idea, but the publishers had been galvanized again into trying to do something about what Variety called the "payment evil."[18]

Profits of the publishers were squeezed particularly hard during 1916 with one report stating they were "forced" to operate under an enormous expense "contracted principally through the payment system which necessitated the expenditure of large sums to insure the popularization of the catalogue numbers. Where the million copy sales were registered, the profits were generally eclipsed by the expense incurred in the 'making.'"[19]

Therefore, it was not surprising that talk of forming another publishers' protective group would surface. However, the idea came from an unlikely source, management of a 5-and-10-cent chain. Their idea was for the publishers to band together to eliminate the existing evils of the business, the chief of which was the payment system. Under this plan each publisher in this fledgling group would post a bond guaranteeing to immediately discontinue the practice of paying professional singers to popularize their numbers. Those who violated the agreement would forfeit their bond. Whether or not a violation had occurred would be determined by a committee composed of men from outside the business. In addition, if found guilty, the 5-and-10-cent stores would stop selling products from the guilty publishers. It was thought that a single example would be enough to forever banish the payment system.

While publishers were said to be desperate to ban payola and while several of the larger ones tentatively agreed to combine under such conditions, the idea didn't come to fruition. One reason was that publishers were suspicious of each other. The Music Publishers' Board of Trade was a short-lived failure as companies ignored its provisions. A more important reason for the failure of this new plan was the publishers' distrust of the dime-store chains. Many of the music men believed the chains actually favored the payola system and that it popularized songs more quickly, creating a big demand for sheet music copies. Why, wondered industry cynics, did the stores now want to eliminate payola? These cynics in the trade worried about the possibility of the chains gaining complete control over the selling end of popular music. They feared the power to exclude all of the company's music from their stores would be wielded like a club to dominate them. Sympathetic to the publishers was another group, theatrical managers, who maintained a neutral stance.[20]

Fears of the retail outlets were not entirely groundless. Back in 1907 several major publishers, including Witmark and Leo Feist, joined forces to create American Music Stores to keep the price of sheet music up in retail stores. Department stores such as Macy's were then selling sheet music at prices lower than publishers desired. This group worked to end a price war that sometimes saw sheet music prices drop to 1 and 2 cents a copy.[21]

Very likely the dime stores were trying to create leverage against the publishers. Sheet music mostly sold for 10 cents a copy. These 10-cent stores were considering raising prices on a host of 10-cent items up to 15 cents. Naturally enough, publishers expected to share in this with a boost in their wholesale prices. Sheet music wholesaled at 6 cents a copy, down from 7 or 8 cents in the recent past. Some publishers occasionally wholesaled at 5.5 cents a copy. Despite increases in their own costs, "in addition to the heavy fee exacted by the professional singers," publishers had not attempted to increase wholesale prices. Some advocated moving to 8 cents, but the music men had made no concerted effort in that direction. If prices rose to 15 cents retail publishers envisioned as much as 10 cents wholesale.[22] Had the chain stores' proposed organization come to pass it might have been more difficult for the publishers to implement price hikes.

As suspicious of each other as they were, the squeeze on profits finally compelled the music men into a group, the Music Publishers' Protective Association (MPPA), formed in April 1917. The driving force behind formation of this group was Sime Silverman, founder of *Variety*, with the help of the United Booking Office, which booked Keith-Albee vaudeville. Representing United Booking Office, Pat Casey suggested that E. C. Mills, then an employee of the Keith organization, become the chief officer of the group. Many years later *Variety* would say the MPPA "became too much of a Chamber of Commerce proposition than a virile trade organization and while it has teeth — a $5,000 fine — there is no enforcement of the anti-payola provisos." This organization still existed in the 1970s when it was known as the National Music Publishers Association.[23]

When the MPPA was formed the music publishers estimated they paid over $200,000 a year in payola to vaudeville singers. Initially, MPPA meetings were held in the offices of the Vaudeville Managers' Protective Association (VMPA). This group was enthusiastically behind the publishers' new trade organization. Speaking at one of the MPPA formation meetings, VMPA spokesman Pat Casey explained how vaudeville acts and bills had been disrupted through the payment system. He left no doubt that in remedying vaudeville evils the VMPA looked upon payment to singers as one of the first priorities. Promising to work hand in hand with them to protect vaudeville Casey told the publishers,

> We see an act in New York. It uses songs and we think it a very good act. It secures a contract for 20, 30 or more weeks to play in V.M.P.A. vaudeville theaters. Later, after the act has its contracts, we see it again somewhere out of town, and it's not the same act because it has changed all of its songs, through one of you publishers having promised to pay it more money than some other publisher did. Then again, in any number of our theaters on Monday morning (rehearsal time), our managers find acts on the bill, sometimes three or four, each insisting it will sing the same song. They are insisting because a publisher is paying each act money to sing that song. It has got to stop.[24]

Sole reason for the formation of the MPPA was the elimination of payments to singers to popularize songs. Enforcement was by a committee of three members, none connected with the music industry. This committee, and the MPPA as a whole, had no mandate in any other aspect of the business of the music publishers. *Variety* noted that most publishers recognized payments to singers as destructive. In addition, the publication claimed singers on the take admitted they would welcome the end of the practice; however, they maintained that if someone else were paid they should be paid also.[25]

One month after its formation the MPPA had 25 publishers as members.

They were the biggest and most influential ones in the country. *Variety* maintained naively that the group "automatically abolished the so-called payment system last week," which represented a saving of several thousand dollars per week.[26]

Just three months after that problems began to surface. Word got out that singers previously paid cash to sing songs were given to understand by the publishers that this loss would be made up to the singers by listing them as cowriters on tunes, thus enabling the vocalists to collect part of the royalties due to the real writers. At its meeting in August 1917 the MPPA, reportedly, plugged this loophole in its rules and eliminated this particular practice.[27]

Toward the end of 1917 only a few song publishers who targeted vaudeville as a means of popularizing their songs were not members of the MPPA. Any that remained outside of the fold starting in 1918 would be completely frozen out of vaudeville as the VMPA had issued an order banning all of the songs from non-MPPA members and the rendition of such in houses controlled by the VMPA. So prevalent was the practice of paying singers around this time that it was reported to be "impossible" for a singer to select his own style of song. Each house tended to "work" on a certain song, with the singer ending up in an auction sale. All too often the vocalist contracted to sing material not really suited to him. With payola supposedly ended houses would work on half a dozen or more tunes at any one time. Without the pressure of being paid, each singer could then look over the market and select material best suited to his style.[28] As with all efforts before or after by the publishers to end payola, this group effort would be ineffective. None would have any impact.

According to *Variety*, the first instance of a song becoming a popular hit after appearing only on a record took place in 1919. George E. Stoddard was the writer; "Mary" was the song. Stoddard wrote it for no stage production nor was it sung upon the stage. Perhaps because of this George offered to sell his interest in the song's royalties for $100. There were no takers. After Victor put "Mary" on a record, demand was immediate with orchestras across the country sending in for orchestrations. "Mary" went on to sell 300,000 copies of sheet music, earning Stoddard about $1,500. While payola wasn't involved here it indicated the powerful effect records would have one day.[29]

In the earliest years of this century the record industry had produced any records they wanted without bothering to obtain permission from the copyright holders. During ensuing court battles the record labels argued the copyright law then in force dealt only with reproduction of "writing" and thus didn't apply to them. In 1908 the U.S. Supreme Court ruled in favor of the labels, allowing them to record and release records without payment to copyright holders. An angry set of publishers — who often owned song copyrights from outright purchases — and songwriters lobbied for changes. This resulted in the Copyright Act of 1909, which contained a compromise between the two warring factions in the music industry. The record industry agreed to a provision requiring them to recognize copyright ownership and pay the holders 2 cents for each copy of each tune they recorded. To gain this the publishers and writers agreed to a compulsory licensing provision for the act. This meant that after a song had been licensed to one label for recording, any other label could record it without obtaining permission from the copyright holder, provided they paid the 2 cents to the holder. One argument in favor of this provision was a fear the record companies claimed to have of being under the thumb of a monopoly industry, there then being no effective antitrust law in place, in the absence of compulsory licensing. Publishers and writers accepted this compromise provision as being better than nothing, but in so doing they lost one of the basic underlying principles of copyright, that of exclusivity. Under compulsory licensing the copyright holder could not refuse to license, could not set a term of time for a license, and could not set whatever rate of payment he wanted. In no other area of artistic or creative endeavor is the copyright holder placed in such a weak position as he is with regard to records.

Obviously, the 2 cent fee was meant to be a ceiling; however, if it was also meant to be a floor it failed, for labels often negotiated a license agreement to record for a lesser amount — which was legal — for say 1.5 cents per copy. In fact, most payments ranged from 1.5 to 2 cents, with many under the 2 cent level. This was usually split equally between the publisher and the songwriter. On a 2 cent royalty with two songwriters involved each got 0.5 cents while the publisher got 1 cent. If the publisher owned the copyright he got the entire 2 cents. Over the years many bills have been introduced in Congress to change or eliminate this compulsory licensing provision from the copyright law. It has always been the record label companies who have argued for keeping it as it is. Usually, they pleaded economic necessity. It was always the publishers and writers who tried to eliminate it, claiming, accurately, that its presence caused them a loss of full bargaining power.

Fifty years after this law was enacted the composers and lyricists "have not been able to obtain the maximum statutory fee under the compulsory license provision."[30] This provision made possible the practice of "covering." When a small label released a record by an unknown singer a major label could release a version with a major singer and take away the small firm's sales. This put pressure on the small firm to try to buy copyright outright so as to at least salvage something in the event of a successful cover version. They would then at least get writer's royalties. The provision allowed racism to be more prevalent, especially noticeable in the

1950s when racist radio stations refused to play, for example, Little Richard, substituting instead a white cover by Pat Boone. This provision has always meant more versions of a record on the market at any one time, each fighting for a share of the market. In turn this has put more pressure on companies to dispense payola.

While the record companies grudgingly paid, the publishing companies were still not happy. A specific song was said to have sold 200,000 disks but when the label paid its royalty to the publisher the statement listed just 25,000 sold. In 1914 the labels paid about $500,000 yearly to the publishers under the copyright legislation. Before making their payments the labels attempted to "shave" the amount due by asking publishers to give them as much as a 25 percent discount on the royalties due before tendering payment.[31]

This was one of the issues that led to the formation of the performing rights society ASCAP (American Society of Composers, Authors, and Publishers) in 1914. The story has it that the catalyst for ASCAP's formation occurred when Victor Herbert entered a café that year only to hear one of his tunes being used without his permission and without remuneration to him. In fact, other issues existed, the rip-off by record labels being one of the major ones. While publishers and songwriters were often at odds, the activities of record labels brought them together to form ASCAP.

In other areas of payola not specifically covered by MPPA rules life continued as before. One publisher was said to have paid a large sum of money to a film producer for the right to have his tunes hitched to the film. Some publishers paid several thousand dollars to secure exclusive song rights to a major film. Other firms went so far as to secure song rights to a particular film company's entire list of productions for the season. This particular vogue dated to the song "Mickey" from the 1919 film of the same name.[32]

Hostility toward song pluggers intensified in the early 1920s. The VMPA considered banning all of them from the back stages of vaudeville houses it controlled. Some of these pluggers performed double duty by representing independent booking agents — already denied backstage access. Backstage they would secure acts for the agents, splitting commissions. To cover this extra expense agents charged more than the going rate in commissions.[33]

Even when they were in the front of the house the pluggers still made themselves a nuisance. It was a custom for publishers to purchase 50 or so tickets to a matinee vaudeville performance at the prestigious Palace in New York if one or more of their songs were to be performed by acts on the bill. These tickets were distributed to pluggers who brought along friends and relations. After the song in question was performed this group would applaud loud and long, out of all proportion to the merits of the performance. More than one house might have representatives at the same performance, leading to several such outbursts. Acts singing rival songs were sometimes booed. Regular patrons and acts began to complain about these disruptions. Houses in the Keith circuit, where pluggers were then barred backstage, were ordered by the head office to curtail such noise when it reached unusual levels. More drastic but unspecified action was contemplated.

Chicago had the same problem with front-of-the-house pluggers. In that city the noisemakers tended to occupy their 50–100 seats right at the front of the auditorium. After their middle appearing act performed these people got up and left in a group. When the headliner appeared he was disconcerted and complained to the management when he faced a house packed in the back rows but empty at the front. A rule was instituted at one house requiring such parties to stay from the beginning of the performance to the end. Any breach would lead to a total ban from the theater. Some theaters considered banning song pluggers totally from their premises. Adding to the problem were some independent agents who got in backstage by pretending to be pluggers. These song promoters didn't just go after singers to use their materials but also chased even silent acts, such as jugglers, who used only incidental music.[34]

Relations between publishers and dime stores remained stormy. The major chains in the early 1920s were Woolworth, Kress, Kresge, Grant, McCrory, and Metropolitan. Woolworth buyer E. Z. Nutting issued a letter to his branches, instructing them not to push any song from certain publishers. Those singled out threatened to withdraw all their songs, which rarely got much display space. Woolworth had its own group of favored houses which received all the display space. Dime stores were rumored to sometimes bankroll publishers short of cash to reap later, unspecified benefits.[35]

While in theory the MPPA had abolished cash payments to vaudeville performers, payola continued in other areas with the group's added rule against cut-ins being ignored totally. Some publishing concerns were voluntarily giving up part of the royalty due them as an inducement to companies making records and piano rolls to use their tunes on the flip side of hits. One large music roll company rejected a music house's offer to record one of their songs for free. In the case of piano rolls, retailing then for $1 to $1.25, a publisher might be willing to take a royalty of 8 or 9 cents instead of the usual 10 or 12 cents. Under this scheme a record company would pay a royalty of 1.5 cents for the hit and flip sides instead of the normal 2 cents. Records retailed for 85 cents to $1.[36]

The Vitaphone, an early version of today's music video, became popular in the middle of the 1920s. A singing team was offered $300 by a publisher to introduce its material on the musical screen while a bandsman signed up to do the same for a $1,000 advance "royalty" plus 50 percent of the profits. The MPPA turned a blind eye to any and all such examples of royalty payola.[37]

One group was understandably upset by all the royalty cut-ins — the songwriters. Near the end of 1920 they formed a union to try to gain some leverage. Spearheading the organization were writers Geoffrey O'Hara and Raymond Hubbell. The group had a number of grievances it wished to have addressed, but the main problem — and reason for forming the union — was the cutting in on authorship of nonwriting performers who took away part of the royalties from the true writers. When a song was accepted by a publishing house, that company's professional manager told the writer that he had to have the song rewritten. Thus, said a contemporary report, "an unwanted collaborator, it is claimed by many writers, is forced on the authorship of a song, frequently not even changing a comma, but having his name on the cover as coauthor and sharing royalties under the same arrangement." A drastic example was one songwriter who received a royalty of 0.1 cent per copy instead of the usual 0.5 cent because four others, who contributed nothing, were cut in. Publishing houses were upset by the formation of this new union, fearing "disagreeable complications." The MPPA responded by pledging to deal fairly with the songwriters and to set up a joint complaint committee with this new group.[38]

Cut-ins became so common that performers found themselves to be the "authors" of too much material. A prominent orchestra leader complained he had overdone it. Many of these songs turned out to be lemons but as his name was on them he felt compelled to push them to try to make them hits. Trying to promote all those lemons forced him to turn down superior material. When a performer was cut in on songs which didn't turn into reasonably selling vehicles he faced the possibility of no more future cut-ins from that house.[39]

When Al Jolson opened his new show *Bambo* in 1923 it did well but lacked a hit song. He got Bud DeSylva and Joe Meyer to write one which, when introduced into the show, proved to be a smash. Jolson took the two writers with him to Remick Music publishers. Al wanted $5,000 cash with a cut of the royalties for himself as the price to place the song with Remick. The publisher said he didn't have that much cash on hand, offering instead $1,000 cash and two notes for $2,000 each. According to Meyer, Jolson responded by saying "fuck you," taking his party to Witmark where that firm handed over $5,000 in cash and published "California Here I Come" with Jolson listed as cowriter.[40]

While most performers listed as cowriters contributed nothing, a few did write songs. Whether the performer was a vaudevillian or an orchestra leader, publishers went out of their way to be fair in determining whether or not to publish such material. It was obvious to the publishers that such a performer would go out of his way to plug his own composition.[41]

Radio became involved with payola almost from its inception. In 1925 radio bands were periodically receiving $25 considerations from publishers for their "cooperation" in playing certain songs over the air. A pair of radio vocalists known as the Radio Franks were heard weekly on New York's WMCA, sponsored by a furniture company. The Franks were said to be known as "weekly recipients of a stipulated sum" from the Irving Berlin house for singing Berlin songs only. Station WPCH barred them from their outlet. Stations WEAF and WJX, both in New York, also banned the Franks from their airwaves for the same reason. In fact, these latter two stations barred any singer if they knew the vocalist performed the songs of just one publishing house. However, this ban didn't apply if a publishing house purchased half an hour or an hour of airtime in which only its songs were sung. In that case WEAF would pick entertainers it knew not to be on the take to sing the songs. The public would not be aware of the sponsorship of the time period since no commercials for the house would be aired. Vocalist "Whispering" Jack Smith was also considered an "out-and-out Berlin house man." On the radio Smith sang nothing but Berlin tunes. It was the same in vaudeville, where a program note claimed his repertoire consisted of 50 numbers with requests welcomed. In fact, Smith knew only a handful of numbers, all from the Berlin house.[42]

Singer Harry Richman, recalling the 1920s, said, "In the old days a well known singer could get anything or anybody he wanted, for whatever purpose, through a music publishing house — all the houses were so anxious for the singers to play their songs." During the early 1920s when Richman made the rounds of publishers to see if they had tunes he could do at appearances he hoped to make, one told him to try to get on radio. If he did the plugger promised him $5 every day he sang a song on the air. "Five dollars a day for plugging a song? I'll plug the living hell out of your songs," said Harry. Shortly after, Richman did land a radio spot but was offered no salary as they told him they had no money but that it would be good experience and exposure for the singer. Harry was about to decline when he remembered what the plugger had told him. After ascertaining he could sing whatever songs he wanted to Harry accepted the spot on New York radio. Thinking about the $5 per day offer Richman decided he would plug that publisher's songs incessantly and that was exactly what he did. Each time he was on the air he sang several numbers, "always the songs that publishers had given me five dollars a day for plugging on the air."[43]

Even in the early days the songwriting field was controlled by a small group of writers. D. M. Winkler, an executive with the publisher DeSylva, Brown, and Henderson, estimated that at the end of the 1920s about 80 percent of the really popular hits "have been written by a group of writers that do not total over fifteen." This closed system would be one reason leading to the later formation of BMI (Broadcast Music Incorporated — a rival performing rights society) to oppose ASCAP and the former's ascendancy with rock when ASCAP was slow to handle the new music. The resultant jealousy would lead ASCAP to attack AMI and rock in the late 1950s under the guise of cleaning out payola.[44]

Over in England payola was just as much a part of the scene as it was in North America. Britain's equivalent to the MPPA was the Associated Publishers of Popular Music who in 1922, passed a resolution binding themselves not to pay artists to sing their songs. That they weren't very serious can be seen from the fact that no penalty of any kind was established for violation of this rule. The MPPA had set a fine of $5,000 for violators who paid singers, although it was never enforced. American vaudeville management stood squarely behind the MPPA in publicly demanding an end to payola. In England the vaudeville circuits were opposed to the end of payments, strongly condemning "free" songs which they feared might be killed by inferior artists at a minor hall, dragging down their own business. To them payola meant exclusivity with performances only by superior artists. In England at that time the average price paid by publishers to singers to boost songs ran from £3 to £6 per week. The latter price went only to headliners. The highest fee was reported to have been £1,000 per year paid by the Lawrence Wright Publishing Company to vocalist Talbot O'Farrell to sing their songs exclusively, principally those written by Horatio Nichols. An average American singer could expect to add $20–$30 weekly to his income in those days from payola sources, more than received by all but English headliners. An American vaudeville single act could get as high as $100 a week or more to plug a specific publisher's catalog. Some singers were "sold" exclusively to one music house by the year.[45]

During the 1920s vaudeville began its descent as the public's time, attention, and money were diverted to newer forms of mass entertainment such as film and radio. The preeminent position the vaudeville singer enjoyed as the major recipient of payola declined along with the medium. Bandsmen such as orchestra leaders or other prominent members of the aggregation began to receive greater and greater shares of payola. Publishers, recognizing the changing structure of the entertainment business, sometimes made sure their numbers appealed specifically to the bandsmen, as opposed to the general public, through fine scoring and arrangement. Failing this they might not be performed. If bands liked a number, no matter what shortcomings the material had, they could make the tune popular with the public.[46]

Besides the payment of cash to the bandsmen, the music men employed emissaries to dispense cigars, fees for "special arrangements," and other petty graft to have certain songs played by the bandsmen. These orchestra members reciprocated by urging the music men to publish their own compositions, most of which were duds. One example was orchestra leader Isham Jones. At his peak he started "writing" numbers with his name on them which all went on to popular success. One year later Jones suffered reverses, almost disbanded his orchestra, and was away from the public spotlight for a couple of years. During that period his name didn't appear on any song. Also mentioned as "songwriters" were vocalist Ruth Etting and Mrs. Jesse Crawford, wife of the organist at New York's Paramount Theater. Film house emcees and organists came in for a share of the payola pot. Legitimate songwriter Gus Kahn rose to the defense of Jones claiming that he, Kahn, wrote the lyrics for many of the numbers on which Jones's name appeared and that Jones did indeed write the melodies for the numbers. In Chicago an unnamed band had been playing film houses for 12 years. The leader had never been known to write a song in his life. Then some publishing houses began to use him as a plug medium. Becoming more popular with the public a year later, he was put on the payroll of various firms. Five of the songs he "wrote" were published over the course of one year. One music house paid him $10,000 a year as one of its staff writers while a second house paid him $7,500.[47]

When bandleader Paul Ash came to New York he was offered cash payments by a number of music publishing houses, including at least four members of the MPPA. Rejecting them all Ash claimed he didn't want to jeopardize his standing through the choice of dubious material. However, it was considered a fact that Ash had "some sort of an arrangement" with Irving Berlin. Music publisher Ager, Yellen and Bornstein had several songs on the market with Ash listed as coauthor. Bornstein was the brother of Saul H. Bornstein, general manager of the Berlin house.[48]

Radio bands were not forgotten as some of them aggressively hustled publishers to be cut in on royalties. Several of these bands, and one in particular, were reported to be making life difficult for publishers by playing only numbers from houses which gave them financial consideration in the form of royalty cut-ins. One musician was a very busy man. In addition to the time spent as a musician he managed to hold down three full-time jobs as a staff writer for three different houses, drawing yearly salaries of $10,000, $7,500, and $10,000 from the three. A fourth publisher used this musician's name, by consent, to promote stock sales.[49]

When Guy Lombardo was starting out with his band, the Royal Canadians, in the early 1920s he recalled a then over-the-hill husband and wife song and dance team still on the vaudeville tour. Taking up most of their small dressing room was a gigantic Hartman trunk. Years earlier it had been a gift to the couple from the music publisher. "Hartman trunks were given by the music houses to all noteworthy vaudeville acts in exchange for exclusively using the firms' songs," said Guy. "The trunks were worth as much as $400. . . . In later days the Hartman trunk song routine would have been called Payola. In the days we were learning about vaudeville and Tin Pan Alley, it was simply another way songs got around the country." According to Lombardo, one bandleader on the take was Abe Lyman who "probably would have become a giant in the band business if he had just played his fine music and stopped looking for those pieces of songs. He had his name on almost as many titles as Irving Berlin, but the difference was that few of them became hits. Phil Spitalny was another."[50]

As the Lombardo band worked their way up the ladder to stardom they passed through cities such as Cleveland and Chicago before finally hitting New York. Along the way they were besieged by pluggers who offered Guy a percentage of "hundreds of songs" over the years. Lombardo insisted he was never on the take and that he steadfastly refused to take a penny although he often plugged the tune anyway. Said Guy, "We were offered some pretty good deals. Some of these guys would give you their wife if you wanted her." During 1927 and 1928 in Chicago publishers by the dozens approached his band. Guy's brother Carmen was the group's composer and vocalist. Guy explained that most of the approaches were from publishers who "simply wanted to put his name on songs — lyrics and music — that had already been written. The idea was that if Carmen Lombardo was mentioned as a cowriter in the title the song was bound to take off. There was the added hope that most of the big bands, including Guy Lombardo, would play it. Carm was being offered a piece of each song for what his name meant to it. It was not an uncommon practice, but my brother would have none of it." Carmen was said to be incensed by the idea, a stance with which Guy heartily agreed. Yet Carmen was willing to listen to the always increasing number of unknown aspiring writers who came to him with lyrics and expected him to produce melodies.[51]

Still in Chicago a year later, Guy related that he was still hounded, that publishers through their pluggers

> were always coming up with theater tickets, admissions to sporting events, suits of clothing, and other gifts designed to make a band leader look with favor on their product. The biggest inducement was to offer the leader a "piece" of a song. And many leaders allowed themselves to be romanced that way. They felt they could make money by promoting a song in which they had been given a financial interest. . . . I knew that if I was pressured into mediocre material, the band would suffer. If we played anything but first-class numbers, our band's reputation could not remain first-class.

Once when a group of song pluggers had assembled Lombardo told them, "First let me put you straight on one thing. Neither my brothers nor I want tickets, to anything. We don't want free booze and we don't want dates with chorus girls. Most important, we don't want to be cut in on any song. We welcome your material, but don't bring it into rehearsals. We'll look over everything you submit and we'll accept whatever we think is for us."[52]

Yet Guy and his brothers became very intimate friends, as Lombardo admitted, with the top song producers and pluggers of the day, such as Irving Berlin and Walter Donaldson. In addition, as one writer noted, "To handle songs written especially for them, the Lombardos started their own publishing firm. 'Heartaches' and 'Whistling in the Dark' were two of their first hits.[53] Owning your own publishing firm was simply a more sophisticated form of payola than straight cash or a royalty cut-in as coauthor." When an unknown songwriter was "convinced" to place his song with a bandleader's publishing firm the leader got half the royalties and even more if he "convinced" the author to cut in the leader as coauthor. If was often the only way an aspiring writer had of breaking into the system. This type of payola came under its closest public scrutiny at the end of the 1950s when Dick Clark was revealed as the owner of numerous publishing firms among other things.

Writing in 1930 of the late 1920s, Rudy Vallee said, "Although it is considered something to be whispered about, something almost unethical, I must mention the practice of being 'cut in on' a song. There is really no reason why the subject should be kept in the dark as though it were a disgrace, because the orchestra leader who is responsible for making a song into a hit has a right to expect a recompense." Rudy mentioned the "unreasonable jealousy" of other leaders who thought they should be cut in on songs, forgetting that their support for a song might mean little or nothing to the public. Vallee claimed he'd never asked for a cut-in and that he did refuse to be cut in on songs in which he had no faith. He knew of orchestra leaders who were "in on as many as twenty songs."[54]

In 1928 Vallee said the Leo Feist publishing firm "put me on a weekly retainer as they had previously done with Guy Lombardo, feeling that our good will and intuition in picking hits was worth it. Further, they agreed to publish any song I would suggest to them." One of the songs closely associated with the singer is "I'm Just a Vagabond Lover," which Rudy first heard in 1927 when it was performed in Indianapolis by local bandleader Charlie Davis. When asked for the words and music Davis refused to give them to the singer. A year later twin girls sang the tune to Vallee, who wrote down the words and music and began to broadcast it from the Heigh-Ho Club. Next he placed the song with Feist for publication, who took it, said Vallee, "merely out of politeness; still the entire verse was written by me (melody and lyric) as well as about forty percent of the changes in the chorus." The tune sold 700,000 copies of sheet music plus a large number of RCA Victor disks. When he was sued for copyright violation by the actual writer, Rudy lost in court. However, even after deducting the cost of his lawyer Vallee figured he still cleared $4,000–$5,000 from the song.[55]

Another song closely associated with Rudy is the University of Maine "Stein Song." It began as a march called "Opie," written in 1902 by Emil Fenstad and published by Carl Fischer, a house specializing in band music. In 1904 two University of Maine students decided to enter a contest to find a Maine song. Adelbert Sprague extracted a portion of the melody of "Opie," and roommate Lincoln Colcord supplied the lyrics. The university adopted the song. Rudy introduced it on radio in the fall of 1930. It was obviously destined to become a hit, based on initial reaction. Fischer approached Vallee to ask what sort of royalty arrangement he should make. Vallee replied, "I've made legitimate changes in the song which I believe add to its commercial value — I think one-third of the composer-author royalties would be agreeable." In the previous two pages of discussing this song in his second book of memoirs, Vallee said nothing about making changes in the song. It also contradicted his statement in his first book of memoirs whereby he said he never asked for a cut-in. The "Stein Song" became a hit but as it turned out Colcord received no royalties as he had no contract with Fischer. The publisher asked Colcord what he wanted to settle the matter, then said Rudy, "Before I could stop him he settled for $3,000," although royalties were very much higher.[56]

Writing in the 1960s about 1929, Vallee said he was besieged by leading publishers in New York to introduce their songs. Admitting they offered him cut-ins, or payola, Rudy reiterated that he felt payola was justified.

> After all, without an entertainer "working" on it, a song very often languishes unheard on the shelf. Throughout the years Jolson, Cantor, Harry Richman, Sophie Tucker, Gene Austin and Vallee have been "cut in" on songs they have made into hits. I would venture to say that Gene Austin who has written many songs made more money from royalties on numbers he had little or no part in composing than he did from his Victor recording payments. His "cut" from some of the tunes he "made" in '25 and '26 when he was the Number One crooner must have run to hundreds of thousands of dollars.[57]

Vallee mentioned a few songs he turned down a cut-in on such as "Body and Soul," but none by name for which he did receive a cut-in.

Throughout the 1920s the MPPA remained ineffective at stopping payola. It didn't really try. The group held a special meeting in March 1920 to repledge themselves to the task. It was necessary as so many members accused each other of engaging in payola. Less than two years later representatives from all MPPA members met again for the same purpose.

As before the meeting was necessary as publishers continued to point fingers at one another.[58]

Things got worse for the MPPA as the decade progressed. While all the major popular music houses were members, outsiders openly paid entertainers. The publisher Harms never joined since it was viewed as a noncommercial house rather than a popular song publisher. Harms quickly stepped into the popular field after formation of the MPPA, successfully putting out a number of popular hits. They did this, said a report, "solely through the medium of singers paid by the firm." Protection afforded by the MPPA didn't exist against such raiders. Several prominent members of the MPPA, such as M. Witmark and Sons and the Edward Marks company, resigned in disgust from the MPPA. It cost money to run the organization and increasingly members saw no benefit accruing. Comparisons were made between the MPPA and ASCAP to which most MPPA members also belonged. Class A publishers paid $125 yearly in dues to ASCAP. In return they received around $5,000 yearly in royalties collected by the group from all users of music under copyright. Publishers in the same class paid $125 monthly in dues to the MPPA for no financial return. In addition extra monthly assessments were regularly made by MPPA to meet various additional expenses. That never happened with ASCAP.

Members of the MPPA were convinced the group didn't deliver on its reason for being — to end payola — as each member believed all the others were flaunting the rules. When radio became an important medium the MPPA rules against using payola were introduced there also. However, the Irving Berlin company, an MPPA member, got around this prohibition by setting up a subsidiary company, not an MPPA member, that openly used payola for radio plugging. It was at that time the Berlin's subsidiary made "Red Hot Mamma" a big hit.

As secretary of the board, E. C. Mills was the man with the power in the MPPA. Relations between him and *Variety* hit rock bottom during the 1920s. Mills attacked the publisher Robbins-Engel for some of its practices. When *Variety* defended the company in print Mills became angered at some things that made it into print that he thought should have remained secret. *Variety* was incensed at what they perceived as Mills's attempt to muzzle the press. Calling Mills a man with "the superior air of a czar" *Variety* slammed his high salary of $20,000 a year in 1927.

According to this publication, Saul H. Bornstein of the Berlin house was on intimate, friendly relations with an MPPA executive. While the man was not named, the reference was clearly to Mills whom they said Bornstein had frequently entertained as his guest. If *Variety* had really believed the naive statements they made a year or so after the formation of the MPPA that payola was stopped, they bitterly scorned the group a decade later. *Variety* wrote, "the M.P.P.A. has since degenerated into a farce. Its executive has repeatedly blinded itself to many discrepancies. He had shut his eyes completely to the cutting-in song angle, acts, and particularly orchestra leaders, being taken care of under the subterfuge of royalties through cuts on his songs." Getting a share of royalties didn't guarantee a performer a specific amount of money as straight cash payments did. The way around this was for a house to pay an "advance royalty" or "drawing account" of a fixed sum, say $50 weekly. This way a performer was protected in case he was cut in on a lemon which produced only minuscule royalty amounts. Mills was attacked by *Variety* as little better than a megalomaniac looking after only himself, having some sort of unethical relationship with at least one publisher while seeking the glory of a Landis in baseball or a Hays in motion pictures. The latter two men had been appointed in their respective fields to clean up after various scandals had blackened both areas in the public mind. Both Landis and Hays enjoyed high public profiles and such media attention. Mills did not. *Variety* also accused Mills — again not referring to him by name — as "bulling himself into the A.S.C.A.P. at an additional $10,000 a year salary."[59]

By the end of the decade payola had changed only in the sense that it was more costly for the music publishers. A system that had once cost them $10 or $15 a week slipped to a vaudeville singer in direct cash payments became one that cost them $1,000 or more a year in payments usually charged to royalty accounts with bandsmen being the major recipients. As one account noted at the time, "It's the same old racket having its clothes made by a more expensive tailor."[60]

3 Everybody Is More or Less Disgusted, 1930–1939

By the beginning of the 1930s the focus of payola had shifted to radio. Song pluggers who had devoted attention to burlesque, beer gardens, music hall singers, illustrated slide singers, vaudeville performers, Broadway revues, film theater presentations and public ballrooms now considered everything to be of minor importance in comparison to the value of a song plug over the radio. The Hollywood picture plug had ceased to be important after a brief life.

Reporting on this change of focus *Variety* wrote,

> Radio now is the thought by day and the dream by night of all song pluggers. They still conspire, they still employ the insinuations of flattery, cases of Scotch, cigars, and floral offerings to bandsmen's wives, but all of the old tricks, gimmicks and ethical sleight-of-hand are now performed with but one purpose, to get on the air. No bandsman without a radio outlet is worth bothering about. A mere vaudeville act is received with modulated enthusiasm. Every plug that used to be important is now treated simply as an incidental by-product, helping to keep the ball rolling after radio has started it, and continues to give it the real shove.... Nothing remains but the radio.[1]

While vocalists had a role on radio they took a backseat to the orchestra and its leader. Far and away they were the most important and influential performers of music on the air. Naturally, it was they who were besieged by the music house pluggers. When an informal poll was taken among song publishers in 1933 to find the musicians with the most value as song publicizers, a total of 17 names was generated—13 band leaders and 4 singers. This list had nothing to do with payola. It was a list of performers felt to have enough popularity and power to move a pop song into the hit category, if it could be moved there at all. The bandsmen were Guy Lombardo, Wayne King, Ben Bernie, Vincent Lopez, Phil Harris, Rudy Vallee, George Olsen, Fred Waring, Paul Whiteman, Abe Lyman, Jack Denny, Ted Weems, and the Casa Loma orchestra. Vocalists mentioned were Morton Downey, Ruth Etting, Kate Smith, and Bing Crosby.

Notable by their absence were Eddie Cantor, Al Jolson, and Harry Richman, whom publishers then regarded as not commercial enough.[2]

Interaction between pluggers and bandleaders pictured the latter as hounded and harassed. While conducting his band in a dance number at a club, the nervous and jumpy leader would furtively search the room with his eyes for a place to which he could retire for a few moments rest when the number was over. Sometimes he enlisted the help of the headwaiter who was instructed to group all song pluggers in the same part of the room. It was easy enough to spot a plugger in the crowd, for, said one account, "Their pockets bulge with orchestrations and contracts for cut-ins. There is a predatory look in their eyes."[3]

When the leader arrived at the radio broadcast station he was pounced on by a throng of pluggers lurking in the anterooms. As he left the station the same gang of pluggers remained lying in wait for the bandsman. There was no escaping them. Once he had bearded a bandleader the plugger's usual spiel was to tell the leader what a great band he had, that only he could really make a song, that his arrangements were special, that the number was a real find, that the plugger was doing him a personal favor by giving the leader first chance at the song, and so on. All in all it was said to be "an exciting chase. The leaders have a great time creating such a fuss. They are followed about like picture stars and no one objects to being flattered."[4]

A major radio bandleader could easily have 10 to 14 pluggers dogging him. An orchestra might perform live in the radio station studio or be broadcast from a "remote" — live as they played at a club. Song pluggers were disliked virtually everywhere they appeared. In 1930 *Variety* noted, "Each week they are barred from more hotels, restaurants and clubs because they congest the doorways and are non-paying guests." At the Ambassador Hotel in Los Angeles pluggers were barred from the Coconut Grove nightclub for cluttering it up and making a general nuisance of themselves by hassling orchestra leaders. The pluggers got together and asked Grove management where bands would get new material if it wasn't for the pluggers doing their job. This tactic worked, for the men were reinstated. Also in Los Angeles pluggers were barred from the sheet music counters in department stores. According to the stores, people who came to the counters after the ban went into effect were doing so in order to buy instead of to be entertained. In addition, the number of girls who hung around while the pluggers worked was reported to be greatly diminished. New York's Hotel Pierre barred pluggers from talking with bandleaders in the dining room. So intense was the feeling here that one of the hotel staff insulted a guest he mistook for a plugger.[5]

When the Lombardo band hit New York early in the 1930s the publishers overwhelmed Carmen with flattery, sending him their best lyricists and urging him to write them a couple of songs. Carmen obliged, said Guy, and "almost every week I would be confronted by a new Carmen Lombardo song presented to me by a plugger." Guy claimed he told them there was no guarantee he would play it just because his brother wrote it — that quality would rule. Playing at New York's Roosevelt Hotel, Lombardo said there would be as many as 50 pluggers in the audience waiting to besiege him. Insisting he was not on the take, Guy said of his socializing with the pluggers, "But when we got together socially with our wives or for a ride on the boat, they all understood that we weren't there to discuss songs."[6]

"You're Driving Me Crazy" became a hit song in 1932 after Guy introduced it. Later that year Lombardo heard that a young bandleader whom Guy had helped get a start, Jack Denny, had complained that he wasn't offered that song first. Shortly after that when Guy, Denny, and others were seated together at a table in a club, Guy mentioned as a gag to one of the party, "See all those song pluggers sitting there in back of the room. They're a pain in the neck. If they didn't cut me in on their songs, I'd throw them the hell out of here." Denny's ears perked up. He announced he would try the same technique. Reported Guy, "He opened at Waldorf with great fanfare and unlimited prospects. But the Waldorf patrons were no longer hearing the beautiful arrangements of tried and true songs that Denny had brought them from the Mont Royal in Montreal. Now they were getting the junk Jack Denny was accepting from every song plugger who promised him a percentage of the profits. He didn't finish out the summer." Lombardo acknowledged that what he did was cruel.[7]

Radio networks often found themselves drawn into the payola fray when they felt it detracted from their program quality with constant repetition. In 1931 CBS declared that a song could be played no more than twice in one evening. All orchestra leaders broadcasting from remotes were ordered by NBC to submit programs in advance as a means of preventing repetition. This network insisted it had no set limit but pluggers agreed that twice per evening had been informally established as the limit since any song penciled in more often was always cut back to two plays. Al Short was in charge of the musical end of NBC's program department in 1933. That year he sent a letter to all the publishers informing them he was opposed to having song pluggers running in and out of NBC. Henceforth, any plugger wanting to talk to somebody on NBC property would have to write to Short requesting an appointment with an NBC act. Apparently this measure failed to work, for two years later NBC's program department issued an order barring all publishers' contact men — as song pluggers came to be called in the 1930s — from the network's studios, offices, and foyers. This came after NBC pages reported several contact men used devious methods of approaching their quarries. One page chased a plugger across the entire length of the RCA building up and down several staircases. Publishers were reaching out to tap new sources to receive payola even at this early stage. Some music men contacted radio advertising agencies whose personnel became friendly with the former and were entertained frequently by them "in the usual manner." These ad men were telling their bands what songs to play whenever they could get away with it. They would make up lists of songs they wanted plugged over the air, ordering the leaders to play them. Many reportedly complied, although "name" bands tended to refuse to be dictated to. Commonly, clauses in their contracts expressly stipulated there was to be no interference in the selection of their musical numbers.[8] Presumably it meant that if payola was to change hands it should be their hands doing the receiving, not those of advertising men.

Even though they were an integral part of the payola system the pluggers occasionally took a stance against the practice. A group of 21 gathered in Chicago in 1930 to denounce specifically "theatrical nights" as practiced by a number of prominent bands in expensive nightclubs with important radio outlets. On their off evenings the bandsmen would invite a roomful of friends, relations, and so on for a night of expensive wining and dining. Also invited were pluggers, who invariably got stuck with the entire bill for the night. Initially, the pluggers' meeting was to be in secret; however, at the last minute they invited a newsman to report on it. Later they got cold feet and asked him not to write a story — to no avail. They worried they would antagonize some VIP and bring down the wrath of their employer if they appeared to be too prominently involved in complaining. These radio bands, felt the pluggers, were making excessive demands. All pluggers denied the suggestion that these excessive demands were hitting them in their wallets once in a while to some extent. None wished to take a public stance of being associated with the hint that their bosses might be niggardly. Speaking of the general position of the plugger, one of them at the meeting said, "Never has there been a body of men so insulted and abused while being exploited as song pluggers. They are belittled, kept out, kicked out, stalled, applesauced and treated with general disrespect." One reason the contact men sometimes publicly opposed payola was self-preservation. They feared that if the situation got even more rampant it might reach a stage where a publisher would just mail out a copy of his newest song along with a check to a musician. Song pluggers would no longer be needed. During this period the pluggers' theme song was said to be, "Sound, Sound, the Clarion; / Fill the Zenith; / To all the Music World Proclaim; / One Radio Band, Say What You Like; / Is Worth a Dozen Without a Mike."[9]

Fears such as these weren't entirely groundless. One unnamed publisher did indeed keep no professional department. He spread around $25 weekly payments for a period of four to six weeks to a selected group of bandleaders who played the number a guaranteed number of times per week. However, this publisher was an exception as virtually all maintained a full-time plugging staff. Orchestra leaders just arriving on the scene were quickly initiated into the payola scene as they were besieged by the houses with all sorts of irregular propositions. One did not have to accept payola but one could not escape being propositioned. Orchestra leaders sometimes took jobs playing in hotels at low rates, even below union scale. The economic desirability of such a job was nil but the various side deals turned it into a lucrative position. Anytime publishers in New York got together to denounce payola and/or establish rules against it branch office personnel in places such as Los Angeles and Chicago doubled over in cynical laughter as they ridiculed the inability of the powers that be to even keep faith with themselves.[10] Almost everyone it seemed was openly on the take during the 1930s, especially during the first half of that period.

One current popular number had three bandleaders cut in on the royalties. One leader was in New York, one in Chicago, and the other in San Francisco. In this case the writer didn't lose any money as the publisher reportedly made up the loss to him. If that was true it was a rare exception. An unnamed orchestra leader was said to be on the payrolls of five different publishing houses with a sixth one paying his room rent while a seventh picked up the insurance payments on his musical instruments. So open was the practice that when a bandleader was cut in on five songs in one week he bragged that he had established a record. Some publishers paid the leader a flat $10 each time one of their songs was played on a radio broadcast. Estimates were that a few leaders were cut in on as many as 20 to 40 songs concurrently, at different times. On occasion the cut-in was a percentage of gross sales, as opposed to a royalty cut-in. Even in these cases the publisher reportedly forced the writer "to stand a portion."[11]

Making special arrangements of tunes was a favorite form of payola with orchestra leaders. In normal, nonpayola circumstances the orchestra leader would be expected to bear the costs of making any special arrangements the bandsman felt was necessary to suit his aggregation. However, what happened when a plugger wanted a band to play a number was that the leader would insist that a special arrangement had to be done by one of his people for which the plugger would have to pay—from $20 up. While this method paid less than a royalty cut-in, it could be milked for a considerable benefit to the leader. The leader charging a plugger $35 for a special arrangement would pocket the entire amount. The band's arranger, paid a salary by the leader, would receive his normal weekly pay. Only if the leader got an extra large arranging fee, say $50, and felt generous was it likely he would slip his arranger an extra sum, say $5. Doing five arrangements each week could bring the bandleader an extra $175.

When complaints about royalty cut-ins grew too loud, as they did from time to time, deals in arrangements tended to increase. Leaders aggressively sought out such deals, telling publishers the practice was okay as everybody was doing it. All promised such deals would be kept strictly secret. Bands playing clubs and roadhouses but lacking radio exposure propositioned publishers to buy them air time. In return these bands promised to play whatever songs the publisher desired.[12]

Bandsmen observed with a jaundiced eye the machinations of publishers as they publicly inveighed against payola corruption, yet couldn't trust themselves as they double-crossed each other before the ink was dry on their pledges to abolish the payment system. The leaders felt there was nothing wrong in cashing in all they could while they could. Their attitude was, "What would you do in my place?" In addition, there was the matter of professional jealousy. When one leader felt another one was on the take, whether he was or was not, that first leader felt he should be collecting also. One leader was openly razzed by his peers for not collecting as much as he could. This was due, thought the razzers, to the fact that "he doesn't even know enough to get in out of the rain." Another leader employed at a prominent New York hotel told one publisher that if it wasn't for all his cut-in deals his orchestra couldn't continue working at the hotel as his own salary wouldn't make it worthwhile. He was dependent on his cut-ins, he said, and had to play them whether they were good, bad, or indifferent.[13]

Variety reported late in 1931 that orchestra leader Paul Whiteman was one of the bandsmen who steadily refused cut-ins or other deals, yet only six months earlier the same publication had said, "Whiteman for a time was 'in' on a few songs but Whiteman during his Feist affiliations at $10,000 a year as a song 'advisor' got more out of the net that way." Other musicians were mentioned by *Variety* in 1931 as on the take:

> Vallee is supposed to state frankly he doesn't feature anything he's not in on and he is supposed to be the No. 1 money-getter on song royalties with his earnings placed at $75,000 from that source. Lombardo, Lopez, Bernie, et al., also figure prominently.... Morton Downey is 'in' on songs too.... On the cut-in box score, they say last year Vallee was in on 75 songs; Lombardo, 65; Lopez 40, and so on down the line. Each will squawk, of course, about the cut-in quotations, but the industry knows which are the take boys and there are very few who won't.[14]

Those on the take rationalized they were performing a vital service by featuring a song. By exploiting the number they afforded "the original writer some value for minimizing the original creator's royalty income," said one account. If offered a cut-in on a song by a publisher featuring an established writer such as Gus Kahn the answer by the bandsmen was almost always an immediate yes. If the writer was a lesser light the leader would usually prefer to try the number out first before becoming its "co-author."

Observers started to worry that payola would destroy the industry. Even orchestra leaders themselves feared publishers would go broke with all the cut-ins and deals they handed out — one publisher cut in nine leaders on one song — leaving little left for a profit. Some feared songwriters, who lost so much of their income to cut-in deals, would write less, bringing about a severe shortage of song material.[15] At the same time others feared losses would cause them to write more — thus flooding the market.

Called into question by *Variety* were the long-term benefits to orchestra leaders from being on the take. They thought it would lead to a band getting a reputation for being stale, of repeating a number many times in one evening. The radio public would notice quickly this undue emphasis, with the result the guilty orchestra would get snubbed or at least not achieve real popularity. Cited was a bandsman in Chicago who left that town having failed to make his mark despite his "excellent organization." He was blunt in his demands for money and notorious for accepting favors from publishers. Constantly dishing up the same material for dances and on the radio doomed this individual. As estimated by this publication, an average bandleader tied up with publishers on 10 to 15 pop songs could expect them to bring in around $2,000 a year from royalty cut-ins on an average batch of tunes. A hit song would mean more than $2,000 for a bandleader. Was this enough money to jeopardize a long-term future? *Variety* added, "The band leaders, although they deny it, are receiving hundreds of letters with adverse criticism from their radio public. They take them to task regarding repetition of certain songs on their broadcasts." Likely this was wishful thinking on the part of *Variety*. Desirous of seeing payola brought to a halt, they knew the recipients were unlikely to shun free money waved in their face. They also knew that any and all talk of the publishers getting together to end payola was "bologna. They loved it."[16] What else could end it? Much later, when Top 40 radio format arrived, it was wildly successful using the formula of taking a small number of songs and playing them over and over and over. It's highly unlikely radio listeners of the 1930s complained of any song repetition.

Publishers often took the attitude that it was cheaper to bribe a band than approach it on a straight song plugging basis. It took time, effort, and staff salaries to convince a musician of the merits of a song, whereas by offering some sort of payola the same results could be obtained in an instant. One publishing house estimated spending $20,000 a year on payola yet felt it saved time and money and accomplished more than it could "without the lubrication." Stage acts, while no longer very important, still got some payola. Unusual services were offered by houses. One house had a "partner" who was a professional boxer. In exchange for a song plug bandsmen got free boxing lessons. Rudy Vallee was said to be learning to handle his dukes that way.[17]

Publishers poured so much money into getting their songs played on the radio that they paid more to radio than radio paid publishers for the right to use the songs. In 1930 a Class A publisher received about $45,000 from ASCAP as its share of royalties from the various institutions which used its songs, by licensing them through ASCAP. About $20,000 of that sum came from radio. Most publishers paid much more than that to radio to have their songs plugged by payola. One house spent almost $100,000 for the year on radio payola. "It is the same with the majority of the other publishers also, whether Class A, or less, each in proportion to their earnings from the A.S.C.A.P.," said one report. Both NBC and CBS were reported to be aware of the situation but would not act against it unless ASCAP requested their aid. Publishers were willing to spend these amounts because a hit song — through sheet music sales — could generate as much or more for a publisher as he would receive from ASCAP for a year.[18] Radio was the major medium for developing a hit. Publishers were willing to pay for it.

One publisher of medium size worked on the economic equation that it was worth it to spend $1,000 to start a song off on the road to becoming a hit and another $1,000 to keep it popular once it showed hit possibilities. Big houses threatened to go into payola on a large scale to drive the small ones out of business, claiming it was they who engaged in a greater proportion of payola. Small houses argued that big houses used their size in various ways to try to drive them out of business, forcing them to revert to payola. Individual houses claimed they had to engage in the practice because everybody else was doing it. If they abstained they would go out of business. Orchestra leaders took the money because they had to; they made so little from playing clubs and so on. Besides, if they didn't take the money offered somebody else would. Why shouldn't it be the orchestra leaders? Publishers had to get their material exposed or they were dead. Bandsmen wouldn't play the songs unless they got a deal; they had to do it. Songwriters were cheated out of their royalties, which meant they would soon stop writing many songs, so causing the business to die for want of material. Or they would write all the more songs to regain lost income, causing the business to die from too much, inferior material. The situation was a mess. *Variety* wrote, "subsidization evil for song plugs has reached the stage where everybody is more or less disgusted."[19] Yet it continued to flourish. The industry badly needed a savior of some sort; however, all they got in the 1930s was the fumbling, stumbling MPPA and later that decade the government.

One of the first actions taken by the MPPA, in June 1930, was to alter the fine structure to be levied against members who paid orchestra leaders for special arrangements. A rule forbidding such deals was then on the MPPA's books. What had been a $1,500 fine for an offense was reduced to $250 for a first offense. Aware that the practice was flagrant but lacking evidence or even complaints to proceed on, the MPPA hoped the fine reduction would make it easier to proceed against violators. They reasoned that $1,500 was too heavy a fine, dissuading publishers from making a complaint against a fellow member.[20]

Less than one year later the MPPA held a meeting to deal with the problem. Complaints had been received about payola for special arrangements as well as various other forms of payola. Unanimity of opinion was expressed at the meeting that trade abuses were more prevalent than at any other time and that some effective means of eliminating these unfair practices had to be found. Head of the MPPA was then executive chairman John G. Paine, who had replaced Mills. Later Paine became the general manager of ASCAP. Paine said, "I don't know yet just what procedure to follow in dealing with this situation but I am determined to find out and when I do something will happen." Unable or unwilling to deal with violations by MPPA members, the group turned to publishers, mostly small ones who weren't members. If those companies refused to join the MPPA in its antipayola pledge the group might be forced, it said, to appeal to the government's Federal Trade Commission (FTC) against those companies on the grounds of unfair competition. The MPPA was also considering an appeal to the New York Better Business Bureau.[21]

So desperate were publishers that they held a meeting themselves — independent of any of their organizations — to consider the matter. One of their number claimed to be so financially pressed from continuous payola outlays that he was forced to reduce his nightly air plug payment to bandsmen from $25 to $5 or $10. Music companies considered cut-ins by orchestra leaders "the worst poison ever interjected into the music trades." Every industry in America was then suffering financially from the effects of the Depression. The music industry was not alone in feeling the pinch from falling revenues, but the publishers did not lay the blame on the Depression but on the evils of payola. Making himself and his peers seem blameless victims, one publisher claimed, "the orchestra leaders were trying to run the music business; that they agree and arrange between themselves how and what to do or play."[22]

When ASCAP held its annual meeting in 1931 it took the unusual step of unanimously passing a resolution to "curb the evil of cut-ins." Any publisher found guilty of splitting royalties with orchestra leaders — or other entertainers — or engaging in any other payola practices such as direct payments for plugs and so on would be placed in ASCAP's nonparticipating class for six months. This meant the publisher would receive no dividends from ASCAP for that time. Since a Class A publisher received about $40,000 annually, the fine was effectively $20,000. This action was urged on ASCAP by the publisher segment because, it said, payola had grown to such a degree that "with the current depressed situation in the music trades, the cut-in practice threatens to disastrously overwhelm the music business, if not abruptly stopped."[23]

On April 20, 1931, ASCAP officially put its antipayola rule into effect. When a manuscript was submitted to a publisher/member for publication the names of all the writers were to appear on the manuscript. If a nom de plume was used knowledge thereof was to be furnished to ASCAP in writing. No action could be taken by ASCAP regarding payola against nonmembers of ASCAP, mostly smaller and newer houses. It was felt these firms would be deterred from payola by their ultimate desire to become ASCAP members at some future time. An application for membership might be refused if the house had openly flaunted ASCAP rules while a nonmember. In addition, the group had no control over orchestra leaders, who were not usually members. All ASCAP could do was hint darkly that it would try to achieve leverage through other means. The implication was that ASCAP would perhaps try to enlist the likes of networks such as NBC and CBS to punish erring bandsmen in some way.[24]

This ASCAP ban was not retroactive, which meant songs published after April 20 with a cut-in would be okay if the deal was made prior to that date. As might be expected, the week or so before April 20 was a period of furious activity. Many publishers, said an account, went "on a wholesale rampage of cutting in band leaders.... Publishers cut in band leaders on many songs which are now still in manuscript form. Some may not be published until a year or more hence. One leader made no bones about telling the publishers that he is now cut in on enough songs to carry him for two years. Another declared he was cut in on nine songs the week before the ruling became effective." Some publishers signed cut-in deals with the bandsmen in the first days after April 20. They skirted the rule by back dating agreements.[25]

Perhaps bewildered by the majority of publishers violating the very rules they had urged ASCAP to adopt, the organization doggedly persisted in trying to eliminate loopholes. All houses were asked by ASCAP to supply them with complete details for all existing cut-in deals, title of song, date of agreement, name of orchestra leader or singer cut in, and so on. It was hoped this would establish a master file, thus eliminating more cut-in deals popping up which claimed to be pre–April 20. If ASCAP suspected a deal was struck after April 20 but back dated they threatened to examine the publisher's books—something permitted under the ASCAP constitution. One month after cut-ins were officially banned by the group, ASCAP had not received so much as one complaint. Without a complaint ASCAP could not act. Despite this it was common knowledge in the music industry that payola had not been eliminated. The best someone would say was that it had been reduced somewhat. Deals were still being made. Usually they were now verbal, the handshake agreement replaced ones in writing. Three months after the rule went into effect ASCAP still had received no complaints. It was then estimated that perhaps half the payola had been eliminated in that period. Publishers had been subdued for a time but were slowly and steadily returning to business as usual.[26]

Payola was never a crime until its nonreporting became a federal offense in 1960. Prior to that it was perfectly legal. Often it was against the rules of an organization, such as the MPPA or ASCAP. Whether it would have stood up against a court challenge is impossible to say. The only criminal law payola may have violated was a commercial bribery statute. However, most states didn't have such a law on the books. It was not under federal jurisdiction. There were many reasons why it would have been almost impossible to obtain a conviction under a bribery statute against a giver or taker of payola. As a result most payola deals, whether royalty cut-ins, straight cash payments for a play, or something else were set down in writing, openly.

Next to try to regulate the industry was the National Recovery Administration (NRA) set up under the National Industrial Recovery Act of 1933. It was all part of President Franklin Roosevelt's New Deal program. Every American industry was to establish a code of fair practice to eliminate corruption and unfair competition within itself. Each industry appointed its own people to draft its code. These then went on to Washington for amendments and ultimate passage into law. The music code addressed a number of issues but focused mainly on eliminating payola.

When the music code was complete one of the currently more popular forms of payola had been omitted. Publishers took a song for publication written by a vocalist or bandsman, paying a hefty advance and then forgetting all about the manuscript. Only on rare occasions was such a number ever published. Said a report, this "payoff method has been found the safest all around. It obviates the cut-in, the cash payment, the jewelry gift, the publisher's wife footing the bill of the maestro's frau at some pleasure resort. . . . One of the first line publishers has a safe full of these leader and songster authored manuscripts, many of them both musically and lyrically impossible. But for each a substantial advance has been exchanged." By using this method a publisher could continue his public condemnation of cut-ins and cash payments at ASCAP or MPPA meetings without fear of a rebound, while the leader or singer could convince himself that what he had engaged in was strictly a business deal between writer and publisher. In Chicago a bandleader placed eight of his songs among three publishers over a six month period. None were published.[27]

Radio was writing its own code at the time and it was announced that the code authorities for both radio and music would work together to eliminate plug bribery practices from radio just as soon as the music code was approved, signed by President Roosevelt, and the committee to administer it was appointed. Broadcasters were said to be fed up with frequent late changes in programs made by orchestras and singers as well as with the poor grade of pop releases that often found their way into repertoires. All of this they blamed on payola practices. When the music code arrived in Washington it contained, naturally, an antibribery clause. NRA officials took the view that any open deal between a publisher and a performer could not be considered an unfair trade practice. They also pointed out it was against NRA policy to hinder honest employment. Therefore, the NRA insisted the antibribery clause be modified. As adopted, this part of the code stipulated that any payoff arrangement was okay provided that the vocalist or bandsman, before playing the number, announced over the air that he had been paid for doing so, how much he received, as well as every detail of the terms and conditions involved. When this revised clause was read to the publishers assembled in Washington the reaction was reported as one "of amusement." It seemed strange to them that the government would ask them to incorporate payola into the music industry code's fair trade practice section. However, since the administration insisted upon it the publishers agreed. The NRA was abolished by Roosevelt in 1935 after the court declared it unconstitutional.[28]

Song pluggers got together for another informal meeting to try to come up with a way of dealing with payola. The old worry about losing their jobs with publishers simply mailing out checks was again on their minds. The meeting was fruitless. Finally, in 1934 ASCAP got a complaint. One publisher complained to that group that a bandleader had double-crossed him. After receiving $25 for a special arrangement the publisher said the bandleader didn't deliver. He wanted his money back. In his defense the leader said that while it was true he didn't deliver an annotated treatment on paper to the publisher, the arrangement his orchestra played wasn't the same as the publisher's stock orchestration. He had, said the leader, given the number a "mental reconstruction" and as long as it differed even slightly from the stock arrangement he felt he had lived up to his end of the deal. Apparently ASCAP was satisfied.[29]

Quietly sitting on the sidelines for a couple of years, the MPPA had been content to let other groups take a shot at eliminating payola. Suddenly, they were jolted back into the fray again. Motivation this time was not of ethical or moral considerations but fear that if the MPPA didn't somehow clean their own house someone else might do it for them, with the results not all necessarily to the MPPA's liking.

Early in 1934 the FTC conducted its own investigation of the music industry, prompted by informal complaints it had received to the effect that bribery was rampant in the business. During this probe the FTC concluded that the MPPA, ASCAP, and a third industry organization, the Music Dealers Service, dominated the trade with the same group of men as directors of each of the three organizations. The FTC's New York representative, C. E. Klein, had a conversation with John Paine, telling him of the probe. Klein told him, "In light of everything else as found about the music business by the commission it is too bad that this bribery situation exists." He added that Paine could count on the FTC for cooperation in bringing bribery to an end but that cooperation meant that the music industry would have to do something for itself. Paine got a clear indication that Klein wanted to see an immediate housecleaning undertaken or face some unstated consequences.

Paine wasted no time in calling an MPPA meeting. Quickly the group adopted yet another antibribery pact which banned all the various payola forms. Fine for a first offense against a publisher would be $1,000, rising to $2,000 for a second offense. The pact included a clause whereby publishers agreed to allow fines levied against them to be collected by the MPPA from their dividends due from ASCAP, a measure adopted to try to ensure fines would be collected. New with this pact, compared to earlier ones, was a reward for informers. Those who tipped off the MPPA to a violation would receive one-third of the fines imposed. On June 11, 1934, this agreement went into effect. Any payola deals made prior to that date were allowed to go through, provided that details of such agreements be filed with Paine and that payments to leaders and singers due under such deals were made through Paine, as chairman of the MPPA. One provision of the antipayola pact — obviously aimed at song pluggers — called for the arbitrary dismissal of a publisher's employee who, on his own, attempted to do anything to violate the terms of the pact. Any such dismissed employee was to be totally blacklisted, banned from the industry. Since the National Association of Broadcasters had a proviso in its rules prohibiting the employment of entertainers who accepted payola from song publishers for performances, it was hoped this would keep them in line.

On the day after the pact took effect the MPPA sent a telegram to 50 or so orchestra leaders outlining the new conditions. It was said they accepted it as being in the best interests of the industry. Publishers enthusiastically supported the new pact with most major houses reported to have signed the pact immediately. One who resisted was Robbins Music Corporation. Jack Bregman, Robbins's general manager, was skeptical. He said his company had resisted the special arrangement deal on its own for six months, becoming martyrs to the cause. Robbins yielded to this payola only when it found its new releases being frozen off the air. Bregman accused the other houses of rushing into this new pact principally because they were low on money. Robbins would become a cosigner to the pact after a time if it proved effective and if the signers abided by it, said Bregman.[30]

Five weeks after the pact went into effect Paine sent a second, much tougher, communication to bandleaders. About 15 of them received a letter telling them that unless they stopped insisting on a payoff for playing a number over the air the MPPA would file complaints against them with radio officials. Paine insisted the leaders inform him in writing of their intention to honor his group's antibribery pact. Failing that, when Paine brought complaints to radio executives he would use as evidence against them checks sent to them from publishers through his office after the pact went into effect, a part of the deal to allow pre–June 11 payola deals to stand, provided payment was made through the MPPA.[31]

Later that summer it was admitted that payola had not been eliminated. In particular, one publisher was openly making cash payments to entertainers. Other publishers feared this could drag in the government. Early in 1935 Paine told a meeting of song pluggers that he had never kidded himself into thinking the pact would completely clean the industry of abuses. He felt payola had been cut by around 50 percent, that things were improving, and that even publishers who had not signed the pact were spending less for plugs. Important orchestra leaders were cooperating with the industry, asserted Paine. It was the minor bands who were the problem.[32]

By July of that year, with the pact only one year old, its true, shaky nature was admitted by Paine in a letter he sent out to publishers. Most publishers had, in fact, not signed up immediately. After one year Paine had signed pledges from just half of the houses. The letter took the companies to task for their lukewarm response to the pact. Unless he had signed pledges from 80 percent of the houses in short order, warned Paine, he would release those who had signed from the pact, feeling it wasn't fair for them to be bound while so many were not bound. Paine painted a picture of rampant payola in this letter saying, "Every conceivable kind of bribery is reported to me; direct payments for plugs, extensive payments for special arrangements, gifts of all kinds both inexpensive and expensive given to orchestra leaders and other performers, increased entertaining at openings and like affairs, purchase of tickets for sporting events, theatrical events and benefits. In short, the industry seems to be running wild." The MPPA chairman urged the houses to pledge to the code of ethics to save the industry. This was a necessary step he said, "First, because the industry cannot afford to indulge in an orgy of wild and useless spending, and, second, because the industry is constantly being charged in Washington at copyright hearings, at all broadcasting conventions and at other public gatherings where the music industry is discussed, with being a racket. This industry cannot at this time afford to permit practices to grow up within it which will give any color whatsoever to that charge." Two months after that, in September 1935, Paine had pledges from 60 percent of the houses. Suddenly, the MPPA pulled a complete about-face. Instead of continuing to fear government intervention, that same month Paine officially asked the FTC to step in and hold a trade conference for the purpose of adopting rules against payola practices that would bind the popular music publishers. Paine promised to continue his efforts to align the industry on the MPPA pact until the FTC could hold its conference.[33] No reason was given for this abrupt turnaround regarding government intervention. Perhaps Paine was just frustrated by the apparent hopelessness of getting the great majority of publishers to sign antipayola pacts and then to live up to them.

Over in England payola was just as prevalent and just as much of a problem as it was in North America. London's *Daily Express* gave the situation front-page coverage for a couple of days in 1933 when it "discovered" it. English publishers were paying bandleaders for plugs over the radio — the BBC. This newspaper had come into possession of a copy of a letter signed by nine London music publishers. It was sent out to bandleaders telling them that henceforth there would be a set scale for plugs. Tired of bidding against each other, the houses united to try to limit this expense by agreeing to pay £1 per tune plugged on the air, with the condition that two each of the nine publishers' songs be included in a program. According to the newspaper officials, the BBC tried their best to eliminate the plug system but claimed that its degree of secrecy was such that they were powerless to stop it. British Broadcasting Corporation officials also said they had "every good reason to believe" that singers on its programs were also on the take from the publishers.[34]

Of about 20 established bands then playing in various London restaurants only 3 — Roy Fox, Lew Stone, and Henry Hall the BBC conductor — were said to be immune from graft. One problem was that the BBC paid no money at all to the bands who played over the airwaves. The prestige of playing on the BBC was supposed to be more than sufficient to compensate them. The one exception was Bert Ambrose who was paid $200 per broadcast. Unpaid bands weren't overly concerned about the lack of BBC money. One leader reputedly made $500 per week for several years, all courtesy of payola. In 1933 the BBC, to combat payola, instituted a policy of paying all bands a minimum salary for their radio work. However, the bands had to give up selection of what music they played. The BBC appointed Alfred Hanson to do the music selection for all the BBC performers. Under payola there had been too much repetition of too few tunes. These moves by the BBC were widely hailed as sure to bring about the death of payola.[35]

First reports claimed that direct cash payments for plugs had indeed been killed. However, the trade in special arrangements continued stronger than ever. A large English music publisher was estimated to spend as much as $125,000 yearly on special arrangements. The standard rate paid to a bandleader was $10 per song, if rendered once on the air, and $5 for each additional rendition. The Music Publishers Association got together to condemn this practice but like their American counterpart were unwilling or unable to take any action. As a report noted, "agreements among publishers are farcical, and as soon as they decide on some unanimous action, some immediately break their pledges." Said publisher Jimmy Campbell, "So the B.B.C., high and mighty, stopped said plugs. It was a vicious system. The B.B.C. said, 'there must be no more paid plugs.' Well, there are no more paid plugs — there are special arrangements. The B.B.C. accepts special arrangements."[36]

A few years later the standard fee for a special arrangement was said to be $42. Publishing houses were so annoyed with the expense that they sent a letter to the BBC, through their association. In it they asked the BBC to cooperate with them in eliminating this practice or they threatened to go back to the old practice of paying cash payments directly to bandsmen in a wholesale manner as in the past. By all appearances they had already done so, with the BBC taking more steps to try to eliminate that which it so recently "killed." New contracts between bands and the BBC would henceforth contain clauses specifically barring the bandsmen from receiving cash payments and special arrangements. Any offenders would be blacklisted by the BBC and not invited to broadcast again. In addition, to compensate dance bands for the loss of payola income under these more stringent rules, the BBC increased the amount it paid such bands by 50 percent. At the end of the 1930s the BBC sent a letter to every band on its payroll. It asked that each give a written undertaking not to accept payola from publishers to play specific songs during a broadcast, saying, "That the acceptance of special orchestrations, gifts or direct or indirect money payments from publishers, in consideration of their performing the works of particular publishers, had become increasingly common. . . . The publishing firms have given an undertaking that no new inducements of any kind would be offered after April 11th." That was the date in 1939 it took effect. Many bandleaders responded angrily, claiming they were clean. A BBC spokesman said, "We have had suspicions that a few leaders might be breaking the clause in their contracts, and the letter was sent out as a reminder of their undertakings. There is no suggestion that the majority are disregarding the clause."[37] Meanwhile, back in America. . . .

Appointed to head the FTC investigation was special agent Joseph M. Klein. During a meeting with Paine and representatives of the major houses this agent explained about the earlier FTC probe. It had come about after complaints by a number of small publishers who claimed that a number of major houses, controlled by motion picture producers, held an unfair competitive advantage due to their ability to retain the best writers, to spend large sums of money for exploitation, and to obtain more performance points with their radio broadcast dominance — which meant a larger share of royalties from ASCAP. Klein said he found this complaint to be unfounded and didn't recommend the FTC order an official hearing of the charges. However, Klein related that during that investigation he found the paying of payola to be fairly universal in the music industry. He asked the assembled MPPA people to cooperate with him in supplying information during this present inquiry.[38]

In July 1936, just one month after that meeting, Paine did another abrupt about-face by asking the FTC to call off its payola investigation. To that point preliminary inquiry by FTC agents revealed that payola "had become so rampant that the publisher who wasn't paying rated as the rare exception." Some firms had called off all limits on the payoff bankroll, and in the competition to get their numbers to the top of the weekly network performance list were shelling out far more than they could expect to collect on such performances from the American Society of Composers, Authors and Publishers, or profit from the sale of sheet music. So serious was it that the FTC felt it seriously interfered with a government-controlled medium, broadcasting. Due to this the commission hoped other government agencies would cooperate with them in their investigation. Paine suddenly wanted the industry to be left alone to clean up its house by itself. He cited two reasons for wanting the FTC called off. One was that with the inevitable disclosures that would emerge things would be made "extremely unpleasant for certain leaders." Second was the reputation of the music industry. Despite having said everyone considered the business a racket only a couple of years previously, now he said the industry had "gained high national recognition and all it needs to have this rating torn down or destroyed is a scandal that might result from the findings of a Government agency."[39]

In response to Paine's request to back off the FTC said neither yes nor no. Instead they retorted they would first have to receive evidence of the industry's sincerity in trying to eliminate payola before giving a firm decision. Adoption of a code of fair trade practices was suggested as one of those gestures. On August 31, 1936, the MPPA put just such a code into effect, signed they said by all the major houses. Publishers were said to be enthusiastic and near unanimous in their confidence that they would abide by it and that it would work. Still, there were a few holdouts. A week before this new pact went into effect NBC banned two songs from its airwaves. They were Broadway Music Company's "Without a Shadow of a Doubt" and Morris Company's "On the Beach at Bali Bali." This ban was lifted a couple of days later on the first song when Broadway agreed to become a signatory to the MPPA pact. Morris stated it would continue to refuse the pact because it was skeptical of the whole proposition. If the pressure became too great Morris threatened to sue the MPPA for an injunction and damages on the grounds of conspiracy and restraint of trade. John Royal, NBC program chief, declared he banned the two songs without knowledge of the pact. Privately it was believed NBC knew of the forthcoming pact. Any of the publishers who didn't sign the pledge could be curbed, said the MPPA, through action by the Federal Communications Commission on the ground that bribing radio performers was interference with the public's rights and that a broadcaster violated his license provisions when he condoned such practices. Unlike previous MPPA codes, this particular one didn't carry any penalty at all. According to the organization, if a signatory violated any of the antipayola clauses all the MPPA had to do was go to court and obtain an order restraining the violator from further breaches of the pact. Subsequent violations would subject the party to contempt of court proceedings. Of this pact *Variety* dryly noted, "On its face, the code looks toothless."[40]

Before the pact was even one month old song pluggers claimed it was working. As evidence they cited the number of plugs a song got each night on the radio. Prior to August 31 it was common for a song to be played five or six times total over NBC and CBS while in September three or four plugs in total were the maximum. A second explanation was that orchestra leaders were showing their annoyance with a decrease in their payola income by playing many more older tunes than before. Not much later Paine announced that his MPPA investigators found "practically complete observation" of the publishers' pledge against paying off for plugs. Acknowledging a few slips, Paine said none were of major importance. Also admitted to exist were a number of orchestra leaders holding out against playing current releases unless they were paid $25 in advance for each arrangement. Just one week after that a complaint was made to Paine about a New York publisher paying for plugs. Paine now said this was the only exception, that all other music men were complying with the pact and that orchestra leaders were showing a strong disposition to cooperate in eliminating payola.[41]

Edward Marks was the major mover, besides Paine, in trying to establish a fair practice code for the industry. Hired as a front man was Joseph V. McKee, a one-time acting mayor of New York. He made several trips to Washington to lobby for the cause. Ultimately, this code plan collapsed as the publishers in general opposed it. Even those who favored the code argued they would have to fall in line with established practices — payola — to survive. One industry observer noted that the movement was torpedoed by the publishers because "that's how they wanted to operate."[42]

Still involved was the FTC whose legal division devised a code of fair trade practices for the music industry. Drafts of this document were sent to the MPPA. Since this code was drafted generally — mentioning bribery but not all the specific forms payola took — it was up to the MPPA to couch the document in more specific language. Even in its draft form the FTC document was said to be far more stringent than the MPPA code. Three separate complaints had been received by the FTC that publishers were violating the pact. One of the three houses named was not a signatory to the pact. Despite this, the FTC would likely have withdrawn by then from its music industry involvement altogether, citing the MPPA pact as evidence of internal housecleaning, except for the fact that the commission was pressured from above with the Department of Justice urging the FTC to pursue an investigation of the music industry. The two groups lethargically passed codes back and forth with the FTC, agreeing to include in the government code practically all of the provisions adopted in the MPPA August pact. Notably left out was the clause specifically mentioning special arrangements as a banned item. The commission felt there was no reason to include this as it was covered implicitly in the general clause in the proposed FTC code that concerned bribery. Stalling for time, the MPPA passed some of the FTC documents on to their legal staff for lengthy study.[43]

When Paine received a report that a bandleader currently playing a Times Square hotel had recently obtained a $500 loan from a major publisher, he rushed out to investigate fearing this was a pact violation. The leader said the report was untrue. He had tried to obtain a loan but found no lenders. Because of this antipayola pact this bandsman asserted he had gone $1,900 in the red during his hotel engagement. He wanted the loan to pay bills. He had contracted for the Times Square job two weeks before the pact took effect.[44] In that period it was uncommon for a bandleader to receive just his weekly salary from an employer. The normal method was for the leader to receive or negotiate a much larger sum per week. However, from this amount he had to pay all his bandmembers, arranging fees, insurance, and various other expenses. What remained was his.

Near the end of 1936 Paine circulated a letter to the trade in which he apprised the status of the FTC code, which he had turned over to lawyers for study before submitting it to the industry for consideration as the FTC had "inserted so many stringent and rigid provisions." Putting publishers on their guard, Paine warned them that when it became effective the FTC code would be far more severe than the MPPA pact then in effect and that it would go into activities of the industry beyond the "mere matter of exploitation."[45]

The following spring several publishers approached Paine, pointing out to him that rampant bribery existed again, stimulated by the arrival in New York of several out-of-town orchestras who were especially amenable to receiving special arrangement fees from a number of major publishers. The previous winter was reported to be mostly payola free as the city was filled with big-name bands that picked their tunes well in advance. Any payola taking place was out in the hinterlands with traveling bands of lesser importance. When these houses approached Paine they asked him to take drastic action to halt this recurrence of large-scale payola, both special arrangement deals and straight cash payments for plays. Doing yet another turnaround, Paine contacted the FTC to ask them if they couldn't speed up the issuance of a code of fair trade practices.[46]

A conference was scheduled by the FTC for October 4, 1937, in Washington to be attended by all publishers who wished to be present. The commission had the power to impose a code of conduct on any group which asked it to promulgate standards. In New York the MPPA hurried around trying to line up the music industry into one united body for the meeting. The procode segment didn't want to be put on the defensive in Washington in front of the FTC by having some MPPA members level charges that the code idea was pushed by houses controlled by motion picture producers so the latter could cut their own exploitation costs and suppress further competition from small publishers. There were worries that many of these smaller houses would fight vigorously in Washington against government intrusion, and that they would argue methods of exploitation should not be restricted to methods favored by large, film-dominated publishing houses through a code of fair practices. Small firms were said to be ready to ask the FTC just how public interest was affected by paying bandleaders for special arrangements, and state that freelance songwriters would become extinct if their publishers, mainly small houses, weren't free to use whatever method was necessary to get airplay. They felt that payola was the only way for these small houses to have any chance to compete and survive.[47]

When the meeting was held the feared fractious division of publisher against publisher failed to materialize. Instead they presented a united front in asking the FTC to establish a code. *Variety* ironically called this apparent harmony a "love feast" and "pattycaking." Paine told hearing chairman Judge George McCorkle that the entire industry would welcome with open arms a code of fair trade and that both big and small publishers would abide by its regulations. The industry had never, he added, willfully violated the old NRA code. Publisher Edward Marks criticized all bandleaders save Lombardo, Murray, Whiteman, and Vallee for taking payola. Since the death of the NRA Marks said "chaos again has been the rule in the music publishing industry." He added that payola was then so brazen "that plugs can now be bought in sets of three, six, or more, and the industry is being hurt because music becomes monotonous and unbearable to listeners who have to hear the same tunes over and over again." Marks also said most bandleaders demanded $15, $25, or even $50 for playing a song on the radio and squawked "louder if payment is not made pronto." Louis Bernstein, president of a small publishing house, attacked payola practices which "had led to some members of the industry being forced to resort to the same methods." Inferior tunes were being forced on listeners because "people are being bribed to perform inferior music and today some of the poorest songs on record are being dinned into the ears of the American public for this reason."[48]

On December 15, 1937, the FTC made public its proposed trade practice rules for the music industry, adopted at the October meeting. A certain amount of time was allowed for public comment and objections. While it outlawed certain things like price discrimination, rebates, advertising allowances, and so on, its focus was on outlawing the various payola practices.[49] These rules were never implemented.

The idea that repetition of songs, especially on radio, destroyed them was not uncommon in the 1930s, despite the fact that the aim of payola is and always has been to have a song played over and over, for this is how it becomes a hit. Among the media aimed at the masses the music industry is unique. Books or films are not produced to be consumed repeatedly by the same person. Anyone with a teenager at home or who ever was one himself can attest to the role of repetition in the song industry. The life of the book, film, or song tends to be equally short. In the 1930s the music industry was in a period of transition. Sheet music sales were still the main way music turned a profit, although this was quickly switching to records. The radio meant people all over the country in previously unheard-of numbers could be exposed to the same songs at once. Repetition was becoming more widespread and instantaneous. The ultimate effect of this new medium of radio upon music was then unknown. Many feared this unknown focusing on possibly negative aspects. There was a strong love-hate relationship between the music industry and radio. It would last a long time and be a major underlying factor in the payola scandal of the late 1950s, with undercurrents of radio bashing and rock bashing strongly evident.

From the peak year of 130 million records sold in 1927 the total fell to just 8 million in 1932. By 1942 it was up to 140 million, with no small thanks due to the impact of radio. During the early 1930s staff announcers at radio stations tended to be jacks-of-all-trades giving news, weather, livestock reports, and so on. They also announced the records played, in a dull, monotonous tone, giving just the basic facts. Breaking that mold and establishing the modern era disk jockey was Al Jarvis, who left a Canadian banking job to arrive in Los Angeles in the early 1930s. He landed a job as a staff announcer at that city's KFWB in 1933. Jarvis began to add patter and chatter about the records he played, to interject his personality. For example, he might say, "Here's a swell new orchestra from England. It has a big sound like Paul Whiteman and the leader is Jack Hylton. The song is a big success in Germany and we think it will soon be up on the Lucky Strike Hit Parade now that they've put English words to it. Let me know what you think of Jack Hylton's brand-new Victor recording of 'Just a Gigolo.'" He bought all the records he played on his program. Al got his information from the trade publications such as *Billboard* and *Variety*. Other staff announcers never read such material. Fan mail began to pour in. Soon other announcers started to imitate his chatty and friendly manner at the mike. By then Jarvis's "Make Believe Ballroom" was a hit, broadcast five to six hours a day. Taking note of these happenings was a young man then working as a library assistant at KFWB. That was Martin Block, who soon moved to New York where he established his own "Make Believe Ballroom" which would take him to greater stardom than that attained by Jarvis. The power of the disk jockeys was cemented in 1942 when Capitol Records announced they would send the most influential jockeys all of their new releases for free. Other labels soon followed suit. Glenn E. Wallichs of Capitol recalled:

> so we devised a personalized sample record for about 50 of America's most influential jockeys. We typed up special labels with their names on both sides, pressed them on expensive, lightweight, unbreakable vinylite compound and then had our limited employee force drive around and distribute each sample personally. It was a service that created a sensation. We made the jock a Big Man, an Important Guy, a VIP in the industry. And we published a little newspaper in which we ran their pictures and biographies. That was how it all started. Even Al Jarvis stopped buying records for airplay. With the money he saved he opened his own record store.[50]

Even as early as 1937 the disk jockey was an important person, for in that year Benny Goodman reportedly paid Jarvis the sum of $500 to play his latest record.[51]

The feud between radio — and by extension, jockeys — heated up in the 1930s. Back in the 1920s ASCAP had to take radio to court as the new medium refused to pay for use of music played over the air. Radio argued that since listeners paid nothing to listen to their sets, radio shouldn't have to pay for the use of the music aired. Courts ruled in ASCAP's favor, causing radio to have to pay a negotiated fee. In 1935, just after signing a five-year pact that gave ASCAP 5 percent of broadcasters' net receipts as a royalty, radio, angered by the amount of such fees, persuaded the federal government to charge ASCAP with a violation of the antitrust law. Radio objected to a price and terms which they claimed ASCAP was able to dictate to them for its then 1,015 songwriters and publishers. The government described ASCAP as a gigantic music trust. One powerful member of ASCAP was Warner Brothers, which owned several music publishing subsidiaries including Witmark, Remick, and Harms. Their music catalogues were estimated at 15–40 percent of the ASCAP material that was broadcast over the air. Warner withdrew all of its music from the air in January 1936, despite the five-year contract ASCAP had with radio. Warner argued that since their contract with ASCAP expired in December 1935 they had every right to withdraw. Radio felt they should be bound by radio's contract with ASCAP for the full five years. Warner was after more money from radio.[52] They used the old argument that repetition of songs on the radio decreased sales. Cynics considered the Warner move as an attack on radio in the continuing feud. In August 1936 Warner returned to the ASCAP fold with all damage suits that had been initiated being dropped. The government antitrust action against ASCAP ended years later — in February 1941 — with ASCAP signing a consent decree in which it pledged to clean up its act by, among other things, paying its writer members on a more equitable basis. Continuing complaints against ASCAP by some of its members led to revised consent decrees being signed by ASCAP and the government in both 1950 and 1960. By the end of the 1930s most industry people accepted that radio plays and repetition itself were helpful in creating hits and were good for the record business in boosting sales.

Songwriter Gene Buck was the president of ASCAP in 1936 when he publicly declared concern that Americans of future generations would not know the songs of today, 1936, the way Buck's generation knew songs like "Sweet Rosie O'Grady" and "The Sidewalks of New York." He said,

> Since the advent of radio, songs of high quality, which deserve to live in the memory of the American people, are so quickly worn threadbare by repetition that they soon lose their appeal. I am greatly disturbed about the future of any music written today. In the old days, prior to radio broadcasting, it took three or four years for an American song to sink into the hearts of the people. Today, with more than 600 broadcasting stations, the popularity of any song, no matter how splendid it is, lasts no more than six weeks. Songs like "Smoke Gets in Your Eyes" by Jerome Kern, and Billy Hill's "The Last Round-Up" should become a part of history but constant use may relegate them to oblivion.

Buck added that if it wasn't for music radio would not last, since 75 percent of the programs depended on music in one form or another.[53]

Variety's Abel Green went so far as to indirectly blame radio as the "biggest single force" in the revival of payola. He saw the problem as resting with radio and advertising men who had no standards other than "the most" of anything. Since all they understood were "most played" tabulations as barometers for popularity and inclusion on their airwaves, this encouraged freer spending of payola among minor bands and acts as the only way to get songs into big national radio shows.[54]

As the various agencies worked on codes during the latter half of the 1930s, song pluggers continued to be a nuisance. The MPPA and network CBS sent a joint letter to publishers, telling them they had to do something about the conduct of their pluggers around the CBS studios and offices. The objections CBS had were to the contact men using CBS property as a lounging area, the practice of groups of them ganging up on artists coming and going from the premises and to annoying them during rehearsals. Future complaints would be submitted directly to the MPPA by the networks. This would serve as a final warning. If the objectionable conduct continued after that CBS would ban the plugger in question from its property. In Chicago there were so many of them in certain hotels and cafés chasing the bandsmen that some of these establishments made these pluggers spend a certain amount in these places for food and drink and so on if they wished to keep working the place.[55]

The pluggers held a meeting with the intention of launching their own national union, the Professional Music Men's Protective Association. Motivating this were the recurrent fears of losing their jobs as their publisher/employers bypassed them to deliver payola directly to the recipients. Some publishers threatened to do just that. Spokesmen were confident that once organized the pluggers could do away with payola. It was intended to make membership in the union compulsory. This fledgling union never got off the ground but another one soon would. In 1937 song pluggers reportedly were paid an average of $100–$250 weekly for the best contactmen, with an additional $25–$100 weekly expense account.[56]

A few radio stations dealt with the payola problem by not allowing their performers to choose their own music. Philadelphia's KYW had its program department select all the music to be played by orchestra leaders and singers appearing on the air. Song pluggers weren't happy with this, arguing that each artist knew what was best suited to his style. Jim Begley, KYW program director, replied that the talent wasn't able to select tunes best suited to it because of the pressure being put on it by pluggers to play certain songs in return for payola.[57]

Orchestra leaders responded to the various attempts to limit payola with some inventive wrinkles. More and more of the bandsmen owned music publishing firms. This allowed them to collect money from ASCAP in the form of royalties. The more often a piece was played the more points accumulated with ASCAP and the more money that meant in royalties. Half a chorus played was enough to qualify a song for one play. Bandleaders took to playing each other's tunes, at least half a chorus worth, a practice that came to be called "logrolling." Some bandsmen who owned publishing houses were Isham Jones, Freddie Rich (CBS staff conductor), Ray Block (CBS conductor), Paul Whiteman, Fred Waring, Guy Lombardo, Jack Denny, and Abe Lyman.[58]

The publishing company Words and Music was formed in 1936 by bandleaders Fred Waring, Paul Whiteman, Guy Lombardo, Abe Lyman, and Jack Denny. Among its hits were "Dream a Little Dream of Me" and "The Night Is Young and You're so Beautiful." Overall, however, the firm generated few money-makers. Whiteman soon quit as a partner and eventually Waring became the sole owner.[59]

John Royal of NBC launched an investigation into logrolling on his network programs with a view to warning some leaders and doing henceforth the actual music selection for other leaders. Royal was also trying to change what he thought were too close relationships existing between publishers' employees and the NBC staff who were involved in selecting music for artists and passing on such music already selected. A third complaint Royal was dealing with concerned outlying NBC stations. Publishers claimed some of them dictated to the publishers whom the houses were to employ as local representatives and how much they were to be paid.[60]

Publishers occasionally tried to gain advantage with bandsmen by hiring a leader's brother or relative. The writing segment of ASCAP was pushing that performing rights group to study more carefully the applications for membership from leader/songwriters and leader/publishers. This organization was then said to be conducting thorough probes as to actual authorship whenever membership applications were submitted which involved bandleaders. At least one such application was rejected. Some leaders were said to have suggested to publishers that they, the leaders, saw no reason why they shouldn't share in the royalties derived by the houses from ASCAP. This was not the usual cut-in but simply a request by bandsmen to the houses to give them some of the money since it was the bandsmen who popularized the tune, leading to the receipt of ASCAP royalties.[61] Apparently, no publishers acceded to this request.

4 Everybody Swears Off Payola, 1940–1949

During the 1940s a considerable shift in payola took place. For one thing it was only beginning in this period that the term payola was used regularly to describe the practice, at least in the trades. The MPPA remained in existence but no longer promulgated codes to stamp it out or solicited pledges against it from its member publishers. Instead, that function fell to the song pluggers who, by the start of the 1940s, had formed their own union, the Music Publishers Contact Employees Association (MPCE). This group would work on stamping out payola in the 1940s just as the MPPA had tried to do in the 1930s. They would promulgate just as many codes and they also would have no real success. Other changes in the decade included the industry laying a good deal of the blame for payola on the song rating system. Disk jockeys became a major force in the music industry for the first time and were immediately linked with payola.

After a long battle over how much radio should pay in fees to ASCAP for the right to use ASCAP's catalog the broadcast industry set up a rival licensing organization, Broadcast Music Incorporated (BMI) in 1940. As a mover in payola BMI also took some heat that decade. An elitist group, ASCAP had always had things go its own way. Bad feelings existed within ASCAP toward BMI and the radio networks behind its formation since BMI was a rival taking business away. Broadcast Music was also disliked because it published all the "junk" ASCAP wouldn't touch such as country, ethnic, and black material. Soon this would include most of the rock and roll music. A relatively small number of establishment writers who turned out Broadway show tunes and the June/moon/spoon type of material — whitebread pap — comprised ASCAP. The group disliked radio also because many of its members feared the rise of radio would somehow reduce music sales, thereby cutting the income of ASCAP members. Of course, that never happened but these irrational fears lingered.

The BMI formation both anticipated and exacerbated the licensing fee dispute between ASCAP and radio in 1940 when the old five-year pact expired. On January 1, 1941, all ASCAP tunes were removed from the air, leaving radio with nothing to play except old material in the public

domain. This strike ended in May of that year when the two sides reached
a new agreement.

Both ASCAP and BMI disliked disk jockeys. For the first time in the
music industry payola was paid to people who had nothing to do with the
music, except to introduce it. In the past the vast majority of payola
receivers were people who performed the music. The rise of the disk jockey
would reverse that pattern forever. None of this had a direct bearing on
payola in the 1940s but it set the stage for the infamous late 1950s charge
on payola.

In the England of the 1940s payola remained the industry's major problem. By June 1941 the price of sheet music had doubled to 20 cents but sales
were only about 25 percent of their prewar levels. With the industry hurting financially, publishers lashed out at the evils of payola with renewed
vigor, citing the practice as "rampant." Name bands, with few exceptions,
were forever demanding from $8 to $20 for each tune they played, while
the fees received by the publishers from the BBC rarely were more than
30 percent of the amount extracted by bandsmen. An example was the
broadcasting of dance music to the armed forces, where publishers paid
band leaders a minimum of $8 per number but received from the BBC only
a little over 25 percent of that amount. Singers on the radio were also singled out as demanding anywhere from $20 to $50 from publishers to sing
one of their songs on the air. Among the handful of singers named who
didn't demand payola were Bea Lillie, Bebe Daniels, and Vera Lynn. The
British record trade was termed "virile" chiefly because there was said to
be no kickback every time a record was played. One account reported,
"Publishers are eagerly awaiting the time when they can trust one another
and dictate to the stick wielders that if they want songs they will have to
play them without fee or reward. But this Utopia looks a long way off."[1]

A few years later payola was reported to have assumed "tremendous
proportions," having increased over 100 percent in just the previous six
months, poised to almost ruin the industry. Bandsmen and singers were
still getting fees from publishers for special arrangements but now they
were also demanding cash payments for plugs as well, with a "pay or else"
attitude.[2]

In a few more years payola was pervasive enough to prod the BBC
into conducting a probe. Specifically, the alleged payola activities of bandleader Harry Roy triggered the investigation. A lawyer by the name of Sir
Valentine Holmes was appointed by Parliament to investigate charges of
bribery, corruption, and favoritism amongst the BBC staff. A wide-rang-
ing inquiry, the probe covered all areas of the BBC—variety, drama departments, not just music. When he reported to Parliament Holmes reported the allegations were without solid foundation. None of the BBC
staff were named in the report with the exception of Mrs. D. H. Nelson,

head of the dance band section. Due to the inquiry BBC governors severely rebuked Nelson, expressing disapproval of her "very unwise" acceptance of gifts.

Despite acknowledging she was open to severe criticism Holmes added in his report that he didn't think she was influenced in any way as a result of accepting gifts. The BBC issued an order banning staffers from accepting gifts. Holmes did deplore the practice of singers and leaders taking money from publishers for song plugging and advised the BBC to set up a committee to come up with a solution to the problem. If it wasn't possible to end payola through the cooperation of publishers then Holmes thought legislation should be considered to bring payola within the provisions of the Prevention of Corruption Act of 1906.[3]

Publisher Reg Connelly thought one of the problems was the BBC bias against popular music. This meant that relatively few of these numbers were played. In turn this led to more competition by the publishers to place their numbers into these slots. One way to do this was through payola. A couple of months after Holmes made his report the BBC responded to payola with what was called the "closed mouth policy." Artists had to submit their music lists to the BBC several weeks in advance of performance. Normally, song pluggers knew or could find out the names of artists slated to appear on the BBC before those song lists were submitted. Thus they were able to offer them payola to get a play. Henceforth, the pluggers wouldn't receive information as to who was booked until after these artists had submitted song lists to the BBC. Any employee found giving advance information to publishers or pluggers would be instantly dismissed.[4]

As a result of the Holmes report the BBC and the Music Publishers Association held a series of meetings at which they hammered out an agreement to end the payola system. Giving some idea as to the extent of payola, publishers said an eradication of payola would save them a minimum of $4,000 on every song. Terms of the deal called for the BBC to ban for life from its airwaves any artist proved guilty of accepting payola and the banning from the air for two years the entire catalog of a publisher similarly proved guilty. Anyone accused of payola would be suspended from the air until proved innocent. Since this move was expected to lessen the income of artists the BBC opened negotiations designed to increase the amount it paid to artists on its programs. This agreement, which one account said was "expected to terminate once and for all the plug bribery that has been rampant here for years," took effect on April 12, 1948.

Only publishers who had signed the agreement could have their music eligible for BBC play. The pact was to run for one year, with options. Less than two months later a major problem had arisen. Negotiations for more money had come to naught and bandsmen, angry at the income loss, essentially stopped playing current popular tunes, dragging ancient oldies in the public domain out of the closet instead. The percentage of current popular songs played on some BBC dance programs fell to as low as 2.5 percent. Jim Davidson, head of the BBC dance music broadcasts, was forced to step in and issue an order to the effect that in the future 60 percent of tunes played by dance bands had to consist of current pop tunes. This rule came after the Music Publishers Association met with the BBC to complain about the situation. Strangest feature of this pact was that the practice of publishers paying bandsmen money for special arrangements was allowed to stand, and even codified. Bandsmen would be allowed to receive as much as $20 from a publisher for a special arrangement: it was written into the pact.[5]

In the United States the pluggers were regarded as much less of a nuisance in the 1940s than they were in the 1930s, at least in terms of media coverage. Only once were they reported barred. That was in 1946 when NBC banished them from virtually all of their premises for interfering with artists. They were limited to a specific small office area. This ban, like all the previous ones, was a short-lived affair. If the pluggers weren't as big a nuisance perhaps it was because they were spending more of their time in their union duties to stamp out payola as they took over what had been mostly an MPPA function during the 1930s. The pluggers unionized in May 1940. At that time they had 430 members who averaged $75 a week. This new union was not concerned with wages or working conditions. A report noted, "Its principal aim is to eliminate the practice of bribing musicians to use a song published by the plugger's employer."[6]

When the MPCE and the MPPA signed an agreement in 1941, the antipayola clauses drafted by the contact men were said to include every conceivable form of payola. Not only were all the conventional forms of payola outlawed, but also publishers were barred from having any corporate or partnership relations with bandleaders, singers, booking agents, or managers. Under the agreement if a leader or singer wanted to get into the publishing business he would have to finance the project himself or get a loan from outside of the industry. Commonly, under payola, a publisher would foot these bills.[7]

Something very unusual happened in 1943 when payola charges were leveled in the industry, with the result that disciplining was actually performed. That year a vocal group called the Three Suns were performing at New York's Piccadilly Hotel from where they were heard over the NBC Red network (NBC was then divided into two sections, the Red and the Blue). For a month or more the Suns had been on the MPCE's blacklist for accepting publisher payola. This was apparently informal punishment since the charges against the group at that time were unproven. This blacklisting must have worked, for the Three Suns went to the MPCE and fingered the men who had paid them. As evidence the group showed their books wherein they had recorded the transactions. As a result of their testimony several contact men were punished by their union. Crawford Music Company's professional manager, Larry Spier, was fined $1,000 for instructing employee Jack Erickson to pay the Suns $50 for two plugs. Erickson was fined $250, which he paid. Benny Alberts of Feist Music was fined $200 for giving the Three Suns hockey game tickets and free records. This fine was suspended, provided he behaved himself. Hugo Rubens of Roy Music pled guilty for which he was suspended from active union membership for six months. Wesley Frazer was also charged with having paid the Three Suns but the charges were withdrawn when it was shown the payments occurred before he became a union member. No action was taken against the publishers who supplied the money. Union officials claimed that other similar cases were in the works. They would never come. When these proceedings were launched the music industry was said to be "flabbergasted," not just by the fact that people were disciplined by the union but because of, said one account, "the circumstances under which the convictions took place. Never before had the actual testimony of a bribe receiver led to a conviction."[8]

Payola continued unchecked while the MPCE quickly grew frustrated. Its president, Jimmy O'Connor, told his members at a meeting that the bribery problem was getting out of hand again, that he knew who was guilty, and that if the payola problem didn't stop the union would again take steps to curb it. Next, at a special meeting of the union's executives, O'Connor summoned two important publishers whom he hauled onto the carpet and interrogated on suspected rule violations. No details of the meeting were released, only that it took place. At a union meeting held in May 1944 one publisher "high up in the field" suggested that the MPCE delete from their bylaws the clauses which governed and imposed penalties on payola violations. After recovering from the shock of this idea, the MPCE flatly rejected it. The publisher reasoned that since payola was then rampant, why not open the field to everyone by eliminating antipayola rules? Other publishers, when questioned, admitted payola was going on but denied it was rampant. In any case throwing out rules on payola would not help.[9]

O'Connor and the pluggers responded by formulating a further list of specific behaviors that publishers were not allowed to engage in. These included such practices as not lending their automobiles to artists, not giving testimonial dinners for artists for any occasion, not giving Christmas gifts to artists above a certain value — such value to be set by the MPCE — as well as the more obvious payola infractions. According to O'Connor trade abuses would not be taken lightly. Those caught violating the rules would get no sympathy.[10]

A group of major publishers banded together in 1945 to advance $20,000 to the MPCE for the purpose of investigating the payola situation. Months passed by with the publishers becoming more and more restless as results were not forthcoming. Ultimately MPCE executives repeatedly told the publishers that a number of cases had been completed with full evidence and that accusations and actions would soon be taken. Nothing more was heard of this investigation.[11]

By 1945 several of the more important publishers were said to be considering approaching the MPCE to press for the idea that only one of their number had recently argued: that the union should scrap the bylaws in its constitution which barred payola. These industry men felt that if payola was to be "allowed by the union to its current extent" then all the restrictions should be removed, leaving every man to shift for himself. This was totally unacceptable to the union because of the fears that had haunted the pluggers for years. Unrestricted payola, said a report, "would eliminate the necessity for staffs, or at least cut them down sharply.... This is the main reason the MPCE will not countenance unrestricted paying." It was also felt that big publishers would drive small firms out of business if they operated under unrestricted payola. The MPCE did discuss this idea because of the considerable pressure from publishers before rejecting it. They rationalized that unrestricted payola would make a bad situation worse; that unrestricted payola then — 1945 — would, for unstated reasons, be very much worse for the music industry than in years past when there was unrestricted buying of plugs. One of the largest of the houses, unnamed, was still reported adamant that payola restrictions should be eliminated. This company was then making plans to fight fire with fire by openly buying performances in the face of the MPCE regulations. The idea was that it would create a situation to force a showdown. This publisher felt the rules were crucifying those who abided by them while not penalizing those firms who ignored them.[12] In just a few short years not only had the responsibility for policing payola violations been shifted from publishers to song pluggers, but the latter were also held to account if the rules weren't effective.

Finally, the MPCE was forced into taking some action for, in fact, the publisher who threatened to openly pay for plugs started doing just that and continued for some months. Pushing the union was the fear the practice would spread to other houses. After considering ways of curbing pay for plugs the union sent a letter to all publishers, suggesting three possible courses. The first suggestion was to seek government aid in the enforcement of the union's bylaws against payola. While the specifics of this idea were not spelled out it was widely believed it meant bringing the Treasury Department into the picture to supply them with information on money changing hands. The assumption was that none of the payola receivers

were reporting this money as income on their tax forms. The second idea
was to appoint a coordinator to police the music business — an industry
czar. The third suggestion was that if the two previous proposals failed or
were rejected then MPCE should seriously consider eliminating antipayola
clauses from the MPCE constitution. By March 1947, several months after
the letter had gone out, the MPCE had received comparatively few returns
from the publishers. Ideas one and two found little favor with this group.
One month later the union indefinitely tabled the entire matter of finding
a method to stop payola since they had received such a small number of
replies from the publishers.[13]

Other than the disciplinary action arising out of the Three Suns case,
almost no other accusations or actions were formally brought to light.
Those that were were very minor, considering the admitted pervasiveness
of payola. In 1947 Herman Schubert, operator of the Pelham Heath Inn,
New York, was erased from the MPCE unfair list. Schubert got on this
suspended list because he asked publishers for money before allowing their
songs to be played at his establishment. After signing an agreement promising not to do it again, Schubert was reinstated in the good books. Irving
Fields and his New York Crest Room made their way onto the unfair list
for similar reasons. Bourne Company plugger Teddy Black and Ben Bornstein, brother of the Bourne owner, came before the union's trial board in
1948 charged with paying for arrangements of tunes to unspecified bands.
Apparently, no conviction was registered.[14]

During 1949 when the union was negotiating with the MPPA for a
new contract — wages and working conditions — they attempted to put
more teeth into the antipayola rules because they said the practice was on
a continuing rise, endangering their jobs. What the union wanted to do
was to eliminate from nightly logging sheets all numbers performed by
offending artists (it was from these sheets that ratings were tabulated). By
doing this the airtime of artists demanding plugs would not be a factor in
ratings, therefore nullifying their payola demands. Publishers quashed this
quickly for two reasons. They claimed that barring certain artists from the
sheets would leave them open to conspiracy suits. Secondly, they said they
didn't want the MPCE holding enough power to say which artists would
be ignored in compiling the ratings.[15]

The next idea tried by the pluggers' union was to set up a top secret
trial board to judge those accused of payola infractions. The MPCE came
up with this idea in recognition of the fact that all MPCE members were
employees of publishers' firms and open to retaliation should they be called
upon to penalize anyone connected with their employers' firms. It had taken
the union about ten years to recognize the impossibility of their situation
with regard to payola — to curb a practice which had always been rampant
and to do that curbing by penalizing the people with the power to fire those

who would attempt to impose penalties. The secret trial board was to be made up of representatives of three small publishers — supposedly too poor to pay for plugs — and three upper management employees of three other publishers. What had always stymied trial action in the past was the almost complete inability of getting anybody to give evidence against another member of the music industry, except out of spite.[16]

Publishers publicly swore off payola at the end of 1949 as a result of a meeting with the MPCE. Herman Starr of the Warner house assembled his staff to tell them as of that time his firm would no longer countenance payola and any employee caught in the act would be fired. Other publishers followed suit. Many issued similar cease and desist orders, with a second faction issuing no such orders as they had never engaged in payola, so they said; therefore, no such order was necessary. Abe Olman of Robbins, Feist, and Miller said his company would be happy to cooperate with the MPCE in every way. Bernie Goodwin of Famous-Paramount said, "We have never countenanced such practices here." Said Louis Bernstein of Shapiro-Bernstein, "We do not pay. There isn't a first-class artist who would accept a bribe. The only ones who take are the ridiculously unimportant bands on the late remotes — and it's stupid to pay for that. If I found anyone paying, I'd fire him." One unnamed company owner said, "Sure, I did the same. You have to make a front, but it's an empty gesture. A skunk is a skunk, and the evil will go on. A band leader can do justice to maybe eight songs in a half-hour show. Almost 350 publishers have 1,000 songs they want on the air so they'll revert to payola under a new disguise. In due time the graft and corruption will resume." Jack Robbins of J. J. Robbins stated, "A payola is the best way to find out if you have a song. Spread $750 around over a couple of weeks as against the $10,000 to $15,000 it would cost in the traditional way of launching a song with a high caliber professional staff, and you'll soon know the potential of your tune." One observer, skeptical of these publishers' public announcements of future cleanliness said, "It looks good for a few months, I guess, because a certain firm has already bought its coming drives on four songs in a package deal."[17]

In regard to that meeting the MPCE sent out a letter to only 15 publishers, requesting they attend to once again try to tackle the problem. When the firms found out the letters went out to only a small number of firms they were angry, feeling they had been singled out as guilty of payola by implication. Nevertheless, representatives of nine firms did show up to kick around old ideas with the union, such as removing names of artists from the sheets for demanding or accepting money. Also considered was the idea of eliminating these sheets altogether, thus making payment unnecessary. These sheets were logs of radio broadcasts, said to be all bought by payola.[18] Making these sheets, many of them late-night New York programs, increased the probability of the tune going on to other, more major programs.

The sheets and rating system in general then in effect in the music business came under fire at the meeting, with the publishers calling them "leading factors in the spread and continuance of payola." Almost all expressed a desire to get rid of the sheets. Such sentiments had been expressed in the past but, while individual publishers had occasionally dropped subscriptions to such services, most soon picked them up again. One major, veteran publisher said of this whole, newfound publisher solidarity, "Pious intentions, sure I'm for cleaning up the industry, but the history of this business proves that publishers just can't pull together. Usually when one of these 'common cause' deals comes up, you'll find that everybody gets altruistic for very personal reasons. Get rid of payola when you find that everybody else is paying the same as you, and it's too competitive to pay. If we got rid of the sheets and kept the Accurate [sheet] confidential for publishers, plenty of publishers would be off to curry favor with some producer and would show him the report every week on the button."[19]

In the early part of this period song ratings were computed by several different organizations. The most referred to of these tabulations, or sheets, was Martin Alexander's Accurate Reporting Service, commonly just called Accurate. All leaned heavily toward counting song plays, or plugs, on late-night New York radio stations which featured orchestras picked up from remote. There was then no method of computing the size of the audience. Also these sheets disproportionately ignored the rest of the country in their tabulations. Songs were listed in order according to how many plugs they had received during the tabulation period, which was mainly one week. It was believed in the industry that it was necessary to get a song played here and tabulated because producers of major programs in more prime-time periods selected material based in part on these sheets. Hence the industry would claim these spots were all bought and paid for as a result of "drives" by publishers to get tabulated and move on to more lucrative exposure. Publishers blamed the orchestra leaders who were picked up remote in those time periods as totally corrupt and totally bought. The whole rating issue came under fire as a major cause of payola.

Around 1943 some music publishers began to agitate for dropping the 1-2-3 type of song listings and using instead an alphabetical list of the top 25 most played songs, with no mention made of the number of plugs each song received. These rating sheets were published regularly in the trade media, such as *Variety*, and readily accessible. Publishers conveniently forgot the past as they erroneously complained that "beautiful ballads . . . and the like are no more, because they can't get started. Everybody's just concentrating on making the sheet."[20] Similar sentiments would be expressed later when rock and roll came to dominate.

The MPCE and the MPPA joined forces in calling for alphabetical ratings to replace the 1-2-3 listings. Sole opposing publisher at a meeting which approved this resolution was Louis Bernstein of Shapiro, Bernstein, and Company, who argued that elimination of most played number totals would only strengthen the advantage of film songs, published by movie companies' subsidiary houses, which would then have an even bigger advantage of being picked by producers of major programs. Standing against this was the weight of opinion that if weekly totals ceased to be the song plugger's major effort, there would be no tendency to exaggerate the plug importance of certain bands. This particular resolve was initiated by the MPCE. Later in 1943 *Variety* started to publish the alphabetical list from Accurate instead of the same company's 1-2-3 list. This publication took a jaundiced view of the situation, warning that if any backsliding took place *Variety* would immediately revert to the 1-2- 3 format. Accurate continued to tabulate in the old format, with such listings still available as before to the music publishers. Theoretically, radio producers, the general public, and so on would no longer know the information. Aware of the obvious ways by which they could convey such information to others, *Variety* wrote, "it is because of this knowledge that all the music men must know how they stand, that the danger persists that the boys will be the boys of yore. It is to be hoped otherwise."[21]

One way around the problem of knowing just how high on the ratings a particular song stood was demonstrated by Nick Kenny, a radio columnist on the *New York Daily Mirror*. He was also a songwriter and a song plugger holding a union card in the MPCE. In one column in the summer of 1943 Kenny listed the three tunes that would have led the list under the old rating method. In second spot was a number written by Kenny. The MPCE hauled him on the carpet, dressing him down after he promised not to repeat the episodes. However, less than three years later Kenny did the same thing. His song "Blue" was again in the number two spot.[22]

In Chicago the MPCE caught one contact man making up numbers. This man hung around the lobby of the publisher's building each week until the messenger from the rating service arrived with the weekly report. After convincing the youngster to let him take the sheets, the plugger disappeared into an empty office where he typed in a bunch of imaginary plugs that were never aired. The MPCE fined him $300. An unusual twist in payola had a bandleader being paid by publishers not to play their songs on his programs. Networks customarily demanded an hour or more between plays of a specific song. Since this particular leader had a spot which didn't count in the rating tabulations but was directly adjacent to an hour which did count, he could prevent a song from being counted by delivering a rendition of it on his program. To avoid this possibility he was paid not to play particular tunes that publishers were then driving.[23]

Despite the change in rating systems, a year later publishers were once again howling about "the rampant increase in the practice of paying for plugs." Searching about for a scapegoat they hadn't yet used, some publishers complained the wartime manpower shortage was at least partly to blame for the latest payola epidemic. This theory had it that salaries for contact men had shot up so high that the plugger could and did pay for plugs himself. The irony of pluggers paying for plugs which kept them earning high enough salaries to keep paying was lost on the music houses. *Variety* said that if the situation didn't improve it would forthwith return to publishing the 1–2–3 system.[24]

A couple of publishers put pressure on John G. Paine, by then general manager of ASCAP, to call a meeting of publishers to discuss payola. Slowly, the publishers came over to the idea of jettisoning the Accurate ratings and replacing them with the Peatman system of tabulating plugs. The major improvement with this system was that it minimized the importance of New York local programs, particularly the remotes after 11 P.M. It was the major publishers who were most instrumental in bringing about this change. Dr. John Peatman was an associate dean at the City College of New York and associate professor of psychology. Radio Research was the name of his organization which turned out the ratings. Peatman began working on his rating system in 1941, encouraged by BMI at the time of the radio-ASCAP fight. Supposedly on the Peatman system, quality of performance was more important than quantity. This meant that daytime and early evening plugs were more important than late-night plays. Also more emphasis was placed on Chicago and Hollywood originations rather than relying almost exclusively on New York plays as well as factors such as listener rating of programs and the count. The Accurate tabulations were still used to form part of the New York base for the Peatman system. In December 1945 *Variety* announced it would go along with industry requests and begin publishing the Peatman sheet in place of the Accurate list. This sheet was an alphabetical list of the top 30 tunes with no plug totals listed.[25]

When Nick Kenny published his 1–2–3 list in 1946 with his song "Blue" in second spot under the old Accurate numeric method it didn't even show up that week in Peatman's alphabetical top 30. A few observers raised the obvious question as to why wouldn't payola change from being paid to night bands to daytime and early evening performers. The rather naive assumption put forth was that "since midday broadcasts . . . are operated by people well paid for their efforts . . . the payola evil will not be able to rear its head very high." In 1945 it was estimated that the amount of money paid out annually in payola by the publishers was in the vicinity of $500,000.[26]

Just a few weeks after the Peatman system was introduced optimism ran high over this new rating method, which publishers said caused "the gradual overcoming of the payola system which it was designed to kill . . . the payola evil has been all but eradicated, that if any is going on it is too small to worry about." Just a few more months after that a more realistic assessment began to emerge. Members of the West Coast faction of the MPCE claimed the Peatman system had not accomplished its aim of forestalling payola. According to them, payola was being handed around at daytime radio shows.[27]

Complaints poured into the MPCE offices about payola. Union president Bob Miller, frustrated and angry, asked the complainers to put up or shut up. From the beginning the music industry had been and remained dogged by complaints. However, when investigations were carried out no one seemed to know anything, with the result that no action could be taken. So frustrated was Miller that he went so far as to suggest a good deal of talk about payola was just that: it might actually be nonexistent. It was started by contact men who couldn't keep pace in the industry, couldn't get their share of legitimate plugs, and raised the cry of payola to cover their own inadequacies. Popularity of the Peatman system as the cure for payola continued to decline. During September 1946 *Variety* published a second group of 25 or so songs from the Peatman tabulations. These were also alphabetically arranged but not mingled with the top 30.[28]

An angry *Variety* published an editorial in October 1947 stating that it had only agreed to publish alphabetical ratings in order to eradicate payola. Claiming this had not happened, *Variety* said it would resume publishing ratings in numeric sequence. Said the publication,

> The fact is that the "drive" persists; so does the payola, in one form or another. And as for the idea of not showing this or that disk company, ad agency, sponsor, recording artist, and what-have-you, which song is No. 1 in performance on the sheet, that's so much eyewash. The 1–2–3, etc., breakdown theoretically for intra-office use, is widely swapped by publishers with outside contacts, to the degree that *Variety* abstaining from publishing said information is not only kidding the music men, but tending rather to insult the intelligence of almost all of their contacts.

So many protests flooded into *Variety* from the industry about this threat that the publication decided to take no immediate action on returning to numerical listing of ratings. None of the protestors denied the existence of payola but all thought the alphabetic ratings had achieved a lot in the right direction. All stressed that a return to numeric ratings would "revitalize an evil which has been considerably suppressed."[29]

The Peatman ratings were carried in *Variety* under the heading "Songs with Largest Radio Audience" in 1947. In September of that year the publication introduced a new record rating survey covering a different area.

This was called "Top Record Talent and Tunes." It was a weekly list of most requested records on disk jockey shows. Fifty top songs were listed numerically with the total number of points scored. The listing published on October 29, 1947 (for the week of October 19), was from 27 disk jockeys who worked in 18 cities. Each was named along with the station. Towns and jockeys were to vary week to week. These ratings had all the negative features which compelled the industry to go to an alphabetical system. It was a perfect setup to give payola to jockeys. That week in question 47 of the top 50 songs were licensed under ASCAP with only three under BMI.[30] This dominance which ASCAP would lose in less than a decade to BMI would strongly underpin the 1950s payola scandal.

In 1941 Fred Ebener, staff conductor for WOW, Omaha, an NBC affiliate, sent out a letter to New York publishers, offering to "cooperate" with them in performing their current tunes on his program fed by WOW to the Red network if they paid him $10 or $15 for each tune for what he called "arrangements." Pluggers got wind of this, turning the information over to Bob Miller, who then notified NBC and BMI. Station WOW licensed only BMI material. So Ebener's letter was sent only to BMI-affiliated publishers. Station manager John J. Gillin of WOW explained that Ebener's band preferred to use special over stock arrangements. To this end the orchestra had four men in the aggregation who got $15 for each arrangement. Gillin added that Ebener had exhausted the station's monthly budget for arrangement when a publisher requested him to play a tune. Ebener sent out the letter because of the budget, not knowing he was violating any rule, and stated as proof the very openness of the letter. Gillin promised that since Ebener now knew the rule the incident would not be repeated.[31]

Some publishers set up "offices" for their favorate bandleaders who came in from about 4 to 6 P.M. to make phone calls all over the country, charging them to the publishers. Loans were often made to bandsmen who were known to be bad pay-back risks. Other common forms of payola in the mid-1940s included, reported *Variety*, "fight tickets, endless meals, presents, entertainment (femme and otherwise) that go to certain recording executives and name bands, or that gift of a Frigidaire; and in another instance, groceries."[32] The "little black book" belonging to one bandleader almost surfaced, to the potential embarrassment of the industry, when the unnamed man was sued for divorce by his wife in 1944. She demanded $175 a week in alimony. When the leader complained, saying that was all he made, his wife retorted, "Oh, no, that's what you make as a musician, but you make much more from the payolas from the music publishers — and I have that little black book with your handwriting to prove it."[33]

Songwriter Peter Tinturin sued bandleader Freddy Martin around the same time for $167,000 for failure to live up to an agreement between them, calling for Martin to record songs and then plug those songs written by Tinturin. In return Martin was to receive half of all Tinturin's earnings from those songs. Martin did not fulfill the deal, claiming he didn't understand all of the provisions. Advance royalties received were split between the two men, said Tinturin, but Martin denied receiving any money. The suit was settled out of court.[34]

Most guests on an ABC radio program called "You're in the Act" were not paid the necessary minimum scale as set by the American Federation of Radio Artists. Instead, music publishers took care of them, in effect paying their salaries by paying those who performed their numbers. An unidentified top commercial radio show which programmed a lot of pop material asked publishers for $100 toward arrangements if they wanted their songs to be performed on the show.[35]

Broadcast Music began to arouse antipathy from other industry factions in the mid–1940s over its business methods. One thing BMI did was to set up bandsmen with the leader's own publishing company, financed fully by BMI. The tunes published were always supposedly written by the leaders involved, which they played on the air a minimum number of times to earn royalties advanced each quarter. Leaders who had such arrangements with BMI included Charlie Spivak and Sammy Kaye. Both of these men were asked to invest in their own publishing houses when the contract with BMI came up for renewal. Generally, these so-called publishing houses received $48 per plug from BMI, after starting up, on the basis of a minimum of 150 plugs per year. Many of the ASCAP-affiliated houses were angered by this ploy, calling it "the worst subterfuge possible." These BMI setups were said to be one of the major motivators behind the ASCAP publishers threatening to go "back" to full-scale payola payments. Noted *Variety*, "These ventures have unquestionably been responsible for a great amount of the violations, but not all. Many ASCAP outfits, and top ones, too, are as guilty of infractions in various ways."[36]

Singers also got involved in publishing ventures. As Frank Sinatra's income grew he entered the publishing field in 1942 or 1943. Ben Barton, who owned the struggling Barton Music, recalled, "I submitted 'If You Are But a Dream' for a plug and wound up in a business with Frank." Quickly, Ben owned one-third of his company with the other two-thirds split between Frank and his associate Hank Sanicola. Barton Music expanded by leaps and bounds after the singer became a partner. Soon it was the owner of Sinatra's radio signature tune, "Put Your Dreams Away." The singer's biographer wrote, "Barton Music, the first of a complex of publishing companies developed by Sinatra, flourished during Frank's big years, floundered and went bankrupt during his decline, and came back strong in 1955."[37]

While Bing Crosby was filming *Dixie* a conflict arose between songwriters Johnny Burke and Jimmy Van Heusen on one side and Paramount officials on the other. The writers wanted to establish their own music publishing firm and to publish their own tunes as part of a publishing combine led by Buddy Morris. Crosby was part of the Morris group, having "shifted his publishing interests from Santly-Joy-Select." Paramount wanted to publish the songs from *Dixie* with its own companies. Despite this conflict, the team finished the songs for the film and Bing proceeded to record them for the sound track. Noted as a quick study, Bing recorded the first number quickly and efficiently. When he attempted the second number, "Sunday, Monday or Always" — expected to be the film's biggest hit — he couldn't get it right, always singing off-key or too high or too low. When asked what was wrong Bing said, "I just don't seem to get it. Just as Paramount doesn't seem to get the Burke and Van Heusen music company. That's understandable: I don't get Johnny and Jimmy's song; Paramount doesn't get their publishing idea." After executives of Paramount held a hurried conference over Bing's "difficulty," Burke and Van Heusen got their publishing company. Bing then recorded the song perfectly in one take.[38]

Cut-ins seemed to play a much less prominent role in the payola scene in the 1940s than they had in the 1930s, though still present to some degree. A few specific examples from earlier times came to light in that decade in court battles during copyright renewals. "Down by the Old Mill Stream" was originally copyrighted in 1910, with Tell Taylor as sole writer. While that was how the original copyright certificate read, printed copies of the song all listed one Earl K. Smith as coauthor. "Heartaches" was written in 1930 by John Klenner and Al Hoffman. They cut in bandsman Ben Bernie as coauthor for one-third of the royalties, with Bernie agreeing to plug the tune. This song enjoyed its greatest popularity and sales during a 1947 revival. As Bernie died in 1943 the two actual authors tried to have Bernie's name removed, arguing that Bernie was in only as long as he plugged the song. The total sum involved was $21,000 in royalties for the 1947 period.[39]

Despite the rather widespread knowledge of payola, particularly within the industry itself and its seemingly large size, the Treasury Department showed no interest in investigating what was very likely a large amount of unreported income until the late 1950s scandal. Once in 1944 it was rumored that Treasury was investigating the issue. The rumor was never confirmed and, in any event, nothing happened.[40]

As 1949 came to a close the contact men were in their usual worry over losing their jobs to the check-is-in-the-mail concept. At one of their last meetings that year the MPCE decided to set a deadline date, after which any member caught in a payoff would be fined or expelled from the union, a policy designed to impress on their membership the urgency of reporting violators and to attempt to enlist the cooperation of publishers.

Attesting to the group's ineptitude and impotence was the fact that they had been trying to do this through the entire 1940s. One account reported, "More and more music firms — and top-drawer outfits are included — are paying off the bandleaders. Many of these firms have been firing pluggers and not replacing them, figuring that it's cheaper to bribe for plugs." As usual with such reports, payola was then reported to have never been worse.

> From all indications during the last two months an average of only two orchestras in New York City were not on the take. The price ranges from a piddling $15 for an alleged "transposition" [the stock arrangement in an altered key] to $90 for an orchestration. A noted society bandleader in one of New York's best known hotels regularly charges the $90 fee. Bands, small groups, trios, etc., on location, in hotels, grillrooms, ballrooms, saloons and anywhere else that had a radio wire, have their price. Many a leader takes a band into a spot for union scale, figuring to make up the difference from the publishers — and usually does quite nicely.

Some leaders reportedly took on so many song commitments paid in advance they were unable to play them all over the air. They went to pluggers, explained the problem and tried to extract more money from them. One leader took $50 for a week's worth of plugs, only to split the scene after delivering just one. So bought were bandsmen that the consensus among publishers and pluggers was, "It's a waste of time to make the spots any more." Song pluggers faced further pressure from the decline of the live plug in favor of the recorded plug. Record promotion specialists were hired, with pluggers fired at some firms. The live plug remained important only for earning royalty points with ASCAP. Soon that function would also decline as live acts disappeared in the wake of television. Often bandsmen would squeeze up to 12 tunes into a 15-minute spot — one chorus of each. Playing one chorus was enough to earn an ASCAP count as if the entire tune had aired. Each music industry faction blamed a different faction for the evil of payola. Said one account, "Song pluggers blame their bosses for making the deals without the pluggers' knowledge. Publishers blame their employees for buying plugs out of their own pockets. The established professional men with solid contacts blame the newcomers and the lazy pluggers for starting the bribe system."[41] Just becoming a major force in the industry at the time was the disk jockey. Soon he would be everybody's fall guy, the "real" cause of payola.

Radio stations have been broadcasting records since they started up but they mostly didn't because at that time it was not considered good broadcasting. The odd time a station did so during those early years of radio there was little or no regard for showmanship, production values, or programming records for variety, pace, and so on. A typical way of introducing a record was then, "And now we bring you a phonograph record." Up into the 1940s the law required that when a disk was played it had to be introduced as recorded — as distinct from live — so the public wouldn't be deceived into thinking the performer was there in person. Pressure for this measure came mainly from the musicians' union, which would have been happiest if all records were banned from the air to save their jobs. Most stations employed many musicians as their live, in-house orchestras. Bands picked up by stations from remotes were, of course, live. While there were disk jockeys, they functioned more as introducers, keeping personality out. Emcees or announcers filled in the dead time from remotes for orchestras as radio couldn't abide even a few seconds of dead air as orchestras moved from one tune to another. They also were mere incidentals to the proceedings, not integral elements.

After Al Jarvis the rise of the disk jockey to rank of superstar in the music industry began in New York in 1935 at New York's independent station WNEW. What happened there had ramifications for all radio stations. In 1935, at a time when radio was totally dominated by a small handful of networks, WNEW was an independent station. Having no network affiliation meant a station had little chance for making any impact or achieving much notice. The events of 1935 at WNEW would forever alter the course that these independent stations would follow in the future as it pointed the way for future programming, though it would be over a decade before a pattern really caught on. These events laid the groundwork for the domination of the music industry in the 1950s and onward by records, independent stations, disk jockeys, rock music, and a famous payola scandal.

Martin Block was by no means the first disk jockey. However, he was the first to become a huge star in the field and he was the first to elevate the position of disk jockey to that of a coveted post. He was the first to understand and implement the concept of music programming on his show — as opposed to randomly putting disks on a turntable. Block arrived broke in New York from California in the winter of 1934. After brief and unsuccessful stints as a salesman, he landed a $25 a week staff announcing job at WNEW in December. Only a year or so old at the time, WNEW was busy blueprinting itself as just another station like all the others with a kid show at the right time, recipes at another, and so on. Also employed at the station was Bernice Judis, who in later years would move up to station manager. She thought WNEW should program against the networks rather than like them. To her it seemed logical that the thing to put opposite network shows was good pop music and lots of it. She recalled, "Nobody at the station really paid much attention to me — until my eyes lighted on Martin Block's tonsils. Then I came into my own. I could finally put into effect my kind of program schedule."

Independently, Block was thinking along similar lines, for one day he asked Judis to listen to a show he wanted to put on the air: something he called "The Make Believe Ballroom." With only a dozen or so disks at the station, Block went across the street to the Liberty Music Shop where he bought a few more to audition for Judis. Bernice recalled, "I was excited. I put him on the air the next morning." That was February 3, 1935. At the time WNEW was carrying live broadcasts of a notorious New York trial in progress, which gave Block a large, built-in audience for "Ballroom" which was aired between pickups from the courthouse. "Ballroom" became an instant hit that soon aired six days a week, 3.5 hours a day. Key to its success was its mood or block booking, the formula of broadcasting carefully selected records in solid, across-the-board blocks. While it's a formula that has been all too obvious for a long time, it was unknown in 1935. Martin avoided intrusive mentioning of the fact that his program's music was recorded. He gave, however, the impression that performers were there in the room with him by talking to them. A typical introduction by Block to a Sinatra number went, "Come on now, Frank, give us a little old song. Hm-m-m?"

In 1947 Block worked under contract with two independent stations and the Mutual network. Reportedly he earned a total of $750,000 a year. Block made more money on the air than such stars as Jack Benny and Fred Allen. These latter two men received a higher gross but both, as was the custom, had to pay costars, singers, actors, musicians, and sometimes writers out of their grosses. Block had only to pay his two secretaries. According to Block, necessary ingredients for the success of a disk jockey were "Long hours on the air every day with great regularity . . . intimacy of conversation . . . the ability to make people feel that you know what you're talking about (even if you don't) . . . and a good basic knowledge of pop music and performance." Judis thought the reasons for Block's success included "Not only his radio personality, those golden pitchpipes and that irresistible selling power. . . . But also good taste. Good taste in everything he does on the air. That plus a wonderful ability to pick talent and a kind of 12th sense about hit tunes. He can pick them like no one else . . . he almost never misses."[42]

Even though Block and his program had achieved the status of institution, imitators were slow to follow. Disk jockeys were still not a position to aspire to in the minds of many. That began to crumble somewhat in October 1946 when Ted Husing, considered the nation's top radio sports announcer, quit his job as director of sports at CBS to become a disk jockey at New York's WHN. Husing's annual salary went from $27,500 at CBS to $130,000 at WHN. At first friends asked Husing not to make the move. After he did and it didn't affect his social standing, more followed. Said observers, "Block made the racket pay, but Husing made it respectable."

Calling his program the "Ted Husing Bandstand," he would introduce a Sinatra number thus: "And now Frank Sinatra steps to the Bandstand to sing the lovely ballad 'Time After Time.'" Trailing off after this, barely discernible to listeners were the two words "on record."

A final crumbling took place when shortly after this trombonist Tommy Dorsey became a disk spinner with a guaranteed salary of $1.5 million over five years. Paul Whiteman traded in his baton and live musicians for a turntable and a stack of wax. Whiteman earned $208,000 a year as a disk jockey. A typical chatter from him went, "Hello gals; this is Paul Whiteman. I've got some wonderful records to spin for you, honey chile, to help you spin out those everlovin', everlastin' household joberoos."

It was a full turnabout for the king of jazz Whiteman who, in 1939, unsuccessfully tried to enjoin WNEW from playing records made by his band. Fought and lost in Whiteman's name, the suit was actually financed and prosecuted by RCA Victor. At that time record makers feared the then only budding growth of disk jockeys. They reasoned that if radio owners could listen free to records they wouldn't buy them. Those worried companies were proved wrong, for in 1946 they sold in excess of 242 million disks, better than 10 times the number sold in 1936. The late 1940s would convince the record companies once and for all that disk jockeys actually powerfully aided the sale of records. "Peg o' My Heart" was revived after over two decades by Eddie Hubbard on Chicago's WIND where he played it doggedly. After that about a dozen record companies issued versions of the old number. In 1947 Kurt Webster at Charlotte, North Carolina's WBT revived the 1930 tune "Heartaches." Webster's listeners alone bought 50,000 copies in a few weeks. A total of more than three million copies of various renditions of "Heartaches" were sold in the fall of that year. Both examples illustrated the burgeoning power of disk jockeys to make a hit song through constant playing.

Head of the American Federation of Musicians (AFM) was James Caesar Petrillo, who led a number of skirmishes in the 1940s when he barred his musicians from recording songs — to keep their jobs as live musicians. He regarded records and radio as involved in a conspiracy to destroy his musicians. Leading this conspiracy were the disk spinners. As they emerged as a new aristocracy in radio they took on a special menace in his eyes. As name bandsmen joined the other side Petrillo remarked, "If the trend continues more and more name band leaders will disband their organizations to take advantage of what is developing into one of the biggest box-office attractions in the radio industry." Of course, all Petrillo's efforts failed. The only small victory he gained was the beginning of a special fund paid into by the record companies. It was to be used by the AFM to relieve unemployment among its members. While its form and the amount collected have varied over time, it remains to this day. Most of us have been exposed to it through free summer music concerts put on by professional musicians, usually in parks, in cities all over North America.[43]

Record companies began to take notice of the disk jockey seriously by around 1946. They started to deliver their new material through emissaries "to distribute baubles among the disk jockeys and by other means invite the amity of those so recently despised. . . . Band leaders and singers who are understandably anxious to encourage large sales of their recordings considerately commit small favors for the disk jockeys. They seldom find it inconvenient, for example, to accept invitations from influential disk jockeys to appear in person on their shows."[44]

In 1947 the MPCE considered a complaint about a disk jockey from one of the major networks, whose demands on pluggers approaching him to play their employers' songs "have become so strong" that numerous complaints were brought about him to the MPCE. As in the past this group found no way of dealing with the situation. In some cases contact men were losing their jobs. Song publishing firm Robbins-Feist-Miller hired Hollywood press agent Barney McDevitt to promote their numbers to jockeys, as opposed to using song pluggers as the firm did in New York. McDevitt serviced 27 disk spinners on the West Coast, providing them with free prerelease records. Publisher Hill and Range fired one of their MPCE members, Wally Schuster, and replaced him with three non–MPCE press agents assigned to contact disk jockeys to promote their material. By 1949 the MPCE got together to petition the publishers to cooperate with them by enlisting MPCE members to service disk jockeys, the pluggers' "natural enemy," wrote Variety.[45]

Nine out of ten radio stations had disk jockey shows in 1947, broadcasting such programs for an average of 2 hours and 12 minutes a day. Most likely time for these shows to run was 7–8 A.M. and 4–5 P.M. with 25 percent of stations airing a disk jockey in each of those periods. During 6–7 A.M. and 11 P.M.–midnight 16 percent of the stations broadcast a disk jockey show in each period.[46]

When record buyers were asked what caused them to buy a particular disk, the most popular reason given by those who responded was that it was played by a jockey — 24 percent. A distant second at 13 percent was label first out with song. Teenagers directly made 10 percent of all record purchases but the biggest pop record buyers were families with teenagers.[47]

Several radio station managers in various Midwest cities clamped down on certain disk jockey activity. One platter spinner was found to have a side interest in a record store, while in another city a disk jockey was found to own a piece of a local record distributing firm. He had to divest it. The Disc-Covery Record Company of Sacramento, California, sent a letter to disk jockeys in 1948, offering them a proposition in which commissions would be paid to the spinners on sales of its records. In the letter the company said it would bypass the normal channels so that all revenue would be divided three ways between "The artist, the announcer and the Disc-Covery Record Co." Station executives were angry over this proposition because it was addressed directly to the jockeys rather than station management. This complaint was passed on to the National Association of Broadcasters (NAB), who apparently took no action.[48]

Also by 1948 jockeys were being involved in record royalties. *Variety* reported, "There have been several instances during recent weeks wherein jocks have been offered contracts calling for cuts on disk earnings in return for plays. . . . Payolas to jockeys are not new, but in the past the methods have been confined to an occasional $10 bill." *Billboard* reported on one jockey who called a meeting of his clients to tell them of a hike in his payola fee. A small independent record company, not involved in that case, made a complaint to the FCC that it could only get its records played through payolas.[49]

Newsweek also commented on the growing power of jockeys, chiding them by reporting, "With all the power in their programs and no directors to ride herd on them, some new jockeys are unrestrained in swiping ideas from anyone. They mercilessly play the records that will do them the most good."[50]

New York's Metropolitan Association of Disk Jockeys (MADJ) responded angrily to these *Billboard* tactics asking them to name names, but the publication declined on the ground of protecting sources while at the same time praising MADJ's stance against the payola "evil." On a wider level the National Association of Disk Jockeys held a fund-raising event, the proceeds of which were to be used to establish scholarships at various music schools. Behind this move lay a desire by the jockey group to "attempt to lift from its members the 'stigma' of being labeled the guys who earn more coin out of playing disks than the artists who make them, meanwhile doing or paying nothing in return."[51]

5 Pictures of Dead Presidents, 1950–1958

During the 1950s there was no organization which even attempted, however ineffectually, to control payola. The song pluggers union dropped the matter as quickly as they had taken it up at the beginning of the 1940s. Nor were the pluggers the subject of much media attention in this period, even though over 600 of them were employed by various music firms in 1955.[1] With no group unofficially policing payola, emphasis shifted away from the givers of payola more to the takers. It must have been these contact men who delivered the bribes to disk jockeys but as they no longer wrung their hands in public over the matter the music houses and pluggers were much less in focus.

Orchestra leader Vincent Lopez was placed on the MPCE's unfair list at the very beginning of 1950, charged by the union with "continued and flagrant practices detrimental to the music publishing industry and to the members of the union." Charges weren't specified but apparently revolved around fees for special arrangements. Lopez denied taking money for plugs but admitted accepting arrangement expenses. "I spend $15,000 a year for arrangements," he said, "and I have bills to prove it." Petrillo said it was perfectly okay to be recompensated for arrangements, and he believed he was within his rights in collecting for them. According to Lopez the cost of an average arrangement was $75. Commenting on being placed on the MPCE's unfair list he said, "I think they need me a lot more than I need them. I've been trying out arrangements for them for the past nine years on experimental time.... If that's what the union wants to do, let them, but you can be sure the publishers will still be coming to see me."[2] Bandsmen rapidly lost their influence and position of power to make hits during this decade.

Singers were mentioned briefly as "flagrantly indulging" in payola with one unnamed top female vocalist demanding everything she could from publishers. "It's either a straight cash deal or some cut-in arrangement on the tune as the price for her wax version," reported one account. Music stores in New York worked their own deals with publishers for plugging numbers over their in-store speaker system. One shop charged the publisher

$50 plus a case of records for each number, cutting two such deals each week. Those free records were sold in the store, netting more profit.[3] However, examples such as these were few and far between as the emphasis zeroed in on disk jockeys.

In England the code between the BBC and the Music Publishers Association (MPA) was effective in 1950, according to John Firman of the Feldman publishing house. Firman claimed the two-year-old pact worked effectively, with his company not having to pay to get its music aired. A few years later jockey Jack Payne said the situation was healthier than it used to be but that payola was not totally ended. Under the BBC and MPA agreement each publisher could select four songs each month to be included in an official play list. From this list of 392 songs — based on the 98 publishers who signed the agreement — a bandleader had to select 60 percent of his music to be performed on the BBC. If a publisher violated the agreement his entire catalogue of music was struck from the BBC. In Payne's early days he recalled having been offered, and declining, 15s to play a certain number. During the war he turned down an offer of £25 to play a number. In the early 1950s he said a particular singer was demanding £50 for featuring a number on a BBC program. Much as in the United States the publishers complained about the financial drain from payola, held meetings at which they pledged to stop it, but almost immediately broke rank to begin dispensing payola again.[4]

At the end of the 1950s Labor M.P. Roy Mason urged the government to get commercial deejay shows taken off the BBC and ITA because of "the discrimination which is taking place." He wanted an inquiry to investigate possible payola arrangements between jockeys, television executives, and record companies. Film actor and jockey Richard Attenborough said, "I get letters from record companies asking me to lunch to discuss a certain record. I tell them I haven't time, but will hear the record if they send it along. They do not send me bottles of whiskey or bundles of pound notes." Deejay Peter Noble said, "I have never been offered any bribes, although I could dine out every day of my life if I accepted half the invitations I got." Jack Payne declared "most emphatically" that Britain's pop music industry was operating under payola. Despite this, the government rejected the call for an inquiry. Radio Luxembourg, which was beamed into Britain, offered the best bet for payola since sponsors could buy time of their own on that outlet. Several of the major labels ran their own shows from that station. If a company was too small to buy an entire program it could buy a plug openly. First the firm had to get the okay from Radio Luxembourg, which issued "limited" permits, then it was allowed to "entertain" a jockey.[5]

In 1962 payola was reported as "dead" in the United Kingdom. Partly it was said to be due to Radio Luxembourg and partly due to the check system. Reportedly it was also less profitable. A plug in the past produced sheet music profits of around $700–$800. A comparable 1950's record plug brought in only $50–$60. A few years after that payola was reported to be rife once more. This time it was the pirate radio stations who were demanding inducements to get records played over their airwaves. The pirate stations usually wanted straight cash, royalty cut-ins, or artists to perform services for the station for free or at reduced rates.[6]

The last mention of British payola surfacing in the U.S. press was in 1971 after the Sunday paper *News of the World* alleged that it had un-covered evidence that payments of cash, prostitutes, and all expenses paid holidays were made by song pluggers to deejays to secure air time for their records.[7]

In the United States by 1950 the jockey was acknowledged to be holding an important position as middle man between the record manufac-turer and the record buyer. "Hundreds" of men had become jockeys by then. A few years later, in 1956, there were about 4,000 in the United States. Many established themselves as personalities and stars in their own right in their own localities. Salaries were large for those in that category. In New York John Gambling (WOR) made $150,000 a year; still going strong after 20 years Martin Block (WABC) got $100,000 locally per year plus network affiliation fees; Ted Husing (WMGM) earned $60,000. In Hollywood Harry Maizlish of WKBW pulled down $200,000 a year, with Peter Potter of KLAC and Al Jarvis of WFWB each getting an estimated $60,000 annually. Howard Miller drew $70,000 in Chicago, with Pitts-burgh's Reg Cordic making an estimated $35,000.[8]

Disk jockey power continued to increase with newspapers in cities such as Detroit and Pittsburgh listing weekly the ten top records, as selected by disk jockeys. Detroit published the selections of six different jockeys each week, rotating amongst those working in the area. Publishers and record companies both frowned upon this practice as they believed it allowed the platter spinners to influence the fate of a song with potential record buyers who didn't even listen to their own shows. If the practice of publishing such lists escalated nationwide, the industry foresaw payola mushrooming to new heights as firms would have to give a bigger "ro-mance" to get themselves a spot on these lists. Disk jockeys were quick to realize the potential for income from other sources as they developed side interests. In 1955 there were 20 percent promoting personal appearance events; another 13 percent tried songwriting; and further 18 percent were engaged in promoting a range of activities such as puppet shows, wrestling events, magic shows, summer theater, record reviewing, publicity and promotion for talent, record distribution, and manufacturing. All of this produced extra income for the deejays. Even the usually anonymous record librarians came in for attention. A large station such as New York's WNEW had three on staff in 1955. It was their job to listen to new material, classify it, file it, and in some cases to act as a censor, putting anything with suggestive lyrics into the "forget" file. At that time WNEW received 75–100 new records each week, representing 150–200 sides to listen to. While they were not on-air personalities, they would still in some cases be offered payola[9]; nothing, of course, like that offered to the disk jockeys who were reported to be widely on the take by the start of the 1950s.

When Murray Arnold, program director of Philadelphia's WIP, addressed a meeting of radio program directors in January 1950 he complained, "Program directors let disc jockeys get away with murder." According to him, payola was common in the industry with spinners being deluged with "gifts, cash and dates . . . if you know what I mean," from record companies. As further evidence Arnold cited a small record manufacturer who bought time on WIP but threatened to withdraw his business unless his disks got a bigger plug, claiming "I could split that $225 a week between your five jockeys and get more plays than I do now. That's what I do on three other stations." When Arnold substituted as a disk jockey himself for one week he said he received three calls from promoters offering from $5 to $10 a week if he played their songs. In Arnold's mind the solution to the problem lay in not allowing the jockeys complete control of programming their own shows. He also urged other program directors not to overestimate the importance of any single spinner, saying, "I can replace any disk jockey and do just as well with another one after a three-month build-up."[10]

A New York disk jockey by the name of Wayne Howell made no attempt to hide what he was doing. He was attempting to package and sell a music show around the country to be titled "House of Music." Howell planned to charge publishers 25 cents per plug, multiplied by the number of stations picking up the program. Thus if it was heard in 100 cities one song played would cost the publisher $25. Industry reaction was divided with some firms interested and some opposed, calling it a legalized form of payola. Apparently, this show didn't get off the ground. Along similar lines was a group formed by certain spinners on the West Coast called DJL (Disk Jockeys and Librarians) to enroll small record companies, play their releases excessively, and share in the profits. The DJL assumed that jockeys around the country could make a hit of a record if they all ganged up on it at the same time. When this group tried to recruit in Chicago the reception was icy. A memo was issued by WGN to its staff not to get involved. Jockey Stan Dale of WJJD called the DJL a group that corrupted the objective purpose of the disk jockeys — to play what the audience wanted to hear while that city's best known jockey, Howard Miller, termed the idea "open-faced payola." The DJL also never got off the ground.[11]

In 1955 spinner Bill Randle, speaking of the situation, said, "There are millions of dollars of payola every year. One well-known jock allegedly received a Cadillac which sat for several weeks in his garage. He hadn't yet learned to drive." At the same time the still largely unknown Alan Freed said he accepted valuable gifts but, he explained, "not in front. If I've helped somebody, I'll accept a nice gift, but I wouldn't take a dime to plug a record. I'd be a fool to; I'd be giving up control of my program."[12]

Another spinner stated, "it is a fact that the publishers come in to 'romance' us regularly; their top executives woo us; the heads of record companies also woo us and, frankly, try to corrupt us." A representative of one of the major labels explained to him that his company had a deejay signed up as their special exploitation man in both Philadelphia and Cleveland. They wanted to do the same with this unnamed jockey in the New York area.[13]

Billboard surveyed the scene in a two-part series at the end of 1950 and the beginning of 1951, concluding, "payola to disk jockeys is at an all-time peak, according to the parties who should know — the publishers and record men who do the paying. They, who must accept the onus for having started the practice, are now moaning the blues." Two platter spinners in a New England town were reportedly on the take. They had their own agreement whereby if one was "driving" a particular number the other one laid off. One usually took his out as a percentage deal with the distributor — say — percent of the gross on all local sales of the disk — while the second man preferred a flat-rate deal of $50–$100 to drive a specific song. A jockey in Ohio commanded as high as $400 to drive a number, while in Philadelphia several spinners worked percentage or flat-rate deals. They were known to tell naive publisher representatives, "Sure we'll play it — 50 bucks a week." Newark, New Jersey, had a spinner on a "fat percentage" arrangement with an important distributor. A New England distributor for a large record company refused to offer payola to a jockey because he was already being paid by five other companies. In retaliation this deejay immediately banned all the label's records. Trying to settle the problem the company sent out a troubleshooter who, after due consideration, recommended the deejay be put on the take.[14]

In the pop music field the brunt of the payola was said to fall on the record distributor, not the parent record company. It was the distributor who paid out the cash although record companies often cooperated in paying off the spinners on flat-rate deals, particularly if the distributor told the record company that a particular spinner was doing a good job on a certain record at $50 a week. In such a case the record company would usually come up with half the bribe. In addition, publishing firms did considerable subsidizing. Besides cash they sent gifts to spinners, cut them in on tunes, and entertained them with lavish all expenses paid trips to New York.[15]

When a deejay plugged a local concert on the air he might get as much as 1 percent of the gross. Some took over an entire concert promotion themselves. Many jockeys opened record stores. If on the take they took their payola in the form of boxes of records, which they then sold in those stores. Others turned to songwriting, publishing, or talent management. Some stations tried to control the situation by limiting the number of air plays a record or label could get during a one-week period. The jockeys felt they deserved whatever they could get. After all, they reasoned, they sold time for their stations, products for advertisers, and records for the music industry; therefore, there was nothing immoral or wrong in what they were doing.[16]

While *Billboard* found the pop music field rife with payola it claimed it was even worse, more rampant and more open in the rhythm and blues field. Payola had permeated rhythm and blues "to the core." Almost unanimously the industry concerns in rhythm and blues stated, "We have to pay, period." This was a not so subtle form of racist attack on black elements of the music industry. It meshed perfectly with the old stereotype of the dishonest black. In home areas of record companies these firms paid deejays directly themselves either on a flat-rate basis per drive or a regular monthly stipend, usually $25–$50. Outside these areas it was the distributor who paid off the spinners in one form or another. One rhythm and blues record manufacturer paid two New York spinners $25 a month each with $15 to a third; $25 to a deejay in Newark; two jockeys at $15 each in Philadelphia with a third at $25; one spinner in Pittsburgh at $15; and for a drive on a specific tune in Detroit he paid $10.[17]

As a side business one deejay had an interest in a nightclub where he was known to bring pressure to bear on singers to work the spot at a lower than usual rate. Failure to do so and the spinner threatened to cut off the singer's records from his show. Another jockey collected $200 from a vocalist to plug her engagement at a local club. A spinner with a television talent show on the side got the talent for free, while several were on the payroll of jazz clubs for delivering on-air commercials for those establishments. The radio stations got nothing. For promoting concerts in New York one deejay commanded 5 percent of the gross, another, less influential, got 3 percent on the concerts he touted. A large city was said to be in the clutches of a lead rhythm and blues jockey who owned several record stores, was programmed on several stations, and was on the payroll of every rhythm and blues distributor in the city. Among other things this man got 200 free copies of every record he played. Admitting to being on the take, one deejay explained, "You don't necessarily have to pay to get on my show. I'll play any records my listeners want. Further, I don't charge anybody up front. If they come to me after I've helped them with a record and want to thank me with cash, I accept it. Also, I declare every dime on my tax return. In my best year the whole deal amounted to $2,200 in payola. I don't need it — I get a percentage of all spot announcements. I'd be happy to see them all cut it out." Record manufacturers claimed they did pay this man cash in advance, an average monthly fee of $25. Regarding the whole payola situation, both in the pop and rhythm and blues fields, *Billboard* concluded, "There's little prospect for a cure."[18]

Over two years later *Variety* claimed payola was more serious in the rhythm and blues field and hillbilly field than in the pop world. Jockeys were said to be making frank pitches for payoffs before agreeing to play a number. Small, independent record companies were said to be much more amenable to paying because the jockeys could move enough copies to make it worthwhile. "As a result, the payola has become a normal part of the indie diskeries' operation. Majors, on the other hand, have been placed in a corner, since there is no other channel to crack the rhythm and blues and hillbilly markets except through deejay spins. In some cases, the majors' distribs are forced to make payola deals with the jocks in order to unload their merchandise."[19]

Articles such as these laid the groundwork for shifting much of the blame for payola away from its source — large, white publishers and record companies — onto weaker elements — small, black indies and deejays — with emphasis on the black spinners. By targeting rhythm and blues and country, focus was also switched to the smaller and weaker BMI licensing agency away from the powerful, white ASCAP. Both rhythm and blues and country were almost completely licensed through BMI. These elements would later come together at the end of the 1950s, where ASCAP versus BMI, black versus white, youth versus age, and rock versus pop would be fought under the guise of a crusade against payola.

Certain cities became known as places where payola was particularly rife. In 1951 it was Boston and Chicago who were reported as the worst of the cities. Soon thereafter Philadelphia came to be viewed as a wide-open payola town for disk jockeys, primarily because of the large number of independent disk companies headquartered there. Prices for steady spins on a deejay's show ranged from $50–$100 weekly, depending on the drawing power of the deejay. Such drives by spinners could produce local hits, with records selling from 20,000–40,000 copies in the area. Major record companies were said to be annoyed by the situation but prepared to pay off in order to get spins. Several independent labels in Philadelphia responded angrily to the assertion in *Variety* about their town. Ivan Ballen, head of Gotham and 20th Century in Philadelphia, claimed he had no trouble getting air play without resorting to payola. Ballen thought the article cast the Philadelphia spinner fraternity under a cloud and that independent companies might have a more difficult time in the future getting plugs — legitimate ones. *Variety* responded by rehashing its early article that the majors were getting a disproportionately lower share of spins in Philadelphia. It was easier to blame payola — rightly or wrongly — for that than to consider that taste in music might be changing. It was still a little before the rock explosion but perceptible shifts were occurring. It was the indies and blacks who were largely supplying the new material, at the expense of the white majors. Philadelphia was one of the cities leading the way. Baltimore was another city which became known as a heavy payola town. Deejays regularly received $5 a spin from the independent record companies. Several radio stations tried to curb the practice by adopting a policy of not spinning records unless the label bought time on the air. In some unexplained fashion this move was supposed to halt payola.[20]

With their power to make or break songs deejays had no trouble getting performers to appear on their show to give interviews without receiving any payment. In response to this both the American Guild of Variety Artists and the American Federation of Musicians banned their members from giving free guest shots and recording their voices on tapes or transcriptions destined for disk jockey use. James Petrillo, president of AFM, argued that through the use of these tapes spinners created the illusion to their audience that the performers were actually in the studio. Still bearing a grudge against canned music Petrillo said these voice tapes were "contributing heavily to the development of the mechanical program. The disk jockey is the only one who benefits because no other music is ever employed and the leader is never paid for his services." George Jay, a Hollywood deejay, found a way to circumvent the AGVA edict that any member appearing on a deejay program emanating from a café must be paid. This ban hit Jay, who aired his four-hour nightly program from the King's Restaurant, particularly hard. Jay interviewed performers between records by phoning them, amplifying both sides of the conversation. If a performer was actually in the restaurant Jay sent them into the café's phone booth, conducting his interview from a distance of a few feet.[21]

Record companies had on their staffs salaried employees known as "a and r" men, standing for artists and repertoire. It was the job of these men to find songs for their companies and then match up a singer under contract with a number suited to his or her style and personality. These are senior-level positions in the industry. One of the best known a and r men was Mitch Miller, who spent many years with Columbia Records in that capacity. These men were also involved in receiving payola in the 1950s, working many of the same deals as did the deejays. Besides taking cash to select particular tunes, some a and r men had their own publishing firms or "working relationships" with established firms. Naturally enough, releases tended to come from these firms. Some a and r men became songwriters, cutting themselves in on tunes with the legitimate writers. Others turned to talent management either directly or indirectly.[22]

On rare occasions jockeys rose against other jockeys out of moral concern or perhaps because they were being left out of the payola pot.

Sixteen Detroit area deejays got together to ban the playing of Coral, Jubilee, Label X, and Kapp records until further notice. They took this action because they believed two area spinners were being paid to give preference to those labels. After monitoring the pair's programming for two years the group of 16 charged that releases from the four labels were played out of all proportion to their popularity. In addition, the pair was accused of doctoring the "Detroit Disk Jockey Association list of the Top 10 records" with the payola labels instead of playing the actual list. Representatives of the four labels somehow ironed out the difficulties.[23]

Not surprisingly, the deejays tended to downplay the prevalence of payola. Most admitted to its existence but claimed its incidence was limited mainly to underpaid spinners working the hinterlands. Rationalizations included the idea that payoffs and kickbacks occurred in many business areas, yet those fields weren't tainted as totally corrupt as was the music business. All the insinuations were running down the entire spinner fraternity as well as making the public confused and suspicious of even legitimate song plugs. Jockeys asserted that due to poor sales record companies and distributors resorted to heavy pressure tactics, making it difficult for the deejays to resist the temptation of payola. One complained that low paid spinners resented the fact that record companies never bought time on their show which would enable them to get a wage hike. "They don't support in their own advertising the media that supports them," he added. Some of the spinners felt the pressure would be off both companies and jocks if manufacturers cut their releases in half. Deejay Art Ford of WNEW felt the industry needed policing, saying, "A policing board founded by a reputable group and comprised of top deejays and distribs could weed out the black sheep."[24]

Radio stations reacted strongly. One, WFMS, issued a booklet to its personnel which stated, "A monster has developed within the past six or seven years known as payola. Announcers are approached by record companies, publishers, music stores, songwriters and record distributors, and asked to push their particular recordings or selections. The payola may be anything from a cigarette lighter, a $10 bill or the down payment on a new car, depending on the announcer's importance.... Any announcer at WFMS who is found guilty of accepting gratuities (payolas) will be immediately discharged." Station WFMS insisted that its deejays refrain from mentioning the name of the label or to express any opinion about a disk. Added the primer, "Keep introductions to recordings short and to the point and avoid giving opinions of records. WFMS announcers are to introduce and announce records. They are not critics and at no time are they to criticize any artists or a recording on the air. By the same token WFMS announcers are not to express their opinion in favor of a record. And labels are not to be credited. The audience is not interested whether it is a

Capitol, Decca, Columbia or Victor release. It is intereted in the selection and the artists." To avoid playing records with "gimmick sounds" and "instrumental gymnastics" spinners were presented with these guidelines from the primer, "if you can't sing it or hum it, don't play it."[25]

When *Variety* editorialized in the summer of 1951 that deejay payola was the music business's "Frankenstein," it set off a spate of public philosophizing over the problem in that paper's issues, which lasted over a year. Songwriter Benny Davis looked at the situation historically, remarking that the spinner had to be romanced today as did the bandleader before him, the Paramount Theater organist before him, and the vaudeville act before him. "First it was Jolson, later it was Tommy Dorsey, and before that and in between a publisher would buy an act its wardrobe, or a wardrobe trunk, or pay for 1,000 theatrical photos, and the like. So, today they don't contact the bands as assiduously as they did, instead, they're wining-and-dining the deejays."[26]

Jock and television personality Robert Q. Lewis was "appalled at the chicanery," admitting that strange bids were made to him to drive certain songs. An anonymous publisher opined that the pop music publishing industry was the only industry which merchandised its output by bribing the consumer who used it. He felt the picture hadn't changed that much, being mostly a shift in power from vaudeville to radio and so on. Addressing *Variety* he said, "You are offended because you feel that the talents of the disk jockey are less apparent than the showmanship of the topflight performers, but, fundamentally, it makes little difference whether the cards are in the hands of the bandleaders, the soprano, or the jockey." No cure to the problem was seen by this publisher except the cure for all the evils of the world — "better people. At this moment the disk jockey is getting a free ride, which seems unjustified, but his day, too, will pass."[27]

Alan W. Livingston, vice president of Capitol Records, defended the spinner, arguing that the deejay couldn't possibly control what the public heard on a large scale, that there were too many jockeys in the country to keep anything hidden, and once the public reacted the jockey had no choice but to play what was demanded. Of the spinner Livingston concluded, "I personally think he is the greatest thing that has happened to the music business in many years." Similar sentiments were echoed by Tony Donald, a jockey at Miami's WQAM, who said the spinners didn't make the hits. In reality it was the listeners who kept contacting the deejay to let him know what they wanted.[28]

On the other side was Bill Randle, a spinner at Cleveland's WERE. Randle held the view that approximately 100 top deejays in the country controlled the popular music business, stating, "Of course, it has to be accepted that these 100 major performers do not consciously act in unison, but it also has to be accepted that somehow, whether because of trade papers, music men, record distributors, or, as is probably true, a combination of these factors, over a period of time they seem to react the same toward tunes, artists, etc. Such power so concentrated means that certain evils are present in the disk jockey business that are harmful to the individual, and to the group of performers." Admitting the real and obvious presence of payola, Randle then seemingly contradicted himself by stating "That it is possible to buy a hit or make an artist by payola, is, by the same token, ridiculous." After pointing out bribery in other industries, Randle further muddied his own waters by claiming bribery in the music business was no worse or more prevalent, it was "simply normal business behavior."[29]

Variety focused further on payola with a lengthy, four-part editorial series on payola in July and August 1954. Written by the magazine's editor, Abel Green, this series didn't appear to start out as a series but perhaps was spontaneously extended due to large interest in the matter. What became part one was not labeled as such nor did it end with "to be continued," while part four, the last installment, was labeled "to be continued." Payola was slowly becoming an issue to gain widespread national prominence. Green called for the curbing of payola, which he said had reached "ridiculous and dangerous proportions." Acknowledging its roots went back to the cradle days of Tin Pan Alley, Green nevertheless focused totally on the present, claiming "the manner in which many a fringe scavenger 'cuts up' and cuts in on a disk" was way off base.[30]

Excesses of some a and r men were outlined in the *Variety* series. A major record company told its man they would pay him $50,000 a year if he would not go on the take. However, the man declined, preferring his then salary of $25,000 plus payola, telling his employer, "since I'm producing the hits for you and the company's stockholders, why worry about 'gifts' from 'grateful' artists and music publishers." A second a and r man said, "So who doesn't like a Christmas present, and if it comes in July, and maybe again in September or April, who can hate a publisher; especially if it's a good song, and it sells."[31]

Observed one publisher, "Gee, how I long for the olden days of good clean payola. It's always been with us ever since publishers came to Jolson or Vallee with cut-ins on songs, but that was a 'clean' payola because a great singer did so much for a song. But today, with the a & r setups being what they are, it looks like the job is a license to steal." Bob Burton of BMI stated, "It's a garbage business and you're bound to get filthy when you play with dirt. . . . But it is ridiculous for anybody to fingerpoint at Broadcast Music Inc. and say that because we pay off on performances that has stimulated the payola to records, record-makers, and record jockeys." Burton felt the problem sprang from the major disk labels and ASCAP publishers. Manie Sacks of RCA Victor said, "I purposely pay our people more to keep them above temptation." Another music man dismissed payola merely as "democracy at work." This series concluded with the words of Mitch Miller (a and r head at Columbia Records), who blamed the current situation on "the abdication of the stations to the disk jockeys," citing the shortsightedness of the spinners as having "spawned the evil of payola."[32]

Having apparently struck a chord, *Variety* published another four-part editorial series by Green just 18 months later, in February and March 1956. Similar to the first series, this one did go a little further in singling out independent record companies for blame, and in the rhythm and blues segment he stated, "All the major labels recognize that in the rhythm and blues field they can't compete with the independents who thrive strictly on the payoff system. And even if they behave, how can they police their more energetic and less ethical competitors? Too often the little labels have knocked off the major brand — a look at the top songs full well indicates that no top brand has a copyright on top sellers. Too often it's the reverse." Reaching new heights of hyperbole Green, speaking of deejay payola, inveighed, "this connivance and skullduggery, in the guise of music biz enterprise, has made a large segment of show biz kin and party to a gigantic corruption. It's a contaminating influence and the sharpshooting and chiselling has gone beyond the realm of sound American enterprise."[33]

Herman Starr, head of Warner Brothers Music, said, "When you play in the mud, some of it has got to come off on you." Said Manie Sacks of RCA Victor, "If I catch any of my men taking I'll fire them on the spot." A third executive stated, "I know from nothing." Green restated the lesser labels were "opportunistic, not circumscribed in their methods of operation, and certainly less ethical" as compared with the majors, before concluding it was time for the music industry to clean house before the government got into the act. It was time, said Green, for the business to rid itself of payola, "a shabby, dishonest, cancerous tentacle. The reformation is long overdue." However, Green had no solution of any kind to offer.[34]

The death of "good music" has been announced by observers of the music industry on many occasions. Such pronouncements would reach their peak in the late 1950s after the rise of rock. However, such pronouncements were not uncommon in the early 1950s, long before rock existed or was enough of an influence to be saddled with the blame. In 1951 writer Paul Weston complained that an artist who recorded a beautiful ballad with a simple background hadn't one chance in a hundred of making the public aware that his record was available because the listener was buried under a deluge of trick sounds, multiple voices, weird instrumentations and various other attention-grabbers. Without gimmicks an artist couldn't get into the best-seller lists. This problem occurred, thought Weston, because there were too many releases — 150 per week, for 75 records —

with payola the inevitable result. Weston's solution was to have the record companies voluntarily limit the number of releases per week.[35]

Nat Hentoff of *Down Beat* claimed in 1952 that "Our level of popular music has become abysmal, and the bottom appears to be fathomless. This is an era of the quick hit, the singer with a gimmick in place of a larynx." Nat refused to go along with the "cynical" majority who blamed the public for its inability to enjoy popular music of quality, stating that in recent years the public hadn't even had the opportunity to choose between good and bad music. Music was pitiful, he said, "not because of the public primarily, but because of the recording directors, the song publishers and, especially, the disk jockeys . . . the contemporary disc jockey has reached a fantastic state of pompous musical ignorance and limitless arrogance in the face of that ignorance. These grotesques would be laughable except that they exercise tremendous power." Hentoff felt deejays decided what their listeners heard, not the other way around. Listeners were passive because they had been benumbed by the jockeys for years. Sending letters to jockeys requesting "good" songs was the solution offered here.[36]

Columnist Jack Mabley agreed that mass taste in records had never been more abominable. "The rise of garbage has coincided exactly with the rise in influence of the disk jockey," he said.[37]

The federal government was informed of the widespread payola in the music industry as early as 1956 during a hearing, not specifically about payola, held by the Antitrust Subcommittee of the House Judiciary Committee. Robert W. Sarnoff, then president of NBC, was questioned about the rash of articles about payola by the committee's Emanuel Celler, who wanted to know about a and r men getting "compensation under the table for the purpose of plugging songs that emanated from Broadcast Music, Inc. And that caused a great deal of irritation to songwriters not affiliated with BMI." Sarnoff said he was aware of the problem and that NBC was trying to keep it under control. He also said that if a performer on NBC was found to have accepted payola, the network could do nothing about it. To the query as to whether or not payola was still extensive on NBC, Sarnoff replied, "To be honest with you, I have not paid too much attention to this, personally. I think it is fairly extensive throughout the whole industry. I do not think it is any more on our network than anybody else's."[38]

The copyright law, with its compulsory license provision, came in for the blame as a prime cause of payola, at least in the eyes of some. A government report in 1960 stated, "The 'compulsory license' provision has been one cause of the vastly increased competition in the record industry in the last 15 years." Noting the healthy aspect of this for greater opportunities, the report added, "It has also had evil effects. The imbalance of supply and demand has made unethical practices (e.g. 'payola') seem to some a virtual necessity for economic survival."[39]

When a rhythm and blues song, invariably from a small label, started to climb the charts, one of the major labels moved in quickly to produce a white cover. Many stations in the early days of rock wouldn't play a tune by a black artist such as Little Richard. Because of compulsory licensing they were able to ask for and quickly receive a white cover version. In this case it was Pat Boone who, in the early years, sold more copies of Little Richard tunes — inferior versions — than Little Richard himself. Other artists victimized this way included Lillian Briggs, whose "I Want You to Be My Baby" was covered by Georgia Gibbs. LaVern Baker's "Tweedle Dee" was also covered by Gibbs. Others included "Melody of Love" by Billy Vaughn (covered by the Four Aces), and "Hearts of Stone" by the Charms (covered first by the Crew-Cuts then by Perry Como). Fats Domino's "Ain't That a Shame" was followed by five covers and stalled at number 17 on the pop charts while a Pat Boone cover reached number one. These covers cost the original artist tens of thousands of dollars in lost income for each number covered, even more in the case of smash hits.[40]

Compulsory licensing meant there were more versions of a song competing to become a hit with a greater urgency to receive air play and reach the top.[41]

During the week of July 2, 1956, the ten most popular songs were available in the following variations: number 1 (10 variations on 8 labels), number 2 (9 on 5), number 3 (5 on 5), number 4 (12 on 11), number 5 (3 on 3), number 6 (4 on 3), number 7 (2 on 2), number 8 (9 on 8), number 9 (5 on 4), and number 10 (3 versions on 3 labels).[42]

A little later one writer commented that just 7–8 percent of a year's record releases were hits — appeared on the charts, got played on the radio, or showed up in jukeboxes — "but the vast majority of records sold each year come from the Top 30. Records that aren't hits, in other words, don't sell at all." One estimate had it that over 60 percent of sides released were never played by anyone.[43]

The disk jockey of 1956 was on the air for an average of 22 hours per week. During that time the deejay played 228 sides, of which 39 were new releases, and 91 percent of the deejays selected the records played on their show. According to them, they relied mostly on best-seller lists and audience polls or requests to aid them in selecting those disks as well as their own personal opinion. With regard to side interests, 32 percent of these jockeys listed themselves as professional performers; 21 percent promoted personal appearances; 13 percent were songwriters; 10 percent were involved in artist management; 3 percent had an interest in a music or record store; 1 percent published music; 1 percent had jukebox ties; and 19 percent reported "other" side interests.[44]

Performing artists took to besieging influential deejays in certain cities in order to get on the air to be interviewed and get publicity for their current releases. It had been customary for artists to drop in unannounced at radio stations. As more and more artists took this route some stations became so clogged that many tightened up on visitor permits. Some adopted a policy of no on-air interviews without advance notice. Besides visiting artists, deejays had to deal with distributors, song pluggers, and managers both in person and over the phone. Chicago's Howard Miller, WBBK, rarely interviewed anyone on his radio program but did a few each week on his TV program, if he had a week or two of advance notice. Robin Seymour of Detroit's MKMH banned drop-in interviews, setting up an advance notice system, as did Cleveland's KYW where at least 24 hours' notice was required. At Boston's WBZ-TV jockey Norm Prescott stopped all interviewing on his radio show on the grounds that listeners wanted to hear music and not talk, even from the artists. In the same city Bob Clayton of WHDH wouldn't interview any artist who appeared within two hours or less on another show before they were booked to appear on his. Barry Kaye of Pittsburgh's WJAS was one deejay who maintained an open-door policy; however, on-air interviews were limited by Kaye to big names. If lesser known artists cooperated with Kaye on local record hop appearances Kaye returned the favor by interviewing them and "making time" for their records on his program.[45]

About 5,000 deejays were filling the airwaves in 1957 with *Time* magazine calling them "not only the big noise in radio; they were teenagers' idols, pooh-bahs of musical fashion and pillars of U.S. low- and middle-brow culture." An influential deejay like Howard Miller was grossing a reported $350,000 per year in 1957 from his various enterprises. Two million listeners tuned to his morning show. In addition, he received 1,200 fan letters a week and boasted 300 fan clubs.[46]

While deejays were reportedly deluged with cash — "the collection of pictures of dead Presidents" as jockeys referred to it — and at times gifts ranging from sports cars, to gasoline credit cards, to tires, to suits, to liquor accounts, and to wall-to-wall carpeting — most denied they were personally involved. Miller commented, "I don't need anybody else's money. I paid taxes on $350,000 last year." Jay Michael of WCAE in Pittsburgh argued, "If you want to stay popular you can't get on any payrolls. They'd hand you a dog and say play it. You have to play what you think the public will buy." *Newsweek* argued that the major record companies were not responsible for the "recent virulence of payola," that while they may have nourished the jockey in his infancy he had turned into an "autocrat to whom they were in virtual bondage." This magazine climbed on the other bandwagon by flatly asserting, "The mushrooming of the little disk firm, the trade feels, is responsible for the current abuses."[47]

As the 1950s came closer to an end, rock, jocks, and small independent labels were often painted as the prime culprits in the payola story.

They began to attack each other. Vic Knight, the owner of Key Records, complained to a meeting of broadcasters that money had to be paid to some jockeys to get them to play certain records, claiming the situation was worse in the Midwest and "not too bad" in Los Angeles. Hollywood deejays were quick to deny the charges or to barely acknowledge the existence of payola. Peter Potter said, "To be frank, something is going on. I've had some of my friends tell me about offers. The business has been very clean up to four or five years ago, then stories started to come back to us." Larry Finley of KFWB declared, "I flatly deny there's such a thing as payola out here. Why, I won't even accept a birthday gift." Finley did admit that in his five years as a Hollywood deejay he'd had two payola offers made to him, both of which he claimed to have declined.[48]

Generally speaking, disk jockeys were said to be playing the records they themselves preferred. Given a free hand the jockeys would program a much higher proportion of ballads, instrumentals, jazz, and dance bands. Jockeys were reportedly straining to "free themselves from the rock and roll straitjacket." Representative of this view were the comments of Ed McKenzie of WXYZ in Detroit who said, "It's a handicap to know anything about music. I can't let my personal taste come into it. I'd ruin myself and my audience would leave me. I don't even want to talk about what I think about the music I play. Not even off the record. I don't want to get myself in a mess. I have to keep on good terms with artists who appear on my shows. I'm not trying to educate the public. I give them what they want." Eddie Chase of CKLW in Detroit added that he avoided listening to new releases as much as possible. "If you think the stuff you hear on the air is bad, you should listen to some of the stuff I get."[49]

Veteran jockey Martin Block said he thought pressure to get airplay by the small record companies was responsible for deejay payola. Calling them fly-by-night outfits, he admitted he didn't always receive new records from these small companies who brushed him off because they thought he "came too high." One distributor said he didn't send new disks to Block because "$20 was our top price for getting the record played." Block said his contact with payola "did not go beyond a $10 bill attached to a new disk." This deejay added, as evidence for the existence of payola, "I get very suspicious when a record comes to me on Monday and I play it on the air for the first time on Monday afternoon, and that's generally when other disk jockeys get it, and Thursday I will receive lists that show this new record is way up on the list in popularity. They haven't had enough time to sell enough copies to know that they're tops in sales." Martin regarded the practice of payola as being in the same category as tipping the headwaiter a few bucks in order to get a ringside seat in the nightclub, or so he said when asked why he had never reported any offers to the district attorney's office.[50]

Mitch Miller joined the rock bashers by observing that "much of the juvenile stuff pumped over the airwaves these days hardly qualifies as music." Blasting the jockeys in a speech titled "The Great Abdication," Miller continued, "You carefully built yourself into the monarchs of radio and abdicated — abdicated your programming to the corner record shop; to the eight to 14-year-olds; to the pre-shave crowd that makes up 12% of the country's population and zero percent of its buying power, once you eliminate the pony tail ribbons, popsicles and peanut brittle." *Variety* seconded that opinion adding that "flash-in-the-platter groups of grunters and soloists in un-pear-shaped notes — with monotonous 'music' to match" had come to dominate the industry. Singer Nat King Cole lambasted what he saw as graft and corruption in the industry, blaming rock and small labels. Cole said, "It's never been proven but it certainly seems clear. It doesn't take talent to get to the top today; it takes connections. . . . We've entered the era of the complete takeover and the payola. . . . Now we've got 2,000 fly-by-night companies all fighting to get their records played by disk jockeys. . . . I know some of these disk jockeys and you can't tell me they like this stuff they're plugging."[51]

Los Angeles station KDAY initiated its own response to payola when it implemented its "test record plan." The station charged record distributors $225 a week to play the record of their choice eight times a day, seven days a week. Station vice president Irving Phillips explained that his station limited the plan to a maximum of three records a week and that it didn't interfere with the playing of nonpaying new records. It was, said Phillips, a product testing system which allowed distributors, for a fee, to find out if a record was a potential hit or not. Calling the plan a test system didn't alter the fact it was in reality payola going directly to the station instead of to the deejays. For unrecorded reasons KDAY dropped this system completely after a few months.[52]

With the rising influence of Top 40 formal listings a certain amount of payola was channeled away from jockeys to record dealers. In large cities more than one radio station would each generate their own Top 40 listing based, supposedly, on local record sales and or audience requests. Record stores usually distributed for free each week all such local listings or "ulcer sheets" as the trade called them. Listing on one of these sheets was believed powerful enough to generate sales among some teens without having heard the record. Also such a listing guaranteed a lot of air play. Distributors would contact record stores, asking them to list a certain record among their top sellers, regardless of sales. The reward was a number of free records which the store then sold. Asked if he thought such methods could convert a dud into a hit one distributor said, "The only way to get it on the air these days is to make it look like a best-seller. Then we hope it sells."[53]

Billboard announced in 1958 that payola, a "cancerous growth . . . is fast growing into a monster that may yet destroy its creators." Record company executives claimed the practice was so widespread that it was no longer possible to measure its effectiveness. In New York City one station brazenly offered a $600 deal to companies which guaranteed six plays per day for six weeks. One small independent label reportedly "bought" more radio time than Pepsi-Cola. Rivaling cash as the most effective payola form was that of "free artists," whereby performers appeared gratis at stage shows and record hops for deejays who benefited by an increased box office take. Defending jockeys was deejay promoter Buddy Basch who said, "It stands to reason the good deejays can't be bought. They're more interested in ratings than a few bucks quickly and oblivion. You can imagine what a record program sounds like made up of tunes the deejay has been paid to play and which probably couldn't get on the air any other way."[54]

Formula radio — as Top 40 format was often called — was well established by the late 1950s, although still decidedly a minority position. It was a tightly controlled format which required deejays to limit their selections mainly to those top 40 tunes with only a few slots left open for new releases, up-and-comers and so on. When deejays, about 1,000 strong, attended their first annual convention in Kansas City in 1958 they overwhelmingly attacked the system, railing against being tied in a straitjacket to these Top 40 lists. One seminar the spinners held was titled, "Is the prime requisite of a disk jockey the ability to count to 40?" What was billed as a battle of individuality versus station conformity was in reality a worry by jockeys that they might become redundant and, more to the point, payola might shift away from the deejays to other station personnel who compiled the Top 40 lists and or record stores which supplied the stations with raw data. Mitch Miller maintained, "It must be more than a coincidence that single record buying went into a decline at the very time the number of stations that program the 'Top 40' and other lists climbed to a new high." Veteran deejay Al Jarvis of KFWB was said to be a contented convert to the Top 40 format while Martin Block had used it for a time before switching to a modified form of it. Any shifting of payola as a result of a Top 40 format was felt by industry executives to work against small independent companies to the benefit of the major labels and distributors. It was easier and cheaper to reach a jockey than someone higher up at the station.[55]

The Top 40 concept was introduced in 1955 by Todd Storz in the Midwestern and Southern states, starting with WTIX in New Orleans and spreading throughout an entire chain operated by a southern pharmaceutical company. *Billboard* charts, then containing country and western and rhythm and blues material, were used for the Top 40. The concept was that this material would attract the largest audience, which was the goal of every radio station. It was a formula that worked. Some ten years later KHJ in Los Angeles hired programmer Bill Drake, who had achieved some success with smaller West Coast radio stations. Drake's formula involved less DJ chatter, shorter station promos, fewer commercial breaks, but more commercials per break and more music. This format featured more music minutes per hour but also involved a tightening of the Top 40 format by reducing the playlist to just 35 records. "Standard" Top 40 featured 40 songs plus 20 others such as album cuts and oldies. Drake had done a survey of listeners to find out what annoyed them most about radio. Forty-seven percent said they changed stations when they heard a song they did not like. Thus Drake cut the play list to minimize the chance of hearing such a song. It worked, for within two years KHJ was the top-rated station in Los Angeles.[56]

The federal government's Internal Revenue Service (IRS) started to seriously investigate the tax implications of payola in the spring of 1956 when they began to quiz jockeys, particularly in the Midwest. Agents asked deejays if they had been specifically cut in on any songs, or if they had received any favors from artists such as appearances at stage shows which may have benefited deejays. On their tax forms the disk jockeys listed paying out certain sums of money to artists for appearances at live shows, while these same artists failed to report receiving any such income. Also scrutinized were the personal living styles of the spinners, with particular attention paid to luxury items such as yachts and expensive homes. Fifteen months later the IRS was still checking things out, this time concentrating on Philadelphia. Distributors included payola money as a promotional expense on their tax papers. The IRS asked them to itemize these expenses so as to check the tax statements of those spinners to see if they were declaring as income the money received by them from distributors.[57]

The battle between ASCAP and BMI became more formal when as early as 1956 Frank Sinatra charged that Mitch Miller tried to force the singer to do BMI numbers when Sinatra was at Columbia. About a year later, in September 1957, Florida Senator George A. Smathers of the Interstate and Foreign Commerce Committee was beginning an investigation and hearings into his proposed amendment to the Federal Communications Act which would force the broadcasters to divest themselves of their interest in BMI, music publishing, and recording. Prodding Smathers into this attempt was ASCAP, then with about 4,000 writer members and 1,000 publisher members. Sinatra sent a telegram to Smathers to support the idea, alleged by ASCAP, that broadcaster control of BMI and a large interest in the recording industry (NBC had RCA Victor while CBS owned Columbia Records, for example) discriminated against ASCAP. In his wire Sinatra stated that Miller admitted accepting "large sums of money" from writers whose songs he, Frank, recorded. Frank quoted Miller as having said, "Bob Merrill (responsible for 'If I Knew You Were Coming, I'd've Baked a Cake' and other hit tunes) would bring all the songs to me first. After the songs were a hit I got a check from his royalties to me. It amounted to $5,000 to $6,000 — different checks." When questioned about this Miller said they were "isolated parts" of previous testimony and that he got his fees for legitimate services, such as editing songs, fixing up lyrics, and so on. Clearly in the ASCAP corner, Smathers said of BMI before he had done much investigating, "Had these (monopolistic) practices been in existence in prior years, many great songs such as 'The Missouri Waltz' might not have been available for the enjoyment of the public."[58]

Thirty years later Mitch still regarded rock as "musical illiteracy." Reflecting back to the late 1950s, Miller stated, "In payola nothing was judged on quality. I mean, before payola, you put a record out and got reaction and other guys had to play it, whereas with most rock 'n' roll you couldn't get the first play without the pay. I couldn't get into the field because of payola." Claiming that Columbia was clean during his days there, Miller recounted that when he approached a major television show about playing a Four Lads rock-flavored number the television man suggested the publishing rights be given to him. Upset by this proposition, Mitch claimed he walked away refusing to deal.[59]

During hearings on the Smathers proposal in March 1958, one of the strongest indictments of BMI was delivered by West Coast entertainment and ASCAP attorney Seymour Lazar who said payola was part of the "corruption from the overall handout of BMI money to promote its own music," with the ultimate purpose being to "suppress ASCAP music to keep ASCAP royalty prices down for broadcasters — not to make profits for BMI." He further claimed that BMI was able to send its "wandering tentacles" into every area of the music world through subsidies to publishers, writers, and performers. These "indiscriminate handouts tempt everyone in the music world to promote BMI music at the expense of ASCAP music." According to the attorney, payola amounted to as much as $300–$500 per week to jockeys over and above hefty salaries for the most influential. Los Angeles was cited by Lazar for having "heavy" payola. Labels such as Specialty, Aladdin, Modern, King, Chess, and Checker were named as being involved in recording and publishing mostly BMI material, with an inference of shady practices involved. "Southern California is known as a payola district," he said. "In order to get your song played by disc jockeys in Los Angeles you must pay cash." He ventured that while not all deejays took cash, "more than half do." Upon hearing Lazar's testimony Hollywood record promoter Bob Stern, who represented almost a score of labels, wired the committee, asking for a chance to refute the testimony but never got a reply, let alone an invitation to appear. Stern contended that with so much competition among Los Angeles jockeys none could take a chance on accepting payola to play poor records which might lose them some of their audience knocking them down the ladder. However, Stern then said, while deejays weren't paid for any specific records, "There may be payola but there's no dictatorial pay-off. . . . At Christmas time we show our appreciation for what they've done in the past year and maybe if a jock's wife is in the hospital her bill might be paid. But we never pay them to play any certain records." Subcommittee Chairman Senator John Pastore (Democrat, Rhode Island) queried Lazar about the major record companies. Seymour admitted they didn't favor BMI music but said the "potential danger" of excluding ASCAP was there. Martha Roundtree, president of a Warrenton, Virginia, radio station, claimed that free records were sent "in floods" to broadcasters with 80–90 percent of them being BMI tunes.[60]

Songwriters' Protective Association attorney, John Schulman, cited *Billboard's* top selling record lists to show the predominance of BMI tunes with those far outnumbering ASCAP's. *Cash Box's* numbers were used to show that BMI single releases outnumbered ASCAP's by 2,047 to 1,175 during the first half of 1957. If anything, these figures underscored BMI's very real dominance of the top tune lists. However, the reason was not BMI control; it was ASCAP's refusal to recognize changing public taste. With some exceptions all rock music came through BMI and it was rock music that sold. There was no way ASCAP would handle such "bad" music, which of course quickly drove them virtually off the hit charts. Magazine writer Booton Herndon called songwriters starry-eyed idealists not interested in money, while the "very tone of voice" of BMI spokesmen indicated to him that they "looked on music only as a commodity." Pastore, perhaps the only objective committee member, waved him out of the witness chair without questions or comment.[61]

During his time in the chair Schulman argued there should be some sort of equal time rule for music on the air — much like that accorded politicians — to equalize the situation between ASCAP and BMI. Pastore asked if the Smathers proposed amendment might not kill off BMI restoring ASCAP to a monopoly position. In reply both Schulman and Lazar claimed ASCAP's monopoly aspects had been exaggerated, with the former arguing that broadcasters had SESAC (European), public domain, and Associated Music Publishers' Catalog (serious music). While that was true, virtually none of this material was ever played on popular music radio stations; only ASCAP and BMI were programmed. Lazar argued that ASCAP could not become a monopoly since its rates were subject to arbitration under its consent decree. The licensing group was under a consent decree precisely because the federal government had in the past judged it to be a monopoly.[62]

Dissident ASCAP members claimed it was impossible for younger composers and publishers to advance under its autocratic, unpredictable, and veiled administration. Publisher Guy Freedman charged that arbitrary classification rulings killed income to the Alec Templeton firm. Insult was added to injury when two other ASCAP publishers then offered to buy the depressed Templeton catalogue. When Templeton bought out Axelrod Publishing, an established ASCAP firm, ASCAP refused to transfer credits due to Axelrod, alleged Freeman. Another charge made was that old-line ASCAP firms got their music placed on big TV network shows. Publisher Fred Fox and Freedman both stated that performances by hit records in their catalogues did not always get logged for ASCAP credit, and that only the old and big ASCAP firms were assured of such credits. This, if true, was in conflict with one provision of the consent decree under which ASCAP functioned.

Surveys of tunes played were supposed to have become "objective" under the consent decree. The ratio, said Freedman, of old music over new was three to one in terms of getting performance credit. Several ASCAP dissident publishers claimed that retroactive payments owed them were still not forthcoming after more than two years of grievance procedure. The strongest block within ASCAP was said to be film-owned publishing houses with firms owned by the likes of Warner Brothers, Paramount, and Loew's. Fred Fox was elected for a two-year term on the ASCAP appeals board but was squeezed out after one year because of disagreements with other board members. When a song was an integral part of a program it received one full performance credit, while if it was just background music on a show it received one one-hundredth of a full performance credit. Natalie Kissell, supervisor of ASCAP performance credit tabulations, testified she was unable to explain why certain theme songs on shows received full credit as against one one-hundredth for others, and ASCAP defenders dismissed the critics as "chronic dissenters." They also claimed that ASCAP board members were above any conflict of interest and that the organization was not geared to prevent small publishers from growing. However, they did agree that ASCAP was structured to give "social security to the twilight years of composers."[63]

The general record industry situation was summarized in a lengthy article in *Broadcasting* magazine in August 1959, just a few months before the big payola scandal broke. With advances in technology the number of record companies in existence was then 1,500-2,000, up from a half a dozen at the time of World War II. Many were one-day wonders which disappeared as quickly as they arrived, to be replaced by another. They remained registered and counted but didn't necessarily ever produce another disk. A record could be turned out for $350 or so. To succeed they had to sell but only with radio exposure was this possible. Many stations

devoted 60–70 percent of their time to records but still they could play only
a fraction of the 50–250 new releases they received each week. Stations using a Top 40 format would play perhaps only 20–40 sides per week outside
of those Top 40 numbers. Local record sales remained the most common
form of selecting the Top 40, with audience polls or phone-ins a distant
second. To select the other numbers some stations used a "jury" of station
personnel such as jockeys, librarians, and program directors. The independent jockey who selected and played tunes on his own, without sticking
rigidly to charts, remained in the majority despite the excessive publicity
devoted to Top 40 format. This format generated more publicity than its
presence warranted because deejays felt it posed such a serious threat to
their independence and ultimately to their very jobs.

Stories of payola continued to abound but never with documentation
or proof. Fancy dinners, plush weekends, nights on the town, liquor, cash
paid on either a retainer or per-record basis, a percentage of sales, a piece
of a company, or records by the case-lot for private resale were some of
the items which came a jockey's way. "Booze, broads, and bribes" came
to signify the situation. The disk jockey convention in Miami Beach in the
spring of 1959 became notorious for the "number, variety and meatiness
of the extra-curricular diversions set up for the boys by the recording companies. Some of the hosts displayed singularly fundamental ideas about
recreation, along with seemingly unlimited sources of supply" — meaning
women. Payola couldn't make into a hit a song the public didn't like, but
payola could get a song played on the radio. Only a song that got air play
had a chance of becoming a hit. Some deejays even had "rate cards" showing how many plays you could expect from your money and discounts for
volume. One legendary story involved a deejay who received a color
television set then called the donor to say "it's too bad that I can't use it
where I live without spending $150 for a special antenna installation!"

Lew Irwin, news director of KPOL- KABC-TV in Los Angeles, did a
series on payola. One of his guests was Seymour Lazar, who reiterated
much of what he said about payola at the earlier Smathers hearing. "I
know it exists because I know of individuals that pay individuals all over
the country for it." At this time he called it a "national" problem, with influential deejays adding $50,000–$150,000 to their salaries via payola.
During another broadcast Irwin stated that gangsters who controlled jukeboxes produced records and turned them into hits through payola as part
of their money-laundering operations. Another Irwin guest was ASCAP
West Coast director Wolfe Gilbert, who claimed that major publishing
firms were not as guilty of payola as the smaller and newer ones. *Broadcasting* acknowledged this as a generally shared concept in the industry.

Jockey Dick Whittinghill, KMPC Los Angeles, said he'd been approached a few times and that he knew for a fact that no one at KMPC

took payola. Al Jarvis, jockey at Los Angeles KFWB, said some distributors engaged in the practice and some didn't. "I think the bigger ones do," he explained, "but I don't think that any first rate disc jockey intentionally plays second-rate records. . . . He still must play to please his public." An executive of a major company in clean repute regarding payola commented, "We'll give them anything they want short of money, so long as it doesn't mean demeaning ourselves." His idea was not to buy specific plays but to keep his "label in favor among as many so-called decision makers as possible."

Hot cities where a record became a hit, or didn't, were said to number 12 in 1959 and were (not necessarily in rank order): Boston, New York, Philadelphia, Pittsburgh, Chicago, Cleveland, Detroit, Minneapolis, St. Louis, Los Angeles, San Francisco, and Seattle. Secondary areas were Texas, New York State, Georgia, and the Carolinas. These were the breakout cities and areas where, presumably, payola was particularly prevalent.[64]

When Berry Gordy established Motown Records in 1959 he said that money and favors were regularly demanded of his struggling new firm. A white Detroit jockey in the process of moving to a new house came to Motown and demanded some "big black bucks" to help him move. Motown dispatched the songwriting team of Holland, Dozier, and Holland to do the moving. A disk jockey in St. Louis would call the record company from his station's control booth during his show. With a Motown number playing in the background the jockey said to Gordy, "I just got this big ticket from the cops and I can't pay it. Can you send me $25." Other jockeys would say they had to fly to New York to meet someone on Gordy's behalf, asking Motown to send them a round-trip plane ticket. It was assumed these jockeys cashed in these tickets rather than use them.[65]

6 Do You Now or Have You Ever? 1959

Formal investigation by the government into payola began in November 1959. One probe was conducted by the office of New York District Attorney Frank S. Hogan. Ongoing at that time for several months into possibly fraudulent television commercials, it expanded to look into the music industry. By far the most important investigation was that initiated by the House of Representatives in Washington through the House Special Subcommittee on Legislative Oversight, chaired by Representative Oren Harris, an Arkansas Democrat. This group was coming off a much publicized investigation of television quiz programs, such as "The $64,000 Question," a study that found many of these shows to be fixed. When the committee moved on from quiz shows it announced it would explore the broader field of commercial tie-ups in general, not just music industry bribery. However, it quickly focused exclusively on payola in the music business. The Harris group didn't formally convene during November but traveling investigators visited various cities taking testimony. One reason for Harris and company to stick to payola only was that it brought the politicians an enormous amount of publicity and media attention, virtually all highly favorable. Mainly it was rock and roll, small record companies and deejays especially, who came under the gun. Lost or deliberately left out in the shuffle were a and r men and major labels. The greater one's position in the establishment the more likely one was to get a cursory or nonexistent look from the Harris probers.

One of the first items to come to the Harris group was a memorandum from Burton Lane, president of the American Guild of Authors and Composers (AGAC), who put the main blame for payola on deejays and alleged rigging of best-seller charts. Lane wrote, "There is no doubt that commercial bribery has become a prime factor in determining what music is played on many broadcast programs and what musical records the public is surreptitiously induced to buy." Among the material Lane sent with his letter was a reference charging that Martin Block, then a deejay on WNEW, "entered into a contract whereby he received $48 for every network performance of certain songs. Another contract provided for an advance payment of $12,000 to Block's publishing company." That firm was with BMI. Even though Lane didn't spell out the BMI connection, *Variety* clearly saw the implications and underlying motives in Lane's charges when the periodical commented, "there is no doubt that the AGAC songwriters will attempt to develop their charges that the broadcast industry has been attempting to promote music not controlled by the American Society of Composers, Authors and Publishers. When Lane mentions the musical records the public is surreptitiously induced to buy he is known to be referring to the rock 'n' roll disks, most of which are licensed by Broadcast Music Inc."[1]

Deejay Murray Kaufman of New York's WINS fired off a telegram in his capacity as president of the National Council of Disk Jockeys to the Harris group. In the wire Kaufman "vehemently" protested the Lane allegation, saying the "charge is without foundation but creates in the mind of the public guilt by inference. For your information, sir, only 5 percent of the country's disc jockeys program the music for their shows. This task is done by record librarians and in turn is dictated by the respective program departments. I respectfully suggest a public statement of apology by your group be made immediately." Of course, Kaufman didn't get one. Mostly the industry ran scared, issued denials, and pointed fingers. It was every jock for himself. One, a major publisher who had been paying a weekly retainer to get his tunes played on a television show, was told the deal was canceled, at least temporarily, when the probe was announced.[2] They needn't have worried for the Harris inquiry would never move away from jockeys, rock and roll music, small labels, and radio.

It wasn't clear during the Harris group's preliminary investigation in November that the House would undertake the full hearing which it finally did. Then it was just a threat. In addition, the FCC threatened to launch a probe of its own. Radio station owners were chilled when FCC commissioner Robert E. Lee stated that if payola existed at stations the owners could lose their license to operate, even if they were unaware of their employees' payola activities. Station managers conducted "Have you ever?" questioning sessions with their deejay staff. Record promotion men found it more difficult at some stations to drop in on jockeys in the easy manner of old as management instituted reception blocks. Record spinners on the take reportedly frantically called distributors and labels telling them to hold off on payments. The wire from Kaufman to the Harris group was not particularly defiant but some jockeys felt a need to distance themselves from even this mild rebuke. Deejay Bill Williams of WNEW argued that Kaufman wasn't in a position to speak for his peers: "This fellow representing himself as a spokesman for disc jockeys is like the bat boy speaking for the New York Yankees." Meanwhile, the board of directors of Disk Jockey Association (unrelated to the Kaufman group) issued a statement which read, in part, "We offer our fullest cooperation to the broadcasting industry in supporting and maintaining the public's confidence in the ethical standards and practices of the broadcasting industry and in the profession of disk jockey and music programmer." Jerry Marshall commented, referring to Kaufman, "No one representing any organization can speak for me. . . . In my 22 years of broadcasting I have never had a payola offer. I've also heard a lot about girls and payola, but I've never even been asked to have a cup of coffee."[3]

Eight months before payola broke as a big story Edmond T. McKenzie resigned as a $60,000 a year jockey from Detroit's WXYZ, saying he could no longer stand present-day formula radio — meaning Top 40 rock. His broadcasting career had begun in 1937. McKenzie was profiled in *Life* magazine in November with an article under his byline. This former jockey told an erroneous story about payola but it was revisionist history the establishment wanted to hear and believe. Thus it got prominent space in a national magazine of wide circulation and repute. Wrote McKenzie, "Payola really got started about 10 years ago. Until then the record business was controlled by the big companies like Decca, Columbia, RCA-Victor and Capitol. When the obscure little record companies started up and began turning out offbeat records by unknown artists, they looked for a way to get their product distributed and played. The answer was payola: offering disk jockeys cash to play records they wouldn't play." While he never took payola himself McKenzie said offers came his way, such as being offered $100 for one week if he would play a number several times each day during that week. According to him, many deejays were on the weekly payroll of 5–10 labels, which could mean a side income of $25,000–$50,000 a year. Phil Chess, coowner of the Chess, Checker, and Argo labels, told McKenzie that the first question many jocks asked him when he made his promotion rounds was, "How many dead presidents are there for me?"[4]

"Payola usually begins when a song plugger or publisher comes to town and takes the jockey out for dinner," explained Edmond. "The sky's the limit on entertainment — drinks, girls, everything. There is always a big follow-up at Christmas. They flood you with liquor, TV sets, hi-fi sets, expensive luggage, big baskets of food, watches, silk shirts, imported sweaters. The flow doesn't stop after the holiday season. A record plugger once offered to install a bar in my basement." Station managers knew about payola, thought McKenzie, but turned a blind eye to it, perhaps because jocks didn't make much money and were entitled to what they could get on the side. Chicago spinner Jim Mills admitted he'd been showered with Christmas presents from promoters over the last three years, with everything from jewelry to clocks to hams to cutlery. Mills said he considered these "trinkets something of a nuisance," while adding that "bribes are mostly used to promote rock 'n' roll."[5]

Station WNEW put four of its deejays, William B. Williams, Pete Myers, Gene Klavan, and Dee Finch on the air, with station management personnel, for a one-hour discussion of payola. All agreed that payola existed but all four spinners denied taking any payola. Only two, Williams and Myers, admitted to even having been approached. "I have always turned it down," explained Myers, "because — well, maybe I am afraid of being caught. Probably that's it. I guess I am as honest as any jockey." Said Williams, "I wish I knew psychologically why I turned it down. I think part of it is something Pete touched on — pride in the fact that I would then not have control over my show." As a payola exposé the show was unsatisfactory for the panelists. As *Variety* noted, it "stayed within the safe borders of generalities, clichés, lack of personal experience, denials, etc. The fact that payola existed was conceded by virtually all of the panelists, but the basics of who, what, when, where and how much were given a side detour." If it was uninformative it at least was properly humble and nondefiant. It played well to the attackers, WNEW must have hoped. Station management stated that payola was impossible on WNEW due to the stature of the deejays and the type of balanced music programming on the station. Manager John Sullivan commented that if he found one of the WNEW spinners was taking payola, "I'm sure that I would probably faint because honestly it would be a foreign or alien realization for me. I know how much money (the jocks) make, and as long as they're worth it, they'll be here unless they begin to augment it from some place else."[6]

During August 1959 Chicago deejay Phil Lind played a tape on his WAIT program. It was an interview with the owner of a small West Coast record label, both unnamed, who detailed his alleged problems in getting record exposure in Chicago without payoffs and citing specific demands for payola. The owner claimed one jockey asked for a $200 a week retainer, a second demanded $100 per week, while a third requested a 2 percent interest in the company. Of 20 spinners the owner had requested to play his company's records, seven were willing to play them on a merit basis while the others all asked for money. If all the monetary demands were met this executive estimated it would cost him $22,000 to get a record going in Chicago alone. No specific names were mentioned during this interview which attracted no notice or comment in the trade or media at the time of its airing. Suddenly, in November it became a hot item. Lind came under police protection after claiming he received anonymous threats as a result of the interview. "If you keep blowing the whistle, you're going to wake up in an alley," threatened one caller. A friend of his was told on the phone, "Phil won't listen to us, so you better tell him as a friend to lay off." Someone reportedly offered to pay $1,000 for the tape, presumably to keep it out of reach. While no names were specified during the interview the owner did name names to Lind off the record after the program. This

executive called Chicago the worst city in the country to get a record promoted, although he had run into payoff demands in other cities as well.
The mystery man was soon identified as Dirk Summers, who headed
Roslyn Records. Summers had sunk his savings of $15,000 into the com-
pany. *Life* magazine featured excerpts from the tape transcript when they
spotlighted McKenzie. Lind was interviewed by most national news
magazines.[7]

At the same time as the Lind revelations, Chicago's top spinner
Howard Miller gave out his confession. Eight years earlier Miller said a
record distributor quit the business but before leaving gave the jockey an
affidavit specifying payments this distributor allegedly made to a top
Chicago deejay. Miller also inspected the canceled checks. This action was
taken by the distributor because he told Miller he wanted someone to have
a record of his experiences in the promotion business. When Miller broke
this information to the media in 1959 he said, "I have no desire to name
individuals. In most cases I couldn't prove what I know. I said in most
cases. It would be unfair to name one or two and victimize a couple of guys
for what is a much more widespread practice. Everybody in the industry
knows payola is running rampant. I'm not speaking only of Chicago
because it's no more prevalent here than elsewhere." Still possessing the
affidavit, Miller was asked what he would do if he were subpoenaed. He
said he would tear up the document first. When reminded he could still be
asked under oath what information this document contained he stated, "In
that case, I'd have to answer all questions to the best of my ability." When
this story became public the spinner expressed surprise at reports that
worry had spread to jockeys all over town. "Anyone who is worried about
what I said must be guilty of something," he said. Even though all the
Miller allegations could be expected to increase the pressure for a full and
formal congressional investigation, Miller insisted he was opposed to such
a probe.[8]

As pressure increased to formally investigate the situation a couple
voices of reason appeared in the media. They were a tiny minority soon
drowned out. *New York Times* television critic Jack Gould noted there
was plenty of corruption in the business world in general and wondered,
"Why just pick on show business?" Given that it was show business being
singled out, Gould cited examples of bribery and corruption, nonmusical,
in film and television. "Cynics in broadcasting wonder," he wrote,
"whether the disk jockeys are not relatively small fry when it comes to payoffs." Gould also understood that the dispute originated "with many of the
country's foremost composers — the writers of Broadway and Hollywood
hit tunes — who have been dismayed to witness the dominance of rock 'n'
roll on the nation's airwaves."[9]

After briefly recapping payola back to the 1920s, *Billboard* editorialized,

"Many frustrated music men — out of step with current song and recording trends — see in the present goings-on a chance to return to a position of eminence. The ranks of the frustrated include artists, songwriters, publishers and record manufacturers — many of whom sigh for the good old days, blame their plight on rock and roll and construe that rock and roll is an outgrowth of payola. The cancer of payola cannot be pinned on rock and roll."[10]

Before the end of November disk jockeys began to be fired. In some cases the deejay admitted to taking payola while in others there appeared to be no proof for such charges. Perhaps some stations took advantage of the situation to clean house, to remove jockeys they didn't like, or to lower the payroll. It should be remembered that payola was not illegal at this time at the federal level. Whether an individual state could have successfully initiated proceedings under a commercial bribery statute was highly problematic. In any event most states didn't have such statutes on the books, indicating that while business corruption may have been rampant in general the state acknowledged its presence and in a sense legitimized it by not even formulating laws against it. Those states that did have bribery laws on the books rarely used them.

The first state to enact such a law was New York in 1881. By 1932 there were 17 states that had some type of commercial bribery statute on the books and by 1980 the number was 34 — this was for private bribery as opposed to bribery of public officials which has always been treated more harshly, at least in theory. Sixty years after it enacted its commercial bribery law New York, the commercial capital of the country, did not have one instance whereby this law had been criminally enforced and the conviction upheld.[11]

Detroit's WJBK fired jockey Tom Clay on November 21, 1959, when he admitted he accepted payola. The 30-year-old Clay, popular with teenagers, said that in his first six months in Detroit he never accepted payoffs, "Then my ratings became number 1 and offers came in. At first I thought 'no don't take it.' Then, because I am human and wanted to give my wife and family security, I accepted payola. I am not saying what I did was right or wrong. I am saying it is a part of business. I never told a person he had to pay me to get records played. They asked me to take money. Were they wrong, or good business men?" Over the previous 18 months Clay, who made $8,000 a year as a jock, admitted to taking between $5,000 and $6,000 in payola. Reportedly, the station forgave Clay in August 1959 for taking $100 in payola but warned him he would be fired if it happened again. When the House investigation began to act the station decided to move against anyone who had taken payola, said Clay.[12]

Philadelphia's Joe Niagara of WBIG resigned after a conference with WBIG management. Niagara, a teenage radio favorite, had planned to resign in a month's time to go to a station out west. No reason was given for his abrupt departure. Later Storer Broadcasting, owner of both stations, announced Niagara would not go west, that he had severed his connection with the company completely. Mickey Shorr was fired from his post as deejay at WXYZ in Detroit. Shorr claimed he had been given an opportunity to resign but refused to do so, feeling he had done no wrong. According to Mickey he had never taken payola. His only interest in the musical field was a part ownership in a firm that bought Australian rights to disks from record companies, said Shorr. Only days before the firing of Shorr, Harold L. Neal, Jr., vice president of WXYZ, responded to the charges made by Ed McKenzie (former WXYZ spinner) stating that WXYZ was not clean of payola. "Information available to WXYZ affirms that no disk jockey now performing on the station, no person who participates in the selection of music for broadcast over WXYZ, nor I, this station manager, has either solicited nor accepted any personal consideration, money or otherwise, to have any record played on WXYZ." Right after that a local rock group, the Royal Tones, asked their former agent, Stuart L. Gorelick, to account for $17,670 of income from records and personal appearances. Gorelick said about 10 percent of that amount went to Mickey Shorr but in repayment of a loan, not payola. Shorr agreed, stating he loaned Gorelick $2,000 "a couple of years ago. I've never taken payola from anyone." Explaining in court that one canceled check for $175 was for entertaining jockeys, Gorelick commented, "When you're with a disk jockey, he seldom reaches into his pocket to pay for anything."[13]

Dale Young, who emceed the "Detroit Bandstand" on WJBK-TV, was suddenly fired with no comment being issued by either side. Jack LeGoff was not a disk jockey but a newscaster on WJBK-TV who editorialized on the air about payola. He criticized the media coverage given the subject by Detroit newspapers adding, "Have there not been other accusations of this same sort in the Federal government, in the Federal Communications Commission, in the garment industry, in any number of international unions? Payola is one form or another of American business. This is certainly not to say that I, or the broadcast industry, condones the practice, but I say, let him who is without sin cast the first stone." For this editorial the six-year WJBK employee was immediately fired. Station manager Bill Michaels asserted, "The completely abominable practice of payola is being investigated at all Storer stations. We are going through every station at the local level with a fine tooth comb. There will be absolutely no compromise on this subject at any station or any level." In an indirect slam at LeGoff's editorial Michaels added, "There has never been any question as to our company's condemnation of and complete prohibition against such dishonest business practice. Nor do we subscribe to the implication that it is knowingly tolerated in American business as a general rule."[14]

Deejay Don McLeod of WJBK resigned suddenly. Boston's WILD fired three of the station's top jocks at the same time, Stan Richards, Bill Marlowe, and Joe Smith. Four deejays at WCMS in Norfolk, Virginia – Bob Power, Lee Whitehead, Joe Hoppel, and Olivia Barbee – got together to prove that even payola couldn't force public acceptance of a bad record. This group played the record "Pahalacaka" continuously, racking up 320 spins in one day. They were starting a second day of the same routine when WCMS fired all four.[15]

Certain stations played loosely with definitions of payola, defining it to suit their own circumstances and believing it perfectly proper for jocks to have ownership interests in publishing, recording, or distributing firms as long as such interests didn't infringe on station programming. Other stations regarded all such ties as taboo. John V. B. Sullivan, general manager of WNEW, said he didn't consider it real payola "unless it affects the music." As a result he had no objections to WNEW deejay Lonny Starr's ownership in a couple of firms, as his investigation showed him they didn't appear on Starr's program. This same policy was followed at New York's WINS where general manager Harold Anderson said the station was aware of spinner Murray Kaufman's publishing and recording activities but didn't think they influenced Kaufman's programming. On the other side Westinghouse Broadcasting commented, "WBC does not condone disk jockeys' ownership of record companies, distributing companies, publishing companies or ownership of talent. This is because of the actual or potential conflict of interest between ownership on the one hand and the creative selection of programming on the other."[16]

Pressure was maintained by the House subcommittee, which announced it had received reports from "all over the place" on payola. Investigators had already traveled from Washington to Philadelphia with forays planned for the near future into several other major cities including Chicago, Los Angeles, Boston, Milwaukee, and Miami. Robert E. Lee of the FCC reiterated his warning that stations permitting payola were in danger of losing their licenses. Lee said payola fell into the category of "sneaky commercial," which violated the Communications Act provision that required that paid sponsorship be mentioned. Both *Billboard* and *Variety* called for an investigation into the music industry, with the latter calling such a probe long overdue while admitting, however, that "few have any illusions that payola will end with the probe." Editor Abel Green of *Variety* let slip his real feelings when he described deejays by saying, "They're nothing but microphone pitchmen. Whatever their con or charm or glibness of gab that's the only reason a deejay exists – to peddle the goods."[17]

New York District Attorney Frank S. Hogan's office subpoenaed the books and financial records of 11 record companies as part of their probe.

One of those companies was King Records of Cincinnati, which acknowledged it had paid payola to promote its records on the air. King said it paid between 12 and 15 jockeys around the country, with none receiving more than $100 per month. All payments were made by check with King promising to turn over all such canceled documents to Hogan's office and to cooperate fully. Company president Sydney Nathan said that King never tried to hide the practice, which it ceased "many months ago." Nathan declared, "It is a dirty rotten mess and it has been getting worse and worse in the last five years. It is getting so you can't get your records played unless you pay."[18]

While in Philadelphia House investigators heard from Edward D. Cohn, owner of Lesco Distributors, who said he paid thousands of dollars to get records played on that city's programs and estimated that 20 of Philadelphia's 200 deejays were on the take. Cohn paid $5–$100 to get his numbers played. "This city has the reputation of being the worst place in the country for payola," stated Cohn. "It got to the point where I would have to spend the profit from 10,000 records just to pay the disk jockeys I'd see." Cohn refused to name any names, asserting, "More often the payments they expected were more like a gratuity than a ransom. . . . After all, there was nothing illegal about it."[19]

House investigators built a dossier on Boston, saying, "We have substantial complaints. It is apparent that a certain amount of payola has been going on in Boston." The Boston file was culled from over 2,000 letters received by the subcommittee. Almost unanimously Boston radio personalities denied the existence of any payola, although one group of four stations discarded rock music for a broad range of standard pops calling some of the rock music "an insult to common intelligence." William H. McGrath, station manager of WHDH, said, "we will not be bought, nor will we tolerate any of our talent being bought. Records will be played purely on a basis of merit and for no other reason." President of WNAC, Norman Knight, declared, "the evils referred to about music selection do not exist at WNAC, WNAC-TV, WRKO-FM or the Yankee network." Spokesmen for WEEI and WORL denied there was any payola at their stations, while W. C. Swartley, vice president of WBZ, said payola "has been expressly forbidden. We have taken every reasonable and practicable precaution against this practice which regrettably has existed for too long in the furiously competitive recording industry."[20]

Meanwhile, a few other revelations came out. Two Detroit stations reportedly would openly play a song for the right price. Station WKHM would play one record or album 114 times a week, with a commercial before and after each spin, for $350 per week with a six-week minimum. Station WJBK had a similar deal. State Record Distributors disclosed they paid deejays, some in Cincinnati, to play records. Company president Mel Herman said his company, which distributed in Ohio and Indiana, made payoffs up until the end of 1958 but then stopped because the practice was becoming too expensive. "We didn't invent payola," he said. "We were the victims of it. We couldn't get our records played in some places without paying."[21]

By far the two most visible deejays who came under fire were Alan Freed and Dick Clark. Freed was the most popular, a star to teenagers almost as big as the performers whom he introduced. It was Freed who was the first white deejay to play black music for a mainly white audience. It was Freed who first applied the term "rock and roll" to black music, which had been called "race" music until the late 1940s, then rhythm and blues. It was Freed who staged the first large interracial stage show dances. After early success in Cleveland Alan hit New York in 1954 on station WINS, taking the city by storm as he quickly became that area's top jockey. Freed was slick and hyper. He didn't care if kids in the audience jumped around on their seats. Police were frequent visitors to his stage shows, and they didn't like the fact that Freed seemed to exercise no discipline over the kids. One time Freed was charged with inciting to riot, while another charge briefly leveled against him was that of anarchy. The establishment harassed him. They wanted him gone. Dick Clark was an establishment man as he rose to the top of the deejay heap chiefly through "American Bandstand." Clark made kids behave themselves, he had a dress code and his guest artists engaged in far fewer pelvic thrusts and gyrations than on other programs. Even though "Bandstand" originated in Philadelphia, which had a substantial black population, a viewer of the program was hard pressed to find a black face among the studio kids. If rock music wouldn't go away then the establishment could live with Dick Clark as the top deejay.

House investigators quizzed Clark in Philadelphia, after being tipped that his record list could stand scrutiny in light of his financial interest in several music firms. Initially, Clark reportedly held a one-third interest in Swan Records, in January Music (a publisher), and two other publishing concerns. For example, Freddie Cannon's "Way Down Yonder in New Orleans," "Okefenokee," and "Tallahassee Lassie" were produced by Swan and played regularly on "Bandstand." After being questioned, the ABC network (Clark's employer) immediately ordered him to drop his "outside" music business activities or leave the ABC network. The network said it was implementing a new policy under which performers and others who selected and played records had to divest themselves of all financial interests in labels, publishing, and allied fields. Clark said he would drop all outside interests. Producer of "Bandstand" was Anthony Mammarella who also owned a one-third interest in many of the companies Clark was involved in. Mammarella was given the same option given to Clark — divest or leave the ABC network. Anthony elected to resign from the show, saying he saw nothing wrong in being the producer of a show that played songs recorded by his own company. Dick Clark refused to issue any statement, leaving that to his employer. The ABC network concluded that "Dick Clark has neither solicited nor accepted any personal consideration — money or otherwise — to have any performer appear or to play any record on any of his programs. . . . We have concluded our investigation with renewed faith and confidence in Dick Clark's integrity."[22]

Later his holdings were listed as being much larger, with Clark having reported links with at least six music publishing houses, seven record labels, two distribution companies, one record pressing company, two production companies, and one talent agency. When asked a month or so later which holdings Clark had divested himself of, ABC vice president Michael Foster replied, "I'm damned if I know . . . I doubt if anyone (at the network) knows. I suppose someone knows."[23]

While Clark was being exonerated Freed was being fired. On November 21 radio station WABC terminated his employment abruptly when he refused to sign a statement that he had never taken gifts or money to promote records. All of the WABC jockeys were then being required to sign such a statement. Alan's refusal was reportedly based on principle with the jockey denying he had ever accepted a bribe. He viewed the document as "an insult to my reputation for integrity." Although Freed worked under a five-year contract signed with WABC in June 1958, station general manager Ben Hoberman said that WABC had a "contractual right" to terminate Freed at any time it felt it was necessary. Hoberman refused to give a specific reason for the dismissal but did say it had nothing to do with payola.

Two days later WNEW-TV terminated Freed's "Big Beat" TV deejay program. Metropolitan Broadcasting Corporation, owner of WNEW-TV, requested Freed sign an affidavit saying he had committed no improper practices while working for the station. Freed complied. His statement read, "At no time during my period of association with said program and Channel 5 have I at any time committed any improper practice or done or committed to do any act or thing for which I might properly be criticized." Despite signing this document, Alan was still fired. Bennett H. Korn, vice president of Metropolitan, said the "agreement to terminate" the deejay had been "long in coming." Korn said the station wanted to resume control of all pop music programs. Freed produced and packaged "Big Beat" as well as emceeing it. Difficulties over the program arose with the American Federation of Television and Radio Artists for failure to pay union-scale wages to performers who appeared on the "Big Beat" where they lip-synched as their records were played. Some of these artists received no pay. Freed said he had disk artists "standing in line" to get on his show so why should he pay them? Asked why he signed a statement for WNEW-TV but not for WABC the jockey said it was because the former "didn't push me." He added, "If I go down the drain so will a lot of others." Alan denied receiving any straight payola to play specific tunes or that he ever accepted money up front for the playing of any record. However, if anyone wanted to thank him, after the fact, for playing a disk Freed saw nothing wrong in accepting a gift "whether it ranged from a bottle of whisky to a Cadillac."[24]

As November 1959 gave way to December pressure and media attention continued intense. The FCC joined the FTC, the House, and Hogan's office in applying formal government pressure.

Early that month former Detroit WJBK spinner Tom Clay went a little more public about his two years as a deejay at that station. During the first 11 months on the job during which Clay was not approached he said,

> The record company guys went to the bigger men here. I didn't care because I knew when I was Number One they would come to me.... When I was finally asked out to dinner, I knew I was Number One. Payola comes to the top disk jockeys, so isn't this the greatest compliment.... I have never demanded money from a record company. When a deejay does that, he's dirty rotten. But it is all right for a man to put down $200 and leave a record for a deejay. If the deejay honestly thinks it is good, then he is justified in taking the $200 because, after all, that money is an investment for the record company. If the deejay turns down the record, the $200 is well spent. It saves the company money — they won't go ahead and make 10,000 records.[25]

Chicago's Chess and Checker record companies got so annoyed with the deejay when he sometimes failed to play records they had paid him for that they didn't send him a Christmas present one year. "That really bugged me," recalled Clay. After a phone call they sent him some silverware. Regular checks came in from other companies with a jockey dutifully listing them on his income tax. "Can I send you something every month?" they would ask him. "That isn't necessary but go ahead if you want to," replied Clay. He almost doubled his yearly salary of $8,000.[26]

Clay's downfall turned out to be Harry Nivins, who managed a rock and roll singer by the name of Melrose Baggy. When Nivins offered the deejay $200 to play a Baggy number on the air Clay refused. Later they went for a ride in Nivins's car where Clay was propositioned again. This time the offer was only $100. "I tell him, like, it was $200 last time," said Clay. "I also tell him this is one record which isn't going to happen. I find out later he has a tape recorder in his clothing." Some of the jockeys at WJBK, unfriendly to Clay, had taken up a collection to rent a tiny tape recorder so Nivins could sandbag Clay. When station manager Harry Lipson was confronted with the evidence he passed it off by delivering a mild reprimand to Clay. Unhappy with this, Nivins got in touch with the Miami headquarters of Storer Broadcasting (owner of WJBK), whose own investigation led to the sacking of Tom Clay.[27]

The deejay then turned up at a dance to answer letters teenagers had written to him. "I have received thousands of letters from you kids and almost all of them say they don't think what I did was wrong," he told them. "This is great for my ego but it's not good for you to think that payola is right." Tearfully, he told the 3,000 teens he had got $5,400 in payola over 18 months. Then he broke down and left the auditorium to the cheers of the youngsters.[28]

Alan Freed also had some things to say. He refused to testify in New York before a grand jury under rules which would have made him liable to prosecution on the basis of his own testimony. Immediately, the district attorney's office began an investigation into the records of two companies, Figure Music and Standford Production, in which Freed had an interest. Acknowledging to reporters that he had received financial consideration and gifts valued at "maybe" $1,000 to $2,000 the jockey called them "consulting fees." When the district attorney's office asked him if he felt they were picking on him Freed replied, "Yes."[29]

By the late 1950s Freed was listed as "author" or "coauthor" of at least 15 songs, including "Sincerely," "Most of All," and Chuck Berry's "Maybelline." On the latter a third coauthor listed was deejay Russ Fratto. Soon after it was published Russ took his name off the author list, admitting he had no part in the song's creation. Berry always maintained that Freed also had absolutely no part in creating "Maybelline," simply forcing his name on the tune. Decades later Berry was still losing half of his royalties to the estate of his "collaborator."[30]

Jerry Blaine of Roulette Records and several other labels came forward to say he had lent Freed $11,000 three years earlier, adding that the jockey made monthly payments against principal and interest for about one year at which time Blaine returned to Freed all interest paid and assigned the mortgage over to Roulette. A second account said Roulette held two mortgages from Freed with a value of $21,000 and $16,493 still owing.[31]

As he hosted his final "Big Beat" broadcast early in December, Freed waded through crowds of sobbing teenagers; accepted a scroll from record distributors for his services; danced with some of the kids; and accepted a subpoena to face the New York grand jury. He still insisted he had never taken payola, only that he had served as a "consultant" for the "major record companies." Freed declared, "Payola may stink, but it's here and I didn't start it. . . . What they call payola in the disk-jockey business, they call lobbying in Washington." He recalled that once "a man said to me, 'If somebody sent you a Cadillac, would you send it back?' I said, 'It depends on the color.'"[32]

Frank Hogan's office continued the probe into payola in addition to conferring for several hours with probers from the House to discuss payola and other matters. Amongst people who were questioned by the Hogan office were singers Bobby Darin, Les Paul, Mary Ford, and Eileen Rodgers, all of whom had made recent appearances on an Alan Freed program. Each denied having paid for their appearances with the deejay. Singer Don Cherry told news reporters that he had never paid to have his records played by disk jockeys. Also quizzed was singer Don Anthony, who told Hogan he had recently paid deejays $5,000 to promote his disks. According to Anthony, after this revelation his home had been stoned by "kids in be-bop hats" who yelled, "Rock 'n' roll isn't going to die; you'll die first." Anthony requested that he be given police protection.[33]

Stories of deejays on the take continued to surface. Ronny Kahn recalled the time he was manager of a San Francisco radio station. A letter came for a jockey who had moved on to another station. By mistake the letter for the departed spinner was opened. It contained a check from a record company for $7,000. An owner of a small record label claimed he had been paying $10,000 a year to jockeys who openly told him that they "expected a little cigarette money, if you get what I mean." A former New York jockey told the *New York Post* he had collected $41,000 a year in payola on top of his regular salary. Part of this payola had to be turned over to a "broker" as commission, he said. Along with 13 other jocks this spinner had taken part in a meeting five years earlier at which the group had compiled a "blacklist of nonpaying record companies and had discussed how to raise the deejays' under-the-table prices for promoting records." So topical had payola become that Bob Hope did a payola skit on one of his television programs in December. The comic played a deejay named Herman Paula of KLIP with Ernie Kovacs portraying an investigating senator. The NBC network objected to merchandise plugs in the script, which Hope defended as part of the comedy routine.[34]

Anthony Mammarella admitted he accepted $7,000 as a one-third share to coauthor the Charlie Grace 1957 hit "Butterfly," although he had nothing to do with the writing of the song. One record promoter stated, "Practically every jock in Chicago is on payola." Some of the jocks didn't personally take the money but had an "associate" whose function supposedly was to do the programming of records for air play. Recalled the promoter, "When I'd approach the jockey with a new record he'd say 'See so-and-so. He's the man who programs my records.'" One such associate regularly accepted $25 in cash, sealed in an envelope, every week. This promoter also paid spinners directly and once paid a prominent jock $300 to push a song for an indefinite period. A record executive with a West Coast firm insisted that the really big moneymaking jockeys couldn't be bribed in cash at all. Citing those spinners who legally or otherwise made $100,000–$200,000 per year he said, "What can you offer a jockey making that kind of money? You going to offer him $50 in cash? He'll laugh in your face.... You offer guys like that paid trips to Las Vegas or vacations with all expenses taken care of." Since such payola was expensive it was not uncommon for record companies to pool funds to accommodate and entertain jockeys. One visiting spinner stayed at a Hollywood hotel, did the town, then spent four days at a Las Vegas hotel on the way home. The whole vacation didn't cost the deejay one cent as two record companies combined forces to pick up the full tab.[35]

All of the pressure and media attention directed toward the industry caused radio stations and networks to make various public responses. Storer Broadcasting announced that at their Philadelphia outlet WBIG a new program control policy would be immediately implemented under which disk jockeys were barred from playing music of their own choice. Storer officials were to select tunes they considered desirable. Harold Anderson, general manager of WINS in New York, sent a letter to 200 record companies around the country asking them if they had ever paid any fees, made any gifts, or in any other way compensated any WINS staff. On the West Coast some stations were asking promotion men when they dropped in to visit to sign affidavits as to whether or not they had "influenced" the stations' jockeys on "what to play."[36]

Dr. Frank Stanton, the president of CBS, issued a memorandum to the network's employees, warning them they would face discharge if they were found to have participated in any form of commercial bribery such as payola in the selection of certain music for shows. One exception was stipulated in the memo, "The foregoing does not apply to the courtesies openly accepted or given as part of the usual business or social amenities." This was an apparent reference to the infamous "business lunch" which was to remain acceptable. The NBC network sent a detailed questionnaire to all the deejays, performers, and executives at the six radio stations which NBC directly owned and operated. The questionnaires were to be filled out by the recipients, notarized, and returned to station managers. Questions asked if the recipients owned recording companies, directly or indirectly, or any distributing or publishing firms; if they acted as agents in any way for artists; if they received royalties from any music licensing society; and whether or not they had ever accepted anything of value for playing a record or presenting an artist on radio or television. To monitor payola activity NBC set up a new department, standards and practices. A directive from CBS radio was issued to its owned and operated stations requiring that jockeys submit to their station manager a list of all records to be played, at least 24 hours before air time. Station WNJR in Newark, New Jersey, also adopted the 24-hour rule. On the West Coast in Santa Monica KDAY utilized a lie detector test to show its personnel were not on the take. The station's jocks took the tests on television with KTLA-TV Los

Angeles broadcasting the event. Plough Broadcasting collected payola denial affidavits from all of its spinners. Management at station KALL in Salt Lake City, Utah, asked its deejays to sign a "Pledge of Good Practice" which began, "I pledge that I have not and will not select any record or news item or plug any commercial product or event in return for any entertainment, gifts or payment from advertisers, agencies or promoters." A violation of this pledge meant instant dismissal.[37]

Under this onslaught of negative publicity few attempted to defend the profession. One who did was Bill Gavin, secretary-treasurer of the Disk Jockey Association, who said the whole payola system involved a small portion of the deejays in the entire country. Gavin feared all deejays would suffer from the greed of a few. "The danger is that the public will feel anybody who is a deejay is accepting bribes, and this is just not true," he said.

> I detect symptoms of fear, frenzy and flight on the part of several station managers. They are hurriedly making protestations of purity by large-scale firings and inquisitions of their program staffs. It smacks of requiring an oath of allegiance to the Ten Commandments. Is it their purpose to convince the Washington investigators that they are just now aware of how record promotion pressures have for years been infiltrating and undermining their programs? Is it their belief that they can cure the evil by publicly sacrificing some of their name disk jockeys? Are they also willing to announce their discontinuance of gifts, rebates and "deals" to time buyers?[38]

A few deejays scurried to try to cover themselves. A number of them in New York were reported to have approached record companies with "consultant" contracts — taking no doubt a cue from Alan Freed — to explain payments made to them in the past. These companies were refusing to sign such after the fact agreements on the ground that it was obvious collusion designed to deceive investigators. Trying to take advantage of the negative light in which spinners were cast was Francis X. McLaughlin, who quit work as an investigator for the Oren Harris subcommittee at the end of 1958 before that group began to investigate payola. McLaughlin set up a detective agency in Washington that specialized in keeping tabs on disk jockeys. This company planned to sell its services to radio and television stations to check up on employees to see if they were taking payoffs for playing records.[39]

Variety reported that more and more stations and jockeys were switching away from the more "raucous" rock and roll records to more "melodic" material. While this trade publication didn't expect rock to fade for "some time," it did believe "the calibre of the performers and the material on upcoming disks will be of pro-calibre in contrast to the anything-goes amateurish quality of so many platter hits over the past few years." This switch over was felt to be a response to payola pressure, a way of playing it safe as "the finger of suspicion is more likely to be pointed now at a disk jockey who is spinning a 'far out' brand of rocking music. One of the basic facts in the payola investigation is that numerous indie disk companies, mostly specializing in the rock 'n' roll idiom, are on the carpet for paying off the jockeys." One example was Boston's WEZE which replaced rock with the "Wonderful World of Music," featuring work by George Gershwin, Rodgers and Hammerstein, the Boston Pops, and so on.[40]

The FTC investigation continued into December with 40 staffers engaged in temporary duty on the payola probe. Complaints brought by the commission would be filed under federal law that barred unfair methods of competition in interstate commerce, including deceptive acts or practices. Payola was regarded by the FTC as a deceptive act. On December 4 the commission accused three record manufacturers and six independent record distributors of deceiving the public and restricting competition by making payoffs to radio and television disk jockeys. Manufacturers charged were RCA, London Records (both in New York), and Bernard Lowe (the Cameo label of Philadelphia). Distributors charged were Edward Barsky, Clips Distributing, Davis Rosen, Universal Record Distributor, Sparks Music Distributors (all of Philadelphia) and Main Line Cleveland (of Cleveland). No disk jockeys were named. According to the FTC each company, alone or in collaboration with others, paid payola to disk jockeys to "expose" records in which the companies had a financial interest. "Exposure" was defined as playing a record day after day, often as much as six times a day and "substantially increasing its sales." This deception had the tendency to mislead people into buying these exposed records which they might not otherwise have purchased. Also asserted by the FTC was that this deception caused the records to advance in popularity polls which in turn tended to increase their sales substantially. Payment of payola, said the commission, had "the capacity to suppress competition and to divert trade unfairly from their competitors in violation of the F.T.C. Act." In concealing payments received spinners were misrepresenting to listeners that records were selected without bias. The FTC's power was limited in this case to issuing cease and desist orders after holding public hearings. Continued violations could then lead to Department of Justice court suits which carried fines as penalties.[41]

Cleveland jockey Joe Finan, of KYW, admitted he had been on the payroll of Main Line as a consultant for the past several months. A spokesman for Edward Barsky told reporters, "Sure we paid disk jockeys. We met competition. Every company was involved in one way or another. We merely fought the battle to sell records, and that was to pay some of the bigger disk jockeys." By the end of the month the FTC was preparing another batch of complaints against record companies. The number of disk jockeys involved was expected to rise into the hundreds. However, the FTC had no jurisdiction over the spinners. That problem of how to deal with the jockeys would have to be left to its sister agency, the FCC, which had jurisdiction over the stations which employed the spinners.[42]

The FTC's complaint against RCA was settled in short order when RCA signed a consent decree on December 15. It was considered one of the fastest actions on an FTC complaint in many years. This agreement stipulated that RCA agreed to give up the practice of paying deejays and others in radio and television stations for playing RCA records on the air — unless the listening public was told that the station or one of its employees was paid for doing so. This meant the FTC considered payola to be an acceptable practice as long as the public was informed. As with all consent decrees this one did not constitute an explicit or implicit admission of guilt on the part of the signatory. What RCA agreed to was to engage in no payola practices in the future without having to say it had ever done so in the past.[43]

The FCC got involved in the payola business when on December 3 it sent an inquiry to every one of its 5,326 broadcast licensees, demanding to know what payments had been received since November 1, 1958, for any material broadcast and for which the person making such payment was not identified to the listeners. Payment meant cash or anything of value received by either the station or any of its employees. A second demand was that each licensee inform the FCC of what steps it had taken to prevent payola in the future. Under the Communications Act, if remuneration was received for material broadcast then the person making such payment must be so identified. Each licensee had to have its information sworn and into the FCC within a month — later somewhat extended. This move by the FCC was sudden and unexpected, increasing the pressure which caused some stations to react strongly in their public posturing about payola. Many licensees interpreted the FCC moves as indicating that the individual licensee (station) would bear total responsibility if payola were uncovered there, even if the licensee claimed to be or was ignorant of it.[44]

Billboard continued to take a reasonable approach to payola. Editor Paul Ackerman, writing in *Nation*, stated, "There is a reason to believe that, proportionately, payola is not nearly so widespread among jockeys. Of the thousands of jockeys now at work across the country, it is doubtful whether more than a few hundred are important enough to be subjected to 'heavy' demanding . . . payola may be ethically deplorable, but it is unlikely that it has ever changed, or even could change, the court of popular American music." In his own magazine Ackerman noted that *Billboard* had dropped its territorial charts of best-selling records while continuing to run national charts when it learned that territorial charts would be "reached." Ackerman urged segments of the music industry — manufacturers, distributors, radio stations, and trade papers — to take up their obligations to clean house because "Failure to face the matter honestly and to act may entail intervention by outside regulatory agencies. The latter possibility is not the most pleasant." He didn't mention jockeys.[45]

Down Beat editorialized in a much more emotional manner. This magazine considered Detroit, Cleveland, Chicago, St. Louis, and Philadelphia as the nation's top payola centers, with Philadelphia being the payola capital of America. There wasn't much bribery in the San Francisco–Oakland market but of that which did exist, "Rock 'n' roll jockeys are the primary offenders." According to *Down Beat*, payola worked in the following manner. Record company executives decided which jockeys were to be paid in which cities. Then they contacted the distributor in a particular city to specify which deejay was to get money. The most powerful jockey in an area was chosen. Then the distributor arranged the payoff by personally, or via a salesman, delivering the payoff. The record company then compensated the distributor by way of a shipment of free records equal in value to the payoff. On the label's books the shipment of free records was written off under the heading of "promotional records."

Grudgingly, *Down Beat* agreed with estimates that something like 200 jockeys were on the take, out of 10,000 in America. "This is probably true. But these are in every case powerful jocks who are in a position to influence public tastes; in other words, because of their location, they are the very ones who are in the best position to do damage. Of these 200 or so . . . there are perhaps 25 in key cities who 'are capable' of making $15,000 to $25,000 a year from payola alone."

Held up as an example was Joe Niagara "with his incessant plugging of the worst type of rock 'n' roll . . . who affected a microphone manner so distasteful that it had to be heard to be believed." For *Down Beat* payola was recent and the fault of rock and jockeys for they wrote, "America was finding out that many disc jockeys were indeed crooked, and that the steady debasement of musical tastes during the past decade may have proceeded from cynical financial motivations." However, they did understand that "politicians were finding out that the subject was an excellent source of headlines."[46]

The Harris inquiry continued its own investigation with Harris announcing that public hearings would be held in Washington in January 1960. Investigators prepared a memo on the situation which was "leaked" to the press. Cited in the memo were 27 major cities from coast to coast where the alleged payola had occurred: Washington, Los Angeles, San Francisco, Chicago, Detroit, Cleveland, Cincinnati, Columbus, Boston, Philadelphia, Pittsburgh, Houston, Dallas, Memphis, Baltimore, New York, Newark, Indianapolis, Hollywood (California), Denver, Atlanta,

Birmingham, Milwaukee, Seattle, Miami, St. Louis, and Nashville. Information had been received by the investigators by telephone, telegrams, letters, and personal interviews. Abuses discovered included cash payments made to station staffers for playing disks; staffers who arranged for plugs sometimes had stakes in the music publishing firms, record labels, or distributors; stations affiliated with networks favored the airing of records made by a record company owned by the network; staffers took kickbacks from talent, including juveniles, appearing on programs; ostensibly "independent" programs were secretly owned by station employees; songwriters whose songs were used extensively on 3,500 radio stations received no compensation for such use; ratings were rigged because key record retailers throughout the country received money to falsely state certain records were the best-sellers; free records were given out to staffers who in turn sold them to retail outlets; record hops were used to promote the outside interests of staffers; payoffs by music publishers and other promoters sometimes took the form of fictitious loans, mortgages, or "consultation fees"; and record manufacturers sometimes required a recording artist to sign away all royalty rights in order to get a record made. Another complaint mentioned in the memo was that the a and r men were "receiving payola in sums far exceeding those paid to disk jockeys."[47]

7 Bad Music Squats in the Dark, Accused, 1960

As 1960 began one writer, noting the pressure being brought on the music industry from various quarters, stated confidently, "there's no doubt that for a long time to come, the payola factor in the making of songs will be held down to a minimum.... While payola existed since time immemorial, the disk jockey phase of this peculiar institution really came into its own with the advent of rock 'n' roll and the accompanying flood of independent labels."[1]

The ASCAP versus BMI battle continued. A group of 33 ASCAP songwriters launched a suit against BMI, charging it and its network owners with a conspiracy to keep ASCAP tunes off the air, thus damaging the songwriters' publishing and recording rights and reducing their incomes. This was a reaction by ASCAP people unwilling or unable to accept changing tastes in popular music; to accept the fact that the era of crooners dominating the charts with June/moon/spoon schmaltz was dead for all time. Rather than accept and adapt, ASCAP preferred to see a conspiracy where none existed.

In 1949 and the very early 1950s the typical Top 100 chart would have something like 97 ASCAP tunes, three BMI. From the mid–1950s onward the ratio would be reversed. This particular lawsuit by ASCAP was six years old in 1960. It would become older still before the plaintiffs would finally fail. Internally, ASCAP had other problems. A second consent decree entered into in 1950 had to be revised and replaced by a third consent decree as changes in the society's methods of sampling airplays, computing credits due, formula for allocating current performance money, and reducing the voting power of the top writers and publishers from a spread of 5,000–1 to around 100–1 were installed. Failure to achieve internal agreement on such issues — producing the third consent decree — would have probably led to a full-scale antitrust suit against the society by the Department of Justice. Within ASCAP a group of young songwriters called the Current Writers Committee were agitating against various practices which they felt to be unfair, particularly to beginning songwriters, such as one proposal which would have allotted 30 percent of writers' royalties to songs one year old or older, regardless of actual percentage of air play. The revenue of ASCAP in 1959 was $28 million.

By the start of 1960 both the NBC and CBS networks had divested themselves of ownership in BMI when both sold their stock back to BMI. Following suit shortly thereafter was ABC, thus establishing BMI as totally free of any ownership by the broadcasting networks.[2] Reasons for divestment were not clear but it is likely that the pressure on BMI by ASCAP and others, the payola scandal, and a fear that the government might indeed see BMI as an antitrust target due to its "monopoly control" by the broadcast networks played a major role in the network decisions to divest.

While the different agencies that came to target corruption in the broadcast industry had entered the arena with a broader scope in mind, such as looking at possible bribery in commercials on television, the focus always narrowed and, as noted by a *Variety* writer, "The central target of the payola crackdown is the disk jockey." Noted with relish was the fact that Freed was among the first deejays to be "frozen out" while ABC had clipped Dick Clark's power; indeed, "the disk jockey again illustrated the maxim: power corrupts; absolute power corrupts absolutely. The deejay called the shots and he made the deals. He was not only wined and dined, clothed and even housed, but he was also cut-in as partner and stockholder."[3]

A nonprofit group of citizens who identified themselves as the Listener's Lobby released the results of a survey they had done in Detroit. Ostensibly, it was a study of radio listening habits and attitudes of students in the greater Detroit area. In reality, it was a sharp attack on disk jockeys and their influence on youngsters. According to this survey popular music was preferred by 36.75 percent, rock and roll by 32 percent, jazz by 15 percent, symphonic music by 5 percent, musical comedy by 3.5 percent, background by 3.25 percent, choral by 2.25 percent, opera by 0.5 percent, and other kinds of music by 1.75 percent. Questionnaires were received from 7,568 students in grades nine through 12. Half of those surveyed accepted the practice of payola in the industry. Other findings indicated that rock and roll was more popular among less proficient students than among superior students; that there was a strong correlation between economic background and musical preference, with students from upper middle-class and middle-class families having more interest in popular and classical music than those from lower and lower middle classes. Said the report,

> It is clear that disk jockey programs are not designed to cultivate musical tastes to set examples of vocabulary or diction, or in any other way to educate their audience. It would appear that in the Detroit area radio's effects oppose the interests and politics of public education. As an institution the disk jockey tends to regulate the whole teen-age group to an

inferior position in the social class structure — and then to keep them there. By his sanctioning the relatively inferior tastes in music and the other arts, his emphasis upon sensation as opposed to analysis, and his limitation of his audience to an extremely narrow range of "favorite" material (all of these being characteristics of the lower social classes), the disk jockey confines teenagers within one of the better-designed, and one of the lowest, compartments of the social structure.[4]

Fear of federal investigators hitting Chicago produced a number of revelations in that city. Al Benson, a veteran rhythm and blues spinner in the Windy City, opened his books to reveal he received $855 a month in total from nine labels and distributors. They were: Vee-Jay Records, $100; Chess Records, $100; All State Distributing, $200; Peacock Records Company, Houston, Texas, $50; Garmise Distributing, $100; King Records, $25; Midwest Distributors, $80; M.S. Distributing, $100; and Apex Records, $100. Some of those monthly payments dated back for many years. With the exception of Herb Kole, sales manager of King, none of those on Benson's books made any immediate comment. Kole, when told of the amounts paid to the others, remarked that he was pleased his contribution was the smallest on the list. None of it was payola said Benson, who claimed the money was for ads run in a magazine he operated or for contributions to defray the expenses of a survey he conducted to give current rating information to record distributors and retailers. "The records on this list have nothing to do with the records I play on my program," he argued. "I won't hide behind the Fifth Amendment. What I'm doing is perfectly legitimate." A little later M.S. head Milt Saltstone admitted his company's arrangement with Benson started 11 years previously: "I was the only distributor in town handling race records and I started out by giving Al free records to play on his program. After a while he started asking for money. He'd come in every month and I'd give him a $100 check. Sometimes he'd ask for two or three months in advance," Saltstone explained. "I didn't see anything wrong with it. Businesswise, it was a good deal. His program sold a lot of records for me. If I didn't pay him and he stopped playing my records, I'd have lost a lot of money." According to Saltstone, M.S. stopped paying Benson just about the time investigators arrived in town.[5]

One anonymous, well-known Chicago radio personality reported that Windy City deejays had set up, printed, and circulated a payola catalogue which listed in detail the prices that could be expected from the various record distributors. Information and revisions to this list were passed around by the jockeys at their trade meetings and conventions. Also on the list were the names of records and firms that should be boycotted. A second unnamed source called Chicago jockey demands for payola "among the worst in America," while deejay Sid McCoy was accused of accepting several hundred dollars from M.S. Saltstone, who termed the money a personal loan which had been repaid. That city's best known and most popular deejay, Howard Miller, was suddenly fired by NBC's Chicago outlet, WMAQ. He continued at WILD. Both parties denied that payola had any part in the dismissal. Miller said the parting came about by mutual agreement; that on their concepts of radio music they were at odds and the jockey was not happy with the type of music played at WMAQ. Investigators were then checking out Miller's relationship with Saltstone since in partnership the pair owned radio station WFOX in Milwaukee.[6]

The FTC continued to lay charges identical to those lodged against the first group of companies in December. At the start of the new year 15 more record labels and distributing concerns were charged. Charles S. Gray, an executive of Cosnat Distributing, one of those charged, said, "We operate our business just like everyone else. I don't want to make any further comment at this time." By February 19, a total of 37 different firms had been charged with payola abuses by the FTC. Near the end of that month 43 complaints had been issued.[7]

After it was charged, London Records challenged the FTC on whether payola was illegal. Admitting it had passed payola "directly and indirectly" to deejays, London denied such a practice was in violation of the Federal Trade Act under whose Section 5 all complaints were filed. Don Robey, president of the charged Duke Records, claimed he was innocent. Asked if he had offered payola to jockeys Robey said, "No, but I have bought time on all Houston stations to promote various artists who are coming to town for a personal appearance." Robey noted that many of the Christmas gifts he traditionally sent to deejays were returned in 1959. "It's all pretty absurd," he said. A Philadelphia record distributor, David Rosen, became the second company to sign a consent order similar to RCA's. A and I Record Distributing Company admitted handing out about $800 in the previous three years to disk spinners but didn't know it was violating any laws by "advancing small amounts of money to certain disk jockeys." The company considered the $800 to be promotional expenses which they deducted from their income tax returns. A and I used the payments as a tool to persuade deejays to play the records privately "and if found worthy to play them over the air." The company stated that no attempt was made to defraud the public as the amounts paid "were so small that it could not possibly cause a disk jockey to play their records unless they were worthy of playing them on their programs." Alpha Distributing Company also conceded "having given valuable consideration to certain individuals in radio stations to test, promote and expose records," but contended these payments were not illegal. It also challenged FTC jurisdiction on the ground that only a small portion of Alpha's sales were out of its New York State headquarters. The FTC could only act on interstate commerce. Another company that resisted the charges was the distributing firm of

James H. Martin, which argued that the number of exposures of a record by a jockey was no guarantee that the public would buy it. Acceptance of a record, said the Martin firm, was dependent on the merit of a record and is "separate and independent from, and unaffected by, the number of exposures." There would be deception only if the public was inveigled into buying an inferior rather than a superior product. "However, as there is no objective standard to determine the superiority of one record over another there is no deception," argued the Martin response to the charges.[8]

Toward the end of February the FTC probe had turned up the names of an estimated 200 deejays, none of whom were named. The FTC and FCC were cooperating and releasing information to each other. In addition, the FTC reportedly was passing along data to the IRS. Pressure for legislation against payola increased. Earl W. Kintner, the FTC chairman, urged that any antipayola legislation cover record distributors and manufacturers as well as deejays and other station employees. Kintner estimated that an "exceedingly high percentage" of the more than 256 distributors and 481 labels had been using payola as a "standard commercial procedure." At the same time the FCC proposed legislation that would authorize fines and imprisonment for deception on radio and television through practices such as payola. This proposed legislation would reach directly to station employees, producers, advertisers, station employees, and others over which the FCC had no jurisdiction. This agency said it was "greatly concerned" over payola, noting that existing law covered payola as applied to a station license but not to station employees. The imposition of a criminal penalty was thought by the FCC to be a remedy to this. Since the FCC was then empowered only to revoke a station license it was rarely used. So drastic was this measure that commissioners would let all but extremely flagrant violations pass instead of invoking what was known in the industry as "the death penalty." Some of the pressure was placed on the FTC and the FCC by the House subcommittee and by Attorney General William P. Rogers, both of whom criticized the sister agencies as already having sufficient powers to police and halt deceptive practices but failing to do so. Both agencies were to be quizzed publicly by the House subcommittee and were scrambling to create a positive impression.[9]

Stanley Adams, president of ASCAP, testified before the FCC that payola was rampant in both radio and television and charged BMI with giving payola out to promote BMI's music. When it learned of this BMI called this charge a distortion, while claiming that ASCAP maintained a "system of rigged payments" to its members that encouraged payola while the BMI system discouraged payola. For some reason no one from BMI was slated to testify before the FCC, although after this uproar BMI was added to the witness list. When Adams made his charges the FCC asked him to be more specific but Adams declined.[10]

Singer Jane Morgan joined those who blamed the death of "good" music on bribery in the business and teens. "Payola," she said, "has damaged the music business in that it paved the way for the popularizing of bad songs and the teenage influence has brought exposure to tunes that for the most part are illiterate and meaningless." Others predicted a decline for rock, if payola was eliminated or declined. R. W. Welpott, vice president of WRCV in Philadelphia, said, "I wouldn't say payola has meant the death of rock 'n' roll, but I would certainly say that it has hurt it." Said John F. Meagher, National Association of Broadcasters vice president for radio, "You'll find, I think, that most of the bribery (payola) was done by makers of rock 'n' roll records, and obviously, if this is going to be quashed, the effect will be less playing of this music." With regard to the small, independent record labels one industry observer stated, "It's going to be tougher for these smaller companies to get hits. When the companies paid off, the disk jockeys plugged the disks so often that they got good exposure and made sales. Now, a lot of this junk won't get on the air."[11]

Radio stations continued to respond in various ways. Many cut back on the amount of rock programmed. Most who did so pretended it was not related to payola publicity. Said WABC general manager Ben Hoberman, "Rock 'n' roll already was on the way out." When Boston's WILD dropped rock, owner Nelson Noble commented, "I never believed in rock 'n' roll in the first place." Station WMAQ in Chicago did admit the payola scandals led it to dropping rock in favor of music for adult, mature audiences. Honolulu's KULA and Denver's KICN both moved away from rock. Chicago's WGN, which had banned rock a couple of years earlier, took the added step of notifying distributors that henceforth visits to the station by promotion men would be banned. In addition, WGN stated that it would immediately begin to purchase all records played on the air. Records were delivered to WGN where they received a preliminary audition. Rejected records were returned to distributors while acceptable ones would have their titles listed on a daily release bulletin given to all on-air staff. If an acceptable record was not played within four weeks it was returned to the distributor. The others were paid for by WGN, which was one of the first outlets to institute the practice of paying for its records. Stations usually received all their disks gratis. The Storer Broadcasting Company had its own quality control system which monitored its programming through tape. Each week the head office picked up some or all of the recorded tapes and compared them with a weekly list of approved record selections to detect variations. One station, WNTA, tried to take advantage of the publicity by setting aside the 4–5 P.M. period Monday to Friday and openly selling the time to labels and distributors. Any record would be played for a price on an "on top of the table basis." The station would announce the company as a paying sponsor. Station manager Irv Lichtenstein said WNTA was doing this because "One thing that the payola probe has proved beyond a doubt is that radio sells records. More than that without radio all record companies would have rough sledding."[12] As with other stations who had tried similar experiments this one was not a success.

Down Beat reached new heights of frenzy in a column on payola. Viewing the investigations as primarily called to judge the impact of radio and television on American culture and society, columnist John Tynan inveighed,

> Yet today we are confronted with such utter moral decay in just one segment of society — the music business — that so-called responsible adults can shuck off the studied subversion of the nation's youth by the crass, crude vulgarity known as rock and roll with a complacent shrug.... Parasitic disc jockeys and self-blinded station owners are beginning to get the message: Rock and roll at last is identified with the rotten practice that helped create it and feeds it sustenance — payola. Today bad music squats in the dark, accused.[13]

Along similar lines was an editorial in the *Instrumentalist* which hailed the FCC investigation and the resultant reduction of rock broadcasting "because most of the payola involved this tawdry substitute for music." Also predicted gleefully was a decline in the number of record companies, many of which stayed in business solely by their sales of "rock 'n' roll trash." The editorial writer stated, "For years most music heard on radio stations has been terrible, devoid of good taste and aimed at destroying one's eardrums and sanity." All readers were urged to write letters to their radio stations requesting more "good" music.[14]

Dominating the payola scene in the first few months of 1960 was the House subcommittee which held public hearings on the issue in Washington. The first deejay to testify before the group was David Maynard of Boston's WBZ. Then on probation at his station because of his admissions, Maynard conceded he had received $6,817 in gifts and cash from record distributing firms. Those payments had been received in 1958 and 1959. Maynard insisted the payments were made to him in appreciation of his promoting disks at record hops outside the station and for advising distributors of their records' potential. However, he did say, "I think I was guilty of bad judgment." Subcommittee member Representative Samuel L. Devine (Republican, Ohio) commented that the jockey had been "considerably less than frank." Oren Harris told Maynard he had testified only to what he "had to testify to." Also at WBZ and on probation was spinner Alan Dary who admitted to receiving $400 to $500 in Christmas gifts in recent years from record distributors, but he insisted he had never been paid to plug records over the air. When asked if he had been shocked to learn of the widespread payola in the industry Dary replied, "I certainly was." Besides Christmas gifts Dary got occasional gifts of liquor and a hi-fi set.[15]

Paul G. O'Friel, general manager of WBZ, testified that Dary and Maynard were each suspended for five weeks the previous November after the station conducted its own investigation. When reinstated O'Friel said it was under "strict supervision." The manager told the subcommittee that he had sent two WBZ employees, George W. Givens, music librarian, and deejay Norman Prescott, to New York to get free records from distributors for the station's "miserably sparse" record library. The pair did as instructed, returning to WBZ with some 1,000 albums valued at $10,000–$15,000. O'Friel claimed he couldn't say if the two men had made any representation that the records would be plugged on the station. Nor did he consider the free records as payola but a "long-standing business practice in the broadcasting industry." When George Givens, then with WORL in Boston, testified he told how he and Prescott got the records in the fall of 1958 from Roulette, Epic, MGM, Decca, Capitol, Atlantic, Mercury, Victor, London, and Columbia. Only Decca was reluctant to furnish the records, he said, but gave the pair 200 disks after promising "never to do it again." Givens stated that all the labels were assured the records would be played on WBZ. He did not feel he had done anything illegal; however, he felt he was "begging for merchandise."[16]

The biggest name slated to testify was deejay Dick Clark. In order to milk maximum publicity value Clark's appearance was held back till later in the hearing with no definite date slated, although his name kept popping up. That the saturation point for investigations had been reached can be seen when the Philadelphia district attorney's office decided to launch a probe of its own. When they sought cooperation the FTC, FCC, and House subcommittee all declined to talk to them and were generally uncooperative, forcing Philadelphia to abandon its probe.[17]

The very first witness to testify before the House group was Norman Prescott, a former jockey. After working in New York, Prescott joined WBZ in 1955 then left that station late in 1959 to become a vice president of Joe Levine's Embassy Pictures. During June 1958 Norman was involved in a $100,000 plagiarism suit that was later dropped. Ruth Green Smolker charged he converted to his own use a television script she had shown him in confidence. The allegation was denied by Prescott, whose attorney later announced the suit had been dropped, producing a letter from Smoler which stated her suit came about as a result of a misunderstanding. Prescott requested and got a private hearing before the subcommittee. Such a request could be granted when testimony might tend to "defame, degrade, or incriminate" any individual. After the two plus hours behind closed doors subcommittee chairman Oren Harris described Prescott as a "very cooperative witness."[18]

Spinner Joseph Finan of Cleveland's KYW testified that in 1958 and 1959 he had received a total of $16,100 from 15 labels and distributors.

When KYW learned of this activity they fired him on December 3, 1959, from his $40,000 per year post. Finan conceded he received $450 from Big Top Records for giving "extra consideration" to their records, and that he had a seven-month deal with the RCA producing team of Hugo and Luigi at $200 per month. Regarding that deal he said, "Of course I was more aware of their records making up my radio show." However, with those exceptions the deejay denied accepting money for pushing songs on the air. Also denied by Finan was an affidavit submitted by distributor Main Line Cleveland, which said Finan agreed to play and give more attention to their disks for $50 each. "I have never granted a single record or a single company air time for the money that we received from these companies," asserted Finan. According to this witness the money was received for his agreement to listen to the records — most of which he did at home — to evaluate the records and to see that hits were not overlooked. The money was for his "advice." When asked how he defined a successful commercial record Finan replied, "It must be in tempo with the psychological impact of the times. Much of our lives are frenetic." After being excused as a witness, Harris termed Finan "pathetic" and told newsmen he thought the jockey's conduct was "illegal." Finan responded that Harris's comments were "grossly unfair."[19]

Dismissed on the same day as Finan was KYW's Wesley Hopkins, who admitted receiving $12,000 in 1958 and 1959 for what he described as listening to records and giving his judgment on their commercial potential. He denied ever having given such records preferential treatment on the air. They paid him, he felt, to keep their records from "getting lost in the shuffle." Local newspapers in Cleveland had reported that a third-floor men's toilet at KYW was known as "the payola booth." Hopkins denied any knowledge of this. In addition, he thought that a disk jockey could not popularize a song simply by playing it. The record had to "have it" to "make it."[20]

Former librarian at KYW Charles Young testified to receiving about $3,000 from labels and distributors, but said it was not payola but only for giving the companies advice on the commercial potential of their records. He did acknowledge that those who offered the money were trying to buy his influence. Young helped Finan and Hopkins program their shows. He denied charges that KYW played one song four times in two hours to pacify one label executive who, unhappy at the lack of exposure of his records, threatened to "go to Washington." Subcommittee member Walter Rogers (Democrat, Texas) sarcastically wondered whether Young thought the companies paid him because they "loved him" and "why the payments stopped when he left the station."[21]

Stan Richards, a former spinner at Boston's WILD, acknowledged receiving $6,225 from two Boston record distributors and that the money was probably paid to influence him in playing records on the air. "But," he asserted, "I have made no deals." Richards insisted he played good music, not rock and roll. Frank Sinatra was this spinner's favorite singer. He charged that news stories made deejays "look like vicious characters, as if we're toting a gun. We're being tried by newspapers." His contract was not renewed by WILD when it expired in December 1959. Comparing money received by disk jockeys to "going to school and giving the teacher a better gift than the fellow at the next desk," Richards commented, "This seems to be the American way of life. It's primarily built on romance. I'll do for you. What will you do for me?'"[22]

When he learned of these comments by Richards President Dwight Eisenhower commented, "when we get to the place where the right of people to use the airwaves under license of the government and then they use this just for personal gain over and above the purposes for which they're hired, then I think there is public morality involved. And I think this fellow, whoever he was, talking that way just hadn't thought through the implications of this . . . alibi that he was setting forth."[23]

One of the big revelations at the hearing was information supplied by the Americana Hotel of Miami Beach, Florida, regarding a disk jockey convention in that city on May 29–31, 1959, attended by an estimated 2,000–2,500 people. According to Americana records, 18 record companies and one radio corporation ran up a hotel bill of $117,664.47 at that convention in entertainment and hotel charges for disk jockeys. Affairs such as receptions and cocktail parties accounted for $68,144 of the total. Biggest spender was Capitol Records with a $19,812 bill, including a cocktail party that cost $12,357. Dot Records's bill at the Americana came to $19,415, which included $14,950 spent on a dinner banquet. Third biggest spender was Roulette Records at $19,158, of which $15,415 was for a barbecue and a breakfast. Columbia Records, Mercury Records, and RCA Victor spent $9,415, $8,843, and $8,569, respectively. With an Americana bill of just $42.69 London Records spent the least. This convention was notorious in that unconfirmed reports had it that "planeloads" of prostitutes were brought in to the convention—two planeloads purportedly originated from Chicago. Further, this information was said to be known to payola probers who balked at the idea about airing such indelicacies at a congressional hearing. Investigators were intrigued by possible Mann Act violations—illegal transportation of a female across state lines for immoral purposes. However, to prove the immoral purpose would require calling the prostitutes to the stand and asking embarrassing questions. In the end this matter was not publicly aired by the Harris Subcommittee.[24]

A WMEX deejay, Arnold Ginsberg, testified he had received $4,400 over the past three years while at WBOS and WMEX (both Boston). He considered the money to be Christmas gifts, "tokens of appreciation" or "goodwill because of my position as a disc jockey." Ginsberg insisted no services had been requested from him by the companies paying him nor was any service rendered by him. Oren Harris snapped, "If you and the rest think we are going to swallow this as though it was just an incident, then you must think we're pretty naive, too." After the hearing Harris said that if the federal agencies had cracked down "we could have a different situation and that some of this rotten stuff foisted on the public would have been cut down."[25]

Cecil Steen with the distributing firm Records, said he paid WMEX $1,400 over 13 weeks for having one of its records picked by the station as its "golden platter of the week." The station played the number about eight times a day, 56 a week, making no mention of payments by Records. In addition, Steen said he paid Boston jockeys $2,050, feeling he received some favoritism in airing records but also thought he had wasted money by making the payments. President Maxwell Richmond of WMEX agreed he had charged distributors for selecting their disks as the "golden platter" but that the charges were for expenses incurred by the station in handling and mailing out 50–75 records supplied by the distributor and mailed out free to listeners. There was no charge for this service until it started to become "burdensome," said Richmond. Charges dropped from a high of $150 weekly down to $10 a week, he said, because the handling and mailing procedures were streamlined. Richmond expressed "shock" when he learned that two deejays at his station accepted money from distributors. After the House began its investigation of payola WMEX started to announce it had received payments for records selected as the golden platter over the air, on the "advice of attorneys." Deejay Mel Miller of WMEX admitted receiving a total of $450 from five record companies but thought the money was for "goodwill." Miller didn't think those payments influenced him but was unsure of the intention of the companies. Amongst the records Miller said he "selected" was the weekly golden platter.[26]

The man who threatened to go to Washington was Jack Gold of Paris Records. One of Gold's records, "Little Billy Boy," had been number two or three in the Boston area when he called Finan at KYW to try to promote it. "I got the clear impression I wouldn't get the record played without changing distributors," he said. Later he visited Cleveland personally to get another record, "Love Me Forever," played and "break the impasse." After talking with Young at KYW Gold said he was again told "I wasn't going to be played on the station because I wasn't with the right distributor." Next Gold took up the matter with station management, who informed him that Young and Finan had denied the charges and that he, Gold, offered payola to Finan. After threatening station management that he was prepared to go to Washington and see the FCC about this "discrimination" Gold said his record was played at least twice that night.[27]

After a few days of hearings the House subcommittee announced it had calculated that Boston radio disk jockeys had been paid a total of $40,472 from 1957 to 1959. Music Suppliers paid $27,121 to 19 jockeys and one station librarian; Dumont Record Distributing paid $8,380 to 12 deejays and one librarian; Mutual Distributors paid $2,121 to 17 disk jockeys; and Records paid $2,850. Of its total, Music Suppliers charged $21,634 to its advertising account. When the vice president of Music Suppliers, Gordon Dinerstein, testified, he said his company paid jockeys to create and maintain goodwill, for promoting records at record hops, and for testing and evaluating his firm's new releases. He denied he talked with jockey Maynard to agree on some "innocent purpose" for which payments to Maynard could be explained. Payments were stopped in December 1959, shortly after the House got involved. Subcommittee member John E. Moss (Democrat, California) commented, "You want me to believe that the number of times your records were played on the air had no bearing on the money?" When Dinerstein replied that was so Moss shot back, "I do not believe you. You impress me as far too practical, far too able to pass out funds willy-nilly." Regarding the payments Dinerstein added that he considered them "to be a general business practice. It may have become a habit. . . . That does not make it right but it was the common business practice in the record business. If the public was harmed that indicates something was wrong." Harris replied that "public indignation is such . . . that the American public is not going to stand for that kind of practice."[28]

Boston jockey Joseph Smith of WILD admitted that four Boston distributors and seven record labels had given him a total of $8,955 in the past three years. But none of the money, he insisted, was for payola: "I felt they [the checks and gifts] were expressions of gratitude for records I had played on the air which in turn made money for them." He added that he had no idea what the intentions of the companies were in giving him money. Coed Records informed him by letter that he would receive two cents for each recording of "Sixteen Candles" that was sold. Copyright in that song was held by January Corporation in which Dick Clark was a principal. "They made the agreement with me," said Smith, "I didn't make the agreement with them." Dale Records cut Smith in on royalties at four or five cents per copy sold in his area. As far as Smith was concerned all of these deals came about without any solicitations on his part. He said, "I accepted the money. There were no strings attached." If a record company wanted to send him money "it's wholly its business." When the House began its investigation in November and the payments to Smith stopped he claimed he had not wondered why. As a deejay Smith was paid $117 a week.[29]

Another witness, Donald Dumont, head of Dumont Distributing, acknowledged his company had given deejays $8,565 in checks in addition to gifts but claimed "it was all given to have disk jockeys test my records at record hops, and listen to my new releases." Irving Lewis, an executive with the American Federation of Television and Radio Artists (AFTRA), testified that his union had received "numerous complaints from artists who appeared on TV shows that they had not been paid." Specific shows cited were the Alan Freed show, the Milt Grant program in Washington, the Buddy Dean show in Baltimore, the Jim Gallant show in New Haven, Connecticut, and Bob Clayton's "Boston Ballroom," aired over WHDH-TV. Lewis said he had received no complaints about the Dick Clark show. When Clayton took the stand he denied that performers on his show had not been paid and also denied ever taking payola. "It would be wrong for me to accept any money from a record company," he said. Clayton did admit to receiving $300 over three years from Music Suppliers, but only as Christmas gifts, and that he had "never engaged in any outside activity my employer did not know about."[30]

Lewis added there was "good reason" for no payment problem about Clark's "American Bandstand" out of Philadelphia. The union made certain before the program aired that checks for appearances on the program would be handled by AFTRA's Philadelphia local as insurance that artists would be paid. When AFTRA put heat on the Clayton show the deejay had performers sign a release form that they'd been paid $40. According to Lewis, about six artists complained they weren't actually paid this minimum after signing the form. However, all complaints except one were anonymous as performers feared reprisals. Only Romance Wilson gave AFTRA his name in connection with the complaint.[31]

After hearing the testimony of Dumont, Representative Moss exploded: "I certainly hope the Internal Revenue Service starts looking at some of these payments . . . made for no good reason at all. You have told us under oath that you bought nothing at all. On the basis of your testimony, it [the $8,565] should be completely disallowed [as an income tax deduction]. I might add, I don't believe your testimony." A promotion man with Music Suppliers told how he helped rig the best-selling charts that were published in the trade paper *Cash Box*. Weiss claimed he obtained Boston radio station letterheads which had the signatures of deejays at the bottom. On these sheets Weiss filled in his version of Boston's top selling records then mailed them to *Cash Box*.[32]

Mutual Distributors general manager Irwin B. Goldstein told the hearing that his company had set up an A, B, C, and D class list for deejay Christmas presents. These gifts, he reminded the House members, were "in appreciation of services and consideration given us," not payola. In the A class — worth a gift of at least $100 in value — were only two jockeys, Bob Clayton and Norman Prescott. The B class contained the names of jockeys and record librarians worth a gift or check in the neighborhood of $50. Fifty-nine names were in the C class. These people got a travel kit valued at $2. Gifts for class D members were valued at around $1.50. Goldstein established the list according to the size and importance of the station.[33]

While Norman Prescott had testified in camera on February 8, this testimony was released on February 17 for unstated reasons. Prescott admitted he had received $9,955 in payola from record distributors in Boston. The money was given to him "with the understanding that he would play eight to ten records a day, anything I wanted to play . . . so long as it was represented by their distributorship." "Payola," he asserted, "keeps rock 'n' roll on the air because it fills pockets." Terming payola "almost a big business," the deejay said he had known of it since he entered radio in 1947 but only personally accepted it over the previous two and a half years. He dated the beginning of payola to 1947. In July 1959 he quit as a jockey at WBZ because he was "so disgusted with myself and with the industry that I just wanted to walk away from it." Prescott told of a "nation-wide ring of disk jockeys to broadcast records for pay." This network was primarily set up by music publishers sometime between 1950 and 1954. When approached, the jockey claimed he turned down an offer to join key spinners in the 15 top markets. Later he would receive calls from spinners in other cities "who assumed I was a part of the network and wanted me to help the total picture. They would ask me at that time to lay on a particular record." Under questioning he said he couldn't recall the names of the companies involved. When a jockey "tested" a new release at a record hop the deejay went to the companies and said, "Look, I think this record has it and the kids like it. Do you want me to lay it on." Then, Prescott added, financial arrangements were made between the jockeys and the companies.

One practice Prescott mentioned was that of record distributors including free records to retail outlets along with their purchases to ensure that when radio stations telephoned for best-seller data the stores would include certain records on the Top 40 lists. "The record may not even have been played on the air yet," he said, "but it was one of the best-selling records." He felt all such Top 40 lists were implausible and that payola was a prime factor in establishing them. Regarding his and George Givens' trip to New York to get free records for WBZ, Prescott said Paul O'Friel instructed the pair to promise companies in New York that WBZ would "lay on" records donated to the station library. He quoted O'Friel as saying, "Just fill up the room." While employed as a deejay at Boston's WORL, Norman charged pressure was used by WHDH Boston through Bob Clayton against record labels and distributors to get exclusive airing on Clayton's show at the expense of other stations and jockeys. When other jockeys held a meeting with distributors to break the WHDH stranglehold, he claimed the distributors just "listened, smiled" and continued the practice. He termed RCA Victor "one of the worst offenders." As far as Prescott was concerned he didn't believe

"rock and roll music would ever have gotten on the air without payola."
He thought that generally station managers were not aware of the payola,
which of course by inference put all the blame on the jockeys. *Broadcasting* magazine criticized the questions as being leading and noted that:
"Mr. Prescott's testimony also was in conflict in some places."[34]

Am-Par Records was a subsidiary of ABC–Paramount Theater, and
it was the ABC network that aired Clark's "American Bandstand." President of Am-Par was Samuel H. Clark (no relation to Dick) who said that
Dick Clark would not play an Am-Par record until it had become an established hit. He felt that ABC leaned over backward to avoid favoring play
on the network of records made by Am-Par. Oren Harris told Samuel
Clark that Dick had played nine Am-Par records 30 times the previous October but then dropped that line of questioning, even though the subcommittee believed that only two of the nine disks might be called hits.[35]

Through March and April the FTC continued to lay charges against
labels and distributors, bringing the total number to about 70 companies.
Nine of these firms signed consent orders of the "I never did it, I won't do
it again" variety. Roulette Records conceded it had given "valuable consideration" to deejays but denied illegal payola. When FTC Chairman Earl
T. Kintner testified before the House group he was asked if his agency had
made any investigation of Dick Clark's activities. Kintner replied that it
had and that "we intend to fully explore Mr. Clark's activities." He added
he was aware of Clark's holdings and understood the deejay had divested
himself of them. Then Kintner stated that his agency had stepped aside for
the present in the Clark case as the subcommittee's investigation was
underway. According to Kintner, the FTC had determined that 255 spinners in over 56 cities in 26 states, or other employees of stations holding
federal licenses, had received payola from labels or distributors. Also he
said seven station licensees themselves had taken payola. The agency head
said the FTC still had about 95 labels and distributors to investigate in its
continuing effort to stamp out payola. It was limiting itself to payola complaints against labels and distributors as a result of a policy decision to
crack down on the "root cause – the dispenser of payola." Names of disk
jockeys uncovered by the FTC were made available to the FCC, the IRS
and the subcommittee itself after Harris requested a copy. When he made
the list available to the House group, Kintner expressed the hope it
wouldn't be made public because his agency had only "ex parte" or off-the-
record information on some of those named. Subcommittee members con-
gratulated Kintner on his antipayola campaign. Representative John Moss
said, in a swipe at the FCC, "I only wish we had some evidence of the same
energy by some of the other agencies."[36]

Meanwhile, in New York Frank Hogan's office continued its investigation although it got little attention. During March a dozen people, mostly

jocks, had been invited to come to the district attorney's office. Only three showed up. Two were jockeys and one of those, Lonny Starr of WNEW, was dropped from his job soon afterward. The station did not elaborate on the dismissal except to say the pair had "parted company." In this probe only Alan Freed had been subpoenaed to testify. It was all voluntary. Books and financial records of more than 100 recording companies were subpoenaed. The grand jury hearing the testimony was trying to determine if the crime of commercial bribery had been committed.[37]

Despite the publicity then attendant on payola, there were indications that in Hollywood, California, at least, it was still going strong. According to one report deejays were still on the take and "Even some unfamiliar paws have gotten into the act." These new takers were said to feel they should not have missed out on easy money in the beginning. Now that it was out in the open they were trying to make up for lost time. Area distributors, while not encouraging the practice, were said to find it easier to move their disks when money was given out. The inference was that many deejays weren't afraid of Harris and his congressional probe.[38]

By filing a 20-page memo with the FCC, ASCAP kept up its own pressure. Stanley Adams, president of ASCAP, argued in his memo that payola was "rampant." According to this group, "Enough evidence has already come to light to warrant ASCAP's opinion that the practice of payola payments to disk jockeys goes much deeper than a few 'isolated' cases." According to figures compiled by ASCAP, at least 146 of the 277 titles which made the Top 50 charts in a trade publication the previous year came from labels accused of payola. This represented 53 percent of the year's most popular records. Predictions were that with future revelations this proportion might rise even further. To stymie the practice ASCAP suggested that Congress make payola in the broadcasting industry a criminal offense. In addition, this group made two suggestions: first, that the FCC should adopt a rule, aimed at BMI, that would bar broadcasters from combining to control a performance rights society; second, they proposed that the FCC adopt a rule under which stations would be prohibited from accepting payment for playing a musical work under any condition. The FCC's own proposal would allow payola, provided it was acknowledged as such over the air to listeners. This was viewed by ASCAP as "sanctioning" payola. In turn ASCAP found itself under pressure from the Justice Department. The result was that new rules adopted by ASCAP, with the approval of the Justice Department, reduced royalty payments to ASCAP members for repeated performances of theme and background music on radio and television. Prior to the new rules each such playing of even a few bars of a song meant as much as $200 in royalties: potential royalties that produced what the Justice Department termed an "incentive for artificially stimulating performance, whether by payola or other means."[39]

Payola continued to permeate the popular consciousness with the subject being the target for quips from television comics. Stan Freberg came out with a comic record "Payola Roll Blues," while Lenny Bruce turned his wit on the topic in his album "I'm Not a Nut, Elect Me!" In Poughkeepsie, New York, WEOK banned the use of the term "disk jockey" on its programs because of "unpleasant association." Station director Blair Walliser announced that henceforth his spinners would be referred to as "musicasters."[40]

On the West Coast a feud developed between "Jumpin' George" Oxford, a white who had been northern California's top rhythm and blues jock for a decade, and a radio station. In 1955 he joined San Francisco's black station KSAN, moving over from Oakland's KWBR. Five years later KDIA (formerly KWBR) lured Oxford back to Oakland. An ugly battle developed as Oxford was bumped off the air several weeks before his scheduled departure for KDIA. During this time Oxford was used by the station as an engineer while a house jockey took Oxford's spot using the name "Jumpin' George" which Oxford had failed to copyright. After he departed KSAN sued Oxford and 20 unnamed labels and distributors for $200,000, charging that Oxford spent time playing records due to payola on his show and that this constituted advertising which should be paid for at the going rate. Oxford received $40,000 in payola while at the station, KSAN contended. Oxford denied the amount but did not deny taking payola "as everyone else in the business has. . . . It was accepted as perfectly all right," he said. Oxford added that KSAN had known for years that he took payola, that he mimeographed and sent out to his "clients" a list detailing how many plays of each record they got each week.[41]

Down Beat became far less strident in attacks on deejays, perhaps feeling that payola was on its way out. In March they reprinted one of their 1947 editorials on payola which noted that spinners on the take for cash "are in the very slim minority." That editorial also worried about jockeys with a financial interest in concerts which they promoted on the air, without telling listeners of their interest, and jockeys getting stock shares in new record companies. Added to this old editorial was the comment of the current editor who said, "we're no longer confident that the minority on the take for dough is so slim." While *Down Beat* loved to bash rock and blame it for 1960s payola, they failed to see the irony in using a 1947 editorial about payola — when rock did not exist. In the same issue a columnist wrote regarding the spinners, "the good guys now outnumber the bad guys but the bad guys smell worse than ever."[42]

Mitch Miller continued to hammer away at rock music and its performers. He saw a golden age of "good" jockeys, music, and station managers on the horizon, "because instead of fearing payola and being burdened by the rock 'n' roll drivel, they are truly more program minded. . . . No upstart, one-hit wonders who burp themselves into a few thousand records on some indie label can survive." Of those rock jocks Miller commented, "They were happenstance accidents of the moment. They parallel those one-platter wonders, the burpers and frog-throated, wild-coiffed characters in open shirts and tight breeches who, for some freakish reason, enjoyed a vogue with the subteeners — and I use 'enjoy' loosely."[43]

The death of rock and roll continued to be trumpeted. One observer claimed that deejay resistance to rock, exacerbated by the payola publicity, had become markedly widespread and "now the diskers are finally in full flight from the rock, the roll, the big beat and the teen tunes." It was a cycle this observer expected to spell bad news for the small, independent labels in particular who got by with an amateur combo who usually wrote their own material and had a garage for a recording studio. Whereas songs by pros had been coming back from the publishers rejected with the comment "It's too good," now this material was on the rise because "these deejays are playing it safe and demanding disks that not only require professional talent but are more expensive to produce. Big sounds from a studio orch cost money which the small indies are not accustomed to spend."[44]

Columnist Charles Suber of *Down Beat* noted that attendance was down at rock concerts. While Suber acknowledged there was little drop in sales of rock and roll records he rationalized, "It takes a while for five years of brainwashing to wear off." Suber also reported that Washington's WGAY had dropped Top 40 programming and changed its call letters to WQMR. Under its new format music by the likes of Percy Faith and Andre Kostelanetz would be featured. No record titles or artists' names would be announced; however, the Disk Jockey Association announced its spring convention would go ahead as planned in 1960. Mindful of the ugly publicity generated in 1959, the jockeys invited many Washington observers and investigators to attend in order that the spinners could show a "new and clean face" to the public.[45]

At least one other politician not directly connected with the House probe came out publicly to bash rock and link it with payola. Representative Emanuel Celler, chairman of the House Judiciary Committee, blamed payola for the rise of rock and roll music. The Brooklyn Democrat said he planned to introduce legislation to make it a federal crime to accept or to give payments as an inducement to play musical works or records on the air. His proposal was similar to a measure recently announced by Oren Harris. Celler said, "payola in the selection of musical works and records for broadcast is a kind of corruption that should have been dealt with years ago by the Federal agency charged with primary responsibility in this area — the Federal Communications Commission."[46]

Finding itself under increasing pressure and as the agency singled out to bear the brunt of the blame for the current state of payola, the FCC began to take action to indicate publicly that they were working to stamp out the practice. Just days before John C. Doerfer, chairman of that agency, was due to testify before the House subcommittee the FCC sent letters to four Massachusetts radio stations telling them that their applications for license renewal would be held up, pending possible public hearings involving payola considerations. The stations were WMEX, WILD, WORK (all in Boston), and WHIL in Medford. The commission indicated in the letters that the stations had failed to comply fully with the FCC questionnaire sent out the previous December, having "failed to disclose pertinent information" or "lacking in candor" in their replies. Also cited were minor variations in programming as compared with filed applications from the previous renewal period. For example, WILD had stated it would devote 9.9 percent of its airtime to news and 1.3 percent to discussion while it delivered, said the agency, only 5.19 percent and 0.19 percent, respectively. However, the major reason for holding up license renewals was the stations' alleged involvement in payola. This marked the first time the FCC had ever done so. Since the Federal Communications Act of 1934 was passed the FCC had never failed to renew a license. All four stations claimed the accusations were not justified. All said safeguards against payola had been instituted at their stations before disclosures involving their staff, that their staffs had been warned against taking payola, and that the stations themselves were not aware at any time that any of their employees were on the take.[47]

When Doerfer testified before the Harris group he told them that preliminary results from the FCC's December questionnaire indicated most stations admitted to receiving free records from labels and distributors while insisting that their judgment as to what records would be aired remained unaffected. According to the FCC head, big metropolitan stations got "virtually all" their records free, and medium-size market stations subscribed to "record services" whereby labels supplied their new records at a fixed annual charge, well below the wholesale list price. Stations in very small markets told the FCC they had trouble getting free or cut-rate records as the labels and distributors didn't feel they were important enough. All of the big stations that received free records denied they sold them to record stores; however, a few admitted to giving some away as prizes to their listeners. In almost all cases these free records were played without announcing the source or terms under which they were received, said Doerfer.[48]

While on the stand Doerfer admitted that George B. Storer had flown him and his wife to Miami Beach from Washington in 1958 in a plane owned by the Storer Broadcasting Company, which owned five television stations and seven radio stations. Then Doerfer spent six days as a guest on

Storer's yacht, "Lazy Girl," which took the party to the Florida Keys for golf, after which Doerfer was flown back to Miami Beach in a private plane. According to the FCC head, he made the flight to and from Florida in Storer's plane with the understanding Storer would be reimbursed. However, some two years after the fact he had still not done so. Several members of the inquiry questioned Doerfer's conduct, saying his testimony reminded them of the conduct of deejays who received money and gifts from record companies. "This was no gratuity," retorted Doerfer, "this was a social occasion." He added, "I don't think a commissioner should be a second-class citizen" and defended his right to pick his friends and social activities as long as the friends did not have matters of a contested nature before the commission of an adjudicating nature. "My conscience is absolutely clean," remarked the FCC head. "So long as I do not violate any law or endanger my independent judgment I think I am entitled to select my social acquaintances." After Doerfer finished testifying Oren Harris told the FCC head that his panel would soon hold hearings into the propriety of his Florida trip. Also revealed was the fact that two years previously, while testifying before a House subcommittee investigating federal regulatory agencies including the FCC, Doerfer was criticized after admitting to having been a guest on Storer's yacht in the Bahamas. At that time the FCC head termed his trip as just a "two-hour cruise."

When Doerfer finished testifying before the Harris panel it was reported that the administration would not censure the FCC head over his acceptance of Storer hospitality. The administration was upset and annoyed with Doerfer but hoped the affair would blow over. Asked after the hearing if he would resign, Doerfer could only manage to say, "A New York newspaper hoped I would never resign." However, the storm would not go away with press criticism of Doerfer being particularly strong. This resulted in a thirty-minute meeting with President Eisenhower, wherein he offered his resignation and Eisenhower accepted it. Less than two weeks after appearing before the Harris panel Doerfer was replaced as FCC chairman by Frederick W. Ford. Nor was Doerfer the first FCC member to resign under fire around that time: FCC member Richard A. Mack left after it came to light that he had accepted money from one of the "interested parties" in the awarding of the license for television channel 10 in Miami.[49]

In response to the escalating idea that the FCC had failed to act in the face of payola, this agency came out with a new rule that required stations that received free records from labels and distributors to announce the fact the disk was furnished and to identify the supplier. The FCC public notice said it was "apparent that consideration has been provided in exchange for the broadcasting of various types of material without an accompanying announcement indicating that consideration was provided, and by whom, in exchange for or as an inducement for the particular broadcast." Replies to its questionnaire had convinced the agency that many stations had failed to comply with Section 317 of the Communications Act, which required that all matter broadcast for which valuable consideration is received must be accompanied by an announcement to that effect. Such public announcement was also to be required when a station used free records in a non-broadcast manner, such as giving them out as prizes to listeners or at record hops. In addition, a station promoting a record hop over the air staged to generate a profit to the station and or its employees must announce the fact. While the FCC acknowledged that past noncompliance may have resulted from misinterpretation of Section 317, inadequate supervision of station employees or reliance on "accepted industry practices" as excuses would no longer be accepted.[50]

This reaction by the FCC was clearly a ploy for winning over the Harris panel to its side, as opposed to a genuine attack on payola. All the major stations got all of their records for free, which of course negated any payola possibilities. However, the Harris group hit out heavily at freebie foraging by WBZ in 1958, terming free records as an "inducement to play." Equally heavily scored was the use of free records as prizes for WMEX promotion and giveaways at WBZ-sponsored record hops.[51]

As expected the stations responded angrily to this new rule. The National Association of Broadcasters (NAB) stated, "We do not believe that the receipt of free records by a broadcasting station destroys that station's objectivity in making its determination as to which music should be aired." The CBS, NBC and ABC networks joined in with comments critical of the rule. All agreed that in general payola was bad. None were sure just how the commission defined payola. Broadcasters wanted more time to hassle over rule making and fine legal points before the edict took effect. The NAB argued that the FCC's suddenly harsh interpretation of Section 317 "makes previously accepted day-to-day broadcast practices illegal and unethical." Before such a sweeping order to identify freebies, free talent, and so on was made effective, the NAB wanted rule making as the new order, necessitating extensive changes in day-to-day operations of almost every station in the country.

Yet no one was given the chance to comment on the document that outlawed practices previously accepted over a period of many years without comment. Further noted by the NAB was that back in 1944 there was a proposal before the FCC to require public announcement of free records played. It was dropped in final rule making. The NAB remarked, "In essence, then, the Commission is adopting the rule it previously rejected, but this time without giving the public and interested parties an opportunity to comment one way or another." Paying for all records would possibly curtail the variety of music available to the public as stations couldn't acquire as large a variety if they were on limited budgets, thought the NAB.

Westinghouse Broadcasting Company announced to the FCC that it had begun to buy all its disks. The NBC network argued that free records were comparable to free press releases that went to newspapers and were not acknowledged by the press as "advertising."[52]

Some stations quickly obeyed the new edict. Station WQXR (New York) notified its staff not to accept any more free records until it got further clarification from the FCC. Also in New York both WNYC and WCBS started to make public announcements that the records they played were received gratis. The announcements of WCBS went, "Broadcast and audition copies of the records played during this quarter-hour were supplied through the manufacturers and distributors of those records." After one week this announcement was stopped when CBS stated that only records purchased by the company would be played. Enterprising station KPHO in Phoenix, Arizona, which made its announcement 30 times a day, managed to sell all these spots to a sponsor. The declaration of KPHO stated, "Records for the following program are furnished by MGM, RCA Victor, Capitol, Mercury, and Decca. Distributors providing records are Kerradio of New York, George Jay and Liberty Records of Los Angeles, and M. B. Krupp and Esskay Distributors of Phoenix. The preceding announcement was presented by Ed Post. When you think of real estate, think of Ed Post, Arizona's leading real estate organization with four convenient offices to serve you. That's Ed Post Realty."[53]

Quickly NBC joined CBS in deciding to purchase all their disks. Some stations made their free records announcement after every spin while others made theirs at regular intervals throughout the day. Small, independent labels were expected to be hardest hit if all stations were forced to buy all of their records. Large, established labels and names were expected to have the inside track if only limited material could be bought. One practice followed by many stations had them accepting free records as before, screening them prior to air use, then buying at wholesale prices the records the stations decided to program. Mostly the industry saw the new rule as an overreaction. Said one industry executive, "It's ridiculous. It is like demanding that the *Saturday Review* or the *New York Times Literary Supplement* pay for the books they're going to review."[54]

That this rule was more a knee-jerk reaction by the FCC to appease its critics than an effort to stamp out payola can be seen by the confusion within the FCC itself regarding the rule. The order was issued by the FCC on March 16; however, no effective date was given, leaving the industry wondering if the issue date was its effective date or some later time. The FCC did not clarify the matter — virtually all such orders from regulatory agencies carry an effective date. Initially, no input by the public was scheduled, but on April 1 the FCC granted interested groups a period of time to file objections. A few days later at the NAB convention broadcasters got a chance to question several FCC commissioners about the rule. The same question evoked different answers from different commissioners. Asked by a broadcaster specifically when a station had to announce a free record, commissioner T. A. M. Craven said he thought stations should "not impose on the public numerous announcements every time a record was played." Commissioner Robert T. Bartley said, "at the time of broadcast," while FCC Chairman Ford said an announcement should be made "once each hour under commission rules." If a station obtained a record at a "nominal charge" then the free announcement was required. Asked what nominal meant Ford replied, "It all depends on the circumstances," while Craven declared that the FCC should not "become involved in determining what is reasonable and what is not in a business deal." One broadcaster asked what would happen if he received 100 records from a distributor, purchased 10, but was stuck with the other 90 free records because the distributor refused to pay the return shipping costs. One commissioner suggested the station must make a free announcement on all 100; a second suggested trashing the 90 and forgetting about it; while a third said the station should hold the 90 records until the FCC could come to a decision. Regarding the problem of how a station could determine which of the records in its existing library were free or purchased Ford said, "If you cannot determine if your library was free or not, the F.C.C. can't. I think the F.C.C. would look at it in a practical way and not be too concerned about existing libraries." Overall, Chairman Ford admitted there were some "uncertainties in the new rule."[55]

That Oren Harris and his House panel may have had more in mind than just stamping out an "evil" such as payola became clear when Harris suggested the group's final report might deal heavily with programming and "good music." Harris said, before his hearings concluded, "If, as is often alleged, any broadcast licensees are allowing their license[d] facilities to be used as little more than 'electronic jukeboxes,' serious public interest questions are raised which require congressional attention." The phrase "electronic jukebox" was a favorite of some opponents of Top 40 format, or rock music. Continuing, Harris added, "Finally the extent to which questionable business practices in the popular music and broadcast industries result in the suppression of genuine talent and in foisting upon the public remunerative but mediocre music, has large implications for the cultural future of America.... Have broadcasters allowed their facilities to become an integral functional part of the merchandising of musical products and, if so, is such a function of broadcasters in the public interest, as required by the Federal Communications Act?"[56]

Meanwhile, the name of Dick Clark continued to bedevil the House subcommittee long before he testified. With Alan Freed dethroned as king of the jocks and well on the road to oblivion and early death, Dick Clark was without doubt the most influential and powerful deejay in the land. He was born on November 30, 1929, in Mount Vernon, New York, to a father who was in radio broadcasting. After graduation from Syracuse University in 1951 Dick went into broadcasting instead of advertising as originally intended. Following a brief stint on a small television station in Utica, New York, Clark moved to WFIL-TV in Philadelphia. A few years later when the emcee job on "American Bandstand" opened up Clark was tapped for the post and began his rise to the top of the disk jockey ladder. In 1959 "Bandstand" aired on 101 ABC affiliates, reaching a daily audience of 20 million people. By 1960 he was earning an estimated $500,000 yearly from his various enterprises. At that time he was described as having a well-scrubbed appearance and looking "not unlike an up-and-coming mid-western insurance salesman." Asked about his appeal to teens, Clark saw himself as a combination "friend, adviser, older brother, or young parent." His show's executive producer, Charles Reeves, thought he represented what the average male teen wanted to become and what the average female teen would some day like to marry. His power to make a record was well known. An appearance on his program by a singer could cause a rush on the market for that artist's records. An observer noted, "It is said that he can make a rock 'n' roll hit by just a few playings. He denies this, but nobody believes him."

Despite the fact that he presented a clean image and rigidly controlled the kids on the program as well as toning down such things as pelvic thrusting by entertainers — as compared to Freed who did none of that — Clark had some enemies. Such was the antipathy to rock music at the time. Said Clark, "I am always puzzled why anybody should dislike me because I am associated with young people, and because I defend teenagers' musical likes and dislikes."[57] Still, if rock couldn't be killed, better to have it controlled and run by the likes of Clark than by the likes of Freed.

A skirmish developed on the House subcommittee between Chairman Harris and member John B. Bennett (Republican, Michigan) on March 4 when Bennett demanded that Harris call Clark to testify saying, "This man obviously is seriously involved in payola." Bennett claimed the subcommittee had gathered more information on Clark than any of the deejays it had questioned and that among the evidence was some that Clark had accepted fur coats, expensive rings, and other jewelry. Harris protested that Bennett had "spread on the record" some material "before the facts are developed." The chairman stated the subcommittee was aware of Clark's interest in 17 companies and that they had the affidavit the deejay had signed for ABC. Continuing to stonewall, Harris said the committee should further develop this "complex" case before calling Clark to testify. Representative Moss joined in to support Oren Harris.[58]

One piece of evidence brought out by Bennett was the charge that the

ABC network had received a royalty of seven cents on each Dick Clark record carrying case sold. These cases were manufactured by a company owned by Clark, Mammarella, and record distributor Edward Barsky. The latter's distribution company was one of those under charge by the FTC. Bennett didn't know if these royalties were actually illegal but believed them at least questionable. He demanded an explanation from Clark and ABC and offered the opinion that the network's investigation of the deejay was casual and superficial. Saying that Clark appeared to have engaged in a "refined type of payola," Bennett added, "If we're really going to expose the evils of payola, we're going to have to do more than call in a few small fry disk jockeys. The fact is that Clark is one of the two or three boys who broadcast nationwide." From the affidavit Bennett released information that Clark had received goods valued at $3,400 from a record distributor in the fall of 1959. While Clark had reportedly insisted on paying for the fur stole, which he was told cost $1,000, Dick gave the distributor only $300. A further charge by Bennett was that Clark had "admitted playing songs that were owned or distributed or pressed by companies that he wholly or partly owned, and that he thereby made a financial profit. Clark's admissions in the affidavit alone make a stronger case against him than any of the disc jockeys we've had as witnesses so far." Joining Harris in delaying tactics was Robert W. Lishman, chief counsel of the subcommittee, who said of the Clark case that it was "open and active but not yet ready for a hearing."[59]

Following the Bennett campaign to get Clark quickly on the stand, Harris issued an order in a memorandum to Lishman barring his fellow payola investigators from information about Dick Clark. This secrecy rule was clearly aimed at Bennett, whose attack on Clark was based on making public information in the ABC affidavit which had not then been made a public document. When it became clear that the Harris order was in violation of House rules Harris backed down by modifying his order. He claimed his order had been misinterpreted and that his only intent had been to prevent subcommittee staff from opening the files to non-subcommittee members. Anyone entitled to see the files — any member of the House of Representatives — "can see them if they'll come to me. I'll arrange it so they can see what they want," said Harris.[60]

Clark was called to the stand at the end of April to testify. A couple of days before that testimony was given by Bernard Goldstein, vice president of Computech, a New York firm engaged in what it termed "data processing." Computech had done a statistical study to determine if records in which Clark held a possible financial interest were played more frequently on "Bandstand" than songs in which the deejay held no financial interest. Every record played between August 5, 1957, and November 30, 1959 — 1,885 records played a total of 15,662 times — was analyzed. Goldstein concluded that there was no difference, despite admitting the "interest" records were played on average about twice as often as "no-interest" disks. Computech's study was ordered and paid for by Dick Clark, at an undisclosed cost. Subcommittee members openly scorned Goldstein and his study as both erroneous and incomprehensible. Included in the study count was Clark's "Bandstand" theme song which, of course, was played twice every day, to open and close the program, a song, aired 1,322 times, in which Clark held no financial interest! Goldstein concluded, "the number of record performances in which there existed a possible interest [for Mr. Clark] is consistent with the number of record performances in which no such potential interest existed. In brief, this analysis established that the playing of interest records was consistent with the popularity of the records based upon independent and authoritative ratings." Statisticians called to the stand all condemned the Computech study. Chief mathematical statistician of the U.S. Census Bureau, Joseph P. Daly, said the conclusions were not supported by the data. Morton S. Raff, U.S. Bureau of Labor statistician, stated the Computech study offered no "real evidence on the point at issue," adding, "The figures do not support the conclusion that preferential treatment was not given Clark-interest records." Finally, Joseph L. Tryon, statistics instructor at Georgetown University, termed the Goldstein study of "practically no value.... For given popularity, Mr. Clark played interest records more frequently and over a longer period." When Moss suggested to Goldstein "You were far more interested in getting the account than in getting the facts," the executive denied it. However, Goldstein admitted that was the first attempt by his company at "data processing with semi-judicial implications." He also admitted to "some errors."[61]

Some of the most incriminating evidence against Clark was given by Harry Finfer, a part owner of Jamie Records as well as vice president of Universal Record Distributing, both of Philadelphia. The latter distributed Jamie disks. Finfer testified that he and his partners invited Clark to become a 25 percent owner in Jamie Records in June 1957 due to his "expert knowledge of records." Clark bought 125 shares for a total of $125. After Clark agreed to divest his holdings in November 1959, Finfer and two others bought the 125 shares for $15,000. In July 1959 Jamie decided to pay Clark a salary of $200 a week, retroactive to May 1958. Later he was paid $225 a week. Up to November 1959, when Clark ended his financial interest in Jamie, his salary payments totalled $16,700, making total receipts to Clark from Jamie of $31,700 — all for a $125 investment. According to Finfer the salary was paid to the deejay for "giving Jamie the benefit of his advice and experience." He would go to Clark, play a new record, and receive advice on how to handle it. Skeptical panel members asked if the deejay was still giving "advice" of this type since he had severed connections with Jamie.

Finfer said yes. Also revealed was that between May 1, 1958, and December 31, 1959, Jamie Records paid around $15,000 to disk jockeys all over the country. There was "no understanding," said Finfer, about the jockeys doing anything at all for the monthly payments. After lengthy questioning the executive finally admitted that the money was to compensate the spinners for both listening to the records and for playing some of them on their shows. Among those who received payments was Anthony Mammarella, who got $500 when his wife had a baby then $1,000 at a later period. Universal paid disk jockeys and others in broadcasting a total of $34,246 between July 1, 1957, and July 1, 1959. Mammarella received $4,000 of this, the first $500 being a "gift" for his newborn child.[62]

Testimony was given about the song "The All-American Boy," composed by Oliver Lunsford and sung by Billy Parsons. Ownership passed from Kane Recording to Fraternity Records which had a pressing contract with RCA Victor. Harry Carlson, president of Fraternity, told that after he switched his pressing contract from RCA to the Clark-interest Mallard Pressing, "The All-American Boy" was played on "Bandstand" 18 times in two months, sending it up near the top of the charts after "Bandstand" pushed it. Carlson claimed he never used payola; however, Lunsford testified that Parsons showed him a royalty statement listing payments to 100 deejays. The one name he remembered was Milt Grant, who denied the charge. Parsons told of being paid $3,000 for travel expenses to promote the record but this was charged to his royalty account. A minimum-scale fee to appear on "Bandstand" to lip-synch the number resulted in no real payment but a credit to his royalty account. The singer said he still was listed as owing Fraternity $6,000 on the account due to promotional expenses. While Parsons was listed as the singer, the vocals were actually provided by Parsons' friend, singer Bobby Bare. Parsons complained to the subcommittee that he had received no royalties for a performance that he had never given.[63]

"Get a Job" by the Silhouettes was originally produced by Philadelphia deejay Kay Williams on his Junior label. The record was then purchased by Ember Records. Before that transaction took place copyright to the number was transferred to Wildcat Music — controlled by Tony Mammarella. Then "American Bandstand" broke "Get a Job" nationally, driving it to smash hit status.[64]

Just before Clark took the stand several witnesses testified before the subcommittee in closed-door sessions. On the eve of Clark's appearance Bennett continued his attack on the deejay by saying Clark accepted payola "the same as many other disk jockeys but on a much larger scale." Harris commented that he assumed "eventually all of the testimony will be made public."[65]

When Clark took the stand the deejay told investigators that he had never taken payola, saying, "I have not done anything that I think I should be ashamed of or that is illegal or immoral and I hope to eventually convince you of this. I believe in my heart that I have never taken payola." The subcommittee produced figures to show that in less than three years the deejay had received $167,750 in salaries plus $409,020 in increased stock values on investments totaling $53,773. Lishman repeatedly charged this money came his way because of his position as the country's most influential disk jockey, while subcommittee member Steven B. Derdunian (Republican, New York) told him, "You say you did not get any payola but you got an awful lot of payola." Appearing in his "best blue serge suit" and carrying a briefcase, he was described as "even more self-possessed than his experienced counsel." Dick Clark's television shows brought in about $5–$6 million in advertising revenue to ABC, 4–5 percent of the network's total billings. On the stand Clark detailed 33 businesses in which he had had some interest. These firms ranged from music publishers, to labels, to film concerns, to a business that made a stuffed kitten for sale and distribution on "Bandstand." It was called "Platter-Puss." None of these firms was set up to "exact tribute" from the music industry, insisted Clark. "The various corporations just grew." Conceding that some songs and records were given to his firms at least in part because "I was a network performer" he went on, "However, the conflict between my position as a performer and my record interest never clearly presented itself to me until this committee raised questions of payola and conflicts of interests." Then he decided it might not look good and so dropped his outside interests, he said. When charged by the subcommittee that he favored records on his program in which he had an interest, and when shown figures that he had played such tunes twice as often on average as ones in which he had no interest, the jockey replied, "The truth, gentlemen, is that I did not consciously favor such records. Maybe I did so without realizing it. I would note that until this committee's activities no one had really pointed out the inconsistency of performing records and owning an interest in record and music companies."[66]

Copyright for 160 songs and profits had passed into the control of Clark-interest companies. Of these, 143 came to him as outright "gifts." Before obtaining the copyright to "Sixteen Candles" Clark played the tune four times over ten weeks on his program. After copyright passed to his company the deejay played it 27 times in less than three months and it soared up the charts. These sales of "Sixteen Candles" grossed the Clark company $12,000. A similar pattern took place for "Butterfly," earning the Clark company $7,000. During a period of 27 months Clark gave much less air time to a then well-established top star like Elvis Presley than to a newcomer named Duane Eddy. The jockey had no interest in Presley but had an interest in companies which managed and recorded Eddy. Goading the jockey with the implication that he had deliberately foisted rock and roll on teens, Representative Moss said, "I don't know of any time in our history when we had comparably bad, uniformly bad music." Clark replied, "Popular music has always become popular because of young people. You can't force the public to like anything they don't want. If they don't want it, it won't become a hit." A 13-year-old named Karen Katz was one of many teens in attendance when Clark testified. Her remarks perhaps typified the feelings of teens in general to their jockey idol. Said Karen, "I don't care if he took payola. He gets to us kids. The reason '16 Candles' took off is because we liked it. They say he didn't play enough Bing Crosby. Look, his show isn't for grandmothers. And Frank Sinatra, who needs him?"[67]

Questioned about his association with Jamie Records, Clark said he was "surprised to learn that some people were apparently shocked" at his financial gain. Explaining that such quick profits were possible in the music industry, he stated, "Believe me this is not as unusual as it may seem. This was good, sound business and no one ever blew the whistle or said, 'This is a bad thing to do.' I think the crime I have committed, if any, is that I made a great deal of money in a short time on little investments. But that is the record business." Asked about the $15,000 in payments by Jamie to other record spinners for "listening" to records, Clark characterized this as payola but added he had nothing to do with it. "I've been pretty busy," he said noting he had little time left for "really close supervision of these various companies." During the period January–October 1958 Clark admitted "American Bandstand" engaged in a kickback arrangement with performers on that program. Entertainers would be booked on the show at union scale; however, part of the salary would then be "reimbursed" by either their managers or labels to the Bandstand Producing Company. This was "common practice" in the television industry, claimed Clark, because of high union scales. When "Butterfly" was recorded by Clark's friend Bernard Lowe, the latter offered the deejay a 25 percent share in the record as a friend with no obligation to do anything for it. Clark told Lowe this was not necessary but at the end of the year, said Clark, he was offered and accepted $7,000 as his share of royalties. After receiving a ring, fur stole, and necklace from a music industry firm Clark claimed he and his wife were "embarrassed." He assured the subcommittee he had done nothing for them, noting as well that he had never worn the ring.[68]

Subcommittee members sniped away at the jockey over other stars he had had a large hand in creating, such as Fabian (Fabian Forte) and Frankie Avalon, and their lack of musical ability. After Clark had finished his two days of testimony Harris dismissed the deejay by saying, "Obviously you're a fine young man. With your influence your responsibilities can be great. I'm sure you have realized that . . . I don't think you're the inventor of the system. I think you're the product."[69]

"Bandstand's" producer Mammarella testified in closed session in January. When this was made public in May it revealed he admitted receiving payments from nine labels and distributors but denied the money was paid to have records aired on "Bandstand." He also claimed that Clark had had no knowledge of these payments until he had informed him of them the previous November. Under questioning Mammarella admitted that Wildcat Music, of which he owned 50 percent, was often given half of a song's copyright in return for the promotion he could give it. Also acknowledged was that songwriter Bernard Lowe, the owner of Cameo label, gave Mammarella one-third of the royalties on "Butterfly" and "100 Ways." Although Lowe wrote both numbers alone, Mammarella was listed as coauthor on both songs under the pen name of Anthony September. At one point Anthony was being paid about $950 a week in salaries from at least four sources. Also made public was prior testimony by George Paxton and Marvin Cane, executives with Coronation Music of New York, who told of how they turned over the copyright of "Sixteen Candles" to the Clark-held January Music. The tune was recorded on Paxton's Coed label. Both men stated the deal was made with the expectation Clark would "give the record a ride." He did, playing it 30 times on "Bandstand" in the three months after the assignment of title, copyright, all the mechanical rights, and half of the performing rights to January in November 1958. Paxton estimated January's take on "Sixteen Candles" at $13,000–$15,000. According to Bernard Lowe, he approached Clark in December 1956, making him an offer of 25 percent cut in on "Butterfly" in return for his help in calling disk jockeys across the country to tell them about the record. Clark refused the offer but helped him plug the record nevertheless. A year later, Lowe stated, he paid Clark $7,000 after receiving a letter referring to their "agreement." George Goldner, owner of Real Gone Music and Gone Records, told the subcommittee he had turned over a number of copyrights to Clark's Sea-Lark Company but that there was no commitment that the jockey would air the tunes. In a display of sucking up or biting sarcasm Goldner told the subcommittee members, "As long as there are people like yourselves I still feel safe as an American citizen, and I want to thank you very much for your interest in the music industry and what you are doing for the industry."[70]

Last to testify before the House panel was Clark's boss and ABC president Leonard Goldenson. Representative Peter F. Mack, Jr. (Democrat, Illinois), asked him, "Don't you think that somebody's going to have to do something — the Government or the networks — if we are going to stop the trash that comes over the airwaves?" Goldenson replied that television was a young industry improving all the time. To which Moss retorted, "How can it be so young and have so many bad habits?" The network chief was hammered over his disclaimer of responsibility to investigate Mammarella as he had quit ABC the previous November and for conducting at best only a cursory examination of Clark. Defending his jockey, Goldenson called Clark an "upright" young man whom he was letting stay on because he was convinced Clark had a "good character." Moss quoted to the ABC chief testimony by Alan Freed—conducted in camera and not released—that this ex-WABC jockey said he was told to "lay heavily on Am-Par records and play only Paramount theaters on your stageshows" by ABC vice president Mortimer Weinbach. Those two companies came under the ABC ownership umbrella. Goldenson called Freed's statements a lie. Moss retorted, "Freed was one of the few comparatively truthful men we've had before the committee in either closed or open hearing." When Bennett suggested to Goldenson that 3–4 percent of Am-Par's gross sales went into payola, the network chief said the word should be "promotion." In any case he claimed to be unaware of any payments by Am-Par to deejays. He felt ABC spinners were not the payola types because they didn't primarily program rock and roll like the "mostly small independent stations." Bennett said, "Didn't Freed program rock and roll?" Goldenson dismissed this by saying that the Freed program was not highly rated and scarcely worth checking on. Mack summed up the panel's feelings by pointing out that they objected most strenuously to the network shutting its eyes to the fact that Clark was "top dog in the payola field" and never even beginning a token investigation until the House subcommittee was breathing down their necks. Some of the congressmen on the subcommittee were convinced the Clark-Goldenson testimony was "evasive" at best and an outright lie at worst. "I don't believe you" was a frequent rejoinder to a response. Some on the panel felt that Clark "on the basis of their findings, had exploited his position as the nation's number one deejay to cut himself in on every possible source of revenue in the music industry, from copyright to distribution."[71]

On its final day of hearings, before adjourning to draft laws, the subcommittee announced it had turned up $263,245 in payola handed over to 207 disk jockeys and other broadcast personnel in 42 cities to play particular records. These figures came from a mail survey. A questionnaire had been mailed to 230 record distributors, of whom 130 had responded.[72]

In New York the six-month Hogan probe came to an end in May 1960 with the arrest of five deejays, two record librarians, and one program director on charges of accepting payola. The eight were charged under the state's commercial bribery statute. Conviction on this misdemeanor offense could bring a maximum of one year in jail and a $500 fine on each count. According to Hogan's office the eight had received payola in the amount of $116,850 from 23 record firms in the previous two years. While the district attorney's office claimed the practice had been going on "for at least ten years," the statute of limitations barred prosecution of violations more than two years old. Alan Freed was named on two indictments. One accused him of accepting $10,000 from one record company in 1958 while the second indictment, including 25 counts, charged that he received a total of $20,650 in bribes from six companies in 1958 and 1959. Freed worked for WINS and WABC during that period. Also charged was deejay Peter Tripp of WMGM, accused of accepting $36,050 in bribes from eight record companies. Others charged were jockeys Tommy Smalls of WWRL, accused of taking $13,385; Harold B. Jackson of WLIB, $9,850; Jack Walker of WOV, $7,420; librarian Joseph Saccone of WMGM, $2,000; librarian Ronald Granger of WINS, $7,550; and program director Mel Leeds of WINS, $9,675. When they were arrested both Freed and Leeds lived in California where both were employed by Los Angeles station KDAY as deejay and program director, respectively. All pled not guilty when arraigned in New York and were released prior to trial.

Tripp was immediately fired by his station when the charges were announced. Hogan's office alleged that Freed had been on the payroll of a number of companies that paid him $100–$700 a month to favor their disks. This led to Freed playing the same record as often as eight or nine times on his four-hour radio show. Tripp, it was claimed, received 0.5 cents on the sale of each copy of two records he had plugged, receiving $4,850 and $13,000 from the two firms for favoring "Sixteen Candles" and "I Wonder Why." Named as "chief offenders" in paying to "promote the success of their records" were four firms: Alpha Distributing which paid $21,650; Superior Record Sales, $18,200; Roulette Records, $12,235; and Cosnat Distributing, $12,950. Nineteen other firms allegedly paid lesser amounts. Irv Phillips, manager of KDAY, publicly supported Freed and Leeds, calling them just "fall guys" in the probe. Phillips said he and his station would stand behind both men, remarking, "we are pleased to have them on staff. . . . We are 200 percent behind both men." These indictments by Hogan's office marked the first time legal moves were taken against alleged payola takers. Companies were not acted against, only the radio staffers because, wrote one observer, "the usual practice is to proceed against only one party to an alleged bribery. The companies therefore had immunity so that officials could testify."[73]

First to come to trial was 35-year-old Peter Tripp, who was then employed as a deejay for San Francisco's KYA where he was paid $250 a week. While at WMGM, where he introduced himself to listeners as "the curly-headed kid on the second row" on his "Your Hits of the Week" program, Tripp earned $45,000 annually. During the trial Tripp's attorneys conceded their client accepted the money; however, they maintained this was not commercial bribery because he wasn't a station employee but an "independent contractor" and therefore allowed to make such deals. Harry Apostoleris of Alpha Distributing testified he paid Tripp $10,400 until the payola stories broke in the newspapers. Apostoleris told of approaching the deejay to ask for air time for records of the 10 to 20 labels he represented. Tripp said he could arrange this and offered to play four on each show. When the distributor asked how much, the jockey replied $1,000 a month. Harry offered $500 with a deal struck at $750. At Tripp's request the checks were made out to the jockey's wife, Marilyn, said Apostoleris. At the same time Laurie Records, one of the labels represented by Alpha, paid Tripp $8,000. Neither Alpha nor Laurie knew that the other was paying the deejay. Coed Records vice president Marvin Cane testified that his company paid Tripp 0.5 cents for each copy of "Sixteen Candles" that was sold. The jockey played this tune repeatedly on his program.[74]

During Tripp's time on the stand the jockey contended he was entitled to make the deals under his contract as an independent contractor. He was given the money, he claimed, for his advice as to what records would be successful, what records to purchase, and what the companies should seek in new sounds and artists. "I never took a dime for playing records," asserted Tripp. Asked why checks for this "advice" were made out to Marilyn Tripp, the jockey explained it was because several people were suing him and he "didn't want any more income in my name." He added he had reported all this money on his income tax returns. Queried about his request to record manufacturer George Goldner for $4,000 in August 1958, Tripp replied he had extra expenses that year, found Goldner "nice," and "thought he could afford to help" with a loan.

On May 15, 1961, Tripp was found guilty on 35 counts of commercial bribery — accepting funds from the companies without his employer's knowledge to influence his official acts — on a unanimous finding by a three-judge panel. Assistant District Attorney Joseph Stone asked that a jail sentence be imposed, arguing that Tripp had "boldly and flagrantly violated the law and should suffer the consequences of his acts.... If you give him a slap on the wrists," he told the judges, "it will be a license to others to engage in this creeping corruption. A jail sentence will serve as a warning to others not to engage in this practice." Benjamin Shedler, the deejay's attorney, argued for leniency for his "penniless" client, saying, "He has suffered more than anyone should for a crime of this sort. He lost his job, he was out of work for seven months, he is hopelessly in debt, his house was foreclosed, his reputation destroyed and his future washed out." On October 16, 1961, Tripp was fined $500 and given a six-month suspended sentence. Outside court the jockey commented, "There is no doubt that I'm the scapegoat and the fall guy for the whole country. Today there are still hundreds involved in payola. Everyone is in on it and yet I was singled out."[75]

Charges against Harold Jackson were dismissed in court after the jockey produced evidence that he was an independent contractor and not an employee of station WLIB. Prosecutor Joseph Stone said there was a question as to whether his office could prove beyond a reasonable doubt that Jackson was an employee and not a contractor. Stone also said there was a need for legislation to outlaw kickbacks to independent contractors who were not covered by the commercial bribery statute.[76]

The first disk jockey in the country tried and convicted for income tax evasion as a result of failing to report income from payola was Hunter Hancock of Los Angeles. During 1956–58 a total of nine distributors paid Hancock a total of $17,000 to spin certain disks on stations KGFJ and KPOP. Hancock testified he had played some records submitted to him as "favors" while others had been "contractually paid for." The latter sums were reported as income by Hancock. That sum was in addition to the $17,000 which he had not reported and for which he faced trial. In 1962 the jock was sentenced to a suspended term of four years in prison on each of the three counts. Internal Revenue Service Intelligence Division chief Robert K. Lund reported that three other Los Angeles area disk jockeys were then under investigation, adding that the majority of deejays had already been cleared after scrutiny by his agents. As part of the Harris list of payola figures, Los Angeles led the nation with $86,954 paid out to 23 individuals employed by 13 stations. In commenting on cleared jockeys Lund commented that "about 50 percent of them did accept payola, but the majority of these reported the payoffs on their income tax returns."[77]

In second place was St. Louis, where $51,850 was paid to 23 individuals. Sixty-four individuals in Chicago were reportedly paid a total of $50,395.[78] When the FCC released findings from their December inquiry they reported they received replies from 4,673 out of a total of 4,842 television, AM, and FM stations on the air. From these replies 59 percent reported receiving no payola at all; 29.4 percent said they received free records only; 1.1 percent reported cash received by employees; 0.4 percent reported cash received by stations; 9.5 percent said they received other types of consideration; and 0.6 percent returned incomplete responses.[79]

After postponements of over a year Alan Freed appeared in court in New York in December 1962 and he pled guilty to accepting a $700 bribe from Superior Records and a $2,000 bribe from Cosnat Distributing. He was sentenced to a $300 fine and a six-month suspended jail sentence. In March 1964 Freed was indicted on charges of evading income taxes during the years 1957–59. According to the IRS Freed, then not employed in radio, underreported his income in those years by a total of $56,652, thus escaping taxes of $37,920. For those three years Freed reported a total of $214,000 in taxable income while the IRS charged it should have been $270,000. Alan Freed died before his case was disposed of.[80]

Throughout 1960 the FTC continued to lay complaints against companies. By the time they stopped in August of that year a total of 106 firms were charged. More than 90 of these concerns signed consent orders with the last eight or so complaints being dropped by the agency in August and

September 1961. By the time those last complaints were dropped Congress had adopted antipayola legislation making further prosecution, said the agency, "an unnecessary expenditure of time, effort and funds," adding that "the protection of the public interest is now fully assured by a recent amendment to the Federal Communications Act making it illegal to bestow gifts on radio and television disk jockeys for broadcasting records."[81]

Earl W. Kintner, chairman of the FTC, said he thought that the labels and distributors had "fallen into line" with the government efforts to wipe out bribery. "I think payola has been pretty well stamped out," he added. However, he warned that his agency would take up the issue again if necessary. This agency could not total the amount of payola involved in its complaints as their investigations had dug up only one or two instances in each complaint, just enough to make a case. Other industry sources were also unable to estimate the total take on payola as the practice took many different forms. By February 1961 many officials at the FTC felt they had stopped payola. Officials credited this supposed success to their moving in so quickly and gaining so many fast consent orders. John T. Walker, assistant to the director of litigation, felt "the time was ripe," and that the subcommittee aided by newspapers

> moved into a good situation. It made our work more effective than it might have been otherwise. The big corporations, you know, are very conscious of public relations, and so with the public accepting the position of the subcommittee we had a good situation.... We feel the big manufacturers are making a real effort to get away from payola and I think we'd know about it if there were companies still using it. After all, this is a competitive field and if one company were slipping around, I think we'd hear about it from competitors.

However, some FTC officials felt payola was the product of a fiercely competitive business and therefore it would return.[82]

Philadelphia finally launched its own payola probe in June 1960 after the previous false start when District Attorney Victor H. Blanc interrogated 39 deejays and other broadcast and record company personnel. When the Harris group ended its hearings Blanc sent members of his staff to Washington. They returned to Philadelphia with a filing cabinet full of documents obtained from the Harris panel. Blanc claimed he had evidence to show that over $300,000 had been paid out in payola in his area. Any prosecutions resulting from this probe would be under the Pennsylvania Bribery Act. All local radio stations were to be represented in the probe with the exception of WFIL — Clark's station — which "has been given a clean bill of health" by the FTC and FCC, said Blanc, who added that the information he and his staff had did not involve Clark. The district attorney publicly stated that Clark was innocent of payola. Dick Clark agreed to head a

local disk jockey association designed to allow the deejays to police themselves against future payola. This association was the brainchild of Blanc.
A few months later Blanc announced he had evidence against deejays and
distributors but could not prosecute them for bribery because they all refused to testify against each other on the ground that their testimony might
tend to incriminate themselves. Blanc solved this by having 21 area deejays
and 11 city distributors permanently enjoined by a city judge from taking
or giving payola. When he granted Blanc's request Judge David L. Al-
moign said the district attorney "Had shown ingenuity in finding a path to
the solution of the payola problem." All of these involved signed consent
decrees, promising not to participate in payola in the future while not admitting they had done so in the past. Participating in payola in the future
would lead to contempt of court proceedings. Among the 21 deejays were
Joe Niagara and Anthony Mammarella. By signing the decrees they were
given immunity on payola charges prior to March 1, 1960. Any who refused to sign — none did — would have been subject to civil proceedings
rather than criminal indictment because of the refusal of the principals to
testify. Blanc noted that distributors agreed to testify against reluctant deejays, saying, "The companies have promised me that if we turn up any evidence of future payola, they will come in and testify against the offending
parties in either civil or criminal proceedings."[83]

At the time the Harris hearings ended the diminishment of rock and
roll on the radio was still being reported with Newark, New Jersey's
WNTA, Austin, Minnesota's KQAQ and Dallas, Texas's KVIL all having
banished rock from their airwaves. Independent record labels reportedly
"have been hurt badly by both the congressional investigating subcommittee and the federal commissions for communications and trade." In their
published study the Harris subcommittee listed a number of areas in the
music industry subject to possible payola abuses. The panel said, "the
record manufacturers' A and R man is in many instances able to extract
tribute from publishers and artists because of his power to affect or prevent
the recording of a song." Citing deals between large music publishers and
television producers, the report said, "The producer arranges to use music
from the publisher's catalogues exclusively or nearly exclusively on the air;
this produces steady royalties for the publisher, who then remits a percentage thereof to the producers."[84] Despite the possible prominence of such
abuses the House panel didn't really touch on them during their investigation. But then these abuses didn't involve deejays, rock and roll, BMI or
small independent record labels.

Representative Thomas P. O'Neill, Jr., wrote to FCC head Frederick
Ford soliciting the latter's view on rock and payola after O'Neill had himself scored the music. Ford sidestepped the issue by replying to the congressman that the FCC had no information "which would enable it to

determine with any degree of certainty "if a relationship existed between payola and the popularity of rock and roll music."[85]

In June 1960 a bill titled Communications Act Amendments, 1960 was approved by Oren Harris's Commerce Committee and then by the House Rules Committee. This bill was designed to eliminate payola as well as other abuses such as quiz rigging and free plugs for products over the airwaves. It contained provisions authorizing the FCC to suspend broadcast licenses for up to ten days and impose fines of up to $1,000 a day for violations. When it reached the House it passed easily by a vote of 208–15, despite lobbying by broadcasters to soften or modify the provisions for suspension and fines. Two attempts led by Representative Bennett to amend the bill to allow FCC regulation of the networks as opposed to individual station licensees were defeated. Bennett argued that the absence of provisions for network regulation penalized stations for the sins of the networks. Without such provisions he called the payola bill "a farce and a sham. It is mere window dressing; a sop to the public for all the big scandal headlines." Inaction of the proposed bill, he said, "will take off the heat which has been built up by 3½ years of investigations. It will be said, and the radio and television networks will do their best to spread the word, that all the evils have been cured by this bill. The public may swallow this story and that will be the end of any reform legislation."[86]

Opposition to the bill intensified when it reached the Senate for debate, causing that body to hold hearings on the license suspension and fine parts of the measure. During those hearings Senator John Pastore (Democrat, Rhode Island), chairman of the Senate Communications subcommittee, exacted concessions from FCC head Ford that his agency didn't really need license suspension power; that it could get results it wanted by revoking licenses, issuing cease and desist orders, or imposing forfeitures. When the Senate hearings were over Pastore ordered the bill redrafted to knock out the suspension provision, provide a one-year statute of limitations on offenses, and a limit on the $1,000 a day fines to a maximum of $10,000. Such fines were to be authorized only when violations were committed "willfully or repeatedly," instead of "negligent or intentional" as went the language in the original House version of the measure. A suspected violator would not be penalized until he had been given written notice and time to prepare a written defense against the allegations.[87]

Senator William Proxmire (Democrat, Wisconsin) tried unsuccessfully to put the license suspension provision back into the bill, claiming the Senate modifications put the licensee in a position to "get away with murder." This modified payola bill (S 1898) passed easily in the Senate and then the House, by voice vote in each at the end of August. Bennett felt the modifications left the bill "inadequate and ineffective." On September 13 President Eisenhower signed the measure into law.[88]

This new antipayola measure didn't actually outlaw payola. It stated that a deejay could not accept any type of "consideration" such as money, gifts, or stock shares, for pushing records on the air without announcing his "sponsor." Thus payola was not illegal. It was failure to publicly announce a payola transaction that was illegal, a violation of the antipayola legislation. A deejay could continue to take money from record firms to push their songs as long as he announced the fact to his listeners. Under Section 507 of the Communications Act, which carried criminal penalties of up to a year in jail as well as fines of up to $10,000, an individual was prohibited from offering or accepting payola without the knowledge of the station manager or owner. Prosecutions for violations of this section had to be undertaken by the Justice Department, not the FCC. Section 317 of this act required stations to disclose on the air any payments they received to broadcast particular programming. Violators of this section were subject to administrative penalties, including fines and license revocation, administered by the FCC.

An exception to this rule was that the FCC withdrew its March edict that prevented stations from accepting free records from companies to be used for broadcasting. Provided the supplier didn't give these records in large quantities to those stations — such as 50 or 100 or expect special treatment — stations could accept such records from labels or distributors, but only to the extent needed in their music programming and not be required to make a public announcement about the "sponsor." Also allowed, without announcement, was that labels and distributors could furnish an entirely new music library to a station changing its format, say from classical to Top 40, and who could not afford to stock a new library. Even though no payola was involved, disk jockeys could draw only "reasonable attention" to the performing talent on a record; praise could be used if it was part of his usual spiel with no announcement needed. However, if the deejay went "overboard" using a special sales pitch or urging listeners to buy the disk then a "donor" announcement was needed. A jockey could say something like, "Listen to this latest release of performer 'X,' a new singing sensation" without sponsor announcement, but not, "This is my favorite new record and sure to become a hit; so don't overlook it."[89]

Even around the time of the passage of the antipayola bill the practice was reportedly far from dead. In Los Angeles several distributors acknowledged they were still passing out money. San Francisco columnist Ralph Gleason surveyed conditions in his area:

> Congressional investigation into payola has altered the form of bribery in the phonograph record business, driving it underground. In some areas, it has increased it. . . . Today, informed observers in the business in this area insist there is just as much payola as there ever was and that

locally it still exists and may be even more prevalent than before. No one
will talk officially for publication. "I signed a consent decree," one man
said, "and I want to keep away from the whole thing." But the consensus
is overwhelming. Pay for play still exists. The form now is cash on the
barrel head. This can't be traced. . . . Guys who never thought they had
a chance before now ask for it openly since they know it existed and some
small labels lay it on the line.

Gleason also reported incidents of payola in Los Angeles and in the East.
Making a reported comeback was the promotion man, once called a song
plugger, who got a record played by personally contacting jockeys and
convincing them of a record's merits through hard work. Some of these
men were employed by labels or distributors directly but more and more
they were self-employed, independent people who took on a specific promotion task. Since these people were more distanced from the record firms
it would be easier to blame payola on these self-employed people than if
they were employees directly on a firm's payroll. They could be future
scapegoats.[90]

Billboard declared that the practice had simply "gone underground."
Scared deejays insisted on strictly cash under the table. The one substitute
for cash was entertainment on a large scale such as hotel bills, bar tabs,
theater tickets, and the like. One independent record manufacturer complained that "today it's more difficult to tell if you're actually getting anything for your money. There's absolutely no guarantee your records will
be played."[91]

Just four months after passage of the antipayola legislation Robert
Lishman, acting on reports that payola was still very much alive, felt compelled to publicly state that the combined efforts of the FTC, FCC, and
Justice Department should be enough to control any resurgence of the
practice. However, he noted that he felt enforcement could use much more
vigor than shown so far. The House subcommittee slammed the FTC by
saying of its handling of payola in 1959, "it seemed clear that the Federal
Trade Commission had been derelict in allowing an intolerable competitive situation to engulf the music business. The music trade press had for
years been lamenting the low estate of competitive practices in music distribution, but until the subcommittee's interest appeared, the Commission
was content to do nothing."[92]

Not until 1967 did the U.S. Tax Court rule on Coed Records' argument
that the $18,769 which it paid out in payola during 1958–59 was a common
practice in the industry and therefore was a legitimate deduction from its
income as a business expense. A company that failed to make such payments, said Coed, would not have its records played and therefore its sales
would suffer. The court did, however, rule against Coed in disallowing
payola payments as a deduction.[93]

8 Surreptitious and Devious Means, 1961–1969

At the start of 1961 *Variety* announced, "The payola boys were reportedly doing business at the same old stand despite the edicts, ukases and decrees of the Federal Trade Commission."[1]

Record stores took advantage of the situation by charging distributors if the latter wanted a window display, choice locations inside the store, or their material played over the store's speaker system. One New York retailer charged distributors a flat $750 for four weeks to get the window display. Free albums numbering from 50 to 1,000 were demanded from distributors by other retailers for the window. To get a single played over the store's speakers could cost a distributor anywhere from $25 to $45 on up, averaging out at $100. This pressure by dealers was said to be nationwide.[2]

A couple of years after passage of the payola legislation payola was reported to be "rearing its ugly head." Some said the government probes just took payola out of the hands of the big labels leaving it to the independents and distributors to handle. In the Eastern United States it was claimed there existed a deejay syndicate which took money from a record pusher then apportioned it out to the ten or so key jockeys in the group. Especially prevalent was said to be the practice of getting entertainers to perform free at deejay concerts in order to get their records played on the jocks' radio programs. Jesse Rand, who managed The Lettermen, said he was "up to his ears" in demands from deejays for free appearances by his artists. He added, "They want free shows or else they won't play your records." Backing up Rand was Voyle Gilmor, a and r man at Capitol, saying, "You're almost blackmailed in this thing. You have to say anything or they won't play your records. . . . It's not payola. It's gone beyond payola. Now it's the demand not the acceptance."[3]

By the mid–1960s one major record company executive claimed that San Francisco had become the worst source of payola in the country. "I can't let you use my name; they'd ruin me," he said. Another executive said, "We have got to do something about this before the business rots to pieces." Referring to deejays, a small, independent label which put out half a dozen records a year stated, "The little guy like me hasn't got a chance.

They bleed us to death. They want a piece of the rights or they want money. And if you don't go along, they'll get on the phone and call all around the country to keep their friends in other cities from playing it too." A distributor complained, "They ask for 35 or 40 copies of an album by the artist sometimes. And if you turn them down, they get very salty." Some claimed to function all right without payola. Saul Zaentz, sales manager of the Fantasy label, reported, "We can sell without it. The hell with them. If they don't want to play it, that's their problem.... Luckily, a lot of guys don't ask for anything."[4]

In 1964 a Hollywood, California, record promoter by the name of Albert Huskey said that record promoters that didn't play the game by paying off the right people might as well be dead as far as getting their clients' recordings on the air at a number of radio stations in southern California. Huskey filed a $230,000 damage suit in Los Angeles court, charging that a conspiracy of station executives, deejays, record companies, and promoters had forced him out of business because he refused to participate in the "surreptitious and devious means" employed by the defendants. Due to this conspiracy Huskey claimed he had lost $30,000 in earnings over the previous three years. In addition, he was asking for $200,000 punitive damages. Among those named as defendants were KFWB Los Angeles (owned by Crowell-Collier), KGFJ Los Angeles, KDAY Santa Monica, KMEN San Bernardino, KDEO San Diego, KRLA Pasadena, and jockeys Wink Martindale (KFWB), Hunter Hancock (KGFJ), and Thomas Smalls (KDAY).[5]

Alleged by Huskey was that the conspiracy resulted in disks getting on the air for the personal gain of the defendants instead of due to the actual public demand. The defendants, he said, "have foisted upon the public by broadcast and otherwise false and misleading information of and concerning records, the desirability and popularity thereof and demand therefore, all to their own personal gain and benefit." Besides deceiving the public, these practices "were and are designed to and do preclude fair and honest competition and have prevented plaintiff and others similarly situated and records and musical compositions from competing upon a fair basis." Among the forms that payola took in addition to payment of cash and doctor and dentist bills, alleged Huskey, were

> the furnishing of prostitutes and female company ... use of apartments and hotel suites, alcoholic beverages, clothing ... participation in ownership of record companies, participation in artists' management fees, delivery of commercial quantities of records without further charge ... the services and appearances of performing artists at so-called "hops" or shows presented by the air personalities, from which they reaped substantial benefits by reason of the appearance and services of such artists without appropriate compensation.[6]

About the time Huskey was initiating his lawsuit the FCC was appearing in closed-door session before the House Appropriations Subcommittee, requesting a budget increase for the next fiscal year. Two months later, May 1964, a transcript of this hearing was made public. FCC staffers told of a "regular sprinkling" of complaints concerning payola which they had received. While they checked out the most promising of the leads, no hard evidence of wrongdoing was then in hand. One of the problems for FCC investigators, they said, was that those who had the facts were not licensees but label and distributor executives over whom the agency exercised no control. In its testimony before the Appropriations Subcommittee the commission said it believed that "payola is still widespread in broadcasting and in certain fields may even have increased." Therefore, it added, "it is believed that a major, nationwide investigation of this and related practices, extending over a period of several months, is highly desirable." Officials added that they simply wished to indicate that the agency thought it would be a worthwhile investigation if funds were available; they had made no decision on launching such an inquiry.[7]

Just two weeks after that transcript became public the FCC issued a series of fuzzy denials. According to the commission, no mention at all of payola was made in that March 5, 1964, meeting before the appropriations group. Back in the summer of 1963, when the FCC submitted its regular request for the next fiscal year to the Budget Bureau, it was mentioned in passing that payola was still thought to be widespread, possibly on the increase, and that an investigation at some time might be desirable. Even then, said the FCC, this was merely a possibility, and no extra funds for such a probe were requested at that time. Somehow, said the commission, a paragraph from 1963 found its way into the release of the March 1964 transcript, sparking rumors of a big payola push by the FCC. "This thing has been blown up beyond all proportion," they complained, and plans for such a probe are not "even in the thinking-about-it stage." Commission staff pointed out that there was a fairly regular number of complaints but not one single complaint had checked out into a case for prosecution under the 1960 antipayola law. Since the practice called for criminal prosecution against individuals, the FCC needed the kind of evidence that could stand trial by jury. Rarely could they get it. Most of the complaints received were just "suspicion." Staffers said they got wholesale accusations that "all the deejays" in a certain area played only the big labels. Many complainers were frustrated record salesmen and songwriters who felt they weren't getting fair exposure on the air. Accusations were generally lodged against disk jockeys, record librarians, and record companies, and only rarely against the licensees — stations — themselves, explained the FCC.[8]

Six months after making this confusing denial of plans to probe payola, the FCC announced in November 1964 that it would indeed conduct an investigation into payola. Initially to be conducted in secret, the inquiry was to be under the direction of FCC chairman E. William Henry because the agency had received allegations "from many sources indicating the continued existence and spread of payola and plugola and other improper related practices." Henry was given formal authority by the commission to subpoena witnesses and documents. The FCC indicated that they had been trying for some time to establish the truth or falsity of payola complaints received but that they had not received full cooperation in their investigation to that point. Thus they gave Henry full power to subpoena during the formal inquiry, as opposed to the more usual voluntary appearances sought.[9]

Jockey William B. Williams of WNEW protested innocence when he said, "it's hard to believe that illegal payments would crop up again in the light of what happened four years ago." Another deejay told of a suburban New York radio station where he used to work, saying, "The music director at the station, who used to be my boss, made about $9,000 a year salary, plus about $100 a month in payola. The money was paid to him by promoters for the fly-by-night record companies, and in return he would play certain records, which the kids accepted as hits and went out and bought."[10]

The FCC continued to act in a confusing manner with regard to the probe by stating, after the probe had been announced, that a major investigation was not contemplated. In response to rumors that the agency would conduct public hearings with big-name stars participating, William Ray, chief of the FCC's Complaints and Compliance division replied, "It's not gong to be that way, at all." The investigation would be limited in scope with no prospect of dramatic revelations, he explained. Executives of radio stations and other broadcasting organizations generally expressed public surprise at the investigation as almost unanimously they disclaimed knowledge of the existence of payola. Lazar Emanuel, president of Newark, New Jersey's WJRZ, said his station didn't permit any one disk to be played more than once or twice per week. Frank Ward, vice president of Long Island's WWRL, stated he was surprised at the FCC probe since he felt all New York area radio stations, including WWRL, had instituted strict controls over music selection and presentation. General manager of WLBI Harry Novik claimed he had heard no reports of payola flourishing. His New York station compiled a daily list of music to be played. Miles David, vice president of the Radio Advertising Bureau (RAB), asserted that RAB was "surprised" by the amount of media attention devoted to the probe, adding, "We doubt that reports of gifts to newspaper columnists would be deemed as meriting equivalent headlines." David argued that payola was based on the premise that deejays had complete control of record selection for airplay. This was incorrect, he said, because an RAB survey of stations in large markets — over 500,000 population — indicated that this was true in just 9 percent of the stations. Rumors that the FCC initiated the probe when it did in order to get a bigger budget request from the Budget Bureau were vigorously denied. One observer wrote that "the FCC is hunting for payola wrongdoers with a peashooter and not the heavy artillery that had been dreaded." Also noted was that the targets remained disk jockeys — with a heavy emphasis on small-time local deejays — and those who paid them, while bigger targets such as major networks and ad agency executives were bypassed. Despite the fact that television insiders felt such a probe could produce a scandal to make the quiz show fixes and 1960 payola probe "look relatively innocuous . . . the FCC — in its newest head hunt — appears to be looking the other way."[11]

For months the FCC investigated the payola situation. It was not until May 1966 that the commission announced it would finally begin to conduct nonpublic hearings, some 18 months after the probe was first announced. In the meantime they had been checking a lengthening list of complaints and had reached a point where officials felt it would be "useful" to take testimony from witnesses. Reportedly, some individuals who had paid out money to have records played had named names. Hearings were to be held behind closed doors to prevent "character assassination," said the agency. "We want corroboration of any charges that are made before they become public. We are trying to conduct this inquiry in the least sensational manner possible." Without naming them, the commission indicated that in certain cities more than one group was involved in payola while in two other cities only one set of people were involved in each case. Carefully studied by the FCC was the Al Huskey case.[12]

The following month the secret hearings began with a 12-day session in Los Angeles. At that time the Huskey case had been inactive for six months and had never moved beyond preliminary stages. Revealing nothing of the testimony it was taking, Joe Stirmer, one of the FCC's four-person team in Los Angeles, commented only that "There are many glib people in this industry. There are a lot of pretty smooth talkers." During this time one of the defendants named by Huskey tried to have the court throw the case out, claiming Huskey refused to cooperate in taking depositions and had refused to answer interrogatory questions put to him by attorneys for the defendant. In July, after 12 days of hearings, the FCC team ended its Los Angeles session, returning to Washington. At that point the FCC could hold private hearings in other cities, pass any information along to the Justice Department for possible prosecution, issue a report, hold public hearings, or do nothing at all. Rumor had it that the agency had found "substantial information" that payola was still in operation. In the previous year the agency also had received more than 200 letters complaining about payola.[13]

As the Los Angeles hearings were ending *Billboard* reported that small, independent labels were free and easy with payola with the program directors at the stations being the "direct targets for the bribes. With the advent of the Top 40 formula programming and the elimination of the power of the disk jockey to select the numbers he plays, the program manager has become the key figure in getting disk exposure on the air. Latest quotation on the payola exchange has set the payoff price for a key program director in the area of $25,000." More sophisticated, harder to detect methods, such as funneling money out of an advertising agency's commission, were favored over the old cash on the barrel head method. Deejays were still on the receiving end but usually only where they had a say in determining what went on the air. When Crowell-Collier Broadcasting's sale of KFWB was approved by the FCC in December 1966, the FCC scorned Crowell-Collier calling the company lax in pressing its own investigation of payola and failing to exercise "special diligence to prevent improper use" of the outlet by employees.[14]

During June 1967 the FCC investigated a complaint against station WAME of Miami, Florida. Deejays at the station received compensation for participating in record hops at which entertainers appeared "sometimes without monetary compensation." These deejays also selected which records were to be played on the air. When the agency got a vague answer from WAME as to what precautions that station was taking to prevent such conflicts of interest arising and no answer to the question of what was being done to make sure records played were those requested by listeners, the FCC announced it was withholding a decision on whether to renew the station's license as it could not determine if the station had fulfilled its obligation to exercise "special diligence."[15]

Nothing much happened in regard to the Los Angeles hearings until July 1968 when the FCC sent investigators back to that city to conduct more follow-up investigations. The Huskey suit was settled out of court four months prior to that. In addition to Los Angeles, FCC probers had conducted investigations in New York, San Francisco, Detroit, Baltimore, Pittsburgh, and Houston. All of these probes were closed. The New York investigation resulted in four disk jockeys for two Spanish-language radio stations being indicted by a federal grand jury for violating the 1960 antipayola legislation and for perjury. These indictments came after secret FCC hearings at which the men denied accepting money and services to play specific records. Charged were Pablo Raul Alarcon of WBNX and Rafael Diaz Guttierez, Freddy Baez, and Hipolito Vega, all of WHOM. Alleged in the indictment was that payola violations occurred between 1964 and 1966. Prosecutors were unable to say how much money was given the four during this period but did say that one label paid $5,000 to promote its records.[16]

Baez was convicted of payola and perjury, receiving a $500 fine and a suspended six month imprisonment. Vega was convicted on the same two charges. He was fined $1,500, in addition to three months imprisonment. At the time of their sentencing in February 1971 *Variety* wrote, "Payola is now believed to be virtually restricted to ethnically oriented radio stations. Here the salaries of the disk jockeys are lower than prevailing standards and there is not the same tight control over personalities as exists in radio stations playing pop songs."[17]

9 Hash Instead of Cash, 1970–1979

In 1970 the House Commerce Subcommittee on Investigations sent staffers to check on the payola files at the FCC, although Dan Minelli of that subcommittee said there was no prospect of formal investigation hearings at that time. At the FCC Bill Ray did not deny that House investigators were sleuthing around his agency. The head of the Complaints and Compliance section of the agency added that in general payola was the hardest of all communications law violations to prove as both giver and receiver were equally liable for penalties. The result was, said Ray, much more inhibition than in the days of the 1950s payola scandal because even if an informant was offered immunity he was often reluctant to talk because he could be "blacklisted" by the industry. The agency had investigated its own leads but none of the complaints were backed up by enough proof to stand up legally. Only licensees could be penalized directly by the FCC. Payola charges against station employees such as deejays, record company executives, and record companies themselves, since these were criminal complaints, could only be brought by the Justice Department after the FCC handed information over to them. A higher standard of proof was needed than the FCC needed to proceed against stations. Ray admitted the agency knew there was "a great deal of real payola going on" and that it went on "all the time."[1]

It became popular to claim that payola took place in nonwhite venues. One report in 1971 said the bribery was "virtually restricted to ethnically oriented radio stations," explaining this was so because the deejay salaries at such outlets were lower than the prevailing standards, plus the tight control over jockeys restricting plays to record lists drawn by program directors was more likely to be absent at such stations. A second account claimed the traditional form of cash payment was "believed to be widespread on the rhythm and blues stations" for the same reasons as above.[2]

Payola as a media issue jumped back into a high profile in March 1972 and thereafter when columnist Jack Anderson wrote that month on the practice, followed by a second column the next month. According to

Anderson, he had "Uncovered evidence of a new payola scandal in the billion dollar record industry. Disk jockeys and program directors across the country are provided with free vacations, prostitutes, cash and cars as payoffs for songplugging." It was rampant across the board in the industry, he alleged. "Not only are the big-time disk jockeys collecting payola but the small station jockeys are clamoring to get their share of the boodle." Among the rhythm and blues jockeys and programmers wholesale lots of free records were supplied for cut-rate resale to local retailers in exchange for song plugging. "The more audacious record promoters have simply bribed the record pluggers with cash or with new cars. . . . Thus an underpaid rhythm and blues jockey may be seen riding around in a $5,000 car, all for pushing a few Top Forty records," the columnist stated. Allegedly, people in the record industry had supplied the columnist with the information in detail on condition they remain anonymous. Ending the column was a shot at the FCC for its failure to move on "the smell of scandal in the teen-age records marketplace." Teens had no inkling of the "gangster-like world which rigs record marketing," thought Anderson. These kids were "dupes," always eager to buy the latest hits, while the FCC hadn't been policing this marketplace sufficiently. Big-time jockeys, wrote the columnist, were repeating the history of the 1960 era of having run up thousands of dollars in bills at Las Vegas pleasure houses, all on the expense accounts of record companies.[3]

Immediately after the first Anderson column appeared the FCC wrote to him, requesting he furnish the agency with any information he had obtained during his own investigation. Also quick to respond was Stanley M. Gortikov, president of the Recording Industry Association of America (RIAA), a lobby group for labels which consisted mostly of the large labels as members with few of the independent labels enrolled in the group. It numbered 54 members in 1972. Speaking for the RIAA, Gortikov deplored payola for both moral and business reasons, calling it "commercial suicide." He also noted that "there are undoubtedly some single 'bad apples' among us, as there are in many businesses. If so, their bad practices must be cleaned out." But he stated, "reported instances of payola do not reflect the true broad profile of the recording industry." Gortikov urged the 54 RIAA member companies to initiate "prompt investigations and actions within their organizations to halt any offenses that might be prevailing without their knowledge and consent." He urged all those industry elements not in the RIAA to also clean house while promising cooperation to the FCC and NAB.[4]

Anderson also suggested that drugs were involved in payola, as a payoff instead of cash in some cases. It was an allegation that the music industry found particularly threatening since drug use in America generally was attracting wide media attention and condemnation. Drug use was an integral part of the hippie movement which establishment forces found so difficult to deal with or understand. After Anderson made his drug charges Gortikov immediately sent a memo to all RIAA members. In it he said he couldn't confirm the accuracy of the allegations but if they were true they "mirror a reprehensible condition for us all, both commercially and morally. These practices and their inevitable revelations invite repercussions that our industry can ill afford ... government investigations, imposition of outside rules and standards, loss of imagery and credibility, financial penalty and personal disasters for individuals. Such a condition also could undermine the industry's support in our fight against drug abuse." Gortikov urged all RIAA members to tighten their internal regulations on payola and to institute parallel programs among distributors, promoters, independent labels, and others in the business as "This is particularly important because your company and our industry can be tarnished by transgressions of those independents beyond your sphere of control."[5]

Investigators for Jack Anderson came across the payola story by "accident" while checking out a story on organized crime infiltration of legitimate business. One person they spoke to became a prime source for payola information. Les Whitten, Anderson's chief investigator, said that after the first story appeared "we got a flood of stuff. It was like popping a boil ... since the narcotic stuff was the newest, and because it was, in a way, the most heinous, we concentrated on that." Asked if he thought payola was widespread, Whitten replied, "tentatively, I would say it is a widespread practice but only by a limited number of companies. In some companies, there may be a promotion man here or there involved in payola, but in others, it is an accepted practice, although it's my guess that the heads of those companies may not know about it. There are also some independent promotion men who are paid by companies and use that money for drugs, without their knowledge. But I don't think it's an industry wide practice." His opinion of rock and roll was "some of it is just pure noise. I can see why you'd have to pay someone to get some of that stuff played." Whitten added that Anderson "and I were really appalled that we had to be the ones to break this story. We were told the music trades had knowledge of it, yet had not done anything about it."[6]

In response to the drug charges one record promoter admitted that the use of marijuana was widespread among those under 30 in the radio business but he thought that addiction to harder drugs was much rarer. Young disk promoters had no moral taboos about swapping pot for plays, he said. "In fact, they think it's more legitimate than paying off in cash, the old fashioned payola way." Major labels were reportedly confident that no payola charges, either hash or cash, could be laid at their doorsteps since they had been careful to stay "clean" since the 1960 probe, "although the commonplace favors of dinners, legit tickets, hotel room hookers, etc., are still dispensed." Egmont Sonderling, president of Sonderling Broadcasting whose chain operated four major black radio stations, denied the then prevalent assumption that payola was widespread in r and b outlets. Addressing the idea that black jockeys were more susceptible because they were underpaid, Sonderling said, "it seems to us that the concept is rather naive when it is implied that the acceptance of graft depends on the amount of money a given individual earns. People are either honest or dishonest whether they are in the record business or the broadcasting business." Columnist Ralph Gleason, also responding to Anderson's charges, said the use of favors of all kinds to gain special treatment was a standard part of American business and politics. "To be righteous about some jock grabbing a fast $100 to play a record when IT&T is trying to buy the government," he wrote, "seems to me to be just a bit off-center." Gleason felt it had been proven over the years that it was "absolutely impossible" to manipulate the record market in any way to make a hit with payola, which he called "the American Way of Life and as far as music is concerned, it doesn't get in the way of good records at all. And it never has." In Gleason's view the rock scandals "are really an illusion and have been used, most of the time, to mask an attack on rock and roll.... In the beginning, the payola scandals erupted basically because of old-line ASCAP publishers [who] woke up and found BMI publishing all the hits."[7]

After exchanging letters with FCC chairman Dean Burch, Anderson met with Bill Ray of that agency. The columnist told the commission he would be glad to furnish his leads to them but that he had to protect his sources. Names of informants could not be revealed due to fear of "job reprisals and Mafia enforcers," he explained. While Anderson had written proof of payoffs in "cash, cars, concubines and the like" as well as in "marijuana, cocaine, LSD and other drugs," he did note "in fairness to the record industry, while payola appears to be epidemic, the drug payola is apparently limited to only a few record companies and radio stations." Moderating further, the columnist said that drug-bribing promotion men "deal mainly in marijuana, although insiders have repeatedly told us cocaine is the 'with it' drug this year in show biz." Plays were bought with $20 lots of marijuana; all night drug parties were staged by an independent promoter-producer; a weekly drug drop was paid by an artist to a record magazine writer — all these were incidents cited by Anderson. After the latter event occurred the record of the artist soared up the publication's popularity charts, even though the artist was unknown, leading Anderson to conclude the magazine had to be basing its charting on a staffer's recommendation rather than on retail sales figures and statistics of radio play. Gortikov continued his efforts by undertaking a phone campaign to RIAA members, urging them once again to crack down on any and all evidence of "pay for play, particularly when drugs are involved."[8]

Sensitive to charges by Anderson that the FCC was either ignorant of payola or chose not to take effective action against the practice, FCC commissioner Nick Johnson explained that his agency was not sitting on a lot of evidence, and that complaints which came in were investigated but the agency had no evidence that the practice was widespread. "But hell," said Johnson, "there's payola in every industry. It's common knowledge that most products and services are sold not just on their interest quality. I mean, payola is just an American Business practice." Ultimately, probers for Anderson turned over to the FCC the names of five record companies and five radio stations they said were involved in payola. Companies passed out drugs and hired deejays as "consultants" in return for airplays. Marijuana was smoked in one of the stations' studios, claimed the probers.[9]

Intense media pressure put the FCC on the defensive. They could only act against the licensee, or station, and then only to impose a fine, for they never used the revocation of license provision. Justice didn't like to take on a case against an individual unless it had solid evidence passed on to it by the FCC, which was rarely the case. Mostly the FCC got, it claimed, only hearsay evidence and complaints from promoters and companies whose records were not being played as often as they thought they should. Their people assumed it was payola paid by other people that kept their disks off the air — assumptions that may or may not have been correct. In addition, the FCC had no jurisdiction over the smoking of grass at a radio station, unless it was a pay-for-play bribe. Failing that, it was up to the Federal Bureau of Narcotics and Dangerous Drugs if action was to be taken at all. Thus the expectation of a sudden, wholesale crackdown on payola which the FCC felt the media and public expected was not going to occur, regardless of the extent of the practice.

As the pressure on the FCC mounted the agency announced it had strengthened its ties with Justice and the Bureau of Narcotics and Dangerous Drugs. William Ray said he thought it was time for his agency to hold public hearings into payola, while calling for radio stations and record company personnel to help stamp out bribery. There would be no "fishing expeditions" said Ray, who noted that when preliminary investigations revealed something the public interest would be served by holding public hearings. Ray couldn't say how widespread the payola situation was then but estimated it was far less than in 1959 when "payola was disclosed at that time to be absolutely universal. My guess is we have far less than in those days, but it was never gotten rid of completely." Ray added that the FCC had refrained from open payola hearings in the past because of a policy determination in 1964 that such proceedings should be held behind closed doors. However, since there was a natural tendency at the FCC to hold public hearings on as many things as possible, "Why should we make payola the one exception to this just because we started out that way?"

Another response by the FCC found the agency asking Congress to enact legislation to authorize it to impose sanctions against all violators, not just licensees. Under this proposal a promoter or deejay engaging in payola would be subject to a maximum fine of $5,000 after repeat violations.[10]

Billboard magazine responded angrily to Anderson's charges that a certain promotion man listed a particular record on his own list, so that when a *Billboard* employee, Miss Cott, called for his list of top-selling dicks payola-backed records would be on it. Anderson did print *Billboard*'s denial that it used that particular promoter's list but didn't print the magazine's denial of having a Miss Cott on staff, then or ever. Denouncing Anderson, the magazine's editor stated, "Anderson's persistent practice of damning our industry by innuendo must stop . . . when he continues to sling mud on our industry, spinning sordid allegations based on questionable quotations from little-known sources, the time has come to call for a halt on this nonsense."[11]

The major payola scandal of the 1970s erupted in June 1973. Earlier that year, in February, the Federal Strike Force Against Organized Crime, in Newark, New Jersey, investigating activities of organized crime, indicted talent manager Pasquale Falcone and several others, including a receptionist for CBS's Columbia Records, on heroin trafficking charges. This investigation turned up the name of David Wynshaw, director of artist relations for Columbia Records, among Falcone's papers. Wynshaw was cleared of any involvement in the Falcone charges when he testified before the strike force, led by Herbert J. Stern, the U.S. attorney for New Jersey. However, he told the investigators that Columbia spent over $250,000 on payola to black radio stations. The federal strike force was interested in payola because of possible violations of tax and mail fraud statutes. According to Wynshaw, this budget of at least $250,000 annually for payola was concealed within Columbia's promotion budget. Its purpose was to push records by its recently assembled group of black artists. Payola at Columbia had begun two years earlier, about the time the company got deeply involved in black music. In February 1971 Columbia began to do distribution for Philadelphia International Records, then acquired distribution of the Memphis-based Stax Records, both black labels. Wynshaw recounted that weekly checks for as much as $7,000 were turned over to the publisher of a tip sheet, whose newsletter supposedly kept the industry subscribers informed of each week's hot records. This publisher passed on the money, as payoffs were said to have gone to record producers and were made through Columbia promotion men whose job it was to plug records at radio stations.[12]

Told of the allegations of payola, a spokesman for Columbia said, "We don't know anything about it and don't think it's true. We have no knowledge of any such activities and no evidence that they were transported." Claiming Wynshaw had nothing to do with promotion activities at Columbia Records, the spokesman added, "so he is not a knowledgeable witness." Officials at black radio outlets responded by angrily denying the allegations. Egmont Sonderling commented he was "sick and tired of reading all these allegations" and that "any payola should be on the record companies — let them be hauled in front of a grand jury . . . the basic fallacy of the report lies in the fact that no D.J.'s deal with promotion men — record play lists are drawn up by music directors or program directors . . . I concede bribery is possible everywhere. But what I'm saying is that it's wrong to assume that a D.J. has the ability to get a song on the list." Sonderling said he had investigated payola reports at his stations and often discharged somebody on suspicion. Music directors, not deejays, selected the play lists at his stations. Lucky Cordell, executive director of the National Association of Television and Radio Announcers — made up largely of black jockeys, announcers, and broadcast personalities — said, "Whenever there's talk about payola the finger's always pointed at the black man. It is an accepted fact that a pop hit in white country is worth four to five times what a hit is worth in rhythm-and-blues country. If there is going to be a great amount of money it would go where it would do the most good, wouldn't it?"[13]

More information from various unidentified sources testifying before the strike force indicated the amount of money earmarked for payola was far in excess of the $250,000 figure. Promotion men routinely concealed payoffs in cash and drugs by turning in falsified expense accounts. Some payoffs from labels or distributors took the form of shipments of large quantities of free records to black stations whose employees sold them to record stores. A Columbia employee who had close contact with Columbia talent said it was not uncommon for him to spend $100 on cocaine for "hospitality" then write it off as an entertainment expense. "It was part of my life-style and theirs," he explained. "It was expected that I could communicate with people and part of the ritual was dope." His cocaine buys were made from a dealer who regularly visited the CBS building at 51 West Fifty-Second Street in New York. Payoffs were made to the publishers of industry tip sheets, as these sheets were used by some radio stations as a guide to what records to add to their play lists. One major label reportedly paid one tip sheet a flat $6,000 to mention a single r and b single and $3,000 to name a new middle of the road pop single. The day after a label promotion man spent 15 minutes on the phone talking to a tip-sheet publisher the label got a bill for $150 for the conversation. One popular form of payola consisted of company promotion men buying expensive airline tickets with company funds, charging them up to expense accounts, then giving them to jockeys who cashed them in. A variation of this was for some jockeys and promotion men to submit bills to companies from advertising firms, florists, and limousine rental outfits. These were dummy companies existing only on paper. A promotion man might give a disk jockey 1,000 free record albums in return for playing one or more specific records on the air. In turn the deejay would sell them to a record store for $2 each. The store told the distributor it had 1,000 surplus records which it would then exchange for better-moving records which the store retailed for the regular price of $4.95 to $5.95. This practice was said to be most prevalent among black deejays. Top record company executives sometimes set up their own publishing companies through intermediaries, then forced artists to cut their publishing company in on royalties. An executive with a secret 10 percent interest could make up to $10,000 on one hit single followed by an album. Normally, an artist would sign with a major publishing house which took half of all royalties or set up his own publishing firm. The executive's cut would be an additional one. A record label was told by a music trade publication executive that the amount of advertising space the label bought in the magazine would play a role in how high the label's records moved on the magazine's top-selling charts.[14]

After Wynshaw testified the FBI passed his name along to CBS executives. Almost immediately Wynshaw was fired — in April. His office was padlocked by CBS, which launched its own investigation. Less than two months after that CBS fired Clive Davis, to whom Wynshaw was an aide. Davis was head of Columbia Records and the number one recording executive in the country. Under his tutelage Columbia Records moved rock from 15 percent to over 50 percent of the label's volume. With 22 percent of the record market Columbia grossed $340 million in sales in 1972. Davis, touted as a future head of the Columbia empire, earned more than $350,000 in 1972. Ostensibly, Davis was fired for misusing company funds to the tune of $94,000, spent mostly on his apartment and a bar mitzvah. However, no one in the industry believed this was the real reason. At worst a high-level executive such as Davis caught in such a situation would be expected to repay the money. Columbia filed a civil suit against Davis to regain the money allegedly misused, naming Wynshaw as an accomplice. Columbia Records accountant Anthony Rubino was also fired for being involved. All of this resulted from a Columbia internal probe. When the payola scandal became public about a week after Davis's dismissal, Columbia said it was starting its own thorough investigation, saying "We have no evidence whatsoever of wrongdoing other than in connection with the discharge of three Columbia Records employees, announced last week for improper use of company funds. However, in light of current rumors concerning other irregularities C.B.S. has initiated investigation" of payola allegations.[15]

Among other revelations was a reputed "suit shop" in San Francisco where deejays ordered up to five suits at a time with the tab being picked up by the record companies. Some labels bought "air time" at large retail record stores to have their albums played over the in-store speaker system while customers browsed. One observer noted, "Ten years ago the disk jockeys were into chicks and free vacations. Now it's grass, hash and coke."[16]

In 1972 record sales in the United States alone totaled $2 billion. The year before that 79 million "folk, rock and teen" record albums were sold nationwide by all companies compared with 28 million in 1965. Most of the record companies had staffs of promotion men who visited the radio outlets. In addition, companies used outside promoters on a contract basis. One of these was Kal Rudman, a former schoolteacher who ran a consulting firm from his Cherry Hill, New Jersey, home. Rudman also published a leading tip sheet for which he charged his 1,000 subscribers $150 each. Other tip sheets were put out by Bill Gavin, Bob Hamilton, and George B. Meier. Sheets put out by these four men were regarded as important in the industry by record companies as radio stations often relied upon them to determine which disks would receive heavy air exposure. Rudman acknowledged he had accepted sums of money, sometimes amounting to thousands of dollars, to promote a company's disks by telling jockeys about them. However, he insisted that when he wrote up his tip sheet, *Friday Morning Quarterback*, those fees did not in any way influence his reporting on which disks were soon to become hits. "Doing this is like being a little bit pregnant," Kal explained. "Once you sell out, your credibility is gone. I'm number one because of my track record. If a record is on Rudman's front page, the odds are very strong that it will become a hit. What makes me so powerful? I am almost always right." Under his second hat as a promoter Rudman wouldn't name which companies had used him as a promoter except to say almost all of them. Warner Brothers, MCA Records, and Capitol Records all said they had been clients of his promotion company. Asked about the recent allegations of payola paid to an unnamed tip sheet, Rudman stated, "I'm clean as the board of health."[17]

While the strike force in Newark continued to probe payola, the Justice Department announced it had evidence of payola, over and above that related to Wynshaw's testimony, that had been uncovered, and that explorations beyond Columbia Records would take place. The FCC was reported to be cooperating with the feds, while in Los Angeles separate industry probes were being conducted by the FBI, the IRS, the Bureau of Customs, and narcotics agents. It was the specter of drug use that brought out the probers in such numbers. A radio program director said, "A major star brings in millions to a record company. If he says he wants some drugs, it's hardly surprising that they try to keep him happy. After all, there's only so much money they can give him, and he could get the same amount of that from another company." A music publicist commented that record companies always had to procure for their stars. "It used to be broads for the top singers in the forties and fifties. Now it's coke, smack, grass or whatever."[18]

An executive with Metromedia Corporation explained his company decided not to go into the production of rhythm and blues records because it had heard so much "unsavory" talk about payola and organized crime in the black music industry. According to Metromedia vice president Arthur Birsh, the company heard "scuttlebutt from agents, performers, record company executives and others about payoffs to some disk jockeys, the use of threats by Mafiosi to keep performers in line and the use of drugs in payola. Here it is 1973, but in 1971 you could hear this stuff on the street. It was no secret that sort of stuff went on. The sniff was so unsavory we said, 'Who needs it?'" Emphasizing what they heard was gossip rather than hard evidence, Birsh added he heard "there was a whole lot going on to influence sales and radio air play of rhythm and blues records aside from their merit." As an entertainment conglomerate with radio and television stations, Metromedia said it was worried about getting into an area where shady practices might affect its position as an FCC licensee. Reportedly, the National Association of Television and Radio Announcers (NATRA) was paid money by record companies to host various events and that these companies had contributed to social causes sponsored by the black deejay organization. Some record executives were uncomfortable with the NATRA operation but none were said to want to risk offending the jockeys, perhaps killing their chances of getting their product exposed. New York's black radio station WWRL joined with other black outlets and personnel in condemning the idea that payola was going mostly to blacks. An editorial was broadcast by WWRL condemning what it termed a "generalized smear and vague insinuation with racial overtones."[19]

The FCC announced it had investigated over 50 complaints of payola in the previous 12 months, turning over some of them to the Justice Department. Justice spokesman John Murphy said that indictments could be expected before long "if the evidence develops as I understand it." Meanwhile, at the strike force probe in Newark Anthony Del Vecchio, a former associate of Falcone and coindictee, turned state's evidence, providing information on payola. He was then placed under protective custody. Also from Newark came word that Rudman was indeed the previously unnamed tip-sheet man who had functioned as a conduit for payola money. Columbia admitted using Kal as a promotion man saying, "He's a good promotion man." Rudman reiterated he was not influenced on his tip-sheet listings by his separate work as a promotion man for the major labels. After being named, Kal denied any payola involvement by stating, "I have no contact whatsoever with black radio. I do not report what they are playing. I do not talk to them. When I started the *Friday Morning Quarter-*

back I decided then that I would stay as far away from black radio as possible because I knew what happened today and yesterday would come up sooner or later." Rudman also wrote columns for two trade publications — the weekly *Record World* and the daily *Hollywood Reporter*.[20]

More publicity about payola was generated by a column authored by William Safire, a former speechwriter for Richard Nixon. He claimed that probers were trying to determine if the music industry was "shot through with a higher dollar volume of venality and corruption than has ever been seen in American business history." Safire felt Columbia was engaged in "what may be the second most massive cover-up of the past twelve months" — Watergate was number one. Safire called on Columbia to assign the investigation of its record arm to its investigative CBS news arm instead of to its own law firm — as was then the case — wherein one of the law partners was also a director of Columbia.[21]

In response to this the Justice Department intensified its investigation of Columbia Records. Columbia also announced it was intensifying its internal investigation, while assuring employees in a memo, "This is not a witch hunt. It is for the protection and reputation of all of us." Top executives were incensed over persistent rumors that Davis had been fired to enable Columbia to cover up a drug scandal. Just a few days after Safire's column appeared CBS announced it had assigned a special reporting team to investigate the allegation against Columbia Records. Richard Salant, president of CBS news, asserted, "There are no holds barred in the investigation.... We are not under any pressure from anyone. We have a free hand to air whatever we want."[22]

Safire's article was also noted by Senator James L. Buckley, the New York conservative Republican who didn't know if the allegations of a CBS coverup were accurate but said they deserved attention. Buckley called for a four-part federal probe into payola charges by the attorney general's office, the FCC, the Senate communications subcommittee, and the White House Office of Telecommunications, to ensure the "broadest possible inquiry." According to the senator, his chief concerns were the view young people might get of corporate morality and the fact that "it is common knowledge that drugs are an integral part of the rock-music scene." Asked if he thought there was an effort to attack CBS's credibility because of its Watergate reporting, the senator replied, "I don't think so." Calling for his proposed investigation, Buckley said, "There is far more at stake here than the allegation of illegal business practices. The industry in question is one that is chiefly supported by the young, and it is my belief that the atmosphere of corruption, drugs, and 'fast-buck' opportunism that allegedly surrounds the industry can, if allowed to go uninvestigated and unchecked, give young Americans the misleading impression that so far as business goes, anything goes."[23]

Gortikov announced that his group would "cooperate fully with any investigating bodies" checking out alleged payola practices within the music industry. He added that the RIAA recognized "the possibility that some of the practices reported in the media might be taking place," and he urged each member company "to establish a system of continuous monitoring and investigation to guard against illegal and unethical practices." Additionally, the RIAA head urged an industry-wide effort at self-examination and audit "to make certain that all of their operations are conducted on a legal and morally sound basis and that appropriate action be taken against offenders."[24]

Buckley stirred up enough fear in the industry that CBS president Arthur R. Taylor met privately with the senator for over one hour to discuss payola. According to Leonard Saffir, the senator's press secretary, Taylor promised that CBS would cooperate fully with Buckley's office. Taylor would not comment publicly on the meeting because "We're in the middle of our own internal investigation." Saffir said that Taylor told Buckley that CBS executives "were trying to get at the heart of the allegations" and "what they said was how, when they fired a guy, they were still accused of trying to cover up." Buckley was prompted to speak out on the issue, said Saffir, because of the recent payola articles in major newspapers and magazines, with the "finale" being Safire's article.[25]

A couple of weeks later Buckley fired off a letter to Gortikov, containing a questionnaire the senator wished Gortikov to bring to the attention of RIAA members. The letter called upon RIAA members to not just cooperate with probers but to each conduct their own investigations to determine if payola existed, and stamp it out if it did. The questionnaire asked the extent of drug use in the music industry from a payola standpoint and simply whether or not rockers and their associates used drugs. Buckley also requested from companies copies of company policy statements on drug use, payola, and music that glamorized drugs. In his letter the senator criticized Gortikov's past performance, suggesting the RIAA chief explain his own attitude toward the music industry's drug problem — citing comments Gortikov made three years earlier where he referred to industry critics as "buck passers and crybabies who badmouthed and tarred the industry concerning drug use, drug lyrics and the entire drug-culture connection with some parts of popular music." One potential weapon wielded by Congress over the recording industry was the Senate Subcommittee on Copyright, headed by John McClellan (Democrat, Arkansas), which was considering new copyright legislation that would, among other things, require broadcasters to pay performance royalties of 2 percent of their annual billings to the performers of music used over the air. McClellan said he instructed the subcommittee to look into payola allegations before considering the possible new copyright changes. Radio then paid royalties only to the copyright owner not the performers. Only days after receiving this letter Gortikov hosted a private meeting of some 20 representatives of major labels who were members of the RIAA. Some companies present were Columbia, London, RCA, Capitol, MGM, MCA, Warner, and Electra. Notable by their absence were Atlantic and Motown. Gortikov refused to say if he had passed Buckley's letter onto the group. All he would say was that the meeting was held to discuss the foundation of a "positive plan of action" to combat allegations of payola and drug use in the industry. The RIAA members present reaffirmed their condemnation of payola and again pledged full cooperation with government investigators. The IRS announced it had begun a broad investigation of the tax records of recording companies.[26]

Less than three weeks after promising full cooperation to Buckley CBS decided not to allow some of the employees of its record division to talk to Buckley's aides, who were conducting a payola investigation, claiming that cooperation "at this time" would "blow the integrity of the federal investigation" then underway in Newark. "[C]orporate officials" but not "operational personnel" were being allowed by CBS to talk to the senator's staff. Appointments already set up with certain individuals were canceled. Saffir retorted, "It is difficult to understand how an organization that boasts of the public's right to know can refuse to cooperate with an extremely important Senate investigation." Buckley was trying to arrange with McClellan's subcommittee for power to subpoena CBS employees.[27]

Next to stonewall Buckley's staff was RCA, which told Saffir its executives would answer only to written questions. When Saffir refused to do this RCA categorically denied access to RCA staff to Buckley and his aides. In a prepared statement RCA said it would cooperate only with a duly authorized "legislative committee." Three weeks after sending out a lengthy questionnaire to record firms Saffir said that none had been returned.[28]

At a press conference held on July 30 Senator Buckley leveled charges of "drugola" and underworld connections against the recording industry. Without naming names the senator said drugs purchased for and used by well-known artists had on at least one occasion been authorized by a prominent recording industry executive. Another charge was that artists were forced to pay up to 25 percent of their box-office receipts to organized crime for protection, in a shake-down racket. Appearing with Buckley was John Phillips, formerly with the group The Mamas and the Papas who, while denying personal knowledge of the senator's charges, alleged at least one major label systematically bilked talent of $60 million in royalties through falsification of sales records. None of this had much to do with payola. Buckley said he and his staff worked closely with the Justice Department and that they served as an unofficial arm of McClellan's Senate

Judiciary Subcommittee on Copyright. The senator described his function as primarily that of a "conduit" for information until a full-scale Senate investigation was underway.[29]

Attempts by Buckley to prod McClellan's subcommittee into a full-scale probe found a cool reception. Tom Brennan, counsel for the subcommittee, called Buckley staffers "neophyte investigators who are talking before they have all the evidence." He added, "I know there is objection also to the fact that Senator Buckley is not a member of a committee which has jurisdiction in this matter."[30]

Meanwhile, the probe in Newark continued. Over a dozen New York area radio stations were subpoenaed to appear before the federal grand jury. Each was instructed to bring three years' worth of files on station personnel as well as correspondence to and from record companies. Among those ordered to appear was station WQXR, which played only classical music, and WMCA, which had switched to an all-talk format almost four years earlier. Ordering such unlikely stations to appear at the probe led to widespread opinion that the Newark probers were simply on a "fishing expedition."[31]

Travel agent Ed Garofalo told Newark investigators that his travel agency wrote about $400,000 worth of airline tickets per year for Columbia Records. Garofalo's contact at Columbia was David Wynshaw. Suddenly, in the spring of 1973 Columbia stopped doing business with him as did other record companies, apparently blacklisting him due to scandal rumors, he thought. Most tickets billed to Columbia were ordered through Wynshaw. Through that connection Garofalo met and started to do business with other companies and industry people, including Pasquale Falcone. A Columbia spokesman said his company stopped using all outside travel agents a few months previously but he did not know why. Also uncovered by Newark investigators was a kickback scheme by two executive employees of Stax Records which netted them around $400,000. While government probers tried to tie this somehow to payola they were unable to do so.[32]

Reaction from labels to all this publicity was varied. On the West Coast officials at Warner Brothers–Reprise Records suddenly refused all media requests for interviews after its accounting records were subpoenaed in Newark. When Motown Records got Buckley's request for information on drug use by performers they sent back a terse one-line reply, stating that the inquiry was "not applicable to our company." Asylum Records declared it had decided to sign no new artists because the company believed frightened radio stations were cutting back on their play lists and turning away from new talent. Said Asylum president David Geffen, "Radio stations are afraid to take a chance on new artists unless they have huge hits because they're afraid they'll be questioned about whether they were paid off to play them." Executives who did talk claimed talk of payola and drugola was greatly exaggerated. Motown vice president Michael Roshkind said, "At Motown, any huge expenses for that sort of thing would immediately be noticed. The only people who might pay off are those with an inferior product." Mike Maitland, president of MCA, commented that, "It certainly doesn't show the industry's best face; it's a nice way to make headlines . . . it would be silly for me to discuss this informally when it's going to be the subject of a formal hearing. At that time I'll have counsel with me."[33]

The RIAA announced a "comprehensive action program" on payola after another one of its meetings. Hailed by Buckley as "an important step forward in establishing a cooperative attitude," the plan called for trade publications to draw up standards for the compilation of their popularity charts of hit records "to assure their credibility and authenticity." In reference to payola in the music industry Roy Innis, national director of the Congress of Racial Equality (CORE), blamed it all on big business corruption through monopoly, claiming that 12 major corporations out of 3,000 "influence or outrightly control every record spun on the turntable." Innis charged the FCC and the FTC with nurturing this atmosphere by "fostering monopolistic practices," which damaged the competitive position of black small businessmen in the record industry.[34]

Columnist Gene Lees summed up the situation late in 1973 by first admitting that dope use was rampant in rock and used as payola. Lees moved quickly to Columbia and his real target — rock music bashing — by writing, "At a fifty percent rock content Columbia was ignoring much that was important in American music. . . . Has there been misuse of money at Columbia? Of course there has — just listen to the records." Decrying the betrayal of the trusting young, Lees said,

> They were fed garbage, and told that it was art by record company press agents. An industry that never even perceived — much less practiced — social and aesthetic responsibility . . . sought the widest (and inevitably lowest) common denominator, and then turned its powers of persuasion to the task of claiming this was "great, new significant, unprecedented" — in a word, "heavy." And if, in the pursuit of profit, they allowed their stoned-out rockers to proselytize their sickness to the impressionable young, all well and good in the corporate view.

Then Lees elevated the record industry to far loftier pinnacles than it ever attained, giving it a far more powerful position in society than it deserved when he said, regarding recent payola and drugola charges, "we are seeing the accelerating decay of the fundamental decency and sense of social responsibility that once made the United States great. This decay is in part reflected in and inspired by the record industry, a kind of feedback of moral irresponsibility. . . . These are critical days in the history of the American record industry even as in the history of the nation itself."[35]

The one area where payola was not a problem was in discos. When they were briefly popular in the 1970s it was possible for a record to become known with relatively little airplay. Payments to disco deejays were legal under payola legislation since discos didn't use the public airwaves.[36]

Shortly after the federal strike force uncovered the Wynshaw connection, the case was handed over to the U.S. attorney in Newark. A federal grand jury was convened, which continued to hear evidence in secret. It would drag on for two years, until the summer of 1975, before anything concrete would happen. Clive Davis was scheduled to appear before this panel but when he was fired by CBS his appearance was mysteriously canceled. As time passed with no indictments issued industry observers became more and more puzzled. Some, like Buckley, took advantage of the situation to drag the issue away from its supposedly major focus — payola — into the area of general drug use. Others, like Lees, tried to turn the issue to condemning the "bad" rock music.

Writing in *Ramparts* magazine, Andrew Kopkind summed up what was happening by noting, "the clear-cut issues of bribery and cultural independence, extortion and free expression, have become decidedly murky. Opportunistic politicians, uptight lawyers and reactionary officials have unfocused the original payola issue for their own needs and ends . . . some people fear that the attacks are really meant to threaten rock culture and Woodstock politics to defang the bite and bitterness of the music, to sterilize free-form radio, and generally to mellow out boogie consciousness into a fox-trot beat." Noting that the IRA had "enshrined" Las Vegas conventions, country club memberships, and the four-martini lunch as legitimate business deductions for general industry, Kopkind wrote, "Payola is part of the American way of life; indeed, it is the American way of life. Manufacturers pay off wholesalers and retailers to push their wares; publishers pay off distributors and newsstands to peddle their papers; why can't record companies pay off music stores and deejays to emphasize their albums?" Regarding charges and insinuations that payola was more rife among blacks, he said, "It's been taken for granted for years that payola is a way of life with black-oriented record companies and radio stations. How much of that assumption is a white fantasy is impossible to tell."[37]

In August 1974 CBS News finally aired its documentary "The Trouble with Rock." The program confirmed allegations of payola, organized crime involvement, and drugs in rock music. According to the documentary a CBS Records employee in the past often bought cocaine for CBS rock stars from an organized crime figure and paid for it with "large quantities of best-selling rock albums easily convertible to cash." A rock management figure was quoted as saying, "if you needed an ounce of cocaine that minute, there was a place at CBS Records you could get it." While not naming any companies, CBS News said it found indications of continuing payola infiltration by organized crime and an unhealthy involvement with drugs among major record labels." A description of CBS Records said it was "almost totally uncooperative" during preparation of the program. A spokesman for the record arm said the parent company's own investigation found "no basis" for payola allegations within CBS Records, adding the documentary was "a completely distorted picture of our industry. . . . I am unaware of the activities they describe." Arthur Taylor's spokesman said the CBS president would make no comment since the documentary involved a dispute "between two of his children" — meaning company subdivisions. The RIAA issued a statement saying the documentary "does not reflect an accurate picture of the music or broadcast industries."[38]

Payola allegations continued to pop up. Songwriters representing the Puerto Rico Society of Authors, Composers, and Editors of Music met with the commonwealth's Justice Department in San Juan to complain about payola. Admitting they had no proof of payola on area radio stations, the composers assumed the practice existed because they could not get recordings of their songs played over the air. Writers of mostly romantic ballads, they claimed they were shut out by local jockeys who pushed mostly salsa and rock "after receiving payola from record companies."

In July 1974 John Dexter Worthington, president of CMCA Records of New York, told Boston media people that WMEX (AM) received $800 in commercials and 500 promotional T-shirts from him in exchange for playing his label's single "Run Around Sue" — a revival of the old Dion hit by the Boston group The Second Society. He charged that WMEX stopped playing the disk when the flow of ads and T-shirts was stopped. At his news conference Worthington said he had lodged a complaint about WMEX with the FCC. That agency reported it had nothing in writing from him, only a telephone call outlining his grievance that the station refused to play the record because he wouldn't come up with any more ads and T-shirts. According to Worthington "Run Around Sue" was a top-requested song by WMEX listeners, in addition to selling well in Boston record stores, when it was pulled from the station's playlist. Worthington was told, he said, by WMEX's program director "that if I bought advertising the record would stay on." Ansel Chaney, WMEX publicity director, denied all the charges, stating the record was pulled only because it was no longer popular. Chaney agreed that Worthington contracted to buy $800 worth of ads and donated 500 promotional T-shirts to the station. These shirts carried the name of the song on one side with the station's logo on the other. These expenditures were all Worthington's idea, said Chaney. After the Second Society performed "Run Around Sue" and other material for a charity event in New Hampshire sponsored by WMEX, the song was taken off the playlist. Then Worthington tried to get the song put back on by offering to buy more and provide more shirts. "He made certain threats, and said he would file complaints — but we can't yield to that kind of pressure," explained Chaney.[39]

During the summer of 1975 a record album retailed for around $6.98. Recording artists received a royalty of 5–15 percent of the retail list price, minus an amount for packaging. Thus a singer with a 10 percent royalty received about 63 cents for each copy sold. Cost of producing the album ranged from $30,000 to $75,000, with an average of perhaps $40,000. Usually, this cost of production was deducted from sales before the singer started to collect his 10 percent royalty. Companies producing records charged a wholesale price of $3.25–$3.75 for the album. In addition to paying the performers, the company had to pay two cents for each song on the album to the writer as well as the same amount to the song's publisher. Other costs absorbed by the label were 28–35 cents to press the disc and 10–12 cents for the jacket. Thus an album that wholesaled for $3.75 would leave the label with a gross profit of around $2.25 for each copy sold. Other costs these earnings had to cover included advertising, promotion, distribution, administration, records that lost money, and so on. Gortikov estimated that 80 percent of single records didn't recover their production costs, with 75 percent of albums also not recovering their production costs. However, an album that became a big hit generated millions of dollars in profits.[40]

At radio stations in smaller towns and at smaller FM stations records were still mostly selected by the deejays who played them. Supposedly, these selections were made on the basis of requests and Top 40 charts compiled by trade magazines and tip sheets. Larger stations increasingly claimed their playlist selection was removed from on-air personalities and assigned to program directors. One of the country's largest pop stations was Chicago's WLS, where program director John Gehron said, "We pick our playlist by calling between 125 and 150 record stores in Illinois, Indiana, and Wisconsin every week to learn which records are most popular. This protects us from suspicion of taking payola and protects us from being hyped; we're able to offer what the people are buying." Of those in the industry some felt payola permeated the music business. It had at least a psychological effect on everyone involved in the industry. Said Mike Baker, program director of KLIF in Dallas, "You hear it's around, I haven't seen it. Everybody's worried about being accused of it. I think the big stations are smart enough not to get involved at all; they don't want to get caught in it, like Watergate." Part of the effort to shift blame for payola away from the labels and distributors onto the radio outlets lay in claiming the industry was virtually in their grip when trying to sell their music. Stanley Cornyn, an executive with Warner-Reprise Records, stated, "We have become, year by year, so dependent on radio exposure of our records that without that play we're cooked. In the last 10 years, and dramatically in the last five, the record business has sold only what it could get played."[41] Radio had been important for at least 25 years at that time, not five. Substitute "vaudeville performers" or "bandleaders" for "radio" in the above quote and you would accurately describe the situation at still earlier points in time. There have always been gatekeepers in the industry. It has always been the structure of the label/distributor end of the business (publishers in the earlier times) — monopoly type control by a few large firms with yet relatively easy access to new companies, one-hit wonders who come and go, all desperately promoting more songs than could be aired — which has given rise to payola.

As the Newark grand jury probe dragged on hearing evidence behind closed doors, rumors abounded that a large number of indictments would be issued any day. One potential problem had to do with whether or not the New Jersey panel had jurisdiction to investigate an industry which was mostly located in New York and Los Angeles. This was solved by holding grand jury investigations in other cities at the same time, although Newark remained the major site for hearings.[42]

Finally, in June 1975, two years after the Newark panel began its probe, U.S. attorneys in Newark, New York, Philadelphia, and Los Angeles indicted 19 people and six corporations for payola offenses as well as other charges such as income tax evasion, mail fraud, perjury, and interstate transportation of stolen property. Jonathan L. Goldstein, Newark U.S. attorney, termed it "the first step," promising it was only "the beginning of the inquiry into payola in the billion-dollar pop-record industry." While deejays and program directors were implicated in receiving payola in 16 cities — Norfolk, Virginia; Chicago; Detroit; Inster, Michigan; New York; Atlanta; St. Louis; Memphis; Washington; Oxon Hill, Maryland; District Heights, Maryland; University City, Missouri; Houston; Philadelphia; Baltimore; and Cleveland, none were indicted because they had been "very cooperative," explained Goldstein. It was understood that in return for their help station personnel were granted immunity from prosecution, a common practice used by the Justice Department.[43]

A grand jury in New York indicted Davis and Wynshaw for income tax evasion and Wynshaw and Falcone for conspiracy and mail fraud. None of these charges were related to payola. In Davis's case he was charged with failing to declare about $90,000 in taxable benefits from his employers. It was the same money which CBS was trying to recover from Davis in a civil suit. Davis, then president of Arista Records, regarded the indictment as a vindication of himself, noting that none of the charges linked him with payola or drugola. In his statement he said, "For two years my family and I have suffered from malicious rumors and insinuations growing out of the investigation of the record industry. The indictment against me today clearly establishes that all those rumors and insinuations were false. What is involved are tax charges. The issues are apparently the same as those raised by the CBS civil suit against me . . . I am innocent of those charges." Clive later pled guilty to one count and was fined $10,000. The Los Angeles grand jury returned an indictment against record promoter Fred Rector, charging him with failing to file income tax returns for a two-year period. The one station employee charged was Paul Burke Johnson, program director of Atlanta's rhythm and blues WAOK-AM, indicted on one count of perjury claiming he lied when he denied receiving payola from Kenneth Gamble.[44]

One of the two major indictments was issued by the Philadelphia grand jury against Gamble and Leon Huff of Gamble-Huff Records. The five other companies, Assorted Music, North Bay Records, Gamble Records, Huga Management, and Cheyenne Productions, were all part of Gamble-Huff. Also charged were five other executives of the Gamble-Huff group, Earl Shelton, Joseph Medlin, Edward Richardson (a.k.a. Lord Gas), Harry Coombs, and Benjamin Krass. These men and their companies were alleged to have paid about $37,000 to radio station personnel in cash, clothing, money orders, and airline tickets, and clothing to a total of $6,000 was provided by Krass Brothers Clothiers of Philadelphia. Benjamin Krass was a partner in both Gamble Records and Krass Brothers Clothiers. Station personnel were given airline tickets to travel to Philadelphia to pick up the clothes. In addition, it was alleged that the defendants traveled to New York, Baltimore, Washington, Atlanta, Detroit, Cleveland, and other cities to meet with and pay in excess of $25,000 in cash to deejays and other station personnel. Charges against Huff were later dropped. Gamble pleaded nolo contendere and was fined $2,500.

The second major indictment was issued in Newark against Nat Tarnopol, who controlled Brunswick Record Corporation, and Dakar Records. Six other officials of these firms charged with him were Peter Garris, Irving Wiegan, Lee Shep, Carl Cavise, Melvin Moore, and Carmine De Noia (a.k.a. Doc Wassel). This indictment alleged the defendants sold records to dealers at less than wholesale on the condition that they pay in cash or goods and services — a scheme said to have produced $343,000 in cash and $28,000 in cars, sporting goods, and household items. Allegedly, these defendants used some of these proceeds to pay deejays and other station personnel "as consideration for the public broadcasting of Brunswick and Dakar musical records." They were said to have traveled to various cities and states to make those payoffs. The RIAA's only comment on the indictments was to say "It would be wrong and unfair to suggest that the practices alleged in the indictments represent typical business behavior in these industries." The Gamble-Huff group were almost exclusively black, recording only a very few white artists. Brunswick and Dakar were also mostly black-oriented — with a slightly larger white representation than the former. Almost in anticipation of criticism, federal investigators "cautioned against drawing the inference that personnel at black-oriented stations had been the record companies' primary target."[45]

After two years of effort the federal authorities had labored mightily yet brought forth only a mouse, although Goldstein emphasized that investigations were ongoing with more indictments expected. One observer noted that the indictments were far less sensational than the revelations from 1959 to 1960, and that a couple of companies selling records for cash that was later funneled to deejays for payola was much less spectacular than the rumor mills had been suggesting. He also noted, "persistent rumors about the use of drugs as currency in the payola trade were nowhere to be seen in the federal indictments. Not only was drugola completely absent from the indictments, but not a single major disk company was named by the federal attorneys." Brunswick was a subsidiary of CBS. A source inside Arista Records felt the feds were using Davis in their series of indictments to provide them with a "headliner," and that Davis was "being used by a grand jury that couldn't come up with shit." U.S. attorney Paul Curran of New York said of Davis, "There are no charges of payments by him to others in the record industry, or any charges that he received benefits other than from his employer." It was not unusual for highly paid corporate executives to have disputes with the IRS over what the executive should or should not declare as taxable income and or what constituted a legitimate deduction from gross income. Normally, such disputes were settled by negotiations by the two sides. It was very unusual for charges to be laid as they were against Davis.[46]

At the trial of the Brunswick seven early in 1976 three music directors of radio stations — testifying under grants of immunity — told how they had received $25–$100 on several occasions from Melvin Moore. When one asked what the cash was for Moore replied, "Just to say thanks." E. Rodney Jones, program director of WVON in Chicago, said he had received a total of $2,000 on six occasions, along with airline tickets from Moore as "a token of his appreciation." Roosevelt Green of WJMO in Cleveland in 1972 claimed that in November of that year Moore gave him Brunswick's latest release along with some cash saying, "Thanks." Despite this testimony, all three asserted that the money received had no influence on their selection of music. Green said he had never played a Brunswick disk that he felt didn't deserve to be played. Said Jones, "Gifts or money have never had any influence on my playing of records. If I didn't believe it was a potential hit it wouldn't have been played." In April four of the men were found guilty of conspiracy and fraud charges. Tarnopol was sentenced to three years in jail and fined $10,000 while Garris, Wiegan, and

Shep were each sentenced to two years in jail along with a $10,000 fine. During the trial defense attorneys argued that payola was a way of life in the record industry and part of the promotion and of the business. Federal District Judge Frederick Lacey replied, "If this is true, then the record industry is a dirty business indeed." Tarnopol said, "I am in the deepest disgrace of my life. The last three years of my life have been the worst you can imagine, possibly because of the fact that I could have done something wrong and not known it." Convictions of all four were reversed by the U.S. Court of Appeals in Philadelphia the following year. Next came a mistrial, then the charges were dropped.[47]

Paul Johnson came to trial with his perjury charge reduced to a single count of payola. He was convicted and given a one-year suspended sentence.[48]

Program director Frankie Crocker of New York's black-oriented WBLS-FM was indicted in July 1976 by the Newark grand jury. Goldstein alleged Crocker had made false statements before the panel the previous September when Crocker denied receiving over $10,000 in 1974 and 1975 from independent record promoter Ellsworth Groce and when he denied ever receiving any money from Philadelphia International Records promotion man Harry Coombs, whereas in fact he had been paid $400 in December 1973. Crocker came out of Buffalo, New York, where his parents ran a drycleaning store. After a start in that city as a prime-time deejay, Crocker worked at stations in Pittsburgh, Los Angeles, and New York's WWRL where Groce was program director. In 1972 Frankie was hired by New York's WLIB-FM (later WBLS-FM) after which he rocketed to stardom with Inner City Broadcasting, the nation's first fully black-owned radio corporation. Nicknamed "Black Satin," he led WBLS to a dominant market position aimed at affluent, college-educated blacks but also succeeded in drawing a white audience as well. Known for an extravagant lifestyle, Crocker had a Rolls-Royce, a Mercedes, and an Excalibur. He collected French antiques from trips abroad, wore designer clothes, and frequented the best clubs wearing tinted glasses with the initials "F.C." set with diamonds in the left lens. His salary was rumored to be $100,000–$150,000, although at his trial Crocker stated his WBLS salary was $60,000 per year, up from a previous $30,000, and that he collected another $5,000 annually from TV commercial voiceovers.

At Crocker's trial Groce initially took the Fifth Amendment as to whether or not he had given Crocker money. After the judge gave him full immunity Groce had to testify or face contempt of court charges. Groce then admitted giving Frankie money when he was promoting albums that Crocker played over the air at WBLS. Also testifying at the trial was Charles Bobbit, manager of singer James Brown, who said he paid Crocker around $6,500 over an eight-year period to play certain records. Brown, who claimed no knowledge of the payoffs, took the stand as a character witness for Crocker but did attest to the jockey's power when he said, "He's the most important one . . . you need his air play to help you get a hit." Crocker denied taking payola to play certain records saying, out of court, "I guess especially with black jockeys the rumors are worse. It's something I have been fighting all my life just to stay in the business. . . . My position was and still is, you can't take money for records and still be number one in the biggest market in the city because then you are obligated to too many people." Convicted of perjury, Crocker was sentenced to one year in prison and fined $1,000. This conviction was later overturned by an appellate court. Crocker was then working as an independent a and r consultant to Polydor Records. Crocker was the last case to be prosecuted as part of the federal probes in Newark and other cities. Some 25 of 60 people indicted on various charges had pled guilty to and been convicted on a variety of charges.[49]

No sooner had the Justice Department investigations at Newark and elsewhere died down than the FCC reentered the picture by announcing on December 23, 1976, that it would schedule hearings into payola again. This probe was launched because, said the agency, it had received "new information and complaints" both inside and outside the broadcast industry. Specifically to be investigated were charges that deejays with outside concert promotion interests gave their artists heavy air promotion without making the required announcement that the jockey benefited financially by such an arrangement. The opening complaint was by two of Washington, D.C.'s top rock concert producers, Cellar Door Productions and Dimensions Unlimited, who complained against WOL — Washington's leading soul radio station — deejays and D.J. Productions (DJP), owned by some of the WOL jockeys. The complainants alleged that some WOL deejays demanded payoffs to DJP in exchange for a promise not to boycott the music of artists due to appear in the competitors' concerts. In other cases cash payments, as high as $14,000, were reportedly required to secure airplay of groups booked by Cellar Door and Dimensions.[50]

Before its hearings opened the FCC insisted its hearings would cover the entire range of payola practices and not be limited to deejay conflict of interest situations. Charles Kelley, chief of the FCC hearing division, said, "We are not out to 'get' anybody. This is an investigation proceeding to let the Commission know just how extensive and how serious the payola situation is." There was a major problem in getting anyone to talk. "Everyone says there's a terrible situation," explained Kelley, "but few facts emerge on particular complaints." He did state that the proceeding was not geared to developing evidence that would lead to the conviction of individuals on payola charges or to a station's loss of license. Such evidence would not be ignored, he said, but "We're trying to find out what the problem is, whether the commission must be concerned, and if so, whether it has the tools for dealing with the problem. . . . Payola and plugola have become much more sophisticated. It's not simply a matter of someone handling a disk jockey a $100 bill and a record he is expected to play. As a result, there may be a question as to whether the statutes and rules now on the books are adequate to deal with the problems the commission first addressed in 1964." A major purpose of the 1977 FCC hearings was to inform licensees of any new types of payola being practiced so they could guard against them. With no long-range plans for the inquiry Kelley said the hearings would go on "in spurts until we exhaust our funds or the testimony."[51]

When the hearings opened in February 1977, first to testify was William Washington, president of Dimensions, who said he and Jack Boyle, president of Cellar Door, jointly put on an Earth Wind and Fire (EWF) concert in Washington, D.C., in June 1974. While making arrangements for the concert Washington said he received a note from EWF's management firm in Los Angeles saying it was "having some trouble with some DJs" in Washington and was "concerned about records being played in the market — especially at WOL." After an exchange of letters with WOL owner Egmont Sonderling, Washington met with WOL general manager James Kelsey and WOL deejays. Then Washington said he monitored the station from April to June 1974, finding nothing unusually wrong with the way the station presented records. From June 1974 through most of 1976 Washington stated he got the impression that a group promoted by DJP got more than a normal amount of airplay with the jockeys plugging their own concerts. When Washington and Boyle promoted a second EWF concert — an April 1975 appearance at Washington's suburban Capital Center — the Dimensions head testified he and his partner paid WOL jockey Melvin Edwards (president of DJP) $14,000 in "blood money" for what he described as "$840 worth of promotion, two sell-out concerts and lots of air-play. . . . By paying them this $14,000 we were assured that their records would be played a lot — a hell of a lot."

After EWF's 1974 concert in Washington, DJP had obtained first refusal rights to the group in the District of Columbia area but, nevertheless, Dimensions got a firm booking for the April 1976 date from EWF's management. Soon after this booking was made EWF management contacted Washington telling him that WOL jockeys would have to be taken care of. Washington testified he understood this to mean the deejays would have to be paid in order to keep them from stopping the playing of EWF records on WOL. "We had to create some kind of situation that would keep them happy," said Washington. To this end an agreement was signed by Washington, Boyle, and Edwards guaranteeing DJP a maximum of $14,000 if the concert grossed over $266,000. D.J. Productions undertook responsibility to emcee the concert and produce any and all commercials for the event. Edwards attached a release under which DJP agreed that performance by EWF at the concert would fulfill completely any prior contractual obligation which EWF had to DJP. The night of the concert Washington and Boyle gave Edwards a check for $14,000. The jockey signed it and gave it immediately back to the promoters who handed over $14,000 in cash. Said Edwards, "that's the power of black radio." Then, said Washington, Edwards "even asked for more money, not for all the disk jockeys, but for himself." Boyle corroborated Washington's testimony. Both of these men made unsuccessful last-minute pleas to be allowed to testify behind closed doors, citing "severe social and economic pressures." Besides Edwards, other WOL deejays involved with DJP were Roger Bethel (air name Raymond St. Jacques), Charles Green (Chuck McCool), Marshall Payne (Bobby Bennett), and Gregory Hines. All the jockeys flatly denied the allegations, with Edwards calling the charges "a lot of lies." He added, "We will probably look bad until we can give our side."[52]

Washington alleged he had problems with other acts he booked in the Washington area in 1974 and 1975, including dates for Aretha Franklin, the Isley Brothers, and Rufus where "a hell of a lot of airplay" was obtained for a cut of the box office take. He said the acts themselves were unaware of these arrangements. "Edwards told me many, many times that if you give us a piece of every concert you do, I'll take care of you and have the other guys do the same," the promoter related. Also alleged was that he was forced to coproduce with DJP a 1975 Al Green date because the jockeys "had gotten to Al Green" with threats of reduced airplay. During a Green date the previous year when DJP promoted a Green concert the station was saturated with the singer's tunes "24 hours a day." Edwards reportedly used his influence to secure a lead-in spot for the rock group Ureaus and a percentage of the gross. Despite this, the concert lost money and Edwards, instead of paying Green the contracted $35,000, went to the singer and got him to accept $13,500 instead. Boyle had an exclusive contract for five years to book rock acts in the Capital Center. He and Washington had an exclusive deal with the area's Carter Barron Amphitheater for its summer bookings. The pair partnered to produce all the black acts booked into the Capital Center. So annoyed did Boyle become at WOL jockeys' payola demands that he tried to buy the station for $3 million, but was unsuccessful.[53]

Another witness to testify was Teddy Powell of TP Productions, New York, who was described as the largest black concert promoter in the country. This promoter told of being blocked from promoting the rhythm and blues group Parliament and Funkadelic in the Virginia cities of Norfolk and Richmond after a successful tour in other cities since "Mel Edwards had first refusal of those two cities. . . . He could give them air play and record play. That was my understanding."[54]

When WOL owner Sonderling testified, he described the system in place to control what was heard over the radio. These checks included daily song sheets filled out by on-air personalities, a station playlist, and 24-hour taping of the station. He could not explain how two records by Ureaus (managed by Edwards) were played on the air by Edwards as the number was not on the station's playlist. However, such station controls did not extend to activities of WOL deejays outside the station. "We object if they are involved in the music business," said Sonderling, but the "music business did not include concert promoting." When a letter of complaint from Washington reached Sonderling in 1974 the owner did not respond because he said the letter was "too indefinite and undefined . . . a crank letter . . . I didn't take it very seriously." He said he didn't then realize that Dimensions Unlimited was one of WOL's biggest advertisers. Only when a second letter of complaint, from Washington and Boyle, was received in April 1976 did Sonderling take action by "terminating the rights of the disk jockeys to promote concerts" and by asking Edwards to resign as the station's music director. Edwards claimed he never held such a position.[55]

Boyle admitted his exclusive contract with the Capital Center gave him an effective veto over any promoter wanting to book the facility. Although he claimed he seldom exercised this power, he added that "under no terms" could DJP use it because of their "business ethics," meaning that the jockeys "put force on groups to play for them at reduced prices" by threatening to stop the playing of records. According to Boyle, the $14,000 paid to DJP for the EWF concert came about because EWF's management was pressured into assigning DJP first refusal rights for a Washington area appearance by the group.[56]

FCC hearing division chief Kelley commented on payola, "The problem is not limited to Washington. . . . It seems to be nationwide in scope and consequently our investigation will try to reflect that. . . . The problem unfortunately seems to focus on black-oriented radio stations at this stage. We don't know where the evidence may go. It's due to the extremely segregated nature of the record companies and the record industry." Al Gee, a spokesman for NATRA, stated, "Their target is black announcers." Sonderling felt the payola allegations against his station were a ploy by rival concert promoters to use the FCC proceedings to buy WOL's license at below market price. If the allegations were true WOL's license could be revoked by the agency and a new buyer could step in. Also it would put an end to the rival DJP. Sonderling insisted that his company's investigation of his deejays found they had done nothing wrong. After the 1976 complaint surfaced WOL introduced its new policy of barring its jockeys from running concerts in the Washington area, barring them from interviewing on the air performers giving concerts, and barring them from ad lib "intros and extros" of records when the performers were appearing in concert in the area because the problem required a new policy for a situation "that was brand new to us." The judge at the hearing was baffled that Sonderling failed to see a conflict of interest situation could exist when deejays had interests in concert promotion and artists.[57]

When WOL deejay Roger Bethel testified he said that many of the daily record sheets showing what records were played on WOL were lost or misplaced. Sometimes the jockeys inadvertently threw them out or never filled them out as they could not find the proper forms. Weekly reports on jockey activities were also not filled out regularly. "I never really understood what kind of information they wanted from me. I really didn't take them all that seriously," explained Bethel. The week before the FCC hearings began Bethel said he had spent a day filling out "25 or 30" weekly reports for 1976.[58]

Mel Edwards testified that he never took any money for playing records on WOL and never exerted pressure on artists to perform under the DJP promotional wing although he admitted "We didn't keep the best books in the world. We were guilty of that." D.J. Productions was ordered disbanded by Sonderling in October 1976. Among documents produced by FCC probers was a contract between Edwards and Terry Bassett of Concerts West, a Dallas promoter, in connection with an August 1975 concert by War at the Capital Center. This contract specified that Edwards and DJP would receive a $5,000 promotional fee for providing services in connection with the concert. Services included a two-week saturation promotion of the concert. In addition, DJP would receive a $2,500 bonus if the concert's net gross receipts exceeded $115,000 and another $2,500 if the net gross exceeded $140,000. Edwards also contracted to "coordinate" a radio commercial time buy of $2,500 on WOL on behalf of Concert West's advertising agency. Payments were to be made in cash on the night of the concert. Asked how he came to twice play a record by Ureaus on his show in spite of its not being on the station's playlist, Edwards first said he did so without going through proper channels. Later that day in his testimony, after conferring with his lawyers, the deejay said he'd asked for and received permission from the program director to play the number. When asked if he was still involved with Ureaus as the group's manager Edwards replied, "I don't know." On the question of the EWF $14,000 payment Edwards claimed he was "forced" to sell his right to Boyle because Boyle had "blocked out" DJP from booking the Capital Center, which was the area's largest arena. After the WOL testimony was completed the FCC temporarily wound down its hearings with one official saying, "We have to decide whether we want to go into this detail everywhere." Rumor had it that FCC attorneys were not altogether convinced the deejays had done anything illegal.[59]

Before FCC hearings resumed Mel Edwards was fired by WOL for "gross insubordination." While DJP had been disbanded under station orders, Edwards continued to promote concerts by setting up a new company. Hearings before the FCC started up again after a two-month delay. Privately, the agency was viewed as not knowing what to do with the information it had gathered. Chief counsel for the agency, Ted Kramer, admitted the current payola statutes might not cover adequately the outside activities of deejays. "It's a question of whether the Communications Act is broad enough," he said.[60]

Another allegation that surfaced at this time, not before the FCC, involved Norfolk, Virginia's WOWI (FM) where two employees were fired after charges were made to station management that they attempted to extort $3,000 from a local promoter for playing the records of groups appearing in the Norfolk area. Bill Douthat, president of Whisper Concerts, reported that on three occasions in late 1976 two WOWI staffers approached him, requesting payments of $500 each for playing the disks of EWF, the Commodores, and Average White Band. Douthat refused to pay. Later Leonard Ware, station operations manager, discovered that the records of the groups had been removed from the studio. After Douthat wrote a letter of complaint to WOWI owner L. E. Willis, Sr., informing him of the actions of his employees, the two men were fired in December 1976.

No formal complaint was made to the FCC because Douthat felt Willis handled the complaint satisfactorily. Ware confirmed the story, saying the men told Douthat if he did not pay them they "would discontinue playing the records," and when he didn't pay "the records would just disappear." The two employees, former operations manager Price Wooten and Arthur Paul Young, former music director, both denounced the charges as "totally false." Wooten admitted meeting with Douthat to discuss fees for acting as host for a series of concerts. Young said there was an ongoing problem of missing records at WOWI. "I approached them about the problem of pilferage," he explained.[61]

At the next round of FCC hearings in May three Sonderling Broadcasting executives testified, with two of them claiming the charges made by Washington against WOL deejays were the result of a "personal vendetta" against Mel Edwards. James L. Kelsey, WOL general manager, said he had looked into the situation at the station and found that records "were being played properly." Kelsey was also questioned about hundreds of dollars worth of clothing he had received, paid for by Kenneth Gamble. These gifts, said Kelsey, were made "strictly out of friendship." Cortez Thompson, WOL programming director, echoed Kelsey's statements about Washington having a vendetta against Edwards and that on one occasion Washington told him "he wanted to send Mel Edwards to jail."

Thompson did admit that the station had received several complaints from a Richmond, Virginia, promoter about Edwards' dealings there.[62]

Al Green told the hearing that he took less money for a poorly attended concert in 1975 when promoters implied they would plug his records on a local radio station. He was told in his dressing room before going on that the date was not a sellout and that he was being offered less money than originally contracted for. Green agreed to accept less because he felt he was in a "pressure point" situation right before the concert with the audience waiting for the show. The jockeys promised the singer the rest would be made up later with airplay, not money, being the method of payment. Washington tried to blame this fee cut on coercion by the DJP people, but Green attributed the cut and the unfairly low estimate of ticket sales to Washington.[63]

When Washington was recalled to the stand he admitted that he had done no monitoring of music played on WOL as he had originally claimed. When asked why he had never complained to WOL station executives about concerts coproduced with WOL, featuring Aretha Franklin, Rufus, EWF, and the Isley Brothers, despite numerous visits to the station, the promoter could only respond, "I can't recall." He blamed some of his false or unproven complaints in his earlier testimony on the fact that he had "relied on his lawyers." Even though Washington had insisted he was forced to buy out DJP's right of first refusal for $14,000 before being allowed to promote an EWF concert, Bob Cavallo, manager of the group, was never contacted by the FCC. Cavallo denied ever being threatened by DJP. "We had to go with Dimensions instead," he explained, "because they could get us into the Capital Center. This is a simple case of competition between promoters — cutthroat, but nothing more. The band likes to give a black promoter the first shot whenever possible. If a black DJ in a town is also a top promoter it makes sense to use him." As the FCC hearings closed down in June 1977 the WOL deejays were largely exonerated of all major charges made against them.[64]

Toward the end of June the FCC voted to continue its payola probing, but only behind closed doors. Its attorneys argued that the constant press coverage from public hearings discouraged many witnesses from coming forward. "The progress of the inquiry might be hampered if conducted in public," said the agency. By the following month a three-man FCC team was in Los Angeles conducting interviews in preparation of in camera hearings for August.[65]

Rather than undergo FCC hearings the WOL licensee, who, according to the agency, "either knew or should have known" of the activity at the station, chose to sell the station under special FCC provisions.[66]

10 *Paper Adds, 1980–1991*

The payola issue disappeared from public view for several years until the early 1980s when writer Steve Coll called for another congressional probe into the music industry. Entertainment insiders told him that payola was "back," with the finger being pointed specifically at independent record promoters who were expending large sums to win airplay for their discs. Said one independent promoter, "The Government has tried over the years to investigate payola. All they've come up with is a few Judases to put on pedestals to take the rap so they've given the radio and record business a license to steal." For large record labels radio was the major way to reach consumers. Radio airplay was by far the single most important way of pitching a record. Very little money was spent by the labels for consumer ads on television or in other media. Independent promoters became more and more important in the business as the successful ones cultivated contacts and special access to program directors at stations in particular regions or cities.

Since labels relied solely on trade sheets to find out how much airplay their records received, promoters concentrated on the small number of stations considered important enough to report their playlists to those trade sheets. The trades did not monitor the stations in any way, accepting the playlists as reflecting the stations' choices and ultimately consumer preferences. Stations which didn't report playlists to the trades used the trade lists in compiling their own playlists. Ultimately, what mattered wasn't airplay but getting a record listed on the playlists of as many of the reporting stations as possible. Labels paid large amounts of money to the independent promoters and then forgot about it. If the independent promoters used some of that money for payola to station programmers the labels could disclaim responsibility. It made it very difficult to legally implicate record companies in any illegal doings. It was a strategy that worked, for the major payola villain of the 1980s, as portrayed in the media, was the independent promoter. The downside to all this for the labels was the increasing amount of money paid to promoters who had indeed cultivated contacts over the years, solidifying their position of power in the industry. Labels had turned loose and created these men, only to find they couldn't always control the power and costs associated with them. At the start of 1982 both Columbia and Elektra Records claimed they were phasing the independent promoters out of their promotion budgets altogether. "It has simply gotten to be too expensive to carry on," said Elektra executive Bill Smith. Artists' managers, and even artists themselves on occasion, sometimes paid for promotion out of their own pockets. But other companies did not follow suit and both firms resumed the use of independents within a year. Falling profits were a major reason, with Warner-Elektra down $27 million. Another advantage of this system for the major labels was that it tended to keep small record companies from competing directly against them since the small labels simply could not afford high-priced promoters. Writer Coll noted, "It is virtually impossible for any small company to break the hold that independent promoters have on radio in the major cities. And the record companies will develop only those acts which fit easily into the constructed formats that evolved as radio programming itself became a profitable corporate endeavor. For consumers, the result is stale, utterly predictable repetition of popular music styles. Innovation is rare, and never so radical as to upset the system of radio marketing." Complaints and insinuations about payola being more prevalent on black-oriented radio — so common in the 1970s — disappeared completely, never to be mentioned in the 1980s. Focus returned to where it belonged — white radio.[1]

Congress took an interest in payola again in the summer of 1984 when the House Oversight and Investigations Subcommittee announced it had finished a probe of record promoters and their influence on radio playlists. Investigators conducted in camera interviews with record producers, radio station management and employees, the RIAA, and other music industry people. This fact-finding study was launched after reports surfaced that independent promoters were using payola on a widespread scale to influence radio playlists. All the data gathered was turned over to Rep. John Dingell (Democrat, Michigan) who determined whether or not public hearings would be held. They weren't. Subcommittee staff director Michael Barrett said their probe turned up "no credible evidence of specific incidents of improper or illegal activity. . . . As a consequence the staff recommends that the subcommittee not undertake a full investigation at this time." He did concede there were "ample opportunities for unlawful payoffs."[2]

Payola in the 1980s became a huge public issue following two segments on "NBC Nightly News" which aired on February 24 and 26, 1986, claiming independent promoters had strong organized crime connections and had established a payola foothold in the record industry. Aired in the same week that the music industry handed out its Grammy awards, the programs generated maximum embarrassment. The report alleged that "record companies pay mafia-connected independent promoters almost $80 million a year . . . essentially to do the dirty work of the industry." According to NBC Joe Isgro and Fred DiSipio were described as "two of the most powerful and feared men in the rock business . . . hired by every major record company to promote records." Also alleged was that Isgro and DiSipio attended a Gambino mafia family meeting early that year with reputed Gambino boss John Gotti. Isgro was also said to have ties to another alleged Gambino boss, Joseph Armone. The NBC network claimed its report was based on dozens of interviews with industry figures; however, only two appeared on camera. One was former deejay Jay McDaniels who said he was "threatened . . . and blackballed in the industry . . . when he tried to start a record promotion business in the South . . . saying publicly he wasn't going to use payola." The other was Dan Cox, a jockey at Miami's WINZ.[3]

Allegedly, Isgro and DiSipio were part of what was known in the business as "the Network," a group of about 30 important independent promoters who received as much as $300,000 from labels to get a disk added to the playlists of the country's 27 key radio stations. Epic label, owned by CBS, had distributed Isgro's Private I label until early 1986, while DiSipio was slated to be involved in a new label to be distributed by CBS. This deal fell through after the notoriety. Regarding the power of the promoters in the Network, one label president said, "They're in a position to keep any record, no matter how good, no matter how much of a hit it is, off enough stations to prevent it from going up the charts and thus becoming a hit. In other words, if the labels don't pay, their records don't get played."[4]

The RIAA held a meeting of top label executives the day after the Grammy awards, after first issuing a statement countering the NBC charges. According to its statement, the trade group

> has no knowledge that any firm or individual with whom our companies do business is engaged in any illegal activity, contrary to reports in recent televised network broadcasts. If law enforcement agencies were to inform us that such individuals or firms are engaged in any illegal activities, we will take immediate and decisive corrective actions. Until such time, we find it unjustified and distressing that the recording industry is so indiscriminately maligned by insidious innuendo. Such broad and unspecified allegations unfairly taint the innocent. They also detract from the monumental contributions of the industry to American and international humanitarian and charitable causes.

More trouble loomed for the industry on February 27 when a New York federal grand jury investigating payola issued a sweeping subpoena to the RIAA, demanding all RIAA documents pertaining to record company relations with independent promoters.[5]

After the television program aired other industry insiders spoke out.

Other estimates were that labels paid $50–$60 million annually to a small group of freelance promoters around the country to promote their disks. While much of that money was used legitimately, an unknown portion went on payola. Biggest spender on independent promoters was thought to be CBS, which shelled out an estimated $10 million per year to promoters. Industry consultant and former programmer with WABC in New York City Rick Sklar said that some "independent promoters are largely money conduits who, by making regular payments to radio executives, exercise total control over the stations' play lists." James Carnegie, publisher of the trade newsletter *Radio Business Report*, stated, "it's done mostly in cash between a Mafia-like network of independent promoters and employees of radio stations and record manufacturers. The independent promoters have taken control of the business. They've carved up the territory. One guy says, 'You take Chicago, I'll take Philadelphia.'" The argument was that while payola was never extinguished after the 1960 scandals it had "surged dramatically" in the two years prior to 1986. This resurgence was due, it was said, to a comeback in that period at many FM radio stations of Top 40 format broadcasting, more generally called then contemporary hit radio (CHR) programming. Besides cash, payola took the form of other considerations such as drugs, women, cars, real estate, and so on to employees of selected radio stations to get them to add records to their playlists that were not hits or report fictitious plays on the air — known in the trade as "paper adds." A second element was that some promoters kicked back part of the promotion money received from labels to executives of those same labels. While this latter charge would surface now and then during the 1980s payola hype, it would never be seriously investigated. An estimate from one source was that promoters received as much as $150,000 from a label to "create" a Top 40 record.[6]

More publicity was generated when just three days after Cox appeared on the NBC program he mysteriously disappeared. When he reappeared Cox claimed he had been beaten by four men and drugged. He spent ten days in the hospital. No police report was filed by Cox nor would he talk to FBI agents who questioned him after the attack. As one news story put it, "the entire account of his disappearance is sketchy and unconfirmed — and likely to remain that way." Described as a "DJ with a flair for self-promotion and a 1981 cocaine conviction," Cox stated that his description of cocaine payoffs on the NBC show referred to the past "late sixties, seventies," and even at that only things he had heard about, not witnessed or been a party to himself. The deejay claimed he was "manipulated" by NBC who interviewed him for 90 minutes, only five minutes of which were with regard to payola. The network responded "We're proud of that story, and . . . not aware of any problems with it."[7]

McDaniel had worked for MCA Records from 1979 to 1985. During his early years with that company he had done local promoting in the Carolinas, where he claimed he was concerned over the fact that station adds he had obtained on particular records were being credited to independent promoters, including Cleveland-based Gary Bird. "I'd call in those adds to Pat Pipolo (former MCA promo vice president) and he'd tell me that Bird had already called them in," McDaniel recalled. "I think that's where my problem began with those guys." At the same time McDaniel told station program directors that they should deal with label promotion people, not the independents who were taking away jobs from staffers. While he had no proof of payola, he stated, "I think a certain percentage [of p.d.'s] were on the take." When he left MCA in March 1985 McDaniel claimed he was fired at the instigation of Bird, due to his vocal opposition to the use of independent promoters. MCA denied having fired McDaniel at all, reporting the parting was amicable; and that McDaniel's position was eliminated during a company restructuring and never replaced. "We are surprised that Mr. McDaniel is making these claims, since upon leaving the company, he acknowledged in writing that he had no claims or concerns of any kind whatsoever against MCA Records." McDaniel agreed he'd signed that statement but did so only because he was broke and MCA offered him $5,000 in severance pay if he'd sign. Immediately after leaving MCA McDaniel set up his own independent record promotion firm, which he claimed was driven out of business within one year because independent promoters threatened to retaliate against any label that did business with him. Bird denied that he was a factor in getting McDaniel fired. He also thought it was strange that McDaniel claimed to be opposed to independent promotion since, when he left MCA, he immediately set up an independent firm of his own.[8]

Within days of the NBC payola stories being aired the major labels responded in dramatic fashion. Warner-Elektra-Atlantic (WEA), RCA, Arista, Capitol-EMI, and MCA Records all publicly severed ties with independent record promoters, while CBS was giving the matter "serious study." A spokesman for Warner said that WEA made a similar move back in 1982, but after seeing their business decline as a result WEA "made the decision to go back" to using them. President Elliot Goldman of RCA said that while RCA and Arista had no knowledge of "wrongdoing by indie promoters they were concerned about the perception of our industry by the public." Goldman said the embargo would hold until investigators were finished and "the facts are known." Besides severing ties with independent promoters, Capitol-EMI announced it had retained a legal firm to review its antipayola program which required all promoters — staffers or independents — "to submit periodic sworn confirmations they do not participate in payola activities." Capitol president Bhasker Menon said, "Although we have no evidence to support the NBC allegations, the necessary and responsible corporate conduct must be to reassure ourselves that our company does not contribute unwittingly to any problem that may exist. Two days after we suspended the use of independent promoters, we learned from the Recording Industry Assn. of America that federal grand juries are investigating the situation. We believe this is the only appropriate manner of determining whether any unlawful activity prevails." MCA records simply announced it had suspended the use of some independent promoters. This was taken to mean specifically Isgro and DiSipio at least.[9]

Response from radio stations to the NBC allegations ranged from ridicule to outrage over the possible damaging effect to the industry from such charges. Program director Larry Berger of WPLJ New York said, "On the subject of payola in regards to WPLJ it's impossible to imagine anyone even offering us payola. . . . In 1966 I was music director at WWRL New York. I went to lunch with a promotion guy who handed me a napkin over the table. I opened the napkin and there was money in it. I handed it back. No one offered it to me since. I play music because I love it. Station WCAU Philadelphia vice president Vince Benedict, Jr., said, "I've run what has been one of the biggest CHRs in the U.S. for several years now. I am not naive, but I simply have not seen payola. No one has ever hinted at offering me anything that could be construed that way." Former station owner Bruce "Cousin Brucie" Morrow said there were enough checks and balances to guard against payola. "What concerns me," he said, "is that we still haven't rallied from the 1950s investigation. . . . The pre-payola days of being able to walk in and get a record played that afternoon. . . . That just doesn't happen anymore." He termed the NBC probe a "witchhunt," a comment echoed by others. Jay Boulely, program director at WSPT Stevens Point, Wisconsin, reported he "has had some indications" of payola from independent promoters over the previous few years but, he said, "I just get off that subject as quickly as possible and return to the business at hand." Those indications never reached the point where he had to refuse to deal with any specific promoter. He added, "There are some stations we laugh at because of the length of their play lists."[10]

The FCC announced that while it was aware of the NBC program the agency was not involved in any ongoing investigation. Chief of the commission's enforcement division, Charles Kelley, stated, "Payola — and getting someone to go on the record with allegations — is a very elusive matter. We have received complaints about payola activities of independent promotion people on a regular basis, but when we run them down, they don't bear fruit. It's very difficult to find people to go on record . . . because they don't want to admit to something that will involve their own illegal activities." In a brief editorial *Billboard* called for the music industry to be more vigilant; it applauded the suspending of independent promoters by some of the labels, while warning the business, "Radio and the record industry have long been sitting on a time bomb. . . . The ticking is getting louder; for radio and the record industry, this may be the last chance to defuse the bomb."[11]

One week after most of the major labels announced the severing of ties with independent promoters the last of the major labels, CBS Records, PolyGram Records, and A and M Records followed suit. Both CBS and PolyGram indicated their moves were provisional and could be reversed, depending on the outcome of the federal investigation. CBS said it was "unaware of any illegal activities involving the domestic independent record promotion firms that we employ," but that it was "concerned about the negative impression of our industry that may have arisen from the recent wave of allegations." By this time it was reported that Los Angeles–based Isgro Enterprises, headed by Joe Isgro, was forced to shut down due to the disastrous impact the industry break had on the company. Isgro executive Danny Davis claimed, "A multi-million dollar operation, in 36 hours, is done, gone and 30 people are in the street." Davis couldn't understand how Isgro could be "charged, tried and convicted by the media and have his empire go down the drain." Philadelphia-based Fred DiSipio's firm had also shut down, according to unconfirmed reports.[12]

Many small, independent record promotion companies who promoted the much less remunerative albums — instead of Top 40 singles — saw their business cut back as all the independent promoters became tainted by the scandal. Generally, they didn't receive bonuses for landing airplay reports on specific stations, as Top 40 promoters often did. Lenny Bronstein of Heavy Lenny Promotions promoted albums at 260 key album rock stations in North America for a fee of a few hundred dollars a week. On average he felt he made less from six months of continuous work on a project than certain Top 40 promoters did in a week. Mark Beaven of Advanced Alternative Media, which did album oriented rock promotion, estimated his fee at about $3,000 to work an album for 10 weeks at college and commercial radio, dance clubs, and retail — over 400 weekly and bi-weekly contacts. After paying his expenses for a staff of six Beaven remarked, "That doesn't leave room for payoffs. There's barely enough to pay salaries."[13]

Major labels such as Capitol-EMI and MCA even cut out independent country music promoters from their Nashville offices, leaving these men to complain since payola had never been publicly associated with country music. One of these affected was a firm called Chart Attacks whose president, Stan Byrd, commented, "There just isn't enough money in country to be passing it on to radio." A group of these promoters got together to discuss forming some type of trade association. A split developed, with some wanting to wait out the storm hoping the majors would resume using them while others took a harder line, suggesting they work at moving disks from small labels at the expense of the majors. The MCA label told its talent not to hire independent promoters personally, while Capitol left that option open to its acts, refusing to advise its artists one way or another. Country promoter Sam Cerami proposed that the group take out an ad maintaining their innocence in *USA Today* or some other national consumer publication, saying, "We've got to show the world — not just the manufacturers — that we're honest." Promoter Beau James argued that the layoffs should not be met with lower fees. "We've got to keep our prices up there," he insisted, "because when this blows over we don't want them to say 'I can get you for $1,000 or $700.'" Country independent promoters then earned reportedly between $1,500 and $2,000 per record.[14]

One group happy with the reported demise of independent promoters was the independent distributor group. They had long felt themselves virtually locked out of CHR, lacking both the money and contacts to push their products in that area. Hiring independent promoters themselves was thought fruitless as they felt the promoters devoted more energy to records from their more lucrative major label contracts. Eric Paulson, president of Midwest independent distribution company Navarre, noted, "How many CHR hits have indie labels-distributors had in the last few years? None, that's how many. Many of our promotion people have no reason to walk into CHR radio. We can't get our records played. Now, things may have been equalized."[15]

Virtually every group associated with the music industry felt compelled to publicly respond to the allegations made by the NBC program. Jeff Baumann, general counsel of the NAB, explained it had long been an NAB practice to inform its members about such issues saying, "I don't think we're going to say anything about all this until we know more about the charges being made." The most recent NAB document on the issue was a "payola alert" in a June 1985 newsletter. Within a couple of weeks of the NBC program, the NAB added payola and its prevention as a formal discussion topic at its forthcoming convention. In addition, the group sent out a special payola primer to its 4,630 radio members. This primer suggested certain "control devices" to be implemented to stop payola. In addition, employees were reminded of their obligations. A sample affidavit of compliance that station employees could sign was also part of the primer. While paper adds didn't appear to break any FCC rules in the opinion of the NAB, the primer read, "the misreporting of such information by phone may violate the Federal Wire Fraud statute. Additionally those engaged in such practices could be opening themselves to civil suits for fraud ... a finding by a court that a station had engaged in fraudulent practices might well be considered by the FCC as bearing on the licensee's character qualifications." Vice president of the National Radio Broadcasters Association (NRBA), Peter Ferrara, said, "we take the position that it's a serious problem — if it's real . . . but I have the feeling the press wants to make more of it than it actually is." He added, "where there's smoke, there's fire," but wondered "if it's a match stick rather than a bonfire." The NRBA sent out a payola primer to its members in 1985, then followed it up with an update later that year.[16]

Pat McLain, a counsel for the House Subcommittee on Oversight and Investigations, which had dropped its probe in 1984 due to no credible evidence, commented, "All we've received this past week is press calls. . . . But no, we haven't heard from anyone coming forward with new allegations." While the names of several independent promoters had surfaced during the House subcommittee probe, no one was able or willing to testify as having witnessed wrongdoing. The subcommittee's doors had been left open during the 17 months that had passed but no one had come forward. "We made it clear that if we were able to find any evidence or anything substantial, we would go to Dingell at once," explained McLain. During the current spate of news stories on the issue McLain read of one individual who told a reporter that the current payola scene would make "Watergate look like a picnic." Recalled McLain, "He was one of the first people we interviewed. He couldn't come up with any evidence either." Federal probes intensified, with investigations reportedly underway in Los Angeles, New York, and Newark involving the IRS, the Justice Department, and the FBI. These investigations were looking into not just payola but the general possible involvement of organized crime in the music industry.[17]

Black music people were relieved by the NBC payola allegations, since the very lack of black involvement in independent promotion at that level meant, said one black manager, "there will be very few black fingers in those pies." Columnist Nelson George summed up the situation when he wrote, "the prevailing view is that the exclusion of black staffers from major labels' pop departments, the lack of black independent promotion people working pop product, and the relatively small budgets given black promotion departments leaves most industry blacks on the outside looking in with this particular issue. If there is a certain smugness in these attitudes, it is because many black music veterans feel that past payola investigations focused, quite unfairly, on black music alone."[18]

Anger over the layoffs of independent promoters was most often expressed by artists' managers. Frank Dileo, a former vice president of promotion for Epic and then manager of Michael Jackson, said he was satisfied when he used the independents for Epic and that it was money well spent. He felt managers couldn't afford to pay for independent promotion themselves, citing a cost of as much as $125,000 for a Top 40 number as opposed to $20,000 for AOR (album oriented radio), which he thought managers might be able to afford for their clients. With regard to the NBC allegations, Dileo remarked,

I think as usual the record companies overreacted to the point where they cut everybody out, which was unnecessary. They did it without even investigating, without even giving anybody a chance to say 'yes' or 'no' or defend themselves. It's kind of sad that they took a guy like Joe Isgro and basically put him out of business and never asked him if anything was true. Who is to say that NBC is correct? I've worked with Joe Isgro, Fred DiSipio — all the guys. They always did a wonderful job for me; they conducted themselves as businessmen. . . . What they did to Joe Isgro is a crying shame. . . . If I was Joe I'd not only sue NBC, I'd sue every fucking record company. I'd sue them for antitrust, for getting together and boycotting him.[19]

Some managers felt the whole issue was generated by the labels to bring down the costs of independent promotion, while others wondered what the labels were doing with the money allocated for independent promotion which was now saved. Steven Machat, who managed John Waite and New Edition, among others, remarked, "I wouldn't be surprised if the record companies concocted the whole thing themselves as a means to bring down the prices they were paying the indies." Foreigner's manager, Bud Prager, noted, "The labels have been waiting for the day when they could stop. It's cost such a fortune. But now, the question is: Will the record companies pocket the money?" Managers mostly supported the use of independent promoters as being very valuable in breaking material and as an essential source of information. Money spent by the labels on independent promotion was considered a marketing expense and was thus not recoupable against artist royalties. However, this was of course taken into consideration when contracts and royalty percentages were negotiated with artists. Doc McGhee, comanager of Motley Crue and Bon Jovi, described independent promoters as a "necessary evil. Anything that costs a lot of money to an artist is an evil to me." Motley Crue went Top 10 with "Smokin' in the Boys Room" without independent help at Elektra, but Doc acknowledged that independents played a large part in breaking Bon Jovi with PolyGram. Butch Stone, manager of Krokus, commented that independent promoters were crucial locally because "When you're on tour you really need to know if there are albums in the stores and to what degree the visibility's there. There's no substitute for having someone who can actually go to the store. . . . I've used the information I've gotten from independents to plug holes more than anything else."[20]

On April 2, 1986, Senator Albert Gore, Jr. (Democrat, Tennessee), announced a full-scale investigation by the Senate's Permanent Subcommittee on Investigations into promotional practices in the record industry and what he called "the new payola." Gore was a member of the 1984 House subcommittee preliminary probe into payola while a representative from Tennessee's sixth district. The senator alleged payola was more extensive than in the past, involved much larger sums of money, and was organized into "fiefdoms" throughout the country. Said Gore, "The cumulative evidence is overwhelming that this practice has gotten completely out of hand and has come to dominate some portions of the industry in their decisions as to what records got on the air and which ones didn't. . . . Recent disclosures in the public media as well as the announcement by the Justice Department that grand juries have been convened to investigate this and other matters, make it clear that something is wrong." While he thought all aspects of the record industry were involved, Top 40 format was the area in which the senator felt payola was most pervasive. Asked about any new evidence uncovered by his staff Gore was unable to answer except to say that "some people in the industry are now more willing to speak up." Denying that he had been approached by record labels to hold an investigation, Gore did say, "the record companies are the ones, I would say, who are most anxious about stamping this out." What had been broken, thought the senator, was the "conspiracy of silence" that prevented the House subcommittee from coming up with credible evidence. Claiming "the tide had turned," Gore believed industry sources would talk. "Our goal is not to establish the basis for criminal prosecutions," he said, "but to determine whether or not current laws are working and whether changes are necessary." Gore promised that after interviews were held in places such as Los Angeles and New York public hearings on payola would be held by the Senate subcommittee. A spokesman from the House Oversight and Investigations Subcommittee, chaired by John Dingell, said they had no plans for any further investigations. "In fact, in the absence of any forthcoming evidence, we certainly won't," he said.[21]

One year after this probe was announced it was "put on hold" and was "way on the back burner." The formal announcement by Gore's staff of the probe's end made official what insiders had suspected for months. No official reason was given but Gore announced that month his intention to seek his party's nomination in the 1988 presidential race. A Gore staffer said problems concerning committee jurisdiction arose when committee assignments changed after the 100th Congress convened in January 1987. Also Gore's former chief investigator in the probe took a job in the private sector.[22]

Another NBC report on payola aired on the "NBC Nightly News" on March 31. This show alleged that CBS Records had been the heaviest user of independent promotion men and that CBS Records president Walter Yetnikoff played a key role in blocking a proposed investigation into independent promotion by the RIAA. Citing no specific errors in the news clip, Thomas Wyman, chairman of the board of CBS, contended that following an "intensive investigation" by CBS the company had "no reason to believe that CBS people have been involved in condoning or participating in the activities suggested. . . . Most especially I would underline to all of you that Walter Yetnikoff has been a leader in the industry in every sense. We are extremely unhappy that this broadcast shed any unfavorable light on his distinguished career." The NBC network stood behind its story claiming Yetnikoff declined repeated requests to appear in the news segment, adding that Wyman's comments "were unfortunate and his words ill-chosen. NBC News does not do second-class work."[23]

Meanwhile, Joe Isgro alleged the RIAA wanted to use electronic surveillance and outside detective agencies as part of its proposed investigation into payola and independent promoters. Isgro said he acquired a copy of an RIAA memo containing estimates from two detective agencies to do the work. According to the promoter, this memo was the product of an initial meeting on the subject of payola by attorneys and "just a few record company presidents." It wasn't a secret document and it was not minutes to the meeting. This was the proposal by the RIAA, given to each person who attended that meeting, to take back to their respective companies for a follow-up meeting to make a decision on the proposals of the two different agencies and which one they should use. I believe at that time, when the attorneys took it back to their companies and presented it to the executives at the labels, from what I gather the presidents went bonkers and said 'what are you planning here?'" The RIAA agreed it had considered a payola investigation but refused to give details of the plan. Regarding the memo Isgro spoke of, the RIAA would neither confirm nor deny its existence, claiming that since all material concerning independent promoters had been subpoenaed by the U.S. attorney the RIAA could not comment.[24]

Rolling Stone reported that early in 1986 at a closed meeting of the RIAA a secret ballot was held among label heads, or their representatives, to determine whether the RIAA should look into independent promotion to see if anything illegal was going on. The CBS label and at least one other voted against it, causing the RIAA not to pursue the investigation since they didn't have unanimous support from the labels. According to this account, rates for independent promotion ranged from $1,500 to $15,000 a week for getting a new record played on a single important radio station. It was reported that CBS Records spent at least $25 million a year on independent promotion out of the estimated $60–$80 million annual total. Some industry sources claimed that major label executives had been getting kickbacks from certain independents, kickbacks that ranged from 10 to 25 percent of what the label paid the independent promoter.[25]

One important music industry trade publication was *Radio and Records* (*R and R*). Each week around 12 of its pages were devoted to listing the records played on approximately 250 CHR stations which reported their play lists to *R and R*. These stations were divided into three groups: Parallel Ones, or P-1s, were the approximately 62 most important stations in the country, stations that reached one million or more listeners as well as being ratings leaders or strong contenders in their markets; P-2s and P-3s were less influential. *R and R*, headquartered in Los Angeles, based its hit record lists on these reports, giving more weight to P-1s than to P-2s and P-3s. Labels and promoters were only interested in these radio stations that reported to *R and R*. If they could get a record added to enough P-1s and P-2s it would look like a potential hit to *R and R*'s editor Ken Barnes, who said: "But we can't be too upset about how it's being used. We can't control how they use it." Commenting on how the top independent promoters functioned as brokers, one label executive said, "They'll be paid a certain amount for a record and they in turn will hire other indies. Instead of dealing with eighty indies, you might hire Fred DiSipio for $100,000 and Joe Isgro for $100,000 and they might dole it out to thirty other indies."

Some independent promoters received a flat fee every week for promoting a certain label's records. In addition, they frequently got a bonus for each station they could deliver. While rates varied, a P-3 station cost about $250–$300, a P-2 cost $500–$1,000 and a P-1 ran as high as $5,000. Some labels reportedly paid double or triple to certain stations, pushing a P-1 as high as $15,000 to get one record added to its playlist. To get this money the independent promoters either actually got the record added to the station playlist or got a "paper add" in which a station reported to *R and R* that it added a disk which it wasn't even playing. Ken Barnes said, "paper adds have been — and, to a lesser extent, continue to be — a problem." Barnes said *R and R* warned 20 stations in 1985 about paper adds and after that the magazine dropped "a couple of stations that were giving us a lot of paper-add information." In some cases the promoter simply paid the station program director to supply him with a list of the actual adds before they were published in *R and R*. The independent promoter then reported to the labels he was responsible for these adds, collecting his fee. According to industry sources, between 18 and 27 of the 62 P-1 stations were "owned" or controlled by the independents. Labels, therefore, worried that if they didn't use and pay these independent men these promoters had the power to keep their disks off the airwaves at those outlets. So they paid them. The independent promoters gave payola in the traditional forms of cash, drugs, other tangibles such as automobiles, fur coats, and women, as well as reports of the use of threats of physical violence to get their records played or at least onto the playlists.[26]

Within a few weeks of the airing of the NBC payola story and the suspension of independent promoters by the major labels, those same promoters were plotting their return. Some started up new businesses — "marketing consulting firms" — and were rumored to be already back on the payrolls of some labels. A phone call to Boston-based promoter Jerry

Brenner was answered, "Northwest Marketing." One band manager said, "As we talk they're working out new arrangements with the record companies." In other cases some of these independent promoters were added to labels as staff. Fred Deane, son of DiSipio, was hired as director of AOR promotion by PolyGram, while Motown Records hired Chuck Cliner who previously worked for Midway Marketing, a DiSipio company. Al Perry, who previously worked for Jerry Brenner, was hired by Geffen Records.[27]

Less than two years after this particular scandal broke the use of independent promoters was reported to be as entrenched as ever. Records from every major label had been worked by independents during the previous few months. Bob Catania, vice president of promotion at Island Records, claimed that during any given week the independents worked about 15 of the Top 20 records. Major labels continued to insist they were not currently using the independents but everyone else in the industry disagreed. Most of the main CHR independent firms who were in operation before the story broke were still in business. Said Catania, "It's 98 percent the same guys. Everybody's still there."

Some of the independents were being paid to get airplay for 20 or more different singles each week. To hide the transactions, labels turned to funneling money to middlemen who in turn dealt with the independents. Cory Robbins, head of Profile Records, commented, "They do it through the managers, they do it through the artists, they do it through the publishers. The checks don't come from the labels themselves in many cases, although the label may actually be paying the bill. Why is that? I use independents, but I pay them a Profile check. I'm not ashamed of it." One of the main CHR independent men said, "Right now the only difference at all is the name on the check. Even though the check may come from the manager, what's the difference? The labels are involved." Fees received by the independents were less than before the scandal. While it was not uncommon for a label to have paid a promoter as much as $150,000 to break a single before this scandal, in early 1988 the top figure was around $80,000. Commonly, the independents were then paid an average of $1,200–$1,500 for each CHR station they got to play a record, with a top of $2,000. In the past promotion money was paid by the labels and was not charged to the artist. Now, when money was funneled to the managers that money was, like a recording budget or tour support, recoupable. If the record became a hit the artist had to pay this money back before collecting royalties. Artists' managers continued to talk about "bought" stations — outlets where the independent promoter effectively controlled the playlist through the program director. Catania, who made extensive use of independents, said, "I pay these guys to help me in places where I can't have as strong a relationship. A lot of these guys have relationships going back ten, fifteen years." In the industry some thought the power of the independent promoter was less than it used to be while others thought it was as great as ever. Helping the independent men to regain their position was the fact that almost two years after this particular payola scandal broke nothing had happened; no indictments had been issued.[28]

Shortly after the scandal broke in 1986 the *National Review* came out with an editorial "In Praise of Payola." They wondered why "a perfectly sensible form of promotion" that benefited both consumers and producers of newer and lesser known products — a type of promotion practiced in most retail businesses — would be considered scandalous when applied to the record industry. "Supermarkets accept 'new product fees,' in exchange for which they provide choice display space to new items seeking a market. Many retailers accept substantial subsidies from producers in the form of below cost prices on heavily promoted items. So how did it become scandalous and illegal, for record companies to pay radio stations to play their records?" Financing the production of a record was not the major cost — promotion of the record was. Therefore, promoting it usually required national marketing muscle, something acquired over the years at a great cost by the major labels. It was this that made a recording contract with a major label so important. This editorial writer argued that allowing simple payola — cash for airplay — made the record business more competitive, making it easier for smaller and newer companies to break into the business. "It is in the collective interest of major record companies to outlaw payola: If artists can't buy their way onto the air, they are dependent on the major companies and their connections. Of course once payola is outlawed it is in the interest of the major companies to break the law, which they apparently do, with the aid of Mafia-linked 'promotional specialists.'" Legal payola, it was argued, would help poorer artists and smaller companies, plus give consumers fewer commercials since stations would have another source of income. In summing up the payola situation this editorial writer remarked, "The old rule still applies. If you hear some dummy shouting unfair competition, look for a ventriloquist owned by a cartel."[29]

Joe Isgro formally demanded a retraction of "false and defamatory statements" made by NBC within a couple of weeks of the airing of the first two segments of its payola story. The segment which aired after Isgro made his demand was notable in that it didn't mention Isgro at all. Described as a hothead who got his own way, Isgro denied all the allegations made against him saying, "I'm destroyed. My whole business was ruined by insidious innuendo. In thirty-six hours I have been accused, tried and found guilty for nothing. My business is destroyed." In his independent promotion firm he had employed 30 people. "We cover the entire West Coast. We probably call 150 radio stations, bring them up to date on the product, make sure they've got the record, promote them on it, tell them what's happening around the rest of the country," he explained.

Isgro did admit he was aware of disreputable independents but would not elaborate.[30]

On April 30, 1986, Joe Isgro filed a multimillion dollar lawsuit against the major record labels and the RIAA, charging them with antitrust violations in their sudden termination of independent promotion services. The only major label not listed was CBS Records. The suit accused those named with conspiring to restrain and monopolize independent promotion starting "at least as early as 1985." The subsequent boycott was characterized in the suit as a "collective refusal spurred by the defendants' intention to eliminate competition for indie promotion services and the spiralling fees that competition produced." In so doing, it was alleged, the labels conspired to fix prices for promotion services, limiting freedom of choice among labels in determining their own means of product promotion.[31]

As time passed most of the 12 labels named in Isgro's suit settled out of court. Amounts and reasons for settlement were not divulged, although Lawrence G. Papale, the promoter's attorney, confirmed the settlements involved payments to Isgro of hundreds of thousands of dollars. "We're looking for some money. This is not an academic exercise. Joe's looking to recoup lost profits," said Papale. These settlements made it easier for all independent promoters to resurface and return to business as usual — along with a lack of grand jury indictments against anyone. These settlements were used by the independents as "proof" that the independents had not violated the law. Promoter Ralph Tashjian, an associate of Isgro, remarked, "Why are all these record companies settling? If everybody is so fucking guilty, why are all the record companies settling?"[32]

Federal grand juries in New York and Los Angeles began investigating payola very soon after the story broke in 1986. Subpoenas were issued to most major labels, requesting documents concerning the companies' use of independent promoters. As time passed nothing came out of these investigations. Some legal sources worried that this "new payola" might not be prosecutable under existing payola laws. Independent promoters were said to be sidestepping payola laws by paying radio program directors broad consultancy fees — thus not directly paying to get specific records on the air. However, rumors at the end of 1987 were that the Los Angeles grand jury had uncovered evidence of more than $1 million exchanging hands between promoters and program directors at radio stations. Rumor had it that at least one programmer testified he had received payola from promoter Ralph Tashjian and that Tashjian would be soon indicted.[33]

By early 1988 the grand jury investigation was still underway, then close to two years old. While all the information gathered was still not public, sources indicated the chief targets were Joe Isgro and Ralph Tashjian who were being probed by the Los Angeles strike force of the U.S. Department of Justice's Organized Crime and Racketeering Section. According to accounts Isgro's operations brought him millions of dollars each year from the major labels. From the early 1980s onward he sent weekly cash payments via Federal Express to radio program directors and musical directors who then submitted station reports favorable to the disks Isgro was working to the industry trade charts. One source said, "A lot of cash went through the mail, between $3,000 and $5,000 a week. The money was split each week among a rotating group of between four and eight program directors and music directors, drawn from a pool of as many as thirty different radio station executives." Tashjian, who worked out of the same suite of offices as Isgro, worked as a subcontractor, sometimes providing cocaine and women to program directors as payola. Said another source, "Ralph was more or less the unofficial social director. He told me that in party situations with program directors, he would sometimes provide the cheap thrills — broads, booze or dope. Isgro knows better than to get near any of that stuff himself, so he would wink and look the other way while Ralph took care of business." Yet another source claimed that Isgro at least once confronted Tashjian about his methods: "Joe Isgro went absolutely fucking berserk. He told him to get rid of the hookers and to get rid of the cocaine." Isgro's attitude was that "everybody had a price. He felt he could buy anybody at any time."

Joe was the liaison to the labels while Ralph worked the radio stations. Often Isgro would receive $150,000 or more per week from the labels. It was Tashjian's job to get the records added to the playlists of radio stations around the country. Ralph worked as many as 60 records each week. Each Wednesday when *Radio and Records* published its weekly lists Tashjian would go over them, totaling up the adds doing some computations. Isgro wrote a check — usually for between $3,000 and $5,000 — to Ralph Tashjian for promotion. Ralph could cash the check immediately, prepare Federal Express envelopes with cash, and send them off to program directors, paying for the adds. Isgro felt he was insulated from the actual cash transactions. An individual program director might receive $1,000 or more each time. "There were twenty or thirty program directors or music directors who consistently got money. Some got it every other week," alleged one insider. Reportedly, Isgro billed record labels for obtaining adds at about 10 stations that neither he nor Tashjian had any relationship with. He simply called the stations the day before the *R and R* lists came out and got the names of their playlist adds, then, claiming responsibility, billed the labels for these record adds. Such claims were said to be common practice among independent promoters, with major labels prepared to look the other way in order to retain favor with powerful independents. Described by one associate as a "Mafia groupie," Isgro was also reported to have threatened anyone else who tried to claim credit for his stations. "I'll wreck you," or "I'll ruin your business," were frequently overheard telephone remarks.[34]

Indictments by the federal grand jury in Los Angeles were finally handed down on February 25, 1988, when two music promoters, the wife of one, and a former radio executive were indicted on charges of tax evasion and paying over $260,000 in cash and cocaine to get records played on the air. Also named, but not indicted, were program directors and other employees of nine radio stations in eight cities as receiving this payola from 1980 to 1986. Some of these people were reported to have cooperated with the authorities. Two of the stations were in Fresno, California, with one each in Atlanta, Cincinnati, El Paso, Kansas City, Jacksonville (Florida), Memphis, and Charlotte (North Carolina). U.S. attorney Robert Bonner said the indicted promoters "were acting on behalf of virtually all record companies in this country but that there was no evidence the record companies had been aware of payments for playing records." He declined to say if more indictments were expected. Charged was Tashjian who was accused of giving cash, cocaine, and other valuable considerations to radio station employees. Among the records he pushed were "Wild Boys" by Duran Duran and "Principle Of" by Robert Plant. Ralph and his wife Valerie were also charged with failure to report income in the amount of $303,988 over a three-year period beginning in 1983. Promoter William Craig of Scottsdale, Arizona, was accused of making illegal payments to get records on the air and attempting to evade income tax. Among artists whose records he promoted were Janet Jackson, Culture Club, New Edition, and the Eurythmics. George Wilson Crowell, a former vice president of station KIQQ in Los Angeles, was charged with failing to file federal income tax returns for 1984, 1985, and 1986. Allegedly, he received $100,000 in payola to play certain records over that period.[35]

Following those indictments, grand juries were said to be at work in several other cities including New York, Newark, Philadelphia, Miami, and Cleveland, along with collateral investigations by various IRS offices. Bonner remarked, "Continuing investigation is needed to probe a payola problem of significant dimensions. It's clear that there continues to be a payola problem in the industry. How pervasive and widespread it is will only be revealed after further investigations." He reiterated that "no evidence has yet been uncovered indicating that the record companies were aware that independent promoters were illegally making payments to radio station personnel . . . just about every label you can imagine and just about every artist you can imagine" had records that were payola pushed by those indicted. It was alleged that Craig, who also worked with Isgro, distributed $212,650 between 1982 and 1986 to radio programmers at five stations. Specifically, it was said he paid $22,700 to Sidney Kennedy of WCIN Cincinnati; $31,300 to Odell Rice, Jr., of KPRS Kansas City; $61,500 to Larry Tinsley of WAOK Atlanta; and $97,150 to Chris Turner of WLOK Memphis, WGIV Charlotte, and WJAX Jacksonville. Rice commented, "I'm just a little guy out here in the Midwest . . . I don't know what's going on," adding that he "never met Bill Craig, never asked for payola in my life," and filed "any money I've ever gotten with the IRS." Bonner singled out Kennedy, Tinsley, and Rice as having cooperated in the investigation. Tashjian was charged with distributing $40,000 and various quantities of cocaine to Johnny Lee Walker of KYNO Fresno, an unspecified amount of cocaine to Edward Carey of KMGX Fresno, and $18,000, cocaine, and other valuable considerations to Robert Brulte of KAMZ El Paso between 1980 and 1985. The Tashjians were arrested on February 25 and released the next day when a U.S. magistrate in San Francisco angrily rejected a government request that Ralph be held without bail. The government was also scorned by the judge for arresting the couple at home in front of their children, despite attempts by the Tashjians to turn themselves in prior to the indictments. Meanwhile, strike force chief John Newcomer was asked why he had given MCA Records a letter several months previously assuring the company "it was not a target" in the record business investigation, even though an active investigation was under way and no advance clearance was therefore warranted at that time. Newcomer explained the clearance didn't relate to payola but to other racketeering allegations involving the record industry then also being probed. Most of the stations named in the indictments had a policy which required their programmers and on-air employees to sign an affidavit stating they were familiar with payola laws and recognized the station did not condone payola.[36]

Estimates were that Isgro was paid $7 million a year or more by the major labels to promote their disks. William Craig acknowledged he had paid hundreds of thousands of dollars to program directors between 1982 and 1986 but claimed those programmers worked for him as consultants and that all payments were declared on his corporate income tax forms. He denied that any of the money was paid out for airplay.[37]

A couple of months after the indictments were handed down investigators with the Los Angeles strike force were reported to be probing involvement in the payola scheme by major label executives, despite Bonner's statements that all such labels were unaware of the alleged illegal activities. Investigators believed some executives were involved in kickback schemes whereby they shared some of the millions of dollars they paid out to the independent promoters. Walter Yetnikoff, CBS Records president, estimated that CBS paid the independents $12.8 million in 1985, although other sources put the figure close to $17 million. Warner Brothers spent nearly $6 million on independents in 1985; MCA spent $9 million; and A and M spent over $2 million. Under oath at a deposition in 1987 Irving Azoff, head of MCA Records, testified that Yetnikoff "once told me that one reason CBS supported the indie system was that he felt it made the cost of entry for, shall we say, new upstart labels so high to get into the record business." During 1985 alone Isgro received $4.5 million from CBS labels for promotion. In addition, Isgro owned a record label, Private I, that was distributed by CBS until early in 1986. Even though CBS conducted its own internal investigation of independent promoters, which disclosed no impropriety, evidence indicated otherwise. Sid Sheinberg, president of MCA, told CBS executives in the fall of 1985, "In our judgment the questions raised by rumors concerning the practices of independent promoters in the record industry require the attention of corporate management." He suggested if something wasn't done about the matter it could erupt into a public scandal—which it did four months later. Mo Ostin, chairman of the board of Warner Brothers Records, acknowledged that he and other executives had been troubled by the activities of independent promoters for years. Reportedly, Bill Craig made a $5,000 kickback payment in the mid-1980s to Jheryl Busby, an MCA executive. Craig admitted making the payment, denied it was a kickback, but couldn't recall the reason for the payment. Being checked by investigators was an alleged payment by Isgro to Ray Anderson, then an executive at CBS's Epic label, of $10,000 worth of "Rodeo Drive clothing." The CBS response to this was, "The whole thing doesn't deserve any comment." Isgro was said to entertain lavishly label executives in Las Vegas, paying all the bills while often carrying over $100,000 in cash with him. Six months after being indicted Tashjian was quoted as saying, "All I know is that my business is doing better than ever."[38]

A year after the indictments were issued the government worked out a plea bargain whereby the Tashjians would be allowed to plead guilty to fewer charges in exchange for Ralph's cooperation. This agreement fell through in court when Valerie broke into tears claiming she had been coerced into pleading guilty in order to save her husband from additional charges. The Justice Department denied this. However, the judge threw the plea bargain out. Subsequently, the three original counts of payola against Ralph were replaced by an indictment listing 168 specific payola charges. These alleged violations took place between January 1984 and October 1985 involving records from the RCA, Epic, A and M, Atlantic, Warner Brothers, Columbia, PolyGram, and Capitol labels. Artists on those records included Cyndi Lauper, Kenny Rogers, Eurythmics, Joe Jackson, The Go-Gos, Billy Joel, Prince, Bruce Springsteen, Paul McCartney, The Pointer Sisters, Queen, Julian Lennon, Mick Jagger, and Rod Stewart. On May 21, 1989, Tashjian pled guilty to one count of payola; specifically "Federal Expressing a small amount of cocaine to Mr. Carey Edwards of KMGX Fresno without reporting it. It was my understanding that it was for consideration for reporting or playing phonograph records." In this August 1984 incident were records of Laura Branigan (Atlantic) and Elvis Costello and Bruce Springsteen (both with Columbia). Tashjian placed on the record that "none of the artists or the two record labels were knowl-edgeable as to the activities alleged." Under terms of the plea all other pay-ola charges were dropped. Ralph also pled guilty to one count of subscrib-ing to a false tax return and one obstruction of justice charge. He faced a maximum sentence of nine years in jail and a $265,000 fine. The govern-ment's sentencing recommendation was to be based on "the extent of the cooperation of Ralph Tashjian as determined by the U.S. Dept. of Justice and the I.R.S." Ralph had agreed to aid the government, presumably pro-viding information on Isgro, still a main target of the feds. This marked the second conviction under the then 29-year-old federal payola statute. In December 1989, after Isgro was indicted, Tashjian was sentenced to 60 days at a half-way house, fined $100,000, ordered to perform 500 hours of community service, and placed on three years probation. Earlier Craig and Crowell had pled guilty. Craig was sentenced to 100 hours of com-munity service, a $60,000 fine, and five years probation.[39]

A source close to Tashjian said there was by then friction between Ralph and Isgro. "Ralph is very annoyed with Joe. I've heard Ralph say, 'Mother-fucker you didn't do anything for me, why should I stay quiet?'" Over at the other camp an Isgro insider reported Isgro as livid over a per-ceived betrayal. "Joe is crazed, fuckin' crazed. He thinks somebody turned on him. Joe feels Ralph gave up his wife, and he thinks that's reprehensible. He figures, 'If he gave up his wife, he must be giving me up.'"[40]

A few months after the NBC story broke in 1986 the FCC went on record to say they were not prompted to launch a probe of their own into payola. The agency's Charles Kelley said of the Gore and grand jury probes, "They're operating on their own. No one has talked to me." He added that the FCC had not received any "substantial allegations" about payola in recent months nor was it on any kind of "special alert" with regard to the subject. Such investigations were Justice Department matters since under federal law payola was a crime "in which the station is a victim." Payola occurred when "outside sources pay employees of broadcast stations to put things on the air without telling the licensee," explained Kelley. "Money is going to the employee for playing, in effect, a commercial." If the licensee knows about the payola he is then culpable not of payola but of violating regulations requiring stations to identify sponsored programming. Broadcasters could lose their license for such infractions.[41]

Two years later the FCC was holding one of its regular hearings to determine if Metroplex Communications, owner of Miami radio station WHYI, should have its license renewed. This renewal was challenged by another company which introduced evidence of payola. It was contended that record promoters gave WHYI's then program director Robert Walker drugs as an inducement to play their records. General manager of WHYI David Ross argued that even if a promoter supplied a station employee with a "vial of cocaine, maybe three or four inches long and maybe an inch in circumference it would not constitute payola unless it could be shown that the program director has added a record to the list in exchange for the drugs." Walker and current program director Frank Amadeo had engaged in reporting paper adds to *Radio and Records*. While this practice was generally condemned as dishonest, it was not illegal. Amadeo testified he knew paper adds were "wrong" but he made them under the direction of Walker as a "favor — to help out a record promoter." He said no paper adds had occurred since May 1985, although other sources said they took place as recently as 1986. During the 1980s record promoters arranged for name artists to perform without fee at concerts promoted by WHYI. Scottie Brothers Entertainment Industries — which included a record promotion arm — was one firm that promoted at WHYI. In early 1986, according to testimony, Scottie Brothers gave Amadeo and Walker four Grammy tickets, worth $1,400, prepaid round-trip airplane tickets to Los Angeles, as well as arranging hotel accommodation. Walker paid the hotel bill when the pair checked out, although he was billed for just one room. Amadeo was billed for the plane tickets by Scottie Brothers but it wasn't paid for a year and a half, by which time WHYI was under investigation.[42]

At the end of April 1988 an FCC representative said the agency would begin an inquiry into payola within the next month or two. It didn't happen. What did happen after the indictment of Tashjian was that House Telecommunications Subcommittee member Jack Fields (Republican, Texas) sent a letter to FCC chairman Dennis Patrick expressing concern about the reemergence of payola, and urged him to reaffirm and, if necessary, toughen antipayola policies. Fields urged the agency to consider an investigation "into the present use of payola in the radio and television industry. I am aware these actions may be complex and time consuming. However, I believe that FCC action now will send a strong signal that payola remains an unacceptable and illegal practice for broadcast licensees." Patrick decided not to hold an investigation, arguing that a 1976 probe turned up one station involved in payola but otherwise "produced little in the way of useful results." He added, "Accordingly I am of the view that such an investigation at this time would be premature and likely duplicative of the efforts of the Justice Department." However, the FCC voted unanimously to issue a "warning" to broadcasters outlining the provisions of the Communications Act that outlawed payola and spelled out the consequences. Patrick said it was a "propitious time to set forth the law and remind those in the broadcasting and record business that the FCC will take appropriate action when warranted. . . . This is a good way to let people know we are alert to the issue and that it is a serious issue from time to time." FCC commissioner Jim Quello commented that payola is not as prevalent as it once was, "but what little we do have, let's stop it."[43]

At the end of November 1989 the Los Angeles grand jury issued a 57-count indictment against Joe Isgro, naming a host of charges including racketeering, conspiracy to defraud Columbia Records, making payola payments to radio stations, mail fraud, filing false tax returns, conspiracy to distribute cocaine, and conspiracy to impede the Internal Revenue Service. Also indicted were Raymond Anderson and Jeffrey Monka, a former business associate of Isgro. Both were charged with conspiracy and engaging in a scheme to defraud Columbia Records through a series of kickbacks and the use of the U.S. mail for illegal activity. If convicted on all charges Isgro faced 200 years in prison and $1.4 million in fines. Isgro's own antitrust lawsuit against the dozen major labels and the RIAA had resulted in an out of court settlement with all the parties, except for MCA Records and Warner Brothers. A judge dismissed Isgro's charges against those two firms in 1988. Specifically, the indictment alleged Isgro dispensed payola in the form of money and cocaine to various personnel of radio stations KIQQ Los Angeles, KYNO Fresno, KMGX Fresno, KAMZ El Paso, and other stations. Money paid out was alleged at $70,000 or more along with an unspecified amount of cocaine. A former federal prosecutor said he was pleased to see the action taken against Isgro but believed the record labels knew of Isgro's activities and that some of their officials should have been charged too. Industry officials watched nervously, fearing Isgro might make damaging allegations against labels and their officials. Said one industry expert, "If he goes down, he'll take people down with him."[44]

In the wake of these indictments most within the industry claimed payola was not widespread. Washington air personality Cerphe Colweel said payola was out there but was certainly not prevalent. Former radio executive Gary Stevens remarked, "With very few exceptions, no one radio station is that important to merit payola." Where it did exist it was felt that Top 40 format outlets were far more susceptible to payola than other formats such as classic rock or album oriented rock because they programmed current hits and more singles than other formats. The Isgro indictment referred to 1985. Since that time all four radio stations named had been sold. Two of them changed their call letters. Simon T, general manager of KQLZ (formerly KIQQ), remarked on the payola indictments: "if 20 stations out of 10,000 are involved in payola, then the amount is only two-tenths of 1 percent." What bothered many in the industry were the vague definitions involved. Just what, they wondered, constituted payola. Scott Shannon, program director at KQLZ (FM) commented, "Only the government calls it payola, but the same thing is rampant in the Defense Department." More cynical was the broadcaster who felt the government was picking on the radio industry. "Congress loves to go after the media," he said. FCC chairman Alfred Sikes admonished, "The combination of drugs and payola, when shown to exist among broadcast licensees, involves a violation of the public trust which cannot be tolerated. The commission will act . . . to assure that our communications systems remain free of these totally improper influences. The commission will be following this matter closely to see if there is licensee involvement."[45]

In an unsuccessful motion to have the charges against him dropped on the ground of government misconduct, Isgro asserted he was "the fall guy" for a government investigation of MCA Records that had gone awry. According to Isgro, the investigation of himself stemmed from a squelched probe of MCA's links to reputed mobster Sal Pisello who was convicted of tax evasion. The promoter's lawyers argued that the government ended the MCA probe for political reasons then decided it had to indict Isgro to justify the wide reaching investigation. Several ranking Justice Department officials reportedly told attorney Marvin Rudnick to halt his investigation of MCA and instead investigate Isgro. Eventually, Rudnick successfully prosecuted Pisello, was removed from the case, and then fired by the Justice Department. Much of these allegations had been made already in the press and on television, causing Isgro's prosecutors to say his motion "seems to have been gleaned from newspaper clippings which featured a disgruntled former Justice Department employee who was discharged" — a reference to Rudnick. The MCA label declined any comment with a terse, "We are not a party to this litigation."[46]

When Isgro and the others came to trial at the end of August 1989 George Crowell testified he had received cash payments of about $100,000 a year from the promoter in the mid–1980s. In return for the money Isgro gave him a list of records each week that were to be played several times a day on KIQQ where Crowell was then general manager. None of the charges against Isgro included any accusations that he engaged in illegal activities at the request of the labels that employed him or that he did so with their knowledge. A one-time head of promotion at Motown and then EMI Records, Isgro went into business for himself as an independent promoter at the end of the 1970s. At the time of this trial some 5,000 records were released annually in the United States, each one trying to become a hit. Industry observers felt that payola was paid to radio stations not to guarantee a hit record but to prevent falling into a competitive disadvantage compared to other companies that were paying off stations. "You can't really buy a hit," said one observer. "What you can buy is access to the gatekeepers, which allows your record to get a shot. But they won't play records that don't get a good response."[47]

Crowell said he got $750 for each add. Every week anywhere from 0 to 10 of Isgro's records would be added to his station's playlist. Often Isgro was so anxious to have certain records broadcast on KIQQ that Crowell would sometimes be offered double payments. Since KIQQ had one of the largest audiences in the country, other stations often followed its programming lead. Payment to Crowell was often made by Isgro's bodyguard, David Michael Smith, in the men's toilet of restaurants in Los Angeles. Smith confirmed Crowell's account. Most of the money was gambled away by Crowell, causing him to tap Isgro for loans, payola advances, and help with his mortgage. Isgro's attorney didn't deny his client may have given money to Crowell but said the funds were not payola, "but to help him out." Tashjian and Carey testified as to the deals they did, with Ralph claiming that every time he told Isgro that he was supplying money or cocaine to radio programmers the response was always: "Be careful, but do what you gotta do."[48]

During the trial Tashjian admitted he had reentered the record promotion business, handling many of the labels he and Isgro had worked in the past. Among the labels he said he indirectly represented through his company, Modern Music Marketing, were Warner Brothers, Atlantic, Elektra, and Island. Admitting he had erred in the past, Ralph said, "everybody deserves another chance." He declined to say how much the labels were paying him.[49]

Not long into the trial federal Judge James M. Ideman called a halt when he ruled the federal prosecutors had violated rules of evidence in the case by withholding a key document from a grand jury and the defense attorneys. Defense lawyers had earlier been told the previous trial testimony did not exist. Ideman adjourned while he studied the earlier material. At issue was the testimony of key government witness Dennis Di Ricco who, said Ideman, in Di Ricco's appearance before the Los Angeles grand jury told "a story against the defendants that was diametrically opposed in every respect" to his statements at his own trial in San Francisco. The two statements by this witness were said to differ on no less than 74 points. In between these two statements Di Ricco cut his own deal regarding sentencing on his trial with the federal authorities. Early in September Ideman dismissed the case against Isgro and others, citing "outrageous government misconduct." Calling the prosecutors' case against Isgro suspect, the judge tongue-lashed the prosecutors for "intentionally withholding evidence because they feared its devastating effect on their case." By dismissing the charges "with prejudice," an extremely unusual measure, Ideman made it virtually impossible for new indictments to be brought against Isgro. Charges could not be refiled unless Ideman's ruling was overturned on appeal. So important was this case to the Justice Department that they deployed senior litigation counsel William S. Lynch from Washington, D.C., to handle it. It was Lynch who let slip in judge's chambers a remark indicating he was aware of the existence of the earlier Di Ricco testimony, which allowed Isgro's side to track it down. The sudden end of this payola probe of several years' duration left many frustrated and the Justice Department with virtually nothing to show for it. Attorney Marvin L.

Rudnick, who led the Los Angeles probe in its early years, remarked, "I'm very disappointed that an experienced prosecutor could have blundered so badly. . . . There is clearly payola going on in the record industry. I wish the U.S. attorney general would make the same effort to find out what went wrong with other prosecutors as when they moved me out" of the case. Isgro said, after the charges were dismissed, that he would return to work as an independent record promoter.[50]

When the case ended no one, except maybe Hipolito Vega, had ever served even one day in jail for payola. The FCC statute against payola was further weakened back in 1979 when the FCC ruled that "social exchanges between friends are not payola." It allowed station employees to do drugs or receive money from promoters, claiming the items were shared on a social basis among friends and not in exchange for plugging a specific disk.[51]

By the end of 1990 Isgro was busy trying to reestablish his record promotion company. Business had fallen off considerably since the publicity over the trial with the result that he had diversified, focusing more on film projects and management of recording artists. Said Isgro, "I've been painted as the bad guy. Yet I've been convicted of nothing. . . . This case has affected me for a good five years and it's been difficult to put it out of my life."[52] In the fall of 1991 the prosecutor's appeal of Isgro's dismissal had been pending for one year. Nothing has been reported since.[53]

Having oneself listed as cowriter of a song one didn't pen remained a part of the music industry in the 1980s and 1990s. Narada Michael Walden, a producer at Columbia Records, was honored by ASCAP in 1986 as Songwriter of the Year for Whitney Houston's "How Will I Know," which he "cowrote." That song was the most performed song in the ASCAP catalog that year, earning the group's Song of the Year award. Actual writing credit belonged to Shannon Rubicam and George Merrill, both members of BMI and not ASCAP. "We were so happy to get the break of having a track on a Houston album," that according to Rubicam and Merrill, they didn't protest too much when Walden insisted on cowriter credit for making arrangement changes in the song's bridge. It was precisely the kind of minor item which producers were expected to do and for which they were paid by their record company employer. Martin Kirkup, spokesman for the two songwriters, said Walden "did some rearranging, and we agreed on a percentage." Rubicam and Merrill lost 20 percent of their royalties to Walden, about $250,000. The director of a major music publishing house remarked in 1992, "Our artists are frequently approached by producers who want coauthor credit for making changes in an arrangement—changes that weren't essential."[54]

Currently payola is not much in the news; which is not to say it has disappeared or has waned to any degree. Chances are it has not. No efforts to eradicate it have succeeded and, given the structure of the music industry, none ever will. When payola does receive widespread media attention it is often because other issues are involved, such as music industry infighting as in ASCAP versus BMI, or attacks on music genres, as in rock bashing. Payola has existed for well over a century, is an integral part of the industry and, for many in the industry, it works.

While the established music business may grumble about payola now and then, they are mostly content to work with it. At times they become annoyed when they feel they are all paying out payola just to avoid having their records fall into the no-play pile, as opposed to receiving extra plays. Even then, though, they see it as useful in helping to keep new companies out of the arena or at least making entry more expensive. Annoyance with payola, on the part of the established industry, becomes greatest when a new company has enough resources behind it to attempt to bid up the payola price for all companies. It is then that cries to eliminate payola may be heard at their loudest.

Normal business practices in other industries could very well be considered payola in the music business. A food manufacturer with a new cereal, for example, often gives grocers a deeper discount on this new product for a time if in return the grocer agrees to give the product a certain amount of shelf space. In both the food and music industries there are far more products than there are spaces to put them. In food merchandising it is a standard business practice; in music merchandising it is payola.

Attempts to eradicate payola by attacking the recipients, or gatekeepers, are doomed to total failure. In response to the 1959–1960 scandal, some radio outlets took away from their disk jockeys the right to create their own playlists for their shows. Instead the station program director took over those duties. As a result the director suddenly found himself on the receiving end of payola. The group which comprises music business gatekeepers has, and will, change but there will always be gatekeepers and payola will always be directed to them.

Payola is also crucial to the industry as it is so dependent on radio airplay, and now to a lesser extent on music video exposure. In the cereal example above if the company could not buy shelf space it could still mount a big ad campaign in magazines, billboards, television, and so on. Rarely does the music industry do anything like that, certainly not for an unknown artist with a first release. Efforts are geared almost exclusively to radio exposure. A record must be played and heard before it is bought.

Long before we had television, or radio, or records, the music industry had payola. It still does. It always will.

NOTES

1. Not Enough Singers to Go Around, 1880–1899

1. "Plug Payolas Perplexed," *Variety*, October 19, 1938, p. 41; "Payola's Roots: Usage of 1960's," *New York Times*, March 6, 1985, p. A14; and Abel Green, "Payola Origins and Angles, " *Variety*, March 16, 1960, p. 56.

2. *Oxford English Dictionary*, 2d ed., Oxford: Clarendon, 1989, vol. 11, p. 381.

3. William Boosey, *Fifty Years of Music*, pp. 26–27.

4. "Music Biz Goes Round and Round," *Life*, May 16, 1960, p. 120.

5. Edward B. Marks, *They All Sang*, p. 32; and Isidore Witmark, *From Ragtime to Swingtime*, p. 95.

6. Witmark, *From Ragtime to Swingtime*, pp. 89–90.

7. Ibid., pp. 60, 63.

8. Goldberg, *Tin Pan Alley*, pp. 112, 125, 126.

9. Ibid., p. 169.

10. Ibid., pp. 169–70.

11. Jim Walsh, "No Copyright on Payola," *Variety*, January 4, 1961, p. 236; "Songs of Sixpence," *Newsweek*, April 1, 1957, p. 104; and Goldberg, *Tin Pan Alley*, p. 206.

12. Goldberg, *Tin Pan Alley*, pp. 206–07.

13. Witmark, *From Ragtime to Swingtime*, p. 150.

14. Ibid., pp. 165, 166, 169, 172.

15. Goldberg, *Tin Pan Alley*, p. 105.

16. Marks, *They All Sang*, p. 4.

17. Ibid., pp. 59, 66; and Bernard Sobel, "Pre-Electronic Plugging: Booze-ville to Vaudeville," *Variety*, January 9, 1957, p. 242.

18. Witmark, *From Ragtime to Swingtime*, p. 222; and Sobel, "Pre-Electronic Plugging: Booze-ville to Vaudeville," p. 242.

19. Goldberg, *Tin Pan Alley*, pp. 200–01.

20. Ibid., pp. 198–99.

2. The Payment Evil Runs Wild, 1900–1929

1. Michael Freedland, *Irving Berlin*, pp. 20–21.

2. Gerald Bordman, *Jerome Kern*, p. 26.

3. Edward B. Marks, *They All Sang*, p. 115.

4. Ray Walker, "Veteran Songplugger Recalls Glamour of Early Tin Pan Alley Era," *Variety*, January 2, 1952, pp. 227, 246; "All Song Pluggers Barred," *Variety*, November 26, 1915, p. 3; and "Plugging 'Sweet Adair,'" *Variety*, January 21, 1916, p. 4.

5. "Among the Music Men," *Variety*, April 9, 1920, p. 23.

6. Walker, "Veteran Songplugger Recalls Glamour of Early Tin Pan Alley Era," pp. 227, 246.

7. Joe Santly, "Life and Plugs of a Music Man," *Variety*, October 20, 1954, p. 59.

8. Ben Bloom, "Song Plugging — Then and Now," *Variety*, January 4, 1950, p. 217.

9. "Published Songs," *Variety*, December 20, 1912, p. 32.

10. "Music Publishing Combine Proposed by Wall Street," *Variety*, November 28, 1913, p. 1; and "Precarious Music Publishing May Be Followed by Reforms," *Variety*, January 9, 1914, p. 7.

11. "Music Publishers' Meeting for Protective Purposes," *Variety*, June 19, 1914, p. 6.

12. "Singers Want Publishers to Stop Plugging," *Variety*, July 3, 1914, p. 6.

13. "Music Publishers' Combine Working Out Satisfactorily," *Variety*, July 24, 1914, p. 6; and "Singers of Song," *Variety*, September 11, 1914, p. 38.

14. "Song Plugging Agents May Be Complained Of," *Variety*, December 3, 1915, p. 5.

15. Isaac Goldberg, *Tin Pan Alley*, pp. 206-7; Jerry Wexler, "Pluggers War on Payola," *Billboard*, October 29, 1949, p. 47; Abel Green, "Corruption in the Music Biz . . . II," *Variety*, February 22, 1956, p. 41; and "Music Men Desperate," *Variety*, February 18, 1931, pp. 69, 74.

16. Abel Green, "Selling Side of Song Plugging," *Variety*, January 7, 1942, p. 156.

17. Marks, *They All Sang*, p. 152.

18. "Paying Music Publishers Threaten Legal Action," *Variety*, May 26, 1915, p. 5.

19. "Music Publishers Expect Prosperous New Season," *Variety*, October 6, 1916, p. 7.

20. "Music Publishers May Get Together for Protection," *Variety*, October 6, 1916, p. 3.

21. Isidore Witmark, *From Ragtime to Swingtime*, pp. 287-93.

22. "Popular Sheet Music Price Going Up If 10¢ Stores Raise," *Variety*, January 19, 1917, p. 5.

23. Abel Green, "Desire to Curb Payolas an Old Story, with Sime the Original Author," *Variety*, May 12, 1943, p. 45; Green, "Corruption in the Music Biz . . . II," p. 41; and Herm Schoenfeld, "Today's Disk Payola New Chapter in Long History of Music Biz Corruption," *Variety*, June 13, 1973, p. 1.

24. "Payments for Singing Songs to Be Stopped by Publishers," *Variety*, April 27, 1917, p. 3.

25. Ibid.

26. "Music Men Meet," *Variety*, May 18, 1917, p. 3.

27. "Music Publishers Meeting," *Variety*, August 24, 1917, p. 3.

28. "Popular Song Publishing," *Variety*, December 28, 1917, p. 8.

29. "Song Hit via Records," *Variety*, April 4, 1919, p. 3.

30. Harry G. Henn, "The Compulsory License Provisions of the United States Copyright Law, 1957," and W. M. Blaisdell, "Economic Aspects of the Compulsory License in the Copyright Law, 1958," both in *General Revision of the Copyright Law*.

31. "Music Publishing Combine Proposed by Wall Street," p. 1; and "Music Publishers' Combine Working Out Satisfactorily," p. 6.

32. "With the Music Men," *Variety*, August 15, 1919, p. 10.

33. "Song Pluggers to Be Barred Back Stage," *Variety*, April 30, 1920, p. 4.

34. "Keith Office Will Shut Off Song Pluggers' Applauding," *Variety*, December 2, 1921, p. 4; "Chicago Plugging Nuisance Gets Managerial Attention," *Variety*, April 28, 1922, p. 4; and "Obnoxious Music Pluggers," *Variety*, April 28, 1922, p. 10.

35. "Among the Music Men," p. 23.

36. "News of the Music Men," *Variety*, May 6, 1921, p. 4.

37. "Plug Seen in Vitaphone's Canning," *Variety*, November 3, 1926, p. 51.

38. "Song Writers' Union Started," *Variety*, November 12, 1920, pp. 5, 7; and "Music Men," *Variety*, December 3, 1920, p. 14.

39. "Cutting-In on Songs Can Work Two Ways," *Variety*, May 6, 1925, p. 49.

40. Herbert G. Goldman, *Jolson*, pp. 131–32.

41. "Among the Music Men," p. 23.

42. Abel Green, "Abel's Comments," *Variety*, March 4, 1925, p. 40; and "Singers Tied Up to Single Music Publishers Barred from WEAK or WJZ," *Variety*, August 31, 1927, p. 6.

43. Harry Richman, *A Hell of a Life*, pp. 25, 97, 98.

44. Goldberg, *Tin Pan Alley*, p. 227.

45. "English Music Publishers Stop Payments to Singers," *Variety*, May 12, 1922, p. 2.

46. Green, "Abel's Comments," p. 40.

47. "Melody Songs Passing — Lyrics Now," *Variety*, February 3, 1922, pp. 1, 7; "Paying the Pluggers," *Variety*, January 4, 1928, p. 29; and "Gus Kahn, Tells of Isham Jones," *Variety*, January 18, 1928, p. 54.

48. "Inside Stuff — Music," *Variety*, June 27, 1928, p. 57.

49. "Radio Orchestra Leaders Now Going for Cut-Ins," *Variety*, March 14, 1928, p. 56; and "Inside Stuff," *Variety*, April 13, 1927, p. 55.

50. Guy Lombardo, *Auld Acquaintance*, pp. 121–23.

51. Ibid., p. 76; and Booton Herndon, *The Sweetest Music This Side of Heaven*, pp. 115, 117–21.

52. Lombardo, *Auld Acquaintance*, pp. 97, 98.

53. Ibid., p. 112; and Herndon, *The Sweetest Music This Side of Heaven*, p. 125.

54. Rudy Vallee, *Vagabond Dreams Come True*, pp. 223, 224.

55. Rudy Vallee, *My Time Is Your Time*, pp. 120–21.

56. Ibid., pp. 129–32.

57. Ibid., pp. 121–22.

58. "With the Music Men," p. 23; and "No Song Plug Pay," *Variety*, January 27, 1922, p. 7.

59. "M.P.P.A. Junk Didn't Stop Independent Becoming Foremost Music Publisher," *Variety*, February 16, 1927, p. 49; and "M.P.P.A. Executive Invites Robbins-Engel, Inc., to Resign," *Variety*, March 2, 1927, pp. 45, 48.

60. "Paying the Pluggers," p. 29.

3. Everybody Is More or Less Disgusted, 1930–1939

1. Tom Landry, "The Song Pluggers' Microphone," *Variety*, December 31, 1930, p. 48.

2. "Chicago Picks 13 Bands, 4 Singers as De Luxe Plugs for Music Biz," *Variety*, October 17, 1933, p. 47.

3. "Leaders Dodging Pluggers," *Variety*, December 31, 1930, p. 49.

4. Ibid.

5. "Pluggers Must Alibi Missing Ether Plugs," *Variety*, November 19, 1930, p. 57; Abel Green, "Publishers Do Forcing of It," *Variety*, April 22, 1931, pp. 67–68; "Ban on Plugs Boosts Coast Music Biz," *Variety*, February 25, 1931, p. 62; and "N.Y. Hotel Wants to Bar Song Pluggers and Doesn't Mince Words," *Variety*, January 9, 1934, p. 37.

6. Guy Lombardo, *Auld Acquaintance*, pp. 123, 132, 133.

7. Ibid., p. 177.

8. "NBC Limiting Music Plugs to 2 Nightly," *Variety*, April 1, 1931, p. 59; "Song Pluggers Now Must Write In for Appointments with NBC Air Acts," *Variety*, July 18, 1933, p. 64; "Song Pluggers Nixed by NBC," *Variety*, September 11, 1935, p. 49; and "Radio Song Plugging Now via Adv. Men," *Variety*, August 6, 1930, p. 66.

9. "Song Pluggers Revolt but Want It Kept Secret," *Variety*, December 3, 1930, pp. 65, 67; "Industry's Reaction to Payoff Evil One of Disgust," *Variety*, August 7, 1935, p. 49.

10. "No Publishers' Cut-In Worry on Coast," *Variety*, March 4, 1931, p. 64.

11. "Inside Stuff—Music," *Variety*, November 12, 1930, p. 73; "Pluggers Must Alibi Missing Ether Plugs," p. 57; "Leaders Taking Song Cuts," *Variety*, December 17, 1930, p. 58; and "Resolution Is Aimed at Evil," *Variety*, April 1, 1931, p. 59.

12. "Inside Stuff—Music," *Variety*, March 12, 1930, p. 55; "Special Arrangement Slip," *Variety*, December 3, 1930, p. 67; "Play from the Pubs," *Variety*, May 13, 1931, p. 92; and "Band's Free Plug Ideas," *Variety*, July 9, 1930, p. 58.

13. Green, "Publishers Do Forcing of It," pp. 67–68; and "Music Men Desperate," *Variety*, February 18, 1931, pp. 69, 74.

14. Green, "Publishers Do Forcing of It," pp. 67–68; and "Whiteman Audition for Song Pluggers Weekly," *Variety*, October 27, 1931, p. 61.

15. Green, "Publishers Do Forcing of It," pp. 67–68.

16. "Cut-ins with Results," *Variety*, April 8, 1931, p. 67; and "Inside Stuff—Music," *Variety*, January 28, 1931, p. 78.

17. "Plug Paying Evil Sticking," *Variety*, May 21, 1930, p. 57; "Pubs Reverting to Stage Acts for Song Plugging," *Variety*, September 17, 1930, p. 64; and "Makes Pugs for Plugs," *Variety*, November 19, 1930, p. 57.

18. "Radio Gives Plugs—Yes, and Takes Coin—Plenty," *Variety*, November 10, 1931, p. 61.

19. "Industry's Reaction to Payoff Evil One of Disgust," p. 49.

20. "M.P.P.A. Cuts Penalty as Means to Enforce No Act-Paying Edict," *Variety*, June 11, 1930, p. 57.

21. "Line of Action to Be Determined by M.P.P.A. on Harmful Practices," *Variety*, February 18, 1931, p. 69; and "Gov't Appeal, Cut-Ins for Small Pubs," *Variety*, March 11, 1931, p. 68.

22. "Music Men Desperate," pp. 69, 74; and "Publishers to Meet Over Chiseling," *Variety*, February 11, 1931, p. 73.

23. "Resolution Is Aimed at Evil," p. 59.

24. "Cut-In Regulations Issued for Guidance of Music Publishers," *Variety*, April 22, 1931, p. 67.

25. "Am. Soc. Cut-In Ban Not Retroactive," *Variety*, April 29, 1931, p. 83.

26. "No Complaints on Cut-Ins, ASCAP Is Asking for All Data to Make a Case," *Variety*, June 2, 1931, p. 57; and "Cut-In Rule Cuts Cut-Ins 50% to Date," *Variety*, July 14, 1931, p. 49.

27. "Music Code's Anti-Bribery Song Plugging Subsidies Out," *Variety*,

July 25, 1933, p. 45; and "Bribery Without Eye-Link Escapes Mention in Music Publisher Code," *Variety*, January 30, 1934, p. 45.

28. "Radio-Music's Get-Together on Bribes," *Variety*, August 21, 1934, p. 39; and "NRA's Paid Plug Joker," *Variety*, November 27, 1934, p. 45.

29. "Name Plug Royalty Out," *Variety*, April 24, 1934, p. 47; and "Inside Stuff — Music," *Variety*, June 5, 1934, p. 47.

30. "MPPA Pact Asks for Squealers," *Variety*, June 19, 1934, p. 62.

31. "Bandmen Face Code Action," *Variety*, July 17, 1934, p. 41.

32. "Inside Stuff — Music," *Variety*, August 28, 1934, p. 43; and "Publishers Ask Paine to Modify Bribery Pact," *Variety*, February 27, 1935, p. 53.

33. "Paine Hands Publishers Written Spanking," *Variety*, July 24, 1935, p. 47; and "Paine, for Publishers, Asks Gov't to Intervene Against Paid Plugs," *Variety*, September 11, 1935, p. 49.

34. "Inside Stuff — Music," *Variety*, April 18, 1933, p. 48.

35. "BBC Takes Hold and Song Plugging Graft Evil Now Looks Dead in Eng.," *Variety*, July 25, 1933, p. 45.

36. "Publishers' Double-X Routine Keeps British Air Plug Evil Alive," *Variety*, May 22, 1935, p. 46; and "So You Think You Got Trouble," *Variety*, June 24, 1936, p. 63.

37. "$42 Arrangers' Fee Evil Bobs Up Again," *Variety*, March 16, 1938, p. 38; "Song Plugging," *News-Sheet of the Bribery and Secret Commissions and Prevention League*, August/September, 1936, p. 57; and "B.B.C. Band Leaders," *News-Sheet of the Bribery and Secret Commissions and Prevention League*, April/May, 1939, p. 17.

38. "Trade Commish Eyes Plugs," *Variety*, July 1, 1936, p. 37.

39. "Paine Promises Self-Cleansing," *Variety*, July 29, 1936, p. 39.

40. "MPPA's Anti-Bribery Code Pledged by Pubs," *Variety*, September 2, 1936, p. 42; and "To Orchestra Leaders, Vocalists and All Other Users of Music," *Variety*, September 2, 1936, p. 43.

41. "Maestros No-Like Anti-Bribery Pledge," *Variety*, September 23, 1936, p. 45; "MPPA Sleuths Find Little Bribery," *Variety*, October 7, 1936, p. 45; and "Chi Bribery Evidence Placed Before Paine," *Variety*, October 14, 1936, p. 49.

42. Paul Ackerman, "Ackerman Statement to Payola Probers," *Billboard*, May 9, 1960, p. 8; and Jerry Wexler, "Pluggers War on Payola," *Billboard*, October 29, 1949, p. 47.

43. "FTC's Own Music Code More Stringent Than Pubs' Rules," *Variety*, November 4, 1936, p. 45; and "MPPA Committee Defers Meeting with FTC Till McKee Studies Gov't's Code," *Variety*, November 18, 1936, p. 53.

44. "Leader, Quizzed on Bribery Rumor, Claims MPPA's Code Has Put Him $1,900 in Red," *Variety*, December 9, 1936, p. 41.

45. Ibid.

46. "Pluggers' Bribery of Dance Bands Again Reported on Increase as New Groups Hit Manhattan Spots," *Variety*, May 19, 1937, p. 47.

47. "Indie and Pop Pubs Plan to Attend FTC Probe on Music Biz," *Variety*, September 22, 1937, p. 45.

48. "Two-Hour Session Before Trade Body," *Variety*, October 6, 1937, p. 46.

49. "Music Trade Rules Ready," *New York Times*, December 16, 1937, p. 42.

50. Dave Dexter, Jr., "Origin of the Species," *Billboard*, December 27, 1969, pp. 56, 58.

51. R. Serge Denisoff, "The Evolution of Pop Music Broadcasting," *Popular Music and Society*, 1972, 2:204 n. 3.

52. "Radio," *Newsweek*, January 11, 1936, pp. 42–43; Orbin E. Dunlap, "Song for Sale," *New York Times*, January 12, 1936, sec. 9. p. 15; and "The Music Goes Round," *New York Times*, January 19, 1936, sec. 9, p. 4.

53. "Buck Holds Radio Kills Songs Today," *New York Times*, September 9, 1936, p. 30.

54. Abel Green, "Songmen's Social Graces," *Variety*, August 11, 1937, p. 47.

55. "MPPA Acting on CBS' Squawk," *Variety*, November 25, 1936, p. 47; and "Chicago Pluggers Out of Pocket as Cafés Operate Plenty Crude," *Variety*, May 4, 1938, p. 47.

56. "Pluggers Forming Own Organization to Suppress Bribery," *Variety*, August 25, 1937, p. 45; and Green, "Songmen's Social Graces," p. 47.

57. "KYW Song Rule No Hit with Pluggers," *Variety*, April 20, 1938, p. 39.

58. "Maestro-Publishers No Menace," *Variety*, March 31, 1937, p. 53.

59. Thomas A. DeLong, *Pops: Paul Whiteman, King of Jazz*, p. 211.

60. "Royal Warning NBC Employees and Outside Music Men on Logrolling," *Variety*, March 2, 1938, p. 39.

61. "Bribery Concerns ASCAP," *Variety*, March 9, 1938, p. 47; and "Gotta Really Write 'Em," *Variety*, March 2, 1938, pp. 39–40.

4. Everybody Swears Off Payola, 1940–1949

1. "English Publishing Biz Falters Along Hampered by Germans and Grafters," *Variety*, June 11, 1941, p. 36.

2. "Payola Rears Its Ugly Head Again in London Town," *Variety*, November 29, 1944, p. 38.

3. "BBC Band, Music Dept. Head Hit on Payola Rap," *Variety*, March 26, 1947, p. 45.

4. "BBC Key to Britain's Pop Tune Payola Evil, Sez Reg Connelly," *Variety*, April 30, 1947, p. 46; and "Song Pluggers Restricted by New Closed Mouth BBC Policy on Tunes," *Variety*, June 4, 1947, p. 42.

5. "BBC-Brit. Pubs Propose Severe Payola Penalties," *Variety*, March 10, 1948, p. 43; "Life for British Plug Bribe Artists' Heave-O; Pubs Nixed 2 Yrs," *Variety*, April 7, 1948, p. 43; "Plug Pay Killed Brit. Pubs Beef Bands Sluff Pops," *Variety*, June 16, 1948, p. 42; and "B.B.C. Statement on Song-Plugging," *News-Sheet of the Bribery and Secret Commissions Prevention League*, June 25, 1948, p. 178.

6. "NBC Bars Out All Pluggers," *Variety*, March 13, 1946, p. 49; and "Song Pluggers Unionize; Bribery Their Problem," *New York Times*, May 5, 1940, p. 12.

7. "Drastic New Anti-Bribery Rules Aim to Outlaw Payola from Music Biz," *Variety*, December 3, 1941, p. 51.

8. "3 Suns 'Sing' on Bribes," *Variety*, April 14, 1943, p. 45.

9. "Pluggers' Proxy Warns Bribery Rife Again," *Variety*, December 1, 1943, p. 37; "Pubs on Carpet as Contact Men's Union Launches Drive Vs. Payola," *Variety*, February 9, 1944, p. 44; and "Suggest Deletion of Payola Rules, But CMU Sez Nix," *Variety*, May 10, 1944, p. 27.

10. "Contact Men's Assn. President Lists 9 Don'ts to Curb Payolas," *Variety*, September 13, 1944, pp. 37–38.

11. "Pubs Still Waiting for Payola Probe Results," *Variety*, July 18, 1945, p. 51.

12. "Music Pubs Mull Pressure on MPCE to Remove Plug Restrictions," *Variety*, August 15, 1945, p. 35; "Lifting Curb on Payolas Generally Agreed as Likely to Hypo Problems," *Variety*, October 17, 1945, p. 42; and "Major Publisher

Plans to Crack Payola Evil by Open Plug-Buying," *Variety*, October 24, 1945, p. 47.

13. "Contactmen Union Finds Publishers Lethargic in Launching of Move Vs. Payola," *Variety*, December 18, 1946, p. 51; "Pluggers Union Weighs 3 Gripes on Payola," *Variety*, March 5, 1947, p. 45; and "Pluggers Table Plans to Control Payola Racket," *Variety*, April 9, 1947, p. 42.

14. "Pluggers Drop Nix Vs. Pelham Heath," *Variety*, November 12, 1947, p. 45; and "Major Pub Up on Payola Charge," *Variety*, May 5, 1948, p. 51.

15. "Payola Situation (Here It Goes Again) Endangers Their Jobs, Pluggers Cry," *Variety*, October 26, 1949, p. 54.

16. "MPCE to Set Up Secret Trial Bd. to Halt Payolas," *Variety*, November 2, 1949, p. 43.

17. Jerry Wexler, "Payola Renunciation Draws Cheers, Jeers," *Billboard*, November 26, 1949, pp. 16, 37.

18. "Pubs Invited to Pluggers Payola Meet Not Subject of Finger-Pointing," *Variety*, November 30, 1949, p. 39; and "Pluggers, Pubs in Closer Tie to Erase Payolas," *Variety*, December 21, 1949, p. 33.

19. Jerry Wexler, "Pubbers Put the Payola Finger on Peatman and Himber Sheets," *Billboard*, December 24, 1949, p. 17.

20. "Plan Plug Bribery Cure," *Variety*, April 21, 1943, p. 43.

21. "MPPA Ok's Plan to End Plug Bribery," *Variety*, May 5, 1943, p. 43; and Abel Green, "Desire to Curb Plug Payolas an Old Story with Sime the Original Author," *Variety*, May 12, 1943, p. 45.

22. "Pluggers Call Kenny for Plug Infractions," *Variety*, August 18, 1943, p. 39; and "Pluggers Wanna Ask Nick Kenny Why He Violated Trade Agreement," *Variety*, April 10, 1946, p. 54.

23. "Inside Stuff — Music," *Variety*, December 1, 1943, p. 36; and "Plugless Payola," *Variety*, June 7, 1944, p. 35.

24. "Variety Back to Old Listings?" *Variety*, August 2, 1944, p. 31.

25. "Blowup Brewing on Payolas," *Variety*, November 21, 1945, p. 49; and "Payola Problem to Peatman," *Variety*, December 5, 1945, pp. 39, 44.

26. "Pluggers Wanna Ask Nick Kenny Why He Violated Trade Agreement," p. 54; and "Payola Problem to Peatman," pp. 39, 44.

27. "Pubs Say Payola System Snafued by Peatman Intro," *Variety*, January 16, 1946, p. 47; and "Payola Beef Breaks Out Anew on Coast, Plugger Investigation," *Variety*, May 22, 1946, p. 51.

28. "New Payola Beefs to Be Aired at MCPE Meet," *Variety*, September 18, 1946, p. 42.

29. Abel Green, "A Lot of Eyewash," *Variety*, October 1, 1947, p. 35; and "A–B–C of Plugs Holds," *Variety*, October 8, 1947, p. 44.

30. "Songs with Largest Radio Audience," *Variety*, October 29, 1947, p. 47; "Top Tunes and Recording Artists," *Variety*, September 17, 1947, p. 46; and "Top Record Talent and Tunes," *Variety*, October 29, 1947, p. 42.

31. "WOW Bandleader Offers BMI Plugs on NBC for $10–15 to Cover Cost of 'Arrangements,'" *Variety*, November 12, 1941, p. 45.

32. Green, "Desire to Curb Plug Payolas an Old Story," p. 45.

33. "Payola Diary Kicks Back," *Variety*, October 18, 1944, p. 39.

34. "Writer Sues Freddy Martin for 167G on Song Plug Pact," *Variety*, February 28, 1945, p. 39.

35. "Payola Beef Breaks Out Anew on Coast," p. 51; and "Pluggers Choose Trial Board to Prosecute Payola Evil," *Billboard*, November 5, 1949, p. 18.

36. "Spivak, Kaye Pub Deals at BMI Set New Basic Pattern," *Variety*, February 14, 1945, p. 43; "Music Pubs Mull Pressure on MPCE to Remove Plug Restrictions," p. 35; and "Major Publisher Plans to Crack Payola Evil by Open Plug-Buying," p. 47.

37. Arnold Shaw, *Sinatra*, pp. 57–58.

38. Barry Ulanov, *The Incredible Crosby*, pp. 186–87.

39. "'Mill Stream' Appeal Decision Seen as Setback to 'Cut-In' Songsmiths," *Variety*, February 28, 1945, p. 36; and "Unique Suit on 'Heartaches,'" *Variety*, November 19, 1947, p. 45.

40. "Income Tax Sleuths on Payola Trails?" *Variety*, July 19, 1944, p. 1.

41. Jerry Wexler, "Pluggers War on Payola," *Billboard*, October 29, 1949, pp. 3, 13.

42. "Martin Block Parlays a $20 a Week Idea into a New Radio Pattern," *Variety*, February 8, 1950, p. 33; and Ed James, "Will Petrillo Unseat the Jockeys?" *American Magazine*, December 1947, pp. 30–31.

43. James, "Will Petrillo Unseat the Jockeys?" pp. 30–31.

44. Ibid., p. 85.

45. "Wanted: A Code for Disk Jockeys," *Variety*, March 12, 1947, p. 52; "Pubs Recognize Effect on Disk Jocks' Hold on Public," *Variety*, April 10, 1946, p. 54; "MPCE to Set Up Secret Trial Bd. to Halt Payolas," p. 43; and "Pluggers Turn Guns on Jock Bally Gentry," *Billboard*, November 26, 1949, p. 16.

46. "The News of Radio," *New York Times*, October 13, 1947, p. 46.

47. "Jockeys Ride Herd on Disk-Buyers," *Variety*, May 19, 1948, p. 1.

48. "Disk Jockey Sidelines and Other Abuses Frowned On by Station Ops.," *Variety*, November 5, 1947, p. 49; and "Cal. Disker Wants to Cut Disk Jocks In on Distribution Gravy," *Variety*, January 14, 1948, p. 54.

49. "Disk Jocks Important Enuf Now to Be Cut In on Record Royalties," *Variety*, May 19, 1948, p. 1; and "Deejay Org. Airs Payola Reply," *Billboard*, February 19, 1949, p. 16.

50. R. Serge Denisoff, "The Evolution of Pop Music Broadcasting," *Popular Music and Society*, 1972, 2: 206 n. 3.

51. "Deejay Org. Airs Payola Reply,'" p. 16; and "Disk Jocks Would Use Shindig Coin to Nip 'Stigma,'" *Variety*, January 7, 1948, p. 196.

5. Pictures of Dead Presidents, 1950–1958

1. "Songpluggers No Vanishing Race," *Variety*, October 19, 1955, p. 44.

2. "MPCE Lists Lopez Unfair on Crack-Down on Payola," *Billboard*, January 14, 1950, p. 21.

3. "Payola — Over 5 Years Earlier," *Variety*, December 9, 1959, pp. 53–54; and "Publishers Annoyed by New Racket," *Billboard*, November 25, 1950, p. 16.

4. "Air Payola in Britain Disappears as Pact Succeeds," *Variety*, September 27, 1950, p. 43; and Jack Payne, "Jack Payne on Song Plugging," *Melody Maker*, July 17, 1954, p. 3.

5. "Labor MP Sees Payola Rearing Ugly Schnozzola," *Billboard*, December 7, 1959, pp. 3, 10; "Payola Charges Vs. British Jockeys Snarled in Parliamentary Debate," *Variety*, December 2, 1959, pp. 55, 68; "Two Tough Moves Against Payola," *Broadcasting*, December 7, 1959, p. 38; and "Press Inquiry into British Payola," *Variety*, December 16, 1959, p. 45.

6. "Payola May Be Hot in U.S., but It's Dead in U.K.," *Variety*, February 28,

1962, p. 51; and "Brit. Publishers Sound Payola Alarm Over Cut-In Demands by Radio Pirates," *Variety*, July 13, 1966, p. 35.

7. "BBC Radio Probes Payola Charges," *Variety*, February 24, 1971, p. 47; and "Scotland Yard Probe of BBC Disk Jockeys," *Variety*, April 7, 1971, p. 2.

8. "Role of Disk Jockey as the Middle Man," *Variety*, February 8, 1950, p. 34; Albert J. Elias, "The Reign of the Disc Jockey," *Etude*, March 1956, p. 18; and "The Richest Guys in Radio," *Variety*, December 29, 1954, p. 21.

9. Mike Gross, "Jock Stranglehold Spreads," *Variety*, August 3, 1955, pp. 41, 48; "Mr. Typical Spinner's Man of Many Talents, Interests," *Billboard*, November 12, 1955, p. 61; and J. P. Shanley, "Men Who Pick Disks for Radio Listeners," *New York Times*, May 1, 1955, sec. 2, p. 11.

10. "Widespread Payola Hurting Disk Jockey Shows, Arnold Warns Programmers' Clinic," *Billboard*, February 4, 1950, pp. 4, 47.

11. "Jock Asks Pubs for 25¢ per Plug: But It's Legal," *Variety*, September 10, 1952, pp. 1, 61; and "Chi Jocks Slap Open Payola," *Variety*, October 27, 1954, p. 51.

12. "Inside Stuff — Music," *Variety*, November 9, 1955, p. 45.

13. "Top Deejay Credits Jock Clan with Saving Sinking Music Biz 15 Yrs. Ago," *Variety*, August 29, 1951, p. 43.

14. "Hungry DJ's a Growing Headache," *Billboard*, December 23, 1950, pp. 1, 11, 42.

15. Ibid.

16. Ibid.

17. Jerry Wexler, "R. and B. Jockeys Ride Payola," *Billboard*, January 13, 1951, pp. 1, 13, 40.

18. Ibid.

19. "Diskeries' New Payola Blues," *Variety*, June 10, 1953, p. 61.

20. "Worst Payola Towns," *Variety*, August 8, 1951, p. 41; "Philly Wide-Open Town for Disk Jocks Among Indie Labels," *Variety*, November 5, 1952, p. 37; "City of Brotherly Love Deejays Plug 'Em for Free," *Variety*, November 26, 1952, p. 43; and "Balto Payola Cues New Style Deejay Plugs," *Variety*, March 3, 1954, p. 49.

21. "AFM Joins AGVA in Banning Deejay Guest Shots but AFRA OK's Cuffolas," *Variety*, September 10, 1952, pp. 39, 45; and "Coast Disk Jock Using Phone to Nix AGVA Ban," *Variety*, October 1, 1952, pp. 1, 121.

22. "Payola Widespread, Wide Open," *Variety*, July 21, 1954, pp. 35, 41.

23. "Jocks Junk Payola Platters," *Variety*, February 16, 1955, p. 39; and "16 Det. Jocks Continue No-Spin Policy on 4 Labels Because of Payola, Tie-ins," *Variety*, February 23, 1955, pp. 41, 46.

24. "Payola Finger Pointing at Lesser D.J.s Cues Public Suspicion of Honest Plugs," *Variety*, July 18, 1951, pp. 41, 44.

25. "Station Primer for Deejays Warns Against Payolas, Cuffolas and Gimmicks," *Variety*, September 3, 1952, pp. 1, 55.

26. "Avers Music Biz Started Payola," *Variety*, August 8, 1951, pp. 41, 46; and "Davis Calls It 'Stop-Music' Biz," *Variety*, August 8, 1951, p. 41.

27. "Copyright Act No Solution to DJ Problem; Plugging Power Shifted," *Variety*, August 22, 1951, p. 49.

28. "Cap's Veep Thinks DJ 'Best Thing to Music Biz in Yrs.,'" *Variety*, August 22, 1951, p. 49; and "Cross-Section DJ Opinion Explores Several Facets of the 'Frankenstein,'" *Variety*, August 15, 1951, p. 45.

29. Bill Randle, "100 Deejays Control Music Biz," *Variety*, October 1, 1952, pp. 73, 92.

30. Abel Green, "The Payola That Pauperizes," *Variety*, July 21, 1954, p. 35.

31. Abel Green, "Payola Part II — Who Me?" *Variety*, July 28, 1954, p. 107.

32. Abel Green, "Payola III — Worse Than Ever," *Variety*, August 11, 1954, pp. 43, 49; and Abel Green, "Payola — Continued," *Variety*, August 18, 1954, p. 47.

33. Abel Green, "Corruption in the Music Biz," *Variety*, February 15, 1956, p. 53; and Abel Green, "Corruption in the Music Biz . . . II," *Variety*, February 22, 1956, p. 41.

34. Abel Green, "Corruption in the Music Biz . . . III," *Variety*, February 29, 1956, p. 49; and Abel Green, "Corruption in the Music Biz . . . IV," *Variety*, March 7, 1956, p. 41.

35. Paul Weston, "Too Many Records," *Variety*, August 15, 1951, pp. 45–46.

36. Nat Hentoff, "DJs Too Powerful?" *Down Beat*, March 21, 1952, p. 11.

37. Jack Mabley, "In 'Music' DJs Still (D)rule Air Waves," *Down Beat*, August 25, 1954, p. 2.

38. "Payola — An Inside Story Told Four Years Ago," *U.S. News and World Report*, December 21, 1959, pp. 81–82.

39. *Songplugging and the Airwaves*, p. 3.

40. Rick Sklar, *Rocking America*, p. 21.

41. "Sees Outmoded Compulsory License in 1909 Act Root of Music Biz Evil," *Variety*, February 15, 1956, p. 43.

42. "Comments and Views on Harry G. Henn. The Compulsory License Provisions of the United States Copyright Law," in *General Revision of the Copyright Law*, p. 40.

43. Simon Frith, *Sound Effects*, pp. 8, 147.

44. "How Jocks Got Going," *Billboard*, November 10, 1956, pp. 82, 85.

45. June Bundy, "Radio Disk Jockeys Bar Doors to Stem Record Artist Flood," *Billboard*, February 16, 1957, pp. 1, 28.

46. "What Makes Howard Spin," *Time*, April 29, 1957, p. 50.

47. "Songs of Sixpence," *Newsweek*, April 1, 1957, p. 104.

48. "DJ's Don't Buy Payola Blast," *Variety*, February 27, 1957, pp. 43, 50.

49. Bill Simon, "Jocks Not Playing Disks They Prefer," *Billboard*, November 11, 1957, p. 38; and "Jocks on Pops, Payola, Polls," *Variety*, August 14, 1957, p. 45.

50. "DJ Payola: Like Headwaiter's Tip," *Variety*, March 25, 1959, p. 57.

51. "Deejay's Responsibility," *Variety*, March 12, 1958, p. 53; Herm Schoenfeld, "Deejay: Performer or Puppet?" *Variety*, March 12, 1958, pp. 1, 60; "Rackets Infest Music Industry, Says Nat Cole," *Variety*, March 25, 1959, p. 57; and "Cole Blasts Music Graft," *Down Beat*, May 28, 1959, p. 9.

52. "Legit Kind of Payola," *Variety*, July 23, 1958, pp. 1, 52.

53. Bernie Asbell, "Top 40 Programming Brings Dealer Payola," *Billboard*, March 17, 1958, pp. 2, 8.

54. "Payola Growing Faster Than Jack's Beanstalk," *Billboard*, October 6, 1958, pp. 2, 14.

55. Schoenfeld, "Deejay: Performer or Puppet?" pp. 1, 60; June Bundy, "Deejay Revolt at Top 40 May Bring Basic Changes," *Billboard*, March 17, 1958, pp. 2, 8; and "Top 40 Puts Payola in Spin," *Variety*, December 10, 1958, pp. 57, 62.

56. R. Serge Denisoff, "The Evolution of Pop Music Broadcasting," *Popular Music and Society*, 1972, pp. 210–11 n. 3; and Geoffrey Stokes, *Star-Making Machinery: The Odyssey of an Album*, p. 165.

57. "T-Men Quizzing D-J's on Extra-Curricular Income," *Billboard*, March 17, 1956, p. 18; and "Revenooers Move In on the Payola," *Variety*, June 26, 1957, pp. 1, 18.

58. "The Voice and Payola," *Time*, September 9, 1957, p. 76.

59. Ted Fox, *In the Groove*, pp. 62–63.

60. Mildred Hall, "Payola Hit at BMI Inquiry; Chairman Calls for Proof," *Billboard*, March 24, 1958, p. 12; and "How Big the Payola in Records?" *Broadcasting*, August 31, 1959, pp. 36, 38.

61. Hall, "Payola Hit at BMI Inquiry; Chairman Calls for Proof," p. 12.

62. Ibid., pp. 2, 12.

63. "ASCAP Wears Halo, Horns in Clashing House Testimony," *Billboard*, March 24, 1958, pp. 2, 68.

64. "How Big the Payola in Records?" pp. 35–36.

65. Peter Benjamin, *The Story of Motown*, pp. 50–51.

6. Do You Now or Have You Ever? 1959

1. Milton Bracker, "Hogan Studies Fraud in TV Ads; Payola Denied by Disk Jockeys," *New York Times*, November 8, 1959, pp. 1, 48; and "Double-Pronged Probe into Payola Slows Charge of the Loot Brigade," *Variety*, November 11, 1959, pp. 1, 57.

2. Ibid.

3. June Bundy, "House-FCC Payola Probe Threat Stirs Aircasters," *Billboard*, November 16, 1959, pp. 2, 11.

4. Ed McKenzie, "A Deejay's Exposé — and Views," *Life*, November 1959, pp. 47–48.

5. Ibid.

6. "WNEW Jocks Answer the Big 'Have You Ever?'" *Billboard*, November 16, 1959, p. 16; and "Payola? It Can't Happen Here on WNEW, Say DJs," *Variety*, November 18, 1959, pp. 60, 66.

7. "DJ Gets Threats Over Payola Talk," *Billboard*, November 16, 1959, pp. 3, 50; "Who's on the Tape That WAIT Aired About Deejays-on-the-Take?" *Variety*, November 18, 1959, p. 60; and "Record Maker Describes Payoff," *Life*, November 23, 1959, p. 48.

8. "DJ Gets Threats Over Payola Talk," pp. 3, 50.

9. Jack Gould, "TV: Assessing Effects of Life Under the Table," *New York Times*, November 20, 1959, p. 63.

10. "Lame, Halt and Blind," *Billboard*, November 30, 1959, p. 2.

11. John T. Noonan, Jr., *Bribes*, p. 578.

12. "Detroit Radio Star Confesses Payola," *New York Times*, November 23, 1959, p. 34; and "Detroit Deejays in Payola Hot Seat," *Variety*, November 25, 1959, pp. 55, 62.

13. "Payola Rocks Philly Jocks," *Variety*, November 25, 1959, pp. 55–56; "Disk Jockey Loses Job," *New York Times*, November 29, 1959, p. 66; and "Detroit Deejays in Payola Hot Seat," pp. 55, 62.

14. "Detroit Deejays in Payola Hot Seat," pp. 55, 62.

15. June Bundy, "Payola Probe Keys Widespread Effect," *Billboard*, November 30, 1959, pp. 1, 2; and "4 Out to Debunk Payola Lose Disk Jockey Jobs," *New York Times*, November 26, 1959, p. 51.

16. Bundy, "Payola Probe Keys Widespread Effect," pp. 1, 2.

17. William M. Blair, "House Unit Spurs Payola Inquiry," *New York Times*, November 19, 1959, p. 79; "NBC Scores Time on Quiz Scandal," *New York Times*,

November 23, 1959, p. 34; and Abel Green, "Payola: Past, Present and Phfft," *Variety*, November 25, 1959, pp. 55–56.

18. Richard E. Shepard, "F.C.C. Chairman Tells TV It Faces Tighter Controls," *New York Times*, November 21, 1959, pp. 1, 48.

19. Ibid.; and "Payola Rocks Philly Jocks," pp. 55–56.

20. "Boston Stations Meet Fed Probers with Blanket Denials of Payola," *Variety*, November 25, 1959, pp. 55, 58.

21. "Block That Schlock," *Time*, November 23, 1959, pp. 63–64; and "Payoffs Disclosed," *New York Times*, November 22, 1959, p. 62.

22. "Dick Clark's Music Ties First Casualty of ABC-TV's Sensitivity to Payola," *Variety*, November 18, 1959, pp. 1, 66; "Payola Blues," *Newsweek*, November 30, 1959, p. 94; and Val Adams, "C.B.S. Weighs New Programming; House Unit to Query Dick Clark," *New York Times*, November 18, 1959, pp. 1, 84.

23. Shields ReMine, "Payola," *American Mercury*, March 1960, pp. 38–39.

24. Richard E. Shepard, "Alan Freed Is Out in Payola Study," *New York Times*, November 22, 1959, pp. 1, 62; Val Adams, "Alan Freed Loses 2d Broadcast Job," *New York Times*, November 24, 1959, p. 31; and "Music Biz Probe Spinning Around All Diskery Cut-Ins and Kickbacks," *Variety*, November 25, 1959, pp. 1, 58.

25. "The Wages of Spin," *Time*, December 7, 1959, p. 47.

26. Ibid.

27. Ibid.

28. "Two Tough Moves Against Payola," *Broadcasting*, December 7, 1959, p. 38.

29. Robert Alden, "Alan Freed Bars Immunity Waiver," *New York Times*, December 1, 1959, p. 34.

30. Carl Belz, *The Story of Rock*, p. 51.

31. "Two Tough Moves Against Payola," p. 36; and "More Names Key Headline Hassles," *Billboard*, December 14, 1959, pp. 2, 138.

32. "Disk Jockeys," *Time*, December 7, 1959, p. 47; and "Jockeys on a Rough Ride," *Newsweek*, December 7, 1959, p. 98.

33. "C.B.S. Chief Issues a Bribe Warning," *New York Times*, December 2, 1959, p. 53; "N.B.C. Bars Rebate," *New York Times*, December 5, 1959, p. 47; and "Two Tough Moves Against Payola," p. 36.

34. "How High the Moola?" *Variety*, December 2, 1959, p. 57; "See Distribs as Payola Key," *Variety*, December 9, 1959, pp. 53, 58; and "More Names Key Headline Hassles," pp. 2, 138.

35. "Payola," *Down Beat*, December 24, 1959, pp. 13–15.

36. "Disk Jockeys Curbed," *New York Times*, December 1, 1959, p. 34; and "More Names Key Headline Hassles," pp. 2, 138.

37. "C.B.S. Chief Issues a Bribe Warning," p. 53; and "Broadcasters Vie in Frantic Payola Combat Scramble," *Billboard*, December 7, 1959, pp. 3, 12.

38. "Payola," p. 14; and "Broadcasters Vie in Frantic Payola Combat Scramble," pp. 3, 12.

39. "The No-Payola Sound of Music," *Variety*, December 2, 1959, pp. 1, 64; and "Payola Detectives Due," *New York Times*, December 9, 1959, p. 54.

40. "The No-Payola Sound of Music," pp. 1, 64.

41. William M. Blair, "F.T.C. to File Suits to Prevent Payola," *New York Times*, December 3, 1959, pp. 1, 75; and William M. Blair, "FTC Complaints Name 9 Concerns in Payola Deals," *New York Times*, December 5, 1959, pp. 1, 47.

42. "See Distribs as Payola Key," pp. 53, 58; Blair, "FTC Complaints Name 9

Concerns in Payola Deals," pp. 1, 47; and "More Complaints on Payola Slated," *New York Times*, December 30, 1959, p. 45.

43. "No Payola in RCA's Future," *Broadcasting*, December 21, 1959, p. 46.

44. "Sworn Report Required of All Stations," *Billboard*, December 7, 1959, pp. 3, 10; "Two Tough Moves Against Payola," pp. 35–36; "No Payola in RCA's Future," p. 46; and "Cancellation Threat Cue to Attitude," *Billboard*, December 7, 1959, pp. 3, 10.

45. Paul Ackerman, "Payola: Sing a Song for Sixpence," *Nation*, December 5, 1959, pp. 414–15; and "Trials and Opportunities," *Billboard*, December 7, 1959, p. 3.

46. "Payola," pp. 13–15.

47. Blair, "FTC Complaints Name 9 Concerns in Payola Deals," pp. 1, 47; "Harris Committee's Yule Greeting to B'casting Industry: 'We've Got a Mountain of Info on Deceits,'" *Variety*, December 16, 1959, p. 24; Felix Belair, Jr., "Near Extortions Laid to Radio, TV," *New York Times*, December 15, 1959, pp. 1, 79; and "A Bill of Particulars on Payola," *Broadcasting*, December 21, 1959, pp. 48–49.

7. Bad Music Squats in the Dark, Accused, 1960

1. Herm Schoenfeld, "Climactic Year for Music Biz," *Variety*, January 6, 1960, pp. 207, 210.

2. Ibid.

3. Ibid.

4. Damon Stetson, "Study Questions Effects of Radio," *New York Times*, February 21, 1960, p. 70.

5. "Payola Pot Boils Merrily in Chi," *Billboard*, January 11, 1960, pp. 2, 53; Jack Pitman, "The Chicago Payola Story," *Variety*, January 13, 1960, pp. 43, 48; and "Shakeup Reaches Chicago," *Down Beat*, February 4, 1960, pp. 9–10.

6. Ibid.

7. "15 More Accused of Disk Payolas," *New York Times*, January 3, 1960, p. 68; Mildred Hall, "FTC Pouring It on Payola," *Billboard*, February 1, 1960, p. 2; and "Payola Is Fair," *Broadcasting*, February 22, 1960, p. 44.

8. "London Admits Payola Practices but Says So What," *Variety*, January 20, 1960, pp. 61, 67; "FTC Gets 3rd Consent Order in Payola Cases," *Broadcasting*, February 8, 1960, pp. 64, 66; "42 on FTC Payola Hit Parade," *Broadcasting*, February 15, 1960, p. 62; and "Payola Is Fair," p. 44.

9. "FCC and FTC in Payola Merger," *Broadcasting*, February 22, 1960, pp. 36, 40; "FCC and FTC Would Outlaw Payola via Broadcaster, Diskery, DJ Clamps," *Variety*, February 10, 1960, pp. 55, 60; William M. Blair, "F.C.C. Urges Law on Deceit on Air," *New York Times*, February 12, 1960, pp. 1, 55; and "Radio-TV Inquiry Calls 2 U.S. Aides," *New York Times*, February 21, 1960, p. 68.

10. "ASCAP Is Prodded for Payola Data," *New York Times*, January 12, 1960, p. 44.

11. "Payola Popularized Bad Songs," *Variety*, January 20, 1960, p. 66; and Stanley W. Penn, "Payola's Impact," *Wall Street Journal*, January 6, 1960, pp. 1, 15.

12. Penn, "Payola's Impact," pp. 1, 15; June Bundy, "New Air Formats, Controls in Wake of Payola Exposés," *Billboard*, February 1, 1960, pp. 3, 26; and "Record Plugs on Sale," *New York Times*, February 27, 1960, p. 39.

13. John Tynan, "A Clean Fresh Wind," *Down Beat*, January 7, 1960, p. 17.

14. "Payola Scandals — An Aid to Good Music," *Instrumentalist*, February 1960, p. 81.

15. *Responsibilities of Broadcast Licensees and Station Personnel* (this is the transcript of the Harris subcommittee hearings and has been used as a reference throughout this section); William Blair, "Disk Jockey Tells of $6,000 Favors, but Denies Payola," *New York Times*, February 9, 1960, pp. 1, 14; and "Harris Drums Up Payola Parade," *Broadcasting*, February 15, 1960, p. 52.

16. Ibid.

17. "Payola Probers in Philly," *Variety*, February 10, 1960, pp. 55–56.

18. "Background on Prescott," *Variety*, February 10, 1960, p. 56; and Blair, "Disk Jockey Tells of $6,000 Favors, but Denies Payola," pp. 1, 14.

19. William M. Blair, "Disk Jockey Tells of Getting $16,100," *New York Times*, February 10, 1960, pp. 1, 29; "Congressional Payola Probe Puts Cleve., Boston Jockeys on Hot Seat," *Variety*, February 10, 1960, pp. 55–56; William M. Blair, "$117,665 Bill Paid for Disk Jockeys," *New York Times*, February 11, 1960, pp. 1, 70; and "Harris Drums Up Payola Parade," p. 52.

20. "Harris Drums Up Payola Parade," p. 52.

21. Blair, "$117,665 Bill Paid for Disk Jockeys," pp. 1, 70; and "Harris Drums Up Payola Parade," p. 52.

22. "Harris Drums Up Payola Parade," p. 52; and Blair, "$117,665 Bill Paid for Disk Jockeys," pp. 1, 70.

23. "Transcript of Eisenhower's News Conference," *New York Times*, February 12, 1960, p. 14.

24. Blair, "$117,665 Bill Paid for Disk Jockeys," pp. 1, 70; and "Harris Might Hang Up on Call Girls," *Variety*, February 24, 1960, pp. 89, 94.

25. William M. Blair, "Station in Boston Received Payola," *New York Times*, February 16, 1960, pp. 1, 75; and "Round Two: Boston Payola Party," *Broadcasting*, February 22, 1960, pp. 40–42.

26. Ibid.

27. Blair, "Station in Boston Received Payola," pp. 1, 75.

28. William M. Blair, "Disk Loans Cited in Payola Study," *New York Times*, February 17, 1960, pp. 1, 38.

29. William M. Blair, "Disk Jockey Says He Got Royalties," *New York Times*, February 20, 1960, pp. 1, 21; and William M. Blair, "Class Conscious Payola Story Lifts Eyebrows at House Inquiry," *New York Times*, February 21, 1960, p. 68.

30. Blair, "Disk Jockey Says He Got Royalties," pp. 1, 21.

31. Les Carpenter, "U.S. Payola Panel Calling FCC and FTC to Stand in March," *Variety*, February 24, 1960, pp. 89, 91.

32. Ibid.

33. Blair, "Class Conscious Payola Story Lifts Eyebrows," p. 68.

34. William M. Blair, "Disk Jockey Ring for Payola Cited," *New York Times*, February 18, 1960, p. 67; and "Round Two: Boston Payola Party," pp. 40–42.

35. William M. Blair, "Inquiry Queries Dick Clark Policy," *New York Times*, February 19, 1960, p. 55.

36. "10 More Concerns Accused of Payola," *New York Times*, March 7, 1960, p. 14; "Boxscore on FTC Payola Charges," *Broadcasting*, March 7, 1960, p. 66; "New Payola Charges," *New York Times*, April 4, 1960, p. 59; William M. Blair, "F.C.C. Head Admits He Got Yacht Trip," *New York Times*, March 5, 1960, pp. 1, 40; and "FTC Unearths Hidden Plug-Uglies Engineered by 8 Firms," *Variety*, March 9, 1960, p. 61.

37. Jack Roth, "Payola Inquiry by Hogan to End," *New York Times*, April 5, 1960, p. 27; and "Disk Jockey Dropped," *New York Times*, April 4, 1960, p. 59.

38. Eddie Kafafian, "L.A.'s Johnny-Come-What-May DJs Now Getting In on Lost Loot," *Variety*, March 16, 1960, pp. 55, 60.

39. "DJ Payola Deep," *Variety*, March 16, 1960, pp. 55, 60; "Outlawing of Payola Urged," *New York Times*, March 16, 1960, p. 75; and "ASCAP Acts to Curb Payola," *New York Times*, March 25, 1960, p. 21.

40. "A Lot of Loot," *Down Beat*, April 14, 1960, p. 11; and "Musicaster, Not Disk Jockey," *New York Times*, March 24, 1960, p. 17.

41. "Frisco Station Sues Disk Jockey," *Variety*, April 6, 1960, pp. 1, 52.

42. "Should D.J.s Take It on the Side?" *Down Beat*, March 3, 1960, p. 11; and Charles Suber, "The First Chorus," *Down Beat*, March 17, 1960, p. 4.

43. Abel Green, "Jockeys Relearning Diskmanship as Payola Probe Helps to Clear Air of Rock 'n' Roll 'Drivel': Mitch Miller," *Variety*, March 9, 1960, p. 55.

44. Herm Schoenfeld, "Music Biz's Classy Comeback," *Variety*, March 16, 1960, pp. 1, 78.

45. Suber, "The First Chorus," p. 4.

46. "Celler Blames Payola for Rise of Rock 'n' Roll," *New York Times*, March 28, 1960, p. 17.

47. "4 Radio Licenses Held Up by F.C.C.," *New York Times*, March 2, 1960, pp. 1, 75; "Four Cited on Payola Data," *Broadcasting*, March 7, 1960, pp. 62, 64; and "Four Boston Stations Answer Payola Charges," *Broadcasting*, April 4, 1960, pp. 92, 94.

48. "Half of Country's Broadcasters Get Disk on the Cuff," *Variety*, March 9, 1960, pp. 1, 69.

49. Blair, "F.C.C. Head Admits He Got Yacht Trip," pp. 1, 40; and "A Lot of Loot," p. 11.

50. "New Blow at Plugs and Freebies," *Broadcasting*, March 21, 1960, pp. 55–56; and "FCC Spells Out Plugolas and Payolas," *Variety*, March 23, 1960, p. 24.

51. Mildred Hall, "B'dcast Protests Soar Against FCC Air Freebie Ruling," *Billboard*, March 28, 1960, pp. 1, 64.

52. "FCC Spells Out Plugolas and Payolas," p. 24; "ASCAP Acts to Curb Payola," p. 21; and Hall, "B'dcast Protests Soar Against FCC Air Freebie Ruling," pp. 1, 64.

53. Richard E. Shepard, "Radio-TV Confused by Order to Identify Donors of Records," *New York Times*, March 24, 1960, p. 26; Val Adams, "Du Pont May Move 2 C.B.S. Programs," *New York Times*, March 23, 1960, p. 75; "Announcements Stopped," *New York Times*, March 31, 1960, p. 67; and "Liability to Asset," *New York Times*, April 12, 1960, p. 46.

54. "Diskers Hit by Cuffola Crisis," *Variety*, March 30, 1960, pp. 55, 59; "Diskery Life Begins at '317,'" *Variety*, April 13, 1960, pp. 45, 50; and "A Tough New Ruling," *Down Beat*, April 28, 1960, p. 15.

55. "F.C.C. May Alter Ruling," *New York Times*, April 2, 1960, p. 47; and Val Adams, "F.C.C. Uncertain on Donors' Ruling," *New York Times*, April 7, 1960, p. 71.

56. "Rep. Harris Wants Answers on Link of Payola and Radio's 'Juke' Sound," *Variety*, April 13, 1960, p. 47.

57. "Teen-Agers' Dreamboat," *New York Times*, March 5, 1960, p. 40.

58. Blair, "F.C.C. Head Admits He Got Yacht Trip," pp. 1, 40.

59. Inquiry Hears A.B.C. Got Royalties from Dick Clark," *New York Times*, March 11, 1960, pp. 1, 8; and "A Lot of Loot," p. 11.

60. "Harris Backs Down on Payola Secrecy," *New York Times*, March 13, 1960, p. 79.

61. Anthony Lewis, "Clark Is Accused of Giving Payola," *New York Times*, April 27, 1960, pp. 1, 41; and "The Clark-Harris Payola Hop," *Broadcasting*, May 2, 1960, pp. 58–60.

62. Anthony Lewis, "Inquiry Is Told of Clark Profit," *New York Times*, April 28, 1960, p. 28; and "The Clark-Harris Payola Hop," pp. 58–60.

63. "The Clark-Harris Payola Hop," pp. 58–60.

64. R. Serge Denisoff, "The Evolution of Pop Music Broadcasting," *Popular Music and Society*, 1972, 2: 208 n. 3.

65. "Clark Took Payola, Congressman Says," *New York Times*, April 29, 1960, p. 25.

66. Anthony Lewis, "Dick Clark Denies Receiving Payola," *New York Times*, April 30, 1960, pp. 1, 47.

67. "Music Biz Goes Round and Round," *Life*, May 16, 1960, pp. 118–20, 122.

68. Lewis, "Dick Clark Denies Receiving Payola," pp. 1, 47.

69. Anthony Lewis, "Dick Clark Got $7,150 for Plug," *New York Times*, May 3, 1960, pp. 1, 78.

70. "Mammarella's Secret Success Saga," *Variety*, May 4, 1960, pp. 45, 62; Shields ReMine, "Payola," *American Mercury*, March 1960, p. 39; and "Comeuppance for Clark," *Down Beat*, June 9, 1960, pp. 11–12.

71. Anthony Lewis, "House Unit Plans Payola Remedies," *New York Times*, May 4, 1960, p. 34; and Mildred Hall, "Payola Hearings Finale Prefaces Fast Solon Action," *Billboard*, May 9, 1960, pp. 2, 27.

72. Lewis, "House Unit Plans Payola Remedies," p. 34.

73. Jack Roth, "Alan Freed and 7 Others Arrested in Payola Here," *New York Times*, May 20, 1960, pp. 1, 62; "Eight Deejays Arrested for Accepting Payola," *Billboard*, May 23, 1960, pp. 3, 9; "Payola Dragnet Yields Eight," *Broadcasting*, May 23, 1960, pp. 80–81; and "Payolateers Arrested," *Down Beat*, June 23, 1960, p. 11.

74. Jack Roth, "First Payola Trial Starts Here with Testimony on Disk Jockey," *New York Times*, April 18, 1961, p. 45; and "Payola Rap Gets Tripp $500 Fine, Suspend Jailing," *Variety*, October 18, 1961, p. 49.

75. "Refused Payola, Disk Jockey Says," *New York Times*, April 29, 1961, p. 47; "Testimony Ended in Disk Jockey Suit," *New York Times*, May 3, 1961, p. 75; Jack Roth, "Tripp Guilty of Taking Payola While Radio Disk Jockey Here," *New York Times*, May 16, 1961, p. 44; and Jack Roth, "Tripp Fined $500 in Payola Case," *New York Times*, October 17, 1961, p. 27.

76. "Payola Case Dropped," *New York Times*, February 10, 1962, p. 19.

77. "Guilty of Payola L.A. Deejay Gets Sentence Feb. 26," *Variety*, February 21, 1962, p. 47; and "DJ Found Guilty of Payola Tax Evasion," *Down Beat*, April 12, 1962, p. 11; and "First Govt. Indictment of DJ on Tax Evasion Rap, Failed to Report Payola," *Variety*, August 30, 1961, p. 45.

78. "Comeuppance for Clark," pp. 11–12.

79. "88% Airers Disclaim Payola," *Billboard*, April 11, 1960, pp. 2, 19.

80. "Freed Sentenced for Payola," *New York Times*, December 18, 1962, p. 3; and "Freed, Ex-Disk Jockey, Indicted in $37,920 U.S. Tax Evasion," *New York Times*, March 17, 1964, p. 38.

81. "3 Payola Complaints Dropped," *New York Times*, April 14, 1961, p. 18; "F.T.C. Dismisses Charges of Payola," *New York Times*, June 21, 1961, p. 37; and "Payola Cases Dropped," *New York Times*, September 1, 1961, p. 11.

82. "F.T.C. Is Finishing Its Payola Inquiry," *New York Times*, August 8, 1960, p. 13; "FTC to Take a Payola Hiatus," *Broadcasting*, July 25, 1960, p. 60; and David Halberstam, "Some in F.T.C. Say Payola Ended," *New York Times*, February 5, 1961, p. 44.

83. "36 Disk Jockeys Dance to Rock-the-Role in Philly Payola Follies," *Variety*, June 8, 1960, pp. 2, 51; "Clark Heads D.J. Payola Police Group," *Billboard*, August 29, 1960, pp. 1, 32; and "21 DJs, 11 Distributors Enjoined Over Payola," *Down Beat*, November 24, 1960, p. 13.

84. "Payola Aftermath," *Down Beat*, June 23, 1960, pp. 12–13; and "Check on Kickbacks on Records Is Urged," *New York Times*, June 16, 1960, p. 67.

85. "Ford Doubts Payola Made R and R Popular," *Billboard*, May 9, 1960, pp. 2, 27.

86. "House Set to Debate Payola," *Broadcasting*, June 20, 1960, pp. 100–01; and "Payola Steamroller Detoured," *Broadcasting*, July 4, 1960, pp. 58–61.

87. "Payola Bill Compromise Coming," *Broadcasting*, August 15, 1960, pp. 80–81.

88. "Senate Okays Revised Payola Bill," *Broadcasting*, August 29, 1960, pp. 60, 62; C. P. Trussell, "House Passes Payola Measure with Senate's Lighter Penalties," *New York Times*, August 31, 1960, p. 19; and Felix Belair, Jr., "Eisenhower Signs Bill on Aged Care," *New York Times*, September 14, 1960, p. 9.

89. "F.C.C. Rule on Citing Use of Free Disks Ends," *New York Times*, September 22, 1960, p. 55; Mildred Hall, "FCC Starts Laying Down Payola Rules," *Billboard*, May 1, 1961, pp. 2, 37; "FCC Issues Final Rules on Payola," *Billboard*, May 18, 1963, p. 27; and "Future Guide to Sponsor Identification," *Broadcasting*, August 15, 1960, p. 81.

90. "L.A. Worst Payola Town in the U.S.," *Variety*, August 3, 1960, pp. 1, 62; "Payola Rears Head Again," *Variety*, October 26, 1960, p. 59; and Bob Rolontz, "Promot'n Men Back in Saddle as Payola Tide Ebbs," *Billboard*, August 8, 1960, pp. 1, 33.

91. June Bundy, "Payola Not Dead," *Billboard*, August 29, 1960, p. 1.

92. Mildred Hall, "3 Federal Agencies Watch for Rumored Payola Resurgence," *Billboard*, December 26, 1960, pp. 1, 18.

93. "Tax Court Rules Payola Is Not Deductible Expense," *New York Times*, January 25, 1967, p. 87.

8. Surreptitious and Devious Means, 1961–1969

1. Herm Schoenfeld, "R 'n' R and Payola Still with the Music Biz," *Variety*, January 4, 1961, p. 207.

2. Eddie Kalish, "That Payola in the Window," *Variety*, September 26, 1962, pp. 47, 51.

3. "Payola Again Hits Disk Biz," *Variety*, February 21, 1962, p. 47.

4. Ralph J. Gleason, "Payola Gets You Nothing," *Variety*, January 8, 1964, p. 196.

5. "Payola Charged by L.A. Promoter," *Broadcasting*, April 27, 1964, pp. 73–74.

6. Ibid.

7. "FCC Tells Congress Payola Has Come Back," *Broadcasting*, May 18, 1964, p. 61.

    8. Mildred Hall, "FCC Payola Probe Hoopla Is Poopla," *Billboard*, June 6, 1964, pp. 1, 8.
    9. Eileen Shanahan, "New F.C.C. Inquiry on Payola Is Set," *New York Times*, November 28, 1964, pp. 1, 19.
    10. Francis X. Clines, "Industry Awaits Payola Inquiry," *New York Times*, November 29, 1964, p. 46.
    11. "FCC Will Revisit the Payola Scene," *Broadcasting*, November 30, 1964, p. 60; "Does Payola Still Exist?" *Broadcasting*, December 7, 1964, p. 63; and George Rosen, "Is FCC Barking Up Wrong Tree?" *Variety*, December 2, 1964, pp. 1, 36.
    12. "FCC Starts Countdown on Payola-Plugola," *Broadcasting*, May 23, 1966, pp. 58, 60; and "Payola Probers Plot Hush Hush Hearings," *Billboard*, May 28, 1966, pp. 1, 66.
    13. Eliot Tiegel, "FCC Trio Steps Up Probe with Afterhours Grilling," *Billboard*, July 9, 1966, pp. 1, 10; Eliot Tiegel, "Payola Probe Spins to DJs," *Billboard*, July 16, 1966, pp. 1, 7; "FCC Winds Up L.A. Probe," *Billboard*, July 23, 1966, p. 3; and "Payola Is Still with Us," *Instrumentalist*, September 1966, p. 43.
    14. Herm Schoenfeld, "Payola Follies of 1966," *Variety*, July 27, 1966, p. 89; and "Coast Station Sold; F.C.C. Scores Owner," *New York Times*, December 10, 1966, p. 22.
    15. "Stations Cautioned on Possible Payola," *Broadcasting*, November 27, 1967, pp. 62–63.
    16. "Payola Study on Coast," *Billboard*, July 6, 1968, p. 3; and "Four Disk Jockeys on Local Stations Indicted," *New York Times*, July 24, 1968, p. 43.
    17. "Low-Paid Ethnic DJ's Most Prone to Payola," *Variety*, March 3, 1971, pp. 1, 70.

9. Hash Instead of Cash, 1970–1979

    1. Mildred Hall, "U.S. Digs at Payola Files," *Billboard*, September 5, 1970, pp. 1, 10.
    2. "Low-Paid Ethnic DJ's Most Prone to Payola," *Variety*, March 3, 1971, pp. 1, 70; and "Drug Use in Disk Payola, If True, Can Sink Industry," *Variety*, April 26, 1972, pp. 1, 70.
    3. Mildred Hall, "FCC Asks Payola Data," *Billboard*, April 15, 1972, pp. 1, 56; and "Here We Go Again," *Variety*, April 5, 1972, p. 93.
    4. Ibid.
    5. "Drug Use in Disk Payola, If True, Can Sink Industry," pp. 1, 70.
    6. "The Background on Payola Columns," *Broadcasting*, May 1, 1972, pp. 56–57.
    7. "Drug Payola Scandal Over Disk Biz Reflects Contemporary Youth Pattern," *Variety*, May 3, 1972, p. 239; "Sonderling Hits Payola Rap on Black Deejays," *Variety*, May 10, 1972, p. 69; and Ralph J. Gleason, "Perspectives: Mom, Apple Pie and Payola," *Rolling Stone*, May 11, 1972, p. 34.
    8. Mildred Hall, "Anderson Agrees to Give FCC's Ray Payola Leads," *Billboard*, May 6, 1972, pp. 1, 6.
    9. "As If Payola'd Ever Left," *Rolling Stone*, May 11, 1972, p. 20; and "Anderson Pins Payola on Five Labels, Stations," *Variety*, May 17, 1972, pp. 1, 69.
    10. "FCC Plus U.S. Agencies Co-Op to Stem Drugs-and-Sex Payola Tide," *Variety*, August 23, 1972, pp. 1, 62; "Is Payola Coming Back to Haunt?" *Broad-*

casting, August 28, 1972, p. 34; and Mildred Hall, "FCC Seeks New Rules to Fight Payola Takers," *Billboard*, September 23, 1972, pp. 1, 43.

11. "Put Up or Shut Up," *Billboard*, August 12, 1972, p. 6.

12. Grace Lichtenstein, "Columbia Payola Put at $250,000," *New York Times*, June 6, 1973, pp. 1, 51.

13. Ibid.; and Fred Ferretti, "Radio Men Spurn Payola Charges," *New York Times*, June 9, 1973, p. 67.

14. Ferretti, "Radio Men Spurn Payola Charges," p. 67; Grace Lichtenstein, "Organized Crime Linked to Payola," *New York Times*, June 7, 1973, pp. 1, 28; and Grace Lichtenstein, "Mob-Linked Conduits Get Subpoenas in Payola Case," *New York Times*, June 8, 1973, p. 24.

15. "The Specter of Payola '73," *Newsweek*, June 11, 1973, pp. 74, 79; Lichtenstein, "Organized Crime Linked to Payola," pp. 1, 28; and Lichtenstein, "Colubmia Payola Put at $250,000," pp. 1, 51.

16. "The Specter of Payola '73," pp. 74, 79.

17. Grace Lichtenstein, "Pop-Music Scandal Laid to Pursuit of Fast Money," *New York Times*, June 11, 1973, p. 71.

18. "Search Is On for Payola in Air Play of Records," *Broadcasting*, June 11, 1973, p. 32; and "Payola Rock," *Time*, June 18, 1973, pp. 80–81.

19. Grace Lichtenstein, "Talk of Payola Influenced Metromedia," *New York Times*, June 15, 1973, p. 31; and Herm Schoenfeld, "Today's Disk Payola New Chapter in Long History of Music Biz Corruption," *Variety*, June 13, 1973, pp. 1, 63.

20. Grace Lichtenstein, "Figure in Heroin Case Said to Talk on Payola," *New York Times*, June 13, 1973, p. 74; "Payola Probe: No Letup Now but Prosecution Lowers Profile," *Broadcasting*, June 18, 1973, p. 77; and Grace Lichtenstein, "Payola Jury Asks Testimony on Tips," *New York Times*, June 20, 1973, p. 27.

21. William Safire, "The Drugola Scandal," *New York Times*, June 21, 1973, p. 41.

22. Grace Lichtenstein, "Pop Music Inquiry Broadened by U.S.," *New York Times*, June 22, 1973, pp. 1, 47; and "C.B.S. TV to Study Charges of Payola at Disk Subsidiary," *New York Times*, June 23, 1973, p. 18.

23. Fred Ferretti, "Buckley Wants Record Industry Investigated by 4 U.S. Agencies," *New York Times*, June 26, 1973, p. 41; and "James Buckley Presses for Probe of Payola," *Broadcasting*, July 2, 1973, pp. 42, 44.

24. Fred Ferretti, "Industry Pledges Payola-Study Aid," *New York Times*, July 2, 1973, p. 14.

25. "Payola Probe Continues," *Broadcasting*, July 9, 1973, pp. 39–40.

26. Fred Ferretti, "Recording Group Meets on Payola," *New York Times*, July 11, 1973, p. 48; and Grace Lichtenstein, "I.R.S. Joins Investigations into Recording Concerns," *New York Times*, July 13, 1973, pp. 1, 71.

27. Grace Lichtenstein, "C.B.S. Limits Help in a Payola Study," *New York Times*, July 14, 1973, p. 55.

28. "N.Y. Pop Outlets' Files Subpoenaed in Payola Probe," *Broadcasting*, July 23, 1973, p. 36.

29. "Buckley Denounces Record Industry," *New York Times*, July 31, 1973, p. 31.

30. "Buckley Is Disputed on Payola Reports," *Broadcasting*, August 6, 1973, pp. 35, 36, 38.

31. Les Ledbetter, "5 Stations Called in Payola Inquiry," *New York Times*, July 18, 1973, p. 40; and George Gent, "8 More Stations Are Subpoenaed," *New York Times*, July 19, 1973, p. 22.

32. Grace Lichtenstein, "Payola Inquiry Turns to Travel," *New York Times*, July 26, 1973, p. 43; and Grace Lichtenstein, "U.S. Details Payola Plot of $406,737," *New York Times*, August 22, 1973, p. 39.

33. Grace Lichtenstein, "Record Industry on Coast Shaken by Payola Studies," *New York Times*, July 22, 1973, p. 40.

34. "Trade Group of Record Industry Endorses Payola Investigation," *New York Times*, July 24, 1973, p. 70; and Rudy Johnson, "Innis Says U.S. Fosters Monopoly in Record Industry," *New York Times*, August 15, 1973, p. 75.

35. Gene Lees, "Bad Days at the Black Rock," *High Fidelity*, September 1973, pp. 70–73.

36. Simon Frith, *Sound Effects*, p. 51.

37. Andrew Kopkind, "Payola: As American as Pizza Pie," *Ramparts*, February 1974, pp. 45–48.

38. Grace Lichtenstein, "CBS News Tells of Payola on Records," *New York Times*, August 10, 1974, p. 59.

39. "P.R. Pop Cleffers Say Payola Boosts Rock and Salsa," *Variety*, September 22, 1976, p. 64; and "Payola Charge Backfires on Small Label's Chief," *Broadcasting*, July 29, 1974, p. 34.

40. Robert Lindsey, "Payola Threatens Recording Profits," *New York Times*, July 23, 1975, p. 20.

41. Ibid.

42. Joe Treen, "Payola: Nothin' from Nothin' Is Nothin'," *Rolling Stone*, October 24, 1974, pp. 10, 26.

43. Murray Schumach, "Payola Indictments Name 19, Including 3 Company Heads," *New York Times*, June 25, 1975, pp. 1, 40; and "Payola Traced to 16 Cities in Indictments of R and B Labels," *Broadcasting*, June 30, 1975, pp. 27–29.

44. Ibid.

45. Ibid.

46. Herm Schoenfeld, "Grand Jury Music Biz Probe Continuing as 19 Individuals, 6 Firms Get U.S. Indictments," *Variety*, July 2, 1975, pp. 59–60; and Christopher Cook, "Music Industry Scandal," *Rolling Stone*, July 31, 1975, p. 13.

47. "Music Directors Testify on Payola," *New York Times*, February 14, 1976, p. 53; "Four Record Company Officers Given Prison Terms for Payola," *New York Times*, April 13, 1976, p. 66; and "Payola Case Sent Back for Retrial," *Broadcasting*, August 29, 1977, pp. 42–43.

48. "An Ex-Atlanta Radio Official Is Convicted in Payola Case," *New York Times*, March 5, 1976, p. 62.

49. "Radio Station Aide Indicted in Newark," *New York Times*, July 23, 1976, p. D13; "Notes on People," *New York Times*, December 18, 1976, p. 19; Christopher Cook, "Frankie Crocker's Payola Blues," *Rolling Stone*, April 21, 1977, pp. 19–20; and "Frankie Crocker Makes His Case," *Variety*, April 5, 1978, p. 74.

50. Mildred Hall, "FCC Payola Probe Attracting Congress," *Billboard*, January 8, 1977, pp. 1, 65.

51. Mildred Hall, "Payola Hearings by FCC Feb. 16," *Billboard*, February 12, 1977, pp. 1, 72; and "Play It Again, Sam, but You'll Have to Tell the FCC Why," *Broadcasting*, February 14, 1977, pp. 48, 55.

52. "Concert Promoter Alleges Payola as FCC Opens Its Investigation," *Broadcasting*, February 21, 1977, pp. 24–25; and "FCC Probe of Payola Spreads Cross Country," *Variety*, February 23, 1977, pp. 1, 70.

53. "FCC Probe of Payola Spreads Cross Country," pp. 1, 70.

54. "Sonderling on Stand in Payola Hearing," *Broadcasting*, February 28, 1977, p. 24.

55. Ibid.

56. Ibid.

57. Louise Sweeney, "Broadcasting Payola Sparks FCC Hearings," *Christian Science Monitor*, March 1, 1977, pp. 1, 6; and Mildred Hall, "WOL DJs Promoter Providing Fireworks, Surprise Revelations," *Billboard*, March 5, 1977, pp. 4, 63.

58. "Disk Jockeys Have Difficulties at Payola Hearings," *Broadcasting*, March 7, 1977, pp. 24–25.

59. Boris Weintraub, "WOL Deejay Refutes Promoters," *Billboard*, March 19, 1977, pp. 6, 78; and "FCC Huddles Over Payola Hearings," *Broadcasting*, March 14, 1977, p. 24.

60. "Payola Issue Cooks Along Outside FCC," *Broadcasting*, April 11, 1977, pp. 45–46.

61. Ibid.; and "Norfolk Story, Second Version," *Broadcasting*, May 2, 1977, pp. 60, 62.

62. "SBC Officials Tell FCC Hearing WOL Personalities Had Clean Hands," *Broadcasting*, May 23, 1977, pp. 49–50.

63. "Green Sings Blues at Payola Probe; Jocks Cut Payoff," *Variety*, May 25, 1977, p. 2; and Mildred Hall, "WOL DJs Largely Cleared of Charges," *Billboard*, June 4, 1977, pp. 4, 6, 14.

64. Hall, "WOL DJs Largely Cleared of Charges," pp. 4, 6, 14; and Michael Duffey, "FCC Payola Probe: Conflict in the Capital," *Rolling Stone*, June 2, 1977, pp. 20, 22.

65. "FCC Payola Probe Shuns Press Glare, Going Non-Public," *Variety*, June 28, 1977, pp. 2, 68; "FCC Probe into Payola Now Closed," *Billboard*, July 2, 1977, pp. 3, 83; and "3-Man FCC Team Probing Possible L.A. Air Payola," *Billboard*, July 23, 1977, p. 3.

66. "FCC Not Prompted to Undertake Own Payola Investigation," *Variety*, May 14, 1986, pp. 85, 88.

10. Paper Adds, 1980–1991

1. Steve Coll, "Again, Payola," *Progressive*, January 1982, pp. 40–42.

2. "House Panel Has Report on Payola Ready for Action," *Variety*, August 8, 1984, pp. 1, 76; and "House Unit Drops Disk Payola Probe," *Variety*, September 19, 1984, p. 115.

3. "Capitol, MCA Drop Indies," *Billboard*, March 8, 1986, pp. 1, 91.

4. Michael Goldberg, "Payola Charges Rock Record Biz," *Rolling Stone*, April 10, 1986, pp. 13–14.

5. "Bandwagon Rolling Over Indie Promo," *Variety*, March 5, 1986, pp. 95–96.

6. Robert Lindsey, "Payola's Return to Records Reported," *New York Times*, March 6, 1985, p. A14; and "Bandwagon Rolling Over Indie Promo," pp. 95–96.

7. "Truth and Consequences," *Rolling Stone*, April 24, 1986, pp. 22, 64.

8. Ken Terry, "MCA Denies It Let Promo Rep Go Because of Pressure from Indie," *Variety*, April 9, 1986, p. 113.

9. "Bandwagon Rolling Over Indie Promo," pp. 95–96; and "Capitol, MCA Drop Indies," pp. 1, 91.

10. Kim Freeman, "Payola Allegations Termed Witchhunt," *Billboard*, March 8, 1986, p. 12.

11. "A Federal Case," *Billboard*, March 8, 1986, p. 91; and "Indie Promotion: A Time for Action," *Billboard*, March 8, 1986, p. 10.

12. Henry Schipper, "CBS PolyGram, A and M Halt Use of Indie Promoters," *Variety*, March 12, 1986, p. 151.

13. Phil DiMauro, "Album Rock Promo Caught in Crunch of Current Scandal," *Variety*, March 12, 1986, p. 152.

14. Bob Millard, "Country Promo in Flux; Labels Shifting Tactics," *Variety*, March 12, 1986, pp. 1, 155; and Edward Morris, "Country Indies Plot Strategy," *Billboard*, March 29, 1986, pp. 1, 75.

15. "Indie Record Distribs Hail Demise of Independent Promotion Forces," *Variety*, March 12, 1986, p. 149.

16. Bill Holland, "Assns. Address Payola," *Billboard*, March 15, 1986, p. 106; and Bill Holland, "Payola Reports Spur Panel at NAB Meeting," *Billboard*, April 19, 1986, pp. 1, 91.

17. "No New Payola Evidence, Says Committee," *Billboard*, March 15, 1986, p. 3; and Michael Goldberg, "Feds Probing Mob Involvement in Record Business," *Rolling Stone*, March 27, 1986, p. 13.

18. George Nelson, "Rhythm and Blues," *Billboard*, March 22, 1986, p. 61.

19. "Dileo on Indies," *Billboard*, March 29, 1986, p. 75.

20. Steve Gett, "Managers Irate Over Indies," *Billboard*, March 29, 1986, pp. 1, 75.

21. "Senate Probe of Payola Launched," *Variety*, April 9, 1986, p. 113; Michael Goldberg, "Senate Begins Payola Probe," *Rolling Stone*, May 22, 1986, pp. 13–14; and Bill Holland, "Senate to Probe Payola," *Billboard*, April 21, 1986, pp. 1, 85.

22. Henry Schipper, "D.C. Investigator on Coast Probing Music, Mob Links," *Variety*, June 18, 1986, pp. 81, 84; and Bill Holland, "Payola Probe Out of the Running," *Billboard*, April 25, 1987, pp. 10, 87.

23. Goldberg, "Senate Begins Payola Probe," pp. 13–14.

24. Steve Gett, "Isgro Slams Probe Effort," *Billboard*, April 12, 1986, p. 85.

25. Michael Goldberg, "Independent Promotion," *Rolling Stone*, April 24, 1986, pp. 21–22, 64.

26. Ibid.

27. Ibid.; and Goldberg, "Senate Begins Payola Probe," pp. 13–14.

28. Michael Goldberg, "Inside the Payola Scandal," *Rolling Stone*, January 14, 1988, pp. 13–15.

29. "In Praise of Payola," *National Review*, May 23, 1986, pp. 16–17.

30. Henry Schipper, "NBC's New Payola Statements Draw Isgro Retraction Demand," *Variety*, April 9, 1986, p. 115; and "Joe Isgro," *Rolling Stone*, April 24, 1986, pp. 21, 64.

31. "Isgro Suit Cites Label Conspiracy," *Billboard*, May 17, 1986, pp. 1, 83.

32. Goldberg, "Inside the Payola Scandal," pp. 13–15.

33. Goldberg, "Senate Begins Payola Probe," pp. 13–14; and Dave DiMartino, "Lawyers Mull Legal Payola," *Billboard*, January 9, 1988, p. 86.

34. Goldberg, "Inside the Payola Scandal," pp. 13–15.

35. "U.S. Indicts Four in a Payola Case," *New York Times*, February 28, 1988, p. 26.

36. Henry Schipper, "Payola Probe Shakes Disk Biz," *Variety*, March 2, 1988, pp. 97–98; and Dave DiMartino, "L.A. Payola Indictments Fuel Probes in Additional Cities," *Billboard*, March 12, 1988, pp. 1, 73.

37. "L.A. Grand Jury Hands Up Payola Indictments," *Rolling Stone*, April 7, 1988, p. 19.

38. "Payola: The Record Label Connection," *Rolling Stone*, April 21, 1988, pp. 15, 114; and Ronald Grover, "Here's a Not-So-Golden Oldie: Payola," *Business Week*, August 15, 1988, p. 90.

39. Michael Goldberg, "Payola Probe Back on Track," *Rolling Stone*, June 15, 1989, p. 22; Dave DiMartino, "New Tashjian Indictment Ups Payola Counts to 168," *Billboard*, May 6, 1989, pp. 4, 91; Jean Rosenbluth, "Tashjian Pleads Guilty to Payola Charge," *Variety*, May 31, 1989, p. 67; Dave DiMartino, "Tashjian Pleads Guilty to Payola," *Billboard*, June 3, 1989, pp. 1, 87; and "Former Record Promoter Sentenced in Payola Case," *Wall Street Journal*, December 12, 1989, p. A6.

40. Goldberg, "Payola Probe Back on Track," p. 22.

41. "FCC Not Prompted to Undertake Own Payola Investigation," *Variety*, May 14, 1986, p. 85.

42. Michael Goldberg, "FCC Hears Payola Allegations," *Rolling Stone*, March 24, 1988, pp. 25, 181.

43. "FCC Planning Inquiry into Payola, Plugola Practices," *Billboard*, April 30, 1988, p. 5; and "FCC Lays Down Law on Payola," *Broadcasting*, May 23, 1988, p. 53.

44. Henry Weinstein, "U.S. Indicts 3 on Music Payola Fraud Charges," *Los Angeles Times*, December 1, 1989, pp. A1, A37.

45. "Taking the Pulse on Payola," *Broadcasting*, December 11, 1989, pp. 38–40.

46. Henry Weinstein, "Isgro Claims He's Fall Guy in MCA Probe," *Los Angeles Times*, April 17, 1990, pp. D2, D20.

47. Larry Rohter, "Payola Trial Opens for a Top Record Promoter of the 80's," *New York Times*, August 21, 1990, pp. B1, B10.

48. Larry Rohter, "At Payola Trial," *New York Times*, August 25, 1990, p. 12.

49. Jube Shiver, "Key Figure in Payola Case Again Promoting Records," *Los Angeles Times*, August 29, 1990, p. D2.

50. Larry Rohter, "Payola Prosecutor Faulted," *New York Times*, August 31, 1990, p. B4; Larry Rohter, "Payola Case Dismissed; Judge Faults Prosecutors," *New York Times*, September 5, 1990, p. B3; Richard Turner, "Outrageous Government Misconduct Is Cited as Judge Dismisses Payola Case," *Wall Street Journal*, September 5, 1990, p. B7; and Jube Shiver, "Judge Abruptly Ends Payola Case Against 3," *Los Angeles Times*, September 5, 1990, pp. A1, A16.

51. Jube Shiver, "Payola Trial a Textbook Case in Bungling," *Los Angeles Times*, September 7, 1990, pp. D1, D11.

52. Jube Shiver, "Central Figure in Payola Case Breaks Silence," *Los Angeles Times*, December 14, 1990, p. D2.

53. Thomas S. Mulligan, "Isgro Still Under Appeal," *Los Angeles Times*, September 14, 1991, p. D2.

54. Fred Goodman, "Sharing Credit: Without Me You're Nothing," *Spy*, February 1992, pp. 22–23.

BIBLIOGRAPHY

"A–B–C of Plugs Holds." *Variety*, October 8, 1947, p. 44.

Ackerman, Paul. "Ackerman Statement to Payola Probers." *Billboard*, May 9, 1960, p. 8.

_____. "Payola: Sing a Song for Sixpence." *Nation*, December 5, 1959, pp. 414–15.

Adams, Val. "Alan Freed Loses 2d Broadcast Job." *New York Times*, November 24, 1959, p. 31.

_____. "C.B.S. Weighs New Programming; House Unit to Query Dick Clark." *New York Times*, November 18, 1959, pp. 1, 84.

_____. "Du Pont May Move 2 C.B.S. Programs." *New York Times*, March 23, 1960, p. 75.

_____. "F.C.C. Uncertain on Donors' Ruling." *New York Times*, April 7, 1960, p. 71.

"AFM Joins AGVA in Banning Deejay Guest Shots but AFRA OK's Cuffolas." *Variety*, September 10, 1952, pp. 39, 45.

"Air Payola in Britain Disappears as Pact Succeeds." *Variety*, September 27, 1950, p. 43.

Alden, Robert. "Alan Freed Bars Immunity Waiver." *New York Times*, December 1, 1959, p. 34.

"All Song Pluggers Barred." *Variety*, November 26, 1915, p. 3.

"Am. Soc. Cut-In Ban Not Retroactive." *Variety*, April 29, 1931, p. 83.

"Among the Music Men." *Variety*, April 9, 1920, p. 23.

"Anderson Pins Payola on Five Labels, Stations." *Variety*, May 17, 1972, pp. 1, 69.

"Announcements Stopped." *New York Times*, March 31, 1960, p. 67.

"As If Payola'd Ever Left." *Rolling Stone*, May 11, 1972, p. 20.

Asbell, Bernie. "Top 40 Programming Brings Dealer Payola." *Billboard*, March 17, 1958, pp. 2, 8.

"ASCAP Acts to Curb Payola." *New York Times*, March 25, 1960, p. 21.

"ASCAP Is Prodded for Payola Data." *New York Times*, January 12, 1960, p. 44.

"ASCAP Wears Halo, Horns in Clashing House Testimony." *Billboard*, March 24, 1958, pp. 2, 68.

"Avers Music Biz Started Payola." *Variety*, August 8, 1951, pp. 41, 46.

"The Background on Payola Columns." *Broadcasting*, May 1, 1972, pp. 56–57.

"Background on Prescott." *Variety*, February 10, 1960, p. 56.

"Balto Payola Cues New Style Deejay Plugs." *Variety*, March 3, 1954, p. 49.

"Ban on Plugs Boosts Coast Music Biz." *Variety*, February 25, 1931, p. 62.

"Bandmen Face Code Action." *Variety*, July 17, 1934, p. 41.

"Band's Free Plug Ideas." *Variety*, July 9, 1930, p. 58.

"Bandwagon Rolling Over Indie Promo." *Variety*, March 5, 1986, pp. 95–96.

"B.B.C. Band Leaders." *News-Sheet of the Bribery and Secret Commissions and Prevention League*, April/May 1939, p. 17.

"BBC Band, Music Dept. Head Hit on Payola Rap." *Variety*, March 26, 1947, p. 45.
"BBC-Brit. Pubs Propose Severe Payola Penalties." *Variety*, March 10, 1948, p. 43.
"BBC Key to Britain's Pop Tune Payola Evil, Sez Reg Connelly." *Variety*, April 30, 1947, p. 46.
"BBC Radio Probes Payola Charges." *Variety*, February 24, 1971, p. 47.
"B.B.C. Statement on Song-Plugging." *News-Sheet of the Bribery and Secret Commissions Prevention League*, June 25, 1948, p. 178.
"BBC Takes Hold and Song Plugging Graft Evil Now Looks Dead in Eng." *Variety*, July 25, 1933, p. 45.
Belair, Felix, Jr. "Eisenhower Signs Bill on Aged Cars." *New York Times*, September 14, 1960, p. 9.
_____. "Near Extortions Laid to Radio, TV." *New York Times*, December 15, 1959, pp. 1, 79.
Belz, Carl. *The Story of Rock*. New York: Oxford University Press, 1972.
Benjamin, Peter. *The Story of Motown*. New York: Grove, 1979.
"A Bill of Particulars on Payola." *Broadcasting*, December 21, 1959, pp. 48–49.
Blair, William M. "Class Conscious Payola Story Lifts Eyebrows at House Inquiry." *New York Times*, February 21, 1960, p. 68.
_____. "Disk Jockey Ring for Payola Cited." *New York Times*, February 18, 1960, p. 67.
_____. "Disk Jockey Says He Got Royalties." *New York Times*, February 20, 1960, pp. 1, 21.
_____. "Disk Jockey Tells of Getting $16,100." *New York Times*, February 10, 1960, pp. 1, 29.
_____. "Disk Jockey Tells of $6,000 Favors, but Denies Payola." *New York Times*, February 9, 1960, pp. 1, 14.
_____. "Disk Loans Cited in Payola Study." *New York Times*, February 17, 1960, pp. 1, 38.
_____. "F.C.C. Head Admits He Got Yacht Trip." *New York Times*, March 5, 1960, pp. 1, 40.
_____. "F.C.C. Urges Law on Deceit on Air." *New York Times*, February 12, 1960, pp. 1, 55.
_____. "FTC Complaints Name 9 Concerns in Payola Deals." *New York Times*, December 5, 1959, pp. 1, 47.
_____. "F.T.C. to File Suits to Prevent Payola." *New York Times*, December 3, 1959, pp. 1, 75.
_____. "House Unit Spurs Payola Inquiry." *New York Times*, November 19, 1959, p. 79.
_____. "Inquiry Queries Dick Clark Policy." *New York Times*, February 19, 1960, p. 55.
_____. "$117,665 Bill Paid for Disk Jockeys." *New York Times*, February 11, 1960, pp. 1, 70.
_____. "Station in Boston Received Payola." *New York Times*, February 16, 1960, pp. 1, 75.
Blaisdell, W. M. "Economic Aspects of the Compulsory License in the Copyright Law, 1958." In *General Revision of the Copyright Law*. Washington, D.C.: U.S. Copyright Office, 1957–60.
"Block That Schlock." *Time*, November 23, 1959, 74: 63–64.
Bloom, Ben. "Song Plugging – Then and Now." *Variety*, January 4, 1950, p. 217.
"Blowup Brewing on Payolas." *Variety*, November 21, 1945, p. 49.
Boosey, William. *Fifty Years of Music*. London: Ernest Benn, 1931.

Bordman, Gerald. *Jerome Kern.* New York: Oxford University Press, 1980.
"Boston Stations Meet Fed Probers with Blanket Denials of Payola." *Variety,* November 25, 1959, pp. 55, 58.
"Boxscore on FTC Payola Charges." *Broadcasting,* March 7, 1960, p. 66.
Bracker, Milton. "Hogan Studies Fraud in TV Ads; Payola Denied by Disk Jockeys." *New York Times,* November 8, 1959, pp. 1, 48.
"Bribery Concerns ASCAP." *Variety,* March 9, 1938, p. 47.
"Bribery Without Eye-Link Escapes Mention in Music Publisher Code." *Variety,* January 30, 1934, p. 45.
"Brit. Publishers Sound Payola Alarm Over Cut-In Demands by Radio Pirates." *Variety,* July 13, 1966, p. 35.
"Broadcasters Vie in Frantic Payola Combat Scramble." *Billboard,* December 7, 1959, pp. 3, 12.
"Buck Holds Radio Kills Songs Today." *New York Times,* September 9, 1936, p. 30.
"Buckley Denounces Record Industry." *New York Times,* July 31, 1973, p. 31.
"Buckley Is Disputed on Payola Reports." *Broadcasting,* August 6, 1973, pp. 35, 36, 38.
Bundy, June. "Deejay Revolt at Top 40 May Bring Basic Changes." *Billboard,* March 17, 1958, pp. 2, 8.
_____. "House-FCC Payola Probe Threat Stirs Aircasters." *Billboard,* November 16, 1959, pp. 2, 11.
_____. "New Air Formats, Controls in Wake of Payola Exposés." *Billboard,* February 1, 1960, pp. 3, 26.
_____. "Payola Not Dead." *Billboard,* August 29, 1960, p. 1.
_____. "Payola Probe Keys Widespread Effect." *Billboard,* November 30, 1959, pp. 1, 2.
_____. "Radio Disk Jockeys Bar Doors to Stem Record Artist Flood." *Billboard,* February 16, 1957, pp. 1, 28.
"Cal. Disker Wants to Cut Disk Jocks In on Distribution Gravy." *Variety,* January 14, 1948, p. 54.
"Cancellation Threat Cue to Attitude." *Billboard,* December 7, 1959, pp. 3, 10.
"Capitol, MCA Drop Indies." *Billboard,* March 8, 1986, pp. 1, 91.
"Cap's Veep Thinks DJ 'Best Thing to Music Biz in Yrs.'" *Variety,* August 22, 1951, p. 49.
Carpenter, Les. "U.S. Payola Panel Calling FCC and FTC to Stand in March." *Variety,* February 24, 1960, pp. 89, 91.
"C.B.S. Chief Issues a Bribe Warning." *New York Times,* December 2, 1959, p. 53.
"C.B.S. TV to Study Charges of Payola at Disk Subsidiary." *New York Times,* June 23, 1973, p. 18.
"Celler Blames Payola for Rise of Rock 'n' Roll." *New York Times,* March 28, 1960, p. 17.
"Check on Kickbacks on Records Is Urged." *New York Times,* June 16, 1960, p. 67.
"Chi Bribery Evidence Placed Before Paine." *Variety,* October 14, 1936, p. 49.
"Chi Jocks Slap Open Payola." *Variety,* October 27, 1954, p. 51.
"Chicago Picks 13 Bands, 4 Singers as De Luxe Plugs for Music Biz." *Variety,* October 17, 1933, p. 47.
"Chicago Pluggers Out of Pocket as Cafés Operate Plenty Crude." *Variety,* May 4, 1938, p. 47.
"Chicago Plugging Nuisance Gets Managerial Attention." *Variety,* April 28, 1922, p. 4.

"City of Brotherly Love Deejays Plug 'Em for Free." *Variety*, November 26, 1952, p. 43.

"The Clark-Harris Payola Hop." *Broadcasting*, May 2, 1960, pp. 58–60.

"Clark Heads D.J. Payola Police Group." *Billboard*, August 29, 1960, pp. 1, 32.

"Clark Took Payola, Congressman Says." *New York Times*, April 29, 1960, p. 25.

Clines, Francis X. "Industry Awaits Payola Inquiry." *New York Times*, November 29, 1964, p. 46.

"Coast Disk Jock Using Phone to Nix AGVA Ban." *Variety*, October 1, 1952, pp. 1, 121.

"Coast Station Sold; F.C.C. Scores Owner." *New York Times*, December 10, 1966, p. 22.

"Cole Blasts Music Graft." *Down Beat*, May 28, 1959, p. 9.

Coll, Steve. "Again, Payola." *Progressive*, January 1982, pp. 40–42.

"Comeuppance for Clark." *Down Beat*, June 9, 1960, pp. 11–12.

"Comments and Views on Harry G. Henn. The Compulsory License Provisions of the United States Copyright Law," in *General Revision of the Copyright Law*. Washington, D.C.: U.S. Copyright Office, 1957–60.

"Concert Promoter Alleges Payola as FCC Opens Its Investigation." *Broadcasting*, February 21, 1977, pp. 24–25.

"Congressional Payola Probe Puts Cleve., Boston Jockeys on Hot Seat." *Variety*, February 10, 1960, pp. 55–56.

"Contact Men's Assn. President Lists 9 Don'ts to Curb Payolas." *Variety*, September 13, 1944, pp. 37–38.

"Contactmen Union Finds Publishers Lethargic in Launching of Move Vs. Payola." *Variety*, December 18, 1946, p. 51.

Cook, Christopher. "Frankie Crocker's Payola Blues." *Rolling Stone*, April 21, 1977, pp. 19–20.

_____. "Music Industry Scandal." *Rolling Stone*, July 31, 1975, p. 13.

"Copyright Act No Solution to DJ Problem; Plugging Power Shifted." *Variety*, August 22, 1951, p. 49.

"Cross-Section DJ Opinion Explores Several Facets of the 'Frankenstein.'" *Variety*, August 15, 1951, p. 45.

"Cut-In Regulations Issued for Guidance of Music Publishers." *Variety*, April 22, 1931, p. 67.

"Cut-In Rule Cuts Cut-Ins 50 Percent to Date." *Variety*, July 14, 1931, p. 49.

"Cut-Ins with Results." *Variety*, April 8, 1931, p. 67.

"Cutting-In on Songs Can Work Two Ways." *Variety*, May 6, 1925, p. 49.

"Davis Calls It 'Stop-Music' Biz." *Variety*, August 8, 1951, p. 41.

"Deejay Org. Airs Payola Reply." *Billboard*, February 19, 1949, p. 16.

"Deejay's Responsibility." *Variety*, March 12, 1958, p. 53.

DeLong, Thomas A. *Pops: Paul Whiteman, King of Jazz*. Piscataway, N.J.: New Century, 1983.

Denisoff, R. Serge. "The Evolution of Pop Music Broadcasting." *Popular Music and Society*, 1972, 2: 204–11 n. 3.

"Detroit Deejays in Payola Hot Seat." *Variety*, November 25, 1959, pp. 55, 62.

"Detroit Radio Star Confesses Payola." *New York Times*, November 23, 1959, p. 34.

Dexter, Dave, Jr. "Origin of the Species." *Billboard*, December 27, 1969, pp. 56, 58.

"Dick Clark's Music Ties First Casualty of ABC-TV's Sensitivity to Payola." *Variety*, November 18, 1959, pp. 1, 66.

"Dileo on Indies." *Billboard*, March 29, 1986, p. 75.

DiMartino, Dave. "L.A. Payola Indictments Fuel Probes in Additional Cities." *Billboard*, March 12, 1988, pp. 1, 73.

_____. "Lawyers Mull Legal Payola." *Billboard*, January 9, 1988, p. 86.

_____. "New Tashjian Indictment Ups Payola Counts to 168." *Billboard*, May 6, 1989, pp. 4, 91.

_____. "Tashjian Pleads Guilty to Payola." *Billboard*, June 3, 1989, pp. 1, 87.

DiMauro, Phil. "Album Rock Promo Caught in Crunch of Current Scandal." *Variety*, March 12, 1986, p. 152.

"Disk Jockey Dropped." *New York Times*, April 4, 1960, p. 59.

"Disk Jockey Loses Job." *New York Times*, November 29, 1959, p. 66.

"Disk Jockey Sidelines and Other Abuses Frowned On by Station Ops." *Variety*, November 5, 1947, p. 49.

"Disk Jockeys." *Time*, December 7, 1959, 74: 47.

"Disk Jockeys Curbed." *New York Times*, December 1, 1959, p. 34.

"Disk Jockeys Have Difficulties at Payola Hearings." *Broadcasting*, March 7, 1977, pp. 24–25.

"Disk Jocks Important Enuf Now to Be Cut In on Record Royalties." *Variety*, May 19, 1948, p. 1.

"Disk Jocks Would Use Shindig Coin to Nip 'Stigma.'" *Variety*, January 7, 1948, p. 196.

"Diskeries' New Payola Blues." *Variety*, June 10, 1953, p. 61.

"Diskers Hit by Cuffola Crisis." *Variety*, March 30, 1960, pp. 55, 59.

"Diskery Life Begins at '317.'" *Variety*, April 13, 1960, pp. 45, 50.

"DJ Found Guilty of Payola Tax Evasion." *Down Beat*, April 12, 1962, p. 11.

"DJ Gets Threats Over Payola Talk." *Billboard*, November 16, 1959, pp. 3, 50.

"DJ Payola: Like Headwaiter's Tip." *Variety*, March 25, 1959, p. 57.

"DJ Payola Deep." *Variety*, March 16, 1960, pp. 55, 60.

"DJs Don't Buy Payola Blast." *Variety*, February 27, 1957, pp. 43, 50.

"Does Payola Still Exist?" *Broadcasting*, December 7, 1964, p. 63.

"Double-Pronged Probe into Payola Slows Charge of the Loot Brigade." *Variety*, November 11, 1959, pp. 1, 57.

"Drastic New Anti-Bribery Rules Aim to Outlaw Payola from Music Biz." *Variety*, December 3, 1941, p. 51.

"Drug Payola Scandal Over Disk Biz Reflects Contemporary Youth Pattern." *Variety*, May 3, 1972, p. 239.

"Drug Use in Disk Payola, If True, Can Sink Industry." *Variety*, April 26, 1972, pp. 1, 70.

Duffey, Michael. "FCC Payola Probe: Conflict in the Capital." *Rolling Stone*, June 2, 1977, pp. 20, 22.

Dunlap, Orbin E. "Song for Sale." *New York Times*, January 12, 1936, sec. 9, p. 15.

"Eight Deejays Arrested for Accepting Payola." *Billboard*, May 23, 1960, pp. 3, 9.

"88 Percent Airers Disclaim Payola." *Billboard*, April 11, 1960, pp. 2, 19.

Elias, Albert J. "The Reign of the Disc Jockey." *Etude*, March 1956, p. 18.

"English Music Publishers Stop Payments to Singers." *Variety*, May 12, 1922, p. 2.

"English Publishing Biz Falters Along Hampered by Germans and Grafters." *Variety*, June 11, 1941, p. 36.

"An Ex-Atlanta Radio Official Is Convicted in Payola Case." *New York Times*, March 5, 1976, p. 62.

"FCC and FTC in Payola Merger." *Broadcasting*, February 22, 1960, pp. 36, 40.

"FCC and FTC Would Outlaw Payola via Broadcaster, Diskery, DJ Clamps." *Variety*, February 10, 1960, pp. 55, 60.

"FCC Huddles Over Payola Hearings." *Broadcasting*, March 14, 1977, p. 24.

"FCC Issues Final Rules on Payola." *Billboard*, May 18, 1963, p. 27.

"FCC Lays Down Law on Payola." *Broadcasting*, May 23, 1988, p. 53.

"F.C.C. May Alter Ruling." *New York Times*, April 2, 1960, p. 47.

"FCC Not Prompted to Undertake Own Payola Investigation." *Variety*, May 14, 1986, pp. 85, 88.

"FCC Payola Probe Shuns Press Glare, Going Non-Public." *Variety*, June 28, 1977, pp. 2, 68.

"FCC Planning Inquiry into Payola, Plugola Practices." *Billboard*, April 30, 1988, p. 5.

"FCC Plus U.S. Agencies Co-Op to Stem Drugs and Sex Payola Tide." *Variety*, August 23, 1972, pp. 1, 62.

"FCC Probe into Payola Now Closed." *Billboard*, July 2, 1977, pp. 3, 83.

"FCC Probe of Payola Spreads Cross Country." *Variety*, February 23, 1977, pp. 1, 70.

"F.C.C. Rule on Citing Use of Free Disks Ends." *New York Times*, September 22, 1960, p. 55.

"FCC Spells Out Plugolas and Payolas." *Variety*, March 23, 1960, p. 24.

"FCC Starts Countdown on Payola-Plugola." *Broadcasting*, May 23, 1966, pp. 58, 60.

"FCC Tells Congress Payola Has Come Back." *Broadcasting*, May 18, 1964, p. 61.

"FCC Will Revisit the Payola Scene." *Broadcasting*, November 30, 1964, p. 60.

"FCC Winds Up L.A. Probe." *Billboard*, July 23, 1966, p. 3.

"A Federal Case." *Billboard*, March 8, 1986, p. 91.

Ferretti, Fred. "Buckley Wants Record Industry Investigated by 4 U.S. Agencies." *New York Times*, June 26, 1973, p. 41.

_____. "Industry Pledges Payola-Study Aid." *New York Times*, July 2, 1973, p. 14.

_____. "Radio Men Spurn Payola Charges." *New York Times*, June 9, 1973, p. 67.

_____. "Recording Group Meets on Payola." *New York Times*, July 11, 1973, p. 48.

"15 More Accused of Disk Payolas." *New York Times*, January 3, 1960, p. 68.

"First Govt. Indictment of DJ on Tax Evasion Rap, Failed to Report Payola." *Variety*, August 30, 1961, p. 45.

"Ford Doubts Payola Made R and R Popular." *Billboard*, May 9, 1960, pp. 2, 27.

"Former Record Promoter Sentenced in Payola Case." *Wall Street Journal*, December 12, 1989, p. A6.

"$42 Arrangers' Fee Evil Bobs Up Again." *Variety*, March 16, 1938, p. 38.

"42 on FTC Payola Hit Parade." *Broadcasting*, February 15, 1960, p. 62.

"Four Boston Stations Answer Payola Charges." *Broadcasting*, April 4, 1960, pp. 92, 94.

"Four Cited on Payola Data." *Broadcasting*, March 7, 1960, pp. 62, 64.

"Four Disk Jockeys on Local Stations Indicted." *New York Times*, July 24, 1968, p. 43.

"4 Out to Debunk Payola Lose Disk Jockey Jobs." *New York Times*, November 26, 1959, p. 51.

"4 Radio Licenses Held Up by F.C.C." *New York Times*, March 2, 1960, pp. 1, 75.

"Four Record Company Officers Given Prison Terms for Payola." *New York Times*, April 13, 1976, p. 66.

Fox, Ted. *In the Groove*. New York: St. Martin's, 1986.

"Frankie Crocker Makes His Case." *Variety*, April 5, 1978, p. 74.

"Freed, Ex-Disk Jockey, Indicted in $37,920 U.S. Tax Evasion." *New York Times*, March 17, 1964, p. 38.

"Freed Sentenced for Payola." *New York Times*, December 18, 1962, p. 3.

Freedland, Michael. *Irving Berlin*. New York: Stein and Day, 1974.

Freeman, Kim. "Payola Allegations Termed Witchhunt." *Billboard*, March 8, 1986, p. 12.

"Frisco Station Sues Disk Jockey." *Variety*, April 6, 1960, pp. 1, 52.

Frith, Simon. *Sound Effects*. New York: Pantheon, 1981.

"F.T.C. Dismisses Charges of Payola." *New York Times*, June 21, 1961, p. 37.

"FTC Gets 3rd Consent Order in Payola Cases." *Broadcasting*, February 8, 1960, pp. 64, 66.

"F.T.C. Is Finishing Its Payola Inquiry." *New York Times*, August 8, 1960, p. 13.

"FTC to Take a Payola Hiatus." *Broadcasting*, July 25, 1960, p. 60.

"FTC Unearths Hidden Plug-Uglies Engineered by 8 Firms." *Variety*, March 9, 1960, p. 61.

"FTC's Own Music Code More Stringent Than Pubs' Rules." *Variety*, November 4, 1936, p. 45.

"Future Guide to Sponsor Identification." *Broadcasting*, August 15, 1960, p. 81.

Gent, George. "8 More Stations Are Subpoenaed." *New York Times*, July 19, 1973, p. 22.

George, Nelson. "Rhythm and Blues." *Billboard*, March 22, 1986, p. 61.

Gett, Steve. "Isgro Slams Probe Effort." *Billboard*, April 12, 1986, p. 85.

_____. "Managers Irate Over Indies." *Billboard*, March 29, 1986, pp. 1, 75.

Gleason, Ralph J. "Payola Gets You Nothing." *Variety*, January 8, 1964, p. 196.

_____. "Perspectives: Mom, Apple Pie and Payola." *Rolling Stone*, May 11, 1972, p. 34.

Goldberg, Isaac. *Tin Pan Alley*. New York: John Day, 1930.

Goldberg, Michael. "FCC Hears Payola Allegations." *Rolling Stone*, March 24, 1988, pp. 25, 181.

_____. "Feds Probing Mob Involvement in Record Business." *Rolling Stone*, March 27, 1986, p. 13.

_____. "Independent Promotion." *Rolling Stone*, April 24, 1986, pp. 21–22, 64.

_____. "Inside the Payola Scandal." *Rolling Stone*, January 14, 1988, pp. 13–15.

_____. "Payola Charges Rock Record Biz." *Rolling Stone*, April 10, 1986, pp. 13–14.

_____. "Payola Probe Back on Track." *Rolling Stone*, June 15, 1989, p. 22.

_____. "Senate Begins Payola Probe." *Rolling Stone*, May 22, 1986, pp. 13–14.

Goldman, Herbert G. *Jolson*. New York: Oxford University Press, 1988.

Goodman, Fred. "Sharing Credit: Without Me You're Nothing." *Spy*, February 1992, pp. 22–23.

"Gotta Really Write 'Em." *Variety*, March 2, 1938, pp. 39–40.

Gould, Jack. "TV: Assessing Effects of Life Under the Table." *New York Times*, November 20, 1959, p. 63.

"Gov't Appeal, Cut-Ins for Small Pubs." *Variety*, March 11, 1931, p. 68.

Green, Abel. "Abel's Comments." *Variety*, March 4, 1925, p. 40.

_____. "Corruption in the Music Biz." *Variety*, February 15, 1956, p. 53.

_____. "Corruption in the Music Biz . . . II." *Variety*, February 22, 1956, p. 41.

_____. "Corruption in the Music Biz . . . III." *Variety*, February 29, 1956, p. 49.

_____. "Corruption in the Music Biz . . . IV." *Variety*, March 7, 1956, p. 41.

_____. "Desire to Curb Payolas an Old Story, with Sime the Original Author." *Variety*, May 12, 1943, p. 45.

_____. "Jockeys Relearning Diskmanship as Payola Probe Helps to Clear Air of Rock 'n' Roll 'Drivel': Mitch Miller." *Variety*, March 9, 1960, p. 55.

_____. "A Lot of Eyewash." *Variety*, October 1, 1947, p. 35.

_____. "Payola: Past, Present and Phfft." *Variety*, November 25, 1959, pp. 55–56.

_____. "Payola—Continued." *Variety*, August 18, 1954, p. 47.

_____. "Payola Origins and Angles." *Variety*, March 16, 1960, p. 56.

_____. "Payola, Part II—Who Me?" *Variety*, July 28, 1954, p. 107.

_____. "The Payola That Pauperizes." *Variety*, July 21, 1954, p. 35.

_____. "Payola III—Worse Than Ever." *Variety*, August 11, 1954, pp. 43, 49.

_____. "Publishers Do Forcing of It." *Variety*, April 22, 1931, pp. 67–68.

_____. "Selling Side of Song Plugging." *Variety*, January 7, 1942, p. 156.

_____. "Songmen's Social Graces." *Variety*, August 11, 1937, p. 47.

"Green Sings Blues at Payola Probe; Jocks Cut Payoff." *Variety*, May 25, 1977, p. 2.

Gross, Mike. "Jock Stranglehold Spreads." *Variety*, August 3, 1955, pp. 41, 48.

Grover, Ronald. "Here's a Not-So-Golden Oldie: Payola." *Business Week*, August 15, 1988, p. 90.

"Guilty of Payola L.A. Deejay Gets Sentence Feb. 26." *Variety*, February 21, 1962, p. 47.

"Gus Kahn, Tells of Isham Jones." *Variety*, January 18, 1928, p. 54.

Halberstam, David. "Some in F.T.C. Say Payola Ended." *New York Times*, February 5, 1961, p. 44.

"Half of Country's Broadcasters Get Disk on the Cuff." *Variety*, March 9, 1960, pp. 1, 69.

Hall, Mildred. "Anderson Agrees to Give FCC's Ray Payola Leads." *Billboard*, May 6, 1972, pp. 1, 6.

_____. "B'dcast Protests Soar Against FCC Air Freebie Ruling." *Billboard*, March 28, 1960, pp. 1, 64.

_____. "FCC Asks Payola Data." *Billboard*, April 15, 1972, pp. 1, 56.

_____. "FCC Payola Probe Attracting Congress." *Billboard*, January 8, 1977, pp. 1, 65.

_____. "FCC Payola Probe Hoopla Is Poopla." *Billboard*, June 6, 1964, pp. 1, 8.

_____. "FCC Seeks New Rules to Fight Payola Takers." *Billboard*, September 23, 1972, pp. 1, 43.

_____. "FCC Starts Laying Down Payola Rules." *Billboard*, May 1, 1961, pp. 2, 37.

_____. "FTC Pouring It on Payola." *Billboard*, February 1, 1960, p. 2.

_____. "Payola Hearings by FCC Feb. 16." *Billboard*, February 12, 1977, pp. 1, 72.

_____. "Payola Hearings Finale Prefaces Fast Solon Action." *Billboard*, May 9, 1960, pp. 2, 27.

_____. "Payola Hit at BMI Inquiry; Chairman Calls for Proof." *Billboard*, March 24, 1958, pp. 2, 12.

_____. "3 Federal Agencies Watch for Rumored Payola Resurgence." *Billboard*, December 26, 1960, pp. 1, 18.

_____. "U.S. Digs at Payola Files." *Billboard*, September 5, 1970, pp. 1, 10.

_____. "WOL DJs Largely Cleared of Charges." *Billboard*, June 4, 1977, pp. 4, 6, 14.

_____. "WOL DJs Promoter Providing Fireworks, Surprise Revelations." *Billboard*, March 5, 1977, pp. 4, 63.

"Harris Backs Down on Payola Secrecy." *New York Times*, March 13, 1960, p. 79.

"Harris Committee's Yule Greeting to B'casting Industry: 'We've Got a Mountain of Info on Deceits.'" *Variety*, December 16, 1959, p. 24.

"Harris Drums Up Payola Parade." *Broadcasting*, February 15, 1960, p. 52.

"Harris Might Hang Up on Call Girls." *Variety*, February 24, 1960, pp. 89, 94.

Henn, Harry G. "The Compulsory License Provisions of the United States Copyright Law, 1957." In *General Revision of the Copyright Law*. Washington, D.C.: U.S. Copyright Office, 1957–60.

Hentoff, Nat. "DJs Too Powerful?" *Down Beat*, March 21, 1952, p. 11.

"Here We Go Again." *Variety*, April 5, 1972, p. 93.

Herndon, Booton. *The Sweetest Music This Side of Heaven*. New York: McGraw-Hill, 1964.

Holland, Bill. "Assns. Address Payola." *Billboard*, March 15, 1986, p. 106.

_____. "Payola Probe Out of the Running." *Billboard*, April 25, 1987, pp. 10, 87.

_____. "Payola Reports Spur Panel at NAB Meeting." *Billboard*, April 19, 1986, pp. 1, 91.

_____. "Senate to Probe Payola." *Billboard*, April 21, 1986, pp. 1, 85.

"House Panel Has Report on Payola Ready for Action." *Variety*, August 8, 1984, pp. 1, 76.

"House Set to Debate Payola." *Broadcasting*, June 20, 1960, pp. 100–01.

"House Unit Drops Disk Payola Probe." *Variety*, September 19, 1984, p. 115.

"How Big the Payola in Records?" *Broadcasting*, August 31, 1959, pp. 36, 38.

"How High the Moola?" *Variety*, December 2, 1959, p. 57.

"How Jocks Got Going." *Billboard*, November 10, 1956, pp. 82, 85.

"Hungry DJ's a Growing Headache." *Billboard*, December 23, 1950, pp. 1, 11, 42.

"In Praise of Payola." *National Review*, May 23, 1986, pp. 16–17.

"Income Tax Sleuths on Payola Trails?" *Variety*, July 19, 1944, p. 1.

"Indie and Pop Pubs Plan to Attend FTC Probe on Music Biz." *Variety*, September 22, 1937, p. 45.

"Indie Promotion: A Time for Action." *Billboard*, March 8, 1986, p. 10.

"Indie Record Distribs Hail Demise of Independent Promotion Forces." *Variety*, March 12, 1986, p. 149.

"Industry's Reaction to Payoff Evil One of Disgust." *Variety*, August 7, 1935, p. 49.

"Inquiry Hears A.B.C. Got Royalties from Dick Clark." *New York Times*, March 11, 1960, pp. 1, 8.

"Inside Stuff." *Variety*, April 13, 1927, p. 55.

"Inside Stuff—Music." *Variety*, June 27, 1928, p. 57.

"Inside Stuff—Music." *Variety*, March 12, 1930, p. 55.

"Inside Stuff—Music." *Variety*, November 12, 1930, p. 73.

"Inside Stuff—Music." *Variety*, January 28, 1931, p. 78.

"Inside Stuff—Music." *Variety*, April 18, 1933, p. 48.

"Inside Stuff—Music." *Variety*, June 5, 1934, p. 47.

"Inside Stuff—Music." *Variety*, August 28, 1934, p. 43.

"Inside Stuff—Music." *Variety*, December 1, 1943, p. 36.

"Inside Stuff—Music." *Variety*, November 9, 1955, p. 45.

"Is Payola Coming Back to Haunt?" *Broadcasting*, August 28, 1972, p. 34.

"Isgro Suit Cites Label Conspiracy." *Billboard*, May 17, 1986, pp. 1, 83.

James, Ed. "Will Petrillo Unseat the Jockeys?" *American Magazine*, December 1947, pp. 30–31, 85.

"James Buckley Presses for Probe of Payola." *Broadcasting*, July 2, 1973, pp. 42, 44.

"Jock Asks Pubs for 25¢ per Plug: But It's Legal." *Variety*, September 10, 1952, pp. 1, 61.

"Jockeys on a Rough Ride." *Newsweek*, December 7, 1959, p. 98.

"Jockeys Ride Herd on Disk-Buyers." *Variety*, May 19, 1948, p. 1.

"Jocks Junk Payola Platters." *Variety*, February 16, 1955, p. 39.

"Jocks on Pops, Payola, Polls." *Variety*, August 14, 1957, p. 45.

"Joe Isgro." *Rolling Stone*, April 24, 1986, pp. 21, 64.

Johnson, Rudy. "Innis Says U.S. Fosters Monopoly in Record Industry." *New York Times*, August 15, 1973, p. 75.

Kafafian, Eddie. "L.A.'s Johnny-Come-What-May DJs Now Getting In on Lost Loot." *Variety*, March 16, 1960, pp. 55, 60.

Kalish, Eddie. "That Payola in the Window." *Variety*, September 26, 1962, pp. 47, 51.

"Keith Office Will Shut Off Song Pluggers' Applauding." *Variety*, December 2, 1921, p. 4.

Kopkind, Andrew. "Payola: As American as Pizza Pie." *Ramparts*, February 1974, pp. 45–48.

"KYW Song Rule No Hit with Pluggers." *Variety*, April 20, 1938, p. 39.

"L.A. Grand Jury Hands Up Payola Indictments." *Rolling Stone*, April 7, 1988, p. 19.

"L.A. Worst Payola Town in the U.S." *Variety*, August 3, 1960, pp. 1, 62.

"Labor MP Sees Payola Rearing Ugly Schnozzola." *Billboard*, December 7, 1959, pp. 3, 10.

"Lame, Halt and Blind." *Billboard*, November 30, 1959, p. 2.

Landry, Tom. "The Song Pluggers' Microphone." *Variety*, December 31, 1930, p. 48.

"Leader, Quizzed on Bribery Rumor, Claims MPPA's Code Has Put Him $1,900 in Red." *Variety*, December 9, 1936, p. 41.

"Leaders Dodging Pluggers." *Variety*, December 31, 1930, p. 49.

"Leaders Taking Song Cuts." *Variety*, December 17, 1930, p. 58.

Ledbetter, Les. "5 Stations Called in Payola Inquiry." *New York Times*, July 18, 1973, p. 40.

Lees, Gene. "Bad Days at the Black Rock." *High Fidelity*, September 1973, pp. 70–73.

"Legit Kind of Payola." *Variety*, July 23, 1958, pp. 1, 52.

Lewis, Anthony. "Clark Is Accused of Giving Payola." *New York Times*, April 27, 1960, pp. 1, 41.

―――. "Dick Clark Denies Receiving Payola." *New York Times*, April 30, 1960, pp. 1, 47.

―――. "Dick Clark Got $7,150 for Plug." *New York Times*, May 3, 1960, pp. 1, 78.

―――. "House Unit Plans Payola Remedies." *New York Times*, May 4, 1960, p. 34.

―――. "Inquiry Is Told of Clark Profit." *New York Times*, April 28, 1960, p. 28.

"Liability to Asset." *New York Times*, April 12, 1960, p. 46.

Lichtenstein, Grace. "C.B.S. Limits Help in a Payola Study." *New York Times*, July 14, 1973, p. 55.

―――. "CBS News Tells of Payola on Records." *New York Times*, August 10, 1974, p. 59.

―――. "Columbia Payola Put at $250,000." *New York Times*, June 6, 1973, pp. 1, 51.

―――. "Figure in Heroin Case Said to Talk to Payola." *New York Times*, June 13, 1973, p. 74.

―――. "I.R.S. Joins Investigations into Recording Concerns." *New York Times*, July 13, 1973, pp. 1, 71.

_____. "Mob-Linked Conduits Get Subpoenas in Payola Case." *New York Times,* June 8, 1973, p. 24.

_____. "Organized Crime Linked to Payola." *New York Times,* June 7, 1973, pp. 1, 28.

_____. "Payola Inquiry Turns to Travel." *New York Times,* July 26, 1973, p. 43.

_____. "Payola Jury Asks Testimony on Tips." *New York Times,* June 20, 1973, p. 27.

_____. "Pop Music Inquiry Broadened by U.S." *New York Times,* June 22, 1973, pp. 1, 47.

_____. "Pop-Music Scandal Laid to Pursuit of Fast Money." *New York Times,* June 11, 1973, p. 71.

_____. "Record Industry on Coast Shaken by Payola Studies." *New York Times,* July 22, 1973, p. 40.

_____. "Talk of Payola Influenced Metromedia." *New York Times,* June 15, 1973, p. 31.

_____. "U.S. Details Payola Plot of $406,737." *New York Times,* August 22, 1973, p. 39.

"Life for British Plug Bribe Artists' Heave-O; Pubs Nixed 2 Yrs." *Variety,* April 7, 1948, p. 43.

"Lifting Curb on Payolas Generally Agreed as Likely to Hypo Problems." *Variety,* October 17, 1945, p. 42.

Lindsey, Robert. "Payola Threatens Recording Profits." *New York Times,* July 23, 1975, p. 20.

_____. "Payola's Return to Records Reported." *New York Times,* March 6, 1985, p. A14.

"Line of Action to Be Determined by M.P.P.A. on Harmful Practices." *Variety,* February 18, 1931, p. 69.

Lombardo, Guy. *Auld Acquaintance.* Garden City, N.Y.: Doubleday, 1975.

"London Admits Payola Practices but Says So What." *Variety,* January 20, 1960, pp. 61, 67.

"A Lot of Loot." *Down Beat,* April 14, 1960, p. 11.

"Low-Paid Ethnic DJ's Most Prone to Payola." *Variety,* March 3, 1971, pp. 1, 70.

Mabley, Jack. "In Music DJs Still (D)rule Air Waves." *Down Beat,* August 25, 1954, p. 2.

McKenzie, Ed. "A Deejay's Exposé—and Views." *Life,* November 1959, pp. 47–48.

"Maestro-Publishers No Menace." *Variety,* March 31, 1937, p. 53.

"Maestros No-Like Anti-Bribery Pledge." *Variety,* September 23, 1936, p. 45.

"Major Pub Up on Payola Charge." *Variety,* May 5, 1948, p. 51.

"Major Publisher Plans to Crack Payola Evil by Open Plug-Buying." *Variety,* October 24, 1945, p. 47.

"Makes Pugs for Plugs." *Variety,* November 19, 1930, p. 57.

"Mammarella's Secret Success Saga." *Variety,* May 4, 1960, pp. 45, 62.

Marks, Edward B. *They All Sang.* New York: Viking, 1935.

"Martin Block Parlays a $20 a Week Idea into a New Radio Pattern." *Variety,* February 6, 1950, p. 33.

"Melody Songs Passing—Lyrics Now." *Variety,* February 3, 1922, pp. 1, 7.

"'Mill Stream' Appeal Decision Seen as Setback to 'Cut-In' Songsmiths." *Variety,* February 28, 1945, p. 36.

Millard, Bob. "Country Promo in Flux; Labels Shifting Tactics." *Variety,* March 12, 1986, pp. 1, 155.

"Mr. Typical Spinner's Man of Many Talents, Interests." *Billboard*, November 12, 1955, p. 61.

"More Complaints on Payola Slated." *New York Times*, December 30, 1959, p. 45.

"More Names Key Headline Hassles." *Billboard*, December 14, 1959, pp. 2, 138.

Morris, Edward. "Country Indies Plot Strategy." *Billboard*, March 29, 1986, pp. 1, 75.

"MPCE Lists Lopez Unfair on Crack-Down on Payola." *Billboard*, January 14, 1950, p. 21.

"MPCE to Set Up Secret Trial Bd. to Halt Payolas." *Variety*, November 2, 1949, p. 43.

"MPPA Acting on CBS' Squawk." *Variety*, November 25, 1936, p. 47.

"MPPA Committee Defers Meeting with FTC Till McKee Studies Govt's Code." *Variety*, November 18, 1936, p. 53.

"M.P.P.A. Cuts Penalty as Means to Enforce No Act-Paying Edict." *Variety*, June 11, 1930, p. 57.

"M.P.P.A. Executive Invites Robbins-Engel, Inc., to Resign." *Variety*, March 2, 1927, pp. 45, 48.

"M.P.P.A. Junk Didn't Stop Independent Becoming Foremost Music Publisher." *Variety*, February 16, 1927, p. 49.

"MPPA Ok's Plan to End Plug Bribery." *Variety*, May 5, 1943, p. 43.

"MPPA Pact Asks for Squealers." *Variety*, June 19, 1934, p. 62.

"MPPA Sleuths Find Little Bribery." *Variety*, October 7, 1936, p. 45.

"MPPA's Anti-Bribery Code Pledged by Pubs." *Variety*, September 2, 1936, p. 42.

Mulligan, Thomas S. "Isgro Still Under Appeal." *Los Angeles Times*, September 14, 1991, p. D2.

"Music Biz Goes Round and Round." *Life*, May 16, 1960, pp. 118–20, 122.

"Music Biz Probe Spinning Around All Diskery Cut-Ins and Kickbacks." *Variety*, November 25, 1959, pp. 1, 58.

"Music Code's Anti-Bribery Song Plugging Subsidies Out." *Variety*, July 25, 1933, p. 45.

"Music Directors Testify on Payola." *New York Times*, February 14, 1976, p. 53.

"The Music Goes Round." *New York Times*, January 19, 1936, sec. 9, p. 4.

"Music Men." *Variety*, December 3, 1920, p. 14.

"Music Men Desperate." *Variety*, February 18, 1931, pp. 69, 74.

"Music Men Meet." *Variety*, May 18, 1917, p. 3.

"Music Publishers' Combine Working Out Satisfactorily." *Variety*, July 24, 1914, p. 6.

"Music Publishers Expect Prosperous New Season." *Variety*, October 6, 1916, p. 7.

"Music Publishers May Get Together for Protection." *Variety*, October 6, 1916, p. 3.

"Music Publishers Meeting." *Variety*, August 24, 1917, p. 3.

"Music Publishers' Meeting for Protective Purposes." *Variety*, June 19, 1914, p. 6.

"Music Publishing Combine Proposed by Wall Street." *Variety*, November 28, 1913, p. 1.

"Music Pubs Mull Pressure on MPCE to Remove Plug Restrictions." *Variety*, August 15, 1945, p. 35.

"Music Trade Rules Ready." *New York Times*, December 16, 1937, p. 42.

"Musicaster, Not Disk Jockey." *New York Times*, March 24, 1960, p. 17.

"Name Plug Royalty Out." *Variety*, April 24, 1934, p. 47.

"NBC Bars Out All Pluggers." *Variety*, March 13, 1946, p. 49.

"N.B.C. Bars Rebate." *New York Times*, December 5, 1959, p. 47.

"NBC Limiting Music Plugs to 2 Nightly." *Variety*, April 1, 1931, p. 59.
"NBC Scores Time on Quiz Scandal." *New York Times*, November 23, 1959, p. 34.
"New Blow at Plugs and Freebies." *Broadcasting*, March 21, 1960, pp. 55–56.
"New Payola Beefs to Be Aired at MCPE Meet." *Variety*, September 18, 1946, p. 42.
"New Payola Charges." *New York Times*, April 4, 1960, p. 59.
"The News of Radio." *New York Times*, October 13, 1947, p. 46.
"News of the Music Men." *Variety*, May 6, 1921, p. 4.
"No Complaints on Cut-Ins, ASCAP Is Asking for All Data to Make a Case." *Variety*, June 2, 1931, p. 57.
"No New Payola Evidence, Says Committee." *Billboard*, March 15, 1986, p. 3.
"No Payola in RCA's Future." *Broadcasting*, December 21, 1959, p. 46.
"The No-Payola Sound of Music." *Variety*, December 2, 1959, pp. 1, 64.
"No Publishers' Cut-In Worry on Coast." *Variety*, March 4, 1931, p. 64.
"No Song Plug Pay." *Variety*, January 27, 1922, p. 7.
Noonan, John T., Jr. *Bribes*. New York: Macmillan, 1984.
"Norfolk Story, Second Version." *Broadcasting*, May 2, 1977, pp. 60, 62.
"Notes on People." *New York Times*, December 18, 1976, p. 19.
"NRA's Paid Plug Joker." *Variety*, November 27, 1934, p. 45.
"N.Y. Hotel Wants to Bar Song Pluggers and Doesn't Mince Words." *Variety*, January 9, 1934, p. 37.
"N.Y. Pop Outlets' Files Subpoenaed in Payola Probe." *Broadcasting*, July 23, 1973, p. 36.
"Obnoxious Music Pluggers." *Variety*, April 28, 1922, p. 10.
"Outlawing of Payola Urged." *New York Times*, March 16, 1960, p. 75.
"Paine, for Publishers, Asks Gov't to Intervene Against Paid Plugs." *Variety*, September 11, 1935, p. 49.
"Paine Hands Publishers Written Spanking." *Variety*, July 24, 1935, p. 47.
"Paine Promises Self-Cleansing." *Variety*, July 29, 1936, p. 39.
"Paying Music Publishers Threaten Legal Action." *Variety*, May 26, 1915, p. 5.
"Paying the Pluggers." *Variety*, January 4, 1928, p. 29.
"Payments for Singing Songs to Be Stopped by Publishers." *Variety*, April 27, 1917, p. 3.
Payne, Jack. "Jack Payne on Song Plugging." *Melody Maker*, July 17, 1954, p. 3.
"Pay-offs Disclosed." *New York Times*, November 22, 1959, p. 62.
"Payola." *Down Beat*, December 24, 1959, pp. 13–15.
"Payola Aftermath." *Down Beat*, June 23, 1960, pp. 12–13.
"Payola Again Hits Disk Biz." *Variety*, February 21, 1962, p. 47.
"Payola — An Inside Story Told Four Years Ago." *U.S. News and World Report*, December 21, 1959, pp. 81–82.
"Payola Beef Breaks Out Anew on Coast, Plugger Investigation." *Variety*, May 22, 1946, p. 51.
"Payola Bill Compromise Coming." *Broadcasting*, August 15, 1960, pp. 80–81.
"Payola Blues." *Newsweek*, November 30, 1959, p. 94.
"Payola Case Dropped." *New York Times*, February 10, 1962, p. 19.
"Payola Case Sent Back for Retrial." *Broadcasting*, August 29, 1977, pp. 42–43.
"Payola Cases Dropped." *New York Times*, September 1, 1961, p. 11.
"Payola Charge Backfires on Small Label's Chief." *Broadcasting*, July 29, 1974, p. 34.
"Payola Charged by L.A. Promoter." *Broadcasting*, April 27, 1964, pp. 73–74.
"Payola Charges Vs. British Jockeys Snarled in Parliamentary Debate." *Variety*, December 2, 1959, pp. 55, 68.

"Payola Detectives Due." *New York Times*, December 9, 1959, p. 54.

"Payola Diary Kicks Back." *Variety*, October 18, 1944, p. 39.

"Payola Dragnet Yields Eight." *Broadcasting*, May 23, 1960, pp. 80–81.

"Payola Finger Pointing at Lesser D.J.'s Cues Public Suspicion of Honest Plugs." *Variety*, July 18, 1951, pp. 41, 44.

"Payola Growing Faster Than Jack's Beanstalk." *Billboard*, October 6, 1958, pp. 2, 14.

"Payola Is Fair." *Broadcasting*, February 22, 1960, p. 44.

"Payola Is Still with Us." *Instrumentalist*, September 1966, p. 43.

"Payola Issue Cooks Along Outside FCC." *Broadcasting*, April 11, 1977, pp. 45–46.

"Payola? It Can't Happen Here on WNEW, Say DJs." *Variety*, November 18, 1959, pp. 60, 66.

"Payola May Be Hot in U.S., but It's Dead in U.K." *Variety*, February 28, 1962, p. 51.

"Payola – Over 5 Years Earlier." *Variety*, December 9, 1959, pp. 53–54.

"Payola Popularized Bad Songs." *Variety*, January 20, 1960, p. 66.

"Payola Pot Boils Merrily in Chi." *Billboard*, January 11, 1960, pp. 2, 53.

"Payola Probe: No Letup Now but Prosecution Lowers Profile." *Broadcasting*, June 18, 1973, p. 77.

"Payola Probe Continues." *Broadcasting*, July 9, 1973, pp. 39–40.

"Payola Probers in Philly." *Variety*, February 10, 1960, pp. 55–56.

"Payola Probers Plot Hush Hush Hearings." *Billboard*, May 28, 1966, pp. 1, 66.

"Payola Problem to Peatman." *Variety*, December 5, 1945, pp. 39, 44.

"Payola Rap Gets Tripp $500 Fine, Suspend Jailing." *Variety*, October 18, 1961, p. 49.

"Payola Rears Head Again." *Variety*, October 26, 1960, p. 59.

"Payola Rears Its Ugly Head Again in London Town." *Variety*, November 29, 1944, p. 38.

"Payola Rock." *Time*, June 18, 1973, pp. 80–81.

"Payola Rocks Philly Jocks." *Variety*, November 25, 1959, pp. 55–56.

"Payola Scandals – An Aid to Good Music." *Instrumentalist*, February 1960, p. 81.

"Payola Situation (Here It Goes Again) Endangers Their Jobs; Pluggers Cry." *Variety*, October 26, 1949, p. 54.

"Payola Steamroller Detoured." *Broadcasting*, July 4, 1960, pp. 58–61.

"Payola Study on Coast." *Billboard*, July 6, 1968, p. 3.

"Payola: The Record Label Connection." *Rolling Stone*, April 21, 1988, pp. 15, 114.

"Payola Traced to 16 Cities in Indictments of R and B Labels." *Broadcasting*, June 30, 1975, pp. 27–29.

"Payola Widespread, Wide Open." *Variety*, July 21, 1954, pp. 35, 41.

"Payola's Roots: Usage of 1960's." *New York Times*, March 6, 1985, p. A14.

"Payolateers Arrested." *Down Beat*, June 23, 1960, p. 11.

Penn, Stanley W. "Payola's Impact." *Wall Street Journal*, January 6, 1960, pp. 1, 15.

"Philly Wide-Open Town for Disk Jockeys Among Indie Labels." *Variety*, November 5, 1952, p. 37.

Pitman, Jack. "The Chicago Payola Story." *Variety*, January 13, 1960, pp. 43, 48.

"Plan Plug Bribery Cure." *Variety*, April 21, 1943, p. 43.

"Play from the Pubs." *Variety*, May 13, 1931, p. 92.

"Play It Again, Sam, but You'll Have to Tell the FCC Why." *Broadcasting*, February 14, 1977, pp. 48, 55.

"Plug Pay Killed Brit. Pubs Beef Bands Sluff Pops." *Variety*, June 16, 1948, p. 42.

"Plug Paying Evil Sticking." *Variety*, May 21, 1930, p. 57.

"Plug Payolas Perplexed." *Variety*, October 19, 1938, p. 41.

"Plug Seen in Vitaphone's Canning." *Variety*, November 3, 1926, p. 51.

"Pluggers' Bribery of Dance Bands Again Reported on Increase as New Groups Hit Manhattan Spots." *Variety*, May 19, 1937, p. 47.

"Pluggers Call Kenny for Plug Infractions." *Variety*, August 18, 1943, p. 39.

"Pluggers Choose Trial Board to Prosecute Payola Evil." *Billboard*, November 5, 1949, p. 18.

"Pluggers Drop Nix Vs. Pelham Heath." *Variety*, November 12, 1947, p. 45.

"Pluggers Forming Own Organization to Suppress Bribery." *Variety*, August 25, 1937, p. 45.

"Pluggers Must Alibi Missing Ether Plugs." *Variety*, November 19, 1930, p. 57.

"Pluggers' Proxy Warns Bribery Rife Again." *Variety*, December 1, 1943, p. 37.

"Pluggers, Pubs in Closer Tie to Erase Payolas." *Variety*, December 21, 1949, p. 33.

"Pluggers Table Plans to Control Payola Racket." *Variety*, April 9, 1947, p. 42.

"Pluggers Turn Guns on Jock Bally Gentry." *Billboard*, November 26, 1949, p. 16.

"Pluggers Union Weighs 3 Gripes on Payola." *Variety*, March 5, 1947, p. 45.

"Pluggers Wanna Ask Nick Kenny Why He Violated Trade Agreement." *Variety*, April 10, 1946, p. 54.

"Plugging 'Sweet Adair.'" *Variety*, January 21, 1916, p. 4.

"Plugless Payola." *Variety*, June 7, 1944, p. 35.

"Popular Sheet Music Price Going Up If 10¢ Stores Raise." *Variety*, January 19, 1917, p. 5.

"Popular Song Publishing." *Variety*, December 28, 1917, p. 8.

"P.R. Pop Cleffers Say Payola Boosts Rock and Salsa." *Variety*, September 22, 1976, p. 64.

"Precarious Music Publishing May Be Followed by Reforms." *Variety*, January 9, 1914, p. 7.

"Press Inquiry into British Payola." *Variety*, December 16, 1959, p. 45.

"Published Songs." *Variety*, December 20, 1912, p. 32.

"Publishers Annoyed by New Racket." *Billboard*, November 25, 1950, p. 16.

"Publishers Ask Paine to Modify Bribery Pact." *Variety*, February 27, 1935, p. 53.

"Publishers' Double-X Routine Keeps British Air Plug Evil Alive." *Variety*, May 22, 1935, p. 46.

"Publishers to Meet Over Chiseling." *Variety*, February 11, 1931, p. 73.

"Pubs Invited to Pluggers Payola Meet Not Subject of Finger-Pointing." *Variety*, November 30, 1949, p. 39.

"Pubs on Carpet as Contact Men's Union Launches Drive Vs. Payola." *Variety*, February 9, 1944, p. 44.

"Pubs Recognize Effect of Disk Jocks' Hold on Public." *Variety*, April 10, 1946, p. 54.

"Pubs Reverting to Stage Acts for Song Plugging." *Variety*, September 17, 1930, p. 64.

"Pubs Say Payola System Snafued by Peatman Intro." *Variety*, January 16, 1946, p. 47.

"Pubs Still Waiting for Payola Probe Results." *Variety*, July 18, 1945, p. 51.

"Put Up or Shut Up." *Billboard*, August 12, 1972, p. 6.

"Rackets Infest Music Industry, Says Nat Cole." *Variety*, March 25, 1959, p. 57.

"Radio." *Newsweek*, January 11, 1936, pp. 42–43.

"Radio Gives Plugs—Yes, and Takes Coin—Plenty." *Variety*, November 10, 1931, p. 61.

"Radio-Music's Get-Together on Bribes." *Variety*, August 21, 1934, p. 39.

"Radio Orchestra Leaders Now Going for Cut-Ins." *Variety*, March 14, 1928, p. 56.

"Radio Song Plugging Now via Adv. Men." *Variety*, August 6, 1930, p. 66.

"Radio Station Aide Indicted in Newark." *New York Times*, July 23, 1976, p. D13.

"Radio-TV Inquiry Calls 2 U.S. Aides." *New York Times*, February 21, 1960, p. 68.

Randle, Bill. "100 Deejays Control Music Biz." *Variety*, October 1, 1952, pp. 73, 92.

"Record Maker Describes Payoff." *Life*, November 23, 1959, p. 48.

"Record Plugs on Sale." *New York Times*, February 27, 1960, p. 39.

"Refused Payola, Disk Jockey Says." *New York Times*, April 29, 1961, p. 47.

ReMine, Shields. "Payola." *American Mercury*, March 1960, pp. 38–39.

"Rep. Harris Wants Answers on Link of Payola and Radio's 'Juke' Sound." *Variety*, April 13, 1960, p. 47.

"Resolution Is Aimed at Evil." *Variety*, April 1, 1931, p. 59.

Responsibilities of Broadcast Licensees and Station Personnel. Washington, D.C.: U.S. Government Printing Office, 1960, 2 parts.

"Revenooers Move In on the Payola." *Variety*, June 26, 1957, pp. 1, 18.

"The Richest Guys in Radio." *Variety*, December 29, 1954, p. 21.

Richman, Harry. *A Hell of a Life*. New York: Duell, Sloan and Pearce, 1966.

Rohter, Larry. "At Payola Trial." *New York Times*, August 25, 1990, p. 12.

_____. "Payola Case Dismissed; Judge Faults Prosecutors." *New York Times*, September 5, 1990, p. B3.

_____. "Payola Prosecutor Faulted." *New York Times*, August 31, 1990, p. B4.

_____. "Payola Trial Opens for a Top Record Promoter of the 80's." *New York Times*, August 21, 1990, pp. B1, B10.

"Role of Disk Jockey as the Middle Man." *Variety*, February 8, 1950, p. 34.

Rolontz, Bob. "Promot'n Men Back in Saddle as Payola Tide Ebbs." *Billboard*, August 8, 1960, pp. 1, 33.

Rosen, George. "Is FCC Barking Up Wrong Tree?" *Variety*, December 2, 1964, pp. 1, 36.

Rosenbluth, Jean. "Tashjian Pleads Guilty to Payola Charge." *Variety*, May 31, 1989, p. 67.

Roth, Jack. "Alan Freed and 7 Others Arrested in Payola Here." *New York Times*, May 20, 1960, pp. 1, 62.

_____. "First Payola Trial Starts Here with Testimony on Disk Jockey." *New York Times*, April 18, 1961, p. 45.

_____. "Payola Inquiry by Hogan to End." *New York Times*, April 5, 1960, p. 27.

_____. "Tripp Fined $500 in Payola Case." *New York Times*, October 17, 1961, p. 27.

_____. "Tripp Guilty of Taking Payola While Radio Disk Jockey Here." *New York Times*, May 16, 1961, p. 44.

"Round Two: Boston Payola Party." *Broadcasting*, February 22, 1960, pp. 40–42.

"Royal Warning NBC Employees and Outside Music Men on Logrolling." *Variety*, March 2, 1938, p. 49.

Safire, William. "The Drugola Scandal." *New York Times*, June 21, 1972, p. 41.

Santly, Joe. "Life and Plugs of a Music Man." *Variety*, October 20, 1954, p. 59.

"SBC Officials Tell FCC Hearing WOL Personalities Had Clean Hands." *Broadcasting*, May 23, 1977, pp. 49–50.

Schipper, Henry. "CBS PolyGram, A and M Halt Use of Indie Promoters." *Variety*, March 12, 1986, p. 151.

_____. "D.C. Investigator on Coast Probing Music, Mob Links." *Variety*, June 18, 1986, pp. 81, 84.

_____. "NBC's New Payola Statements Draw Isgro Retraction Demand." *Variety*, April 9, 1986, p. 115.

_____. "Payola Probe Shakes Disk Biz." *Variety*, March 2, 1988, pp. 97–98.

Schoenfeld, Herm. "Climactic Year for Music Biz." *Variety*, January 6, 1960, pp. 207, 210.

_____. "Deejay: Performer or Puppet?" *Variety*, March 12, 1958, pp. 1, 60.

_____. "Grand Jury Music Biz Probe Continuing as 19 Individuals, 6 Firms Get U.S. Indictments." *Variety*, July 2, 1975, pp. 59–60.

_____. "Music Biz's Classy Comeback." *Variety*, March 16, 1960, pp. 1, 78.

_____. "Payola Follies of 1966." *Variety*, July 27, 1966, p. 89.

_____. "R 'n' R and Payola Still with the Music Biz." *Variety*, January 4, 1961, p. 207.

_____. "Today's Disk Payola New Chapter in Long History of Music Biz Corruption." *Variety*, June 13, 1973, pp. 1, 63.

Schumach, Murray. "Payola Indictments Name 19, Including 3 Company Heads." *New York Times*, June 25, 1975, pp. 1, 40.

"Scotland Yard Probe of BBC Disk Jockeys." *Variety*, April 7, 1971, p. 2.

"Search Is On for Payola in Air Play of Records." *Broadcasting*, June 11, 1973, p. 32.

"See Distribs as Payola Key." *Variety*, December 9, 1959, pp. 53, 58.

"Sees Outmoded Compulsory License in 1909 Act Root of Music Biz Evil." *Variety*, February 15, 1956, p. 43.

"Senate Okays Revised Payola Bill." *Broadcasting*, August 29, 1960, pp. 60, 62.

"Senate Probe of Payola Launched." *Variety*, April 9, 1986, p. 113.

"Shakeup Reaches Chicago." *Down Beat*, February 4, 1960, pp. 9–10.

Shanahan, Eileen. "New F.C.C. Inquiry on Payola Is Set." *New York Times*, November 28, 1964, pp. 1, 19.

Shanley, J. P. "Men Who Pick Disks for Radio Listeners." *New York Times*, May 1, 1955, sec. 2, p. 11.

Shaw, Arnold. *Sinatra*. New York: Pocket Books, 1969.

Shepard, Richard E. "Alan Freed Is Out in Payola Study." *New York Times*, November 22, 1959, pp. 1, 62.

_____. "F.C.C. Chairman Tells TV It Faces Tighter Controls." *New York Times*, November 21, 1959, pp. 1, 48.

_____. "Radio-TV Confused by Order to Identify Donors of Records." *New York Times*, March 24, 1960, p. 26.

Shiver, Jube. "Central Figure in Payola Case Breaks Silence." *Los Angeles Times*, December 14, 1990, p. D2.

_____. "Judge Abruptly Ends Payola Case Against 3." *Los Angeles Times*, September 5, 1990, pp. A1, A16.

_____. "Key Figure in Payola Case Again Promoting Records." *Los Angeles Times*, August 29, 1990, p. D2.

_____. "Payola Trial a Textbook Case in Bungling." *Los Angeles Times*, September 7, 1990, pp. D1, D11.

"Should D.J.s Take It on the Side?" *Down Beat*, March 3, 1960, p. 11.

Simon, Bill. "Jocks Not Playing Disks They Prefer." *Billboard*, November 11, 1957, p. 38.

"Singers of Song." *Variety*, September 11, 1914, p. 38.

"Singers Tied Up to Single Music Publishers Barred from WEAK or WJZ." *Variety*, August 31, 1927, p. 6.

"Singers Want Publishers to Stop Plugging." *Variety*, July 3, 1914, p. 6.

"16 Det. Jocks Continue No-Spin Policy on 4 Labels Because of Payola, Tie-ins." *Variety*, February 23, 1955, pp. 41, 46.

Sklar, Rick. *Rocking America*. New York: St. Martin's, 1984.

"So You Think You Got Trouble." *Variety*, June 24, 1936, p. 63.

Sobel, Bernard. "Pre-Electronic Plugging: Booze-ville to Vaudeville." *Variety*, January 9, 1957, p. 242.

"Sonderling Hits Payola Rap on Black Deejays." *Variety*, May 10, 1972, p. 69.

"Sonderling on Stand in Payola Hearing." *Broadcasting*, February 28, 1977, p. 24.

"Song Hit via Records." *Variety*, April 4, 1919, p. 3.

"Song Pluggers Nixed by NBC." *Variety*, September 11, 1935, p. 49.

"Song Pluggers Now Must Write In for Appointments with NBC Air Acts." *Variety*, July 18, 1933, p. 64.

"Song Pluggers Restricted by New Closed Mouth BBC Policy on Tunes." *Variety*, June 4, 1977, p. 42.

"Song Pluggers Revolt but Want It Kept Secret." *Variety*, December 3, 1930, pp. 65, 67.

"Song Pluggers to Be Barred Back Stage." *Variety*, April 30, 1920, p. 4.

"Song Pluggers Unionize; Bribery Their Problem." *New York Times*, May 5, 1940, p. 12.

"Song Plugging." *News-Sheet of the Bribery and Secret Commissions and Prevention League*, August/September, 1936, p. 57.

"Song Plugging Agents May Be Complained Of." *Variety*, December 3, 1915, p. 5.

"Song Writers' Union Started." *Variety*, November 12, 1920, pp. 5, 7.

"Songpluggers No Vanishing Race." *Variety*, October 19, 1955, p. 44.

Songplugging and the Airwaves. Washington, D.C.: Committee on Interstate and Foreign Commerce, 1960.

"Songs of Sixpence." *Newsweek*, April 1, 1957, p. 104.

"Songs with Largest Radio Audience." *Variety*, October 29, 1947, p. 47.

"Special Arrangement Slip." *Variety*, December 3, 1930, p. 67.

"The Specter of Payola '73." *Newsweek*, June 11, 1973, pp. 74, 79.

"Spivak, Kaye Pub Deals at BMI Set New Basic Pattern." *Variety*, February 14, 1945, p. 43.

"Station Primer for Deejays Warns Against Payolas, Cuffolas and Gimmicks." *Variety*, September 3, 1952, pp. 1, 55.

"Stations Cautioned on Possible Payola." *Broadcasting*, November 27, 1967, pp. 62–63.

Stetson, Damon. "Study Questions Effects of Radio." *New York Times*, February 21, 1960, p. 70.

Stokes, Geoffrey. *Star-Making Machinery: The Odyssey of an Album*. Indianapolis: Bobbs-Merrill, 1976.

Suber, Charles. "The First Chorus." *Down Beat*, March 17, 1960, p. 4.

"Suggest Deletion of Payola Rules, But CMU Sez Nix." *Variety*, May 10, 1944, p. 27.

Sweeney, Louise. "Broadcasting Payola Sparks FCC Hearings." *Christian Science Monitor*, March 1, 1977, pp. 1, 6.

"Sworn Report Required of All Stations." *Billboard*, December 7, 1959, pp. 3, 10.

"Taking the Pulse on Payola." *Broadcasting*, December 11, 1989, pp. 38–40.

"Tax Court Rules Payola Is Not Deductible Expense." *New York Times*, January 25, 1967, p. 87.

"Teen-Agers' Dreamboat." *New York Times*, March 5, 1960, p. 40.

"10 More Concerns Accused of Payola." *New York Times*, March 7, 1960, p. 14.

Terry, Ken. "MCA Denies It Let Promo Rep Go Because of Pressure from Indie." *Variety*, April 9, 1986, p. 113.

"Testimony Ended in Disk Jockey Suit." *New York Times*, May 3, 1961, p. 75.

"36 Disk Jockeys Dance to Rock-the-Role in Philly Payola Follies." *Variety*, June 8, 1960, pp. 2, 51.

"3-Man FCC Team Probing Possible L.A. Air Payola." *Billboard*, July 23, 1977, p. 3.

"3 Payola Complaints Dropped." *New York Times*, April 14, 1961, p. 18.

"3 Suns 'Sing' on Bribes." *Variety*, April 14, 1943, p. 45.

Tiegel, Eliot. "FCC Trio Steps Up Probe with Afterhours Grilling." *Billboard*, July 9, 1966, pp. 1, 10.

_____. "Payola Probe Spins to DJs." *Billboard*, July 16, 1966, pp. 1, 7.

"T-Men Quizzing D-J's on Extra-Curricular Income." *Billboard*, March 17, 1956, p. 18.

"To Orchestra Leaders, Vocalists and All Other Users of Music." *Variety*, September 2, 1936, p. 43.

"Top Deejay Credits Jock Clan with Saving Sinking Music Biz 15 Yrs. Ago." *Variety*, August 29, 1951, p. 43.

"Top 40 Puts Payola in Spin." *Variety*, December 10, 1958, pp. 57, 62.

"Top Record Talent and Tunes." *Variety*, October 29, 1947, p. 42.

"Top Tunes and Recording Artists." *Variety*, September 17, 1947, p. 46.

"A Tough New Ruling." *Down Beat*, April 28, 1960, p. 15.

"Trade Commish Eyes Plugs." *Variety*, July 1, 1936, p. 37.

"Trade Group of Record Industry Endorses Payola Investigation." *New York Times*, July 24, 1973, p. 70.

"Transcript of Eisenhower's News Conference." *New York Times*, February 12, 1960, p. 14.

Treen, Joe. "Payola: Nothin' from Nothin' Is Nothin'." *Rolling Stone*, October 24, 1976, pp. 10, 26.

"Trials and Opportunities." *Billboard*, December 7, 1959, p. 3.

Trussell, C. P. "House Passes Payola Measure with Senate's Lighter Penalties." *New York Times*, August 31, 1960, p. 19.

"Truth and Consequences." *Rolling Stone*, April 24, 1986, pp. 22, 64.

Turner, Richard. "Outrageous Government Misconduct Is Cited as Judge Dismisses Payola Case." *Wall Street Journal*, September 5, 1990, p. B7.

"21 DJs, 11 Distributors Enjoined Over Payola." *Down Beat*, November 24, 1960, p. 13.

"Two-Hour Session Before Trade Body." *Variety*, October 6, 1937, p. 46.

"Two Tough Moves Against Payola." *Broadcasting*, December 7, 1959, pp. 35–36, 38.

Tynan, John. "A Clean Fresh Wind." *Down Beat*, January 7, 1960, p. 17.

Ulanov, Barry. *The Incredible Crosby*. New York: McGraw-Hill, 1948.

"Unique Suit on 'Heartaches.'" *Variety*, November 19, 1947, p. 45.

"U.S. Indicts Four in a Payola Case." *New York Times*, February 28, 1988, p. 26.

Vallee, Rudy. *My Time Is Your Time*. New York: Obolensky, 1962.

_____. *Vagabond Dreams Come True*. New York: Grosset and Dunlap, 1930.

"Variety Back to Old Listings?" *Variety*, August 2, 1944, p. 31.

"The Voice and Payola." *Time*, September 9, 1957, p. 76.

"The Wages of Spin." *Time*, December 7, 1959, p. 47.

Walker, Ray. "Veteran Songplugger Recalls Glamour of Early Tin Pan Alley Era." *Variety*, January 2, 1952, pp. 227, 246.

Walsh, Jim. "No Copyright on Payola." *Variety*, January 4, 1961, p. 236.

"Wanted: A Code for Disk Jockeys." *Variety*, March 12, 1947, p. 52.

Weinstein, Henry. "Isgro Claims He's Fall Guy in MCA Probe." *Los Angeles Times*, April 17, 1990, pp. D2, D20.

_____. "U.S. Indicts 3 on Music Payola Fraud Charges." *Los Angeles Times*, December 1, 1989, pp. A1, A37.

Weintraub, Boris. "WOL Deejay Refutes Promoters." *Billboard*, March 19, 1977, pp. 6, 78.

Weston, Paul. "Too Many Records." *Variety*, August 15, 1951, pp. 45-46.

Wexler, Jerry. "Payola Renunciation Draws Cheers, Jeers." *Billboard*, November 26, 1949, pp. 16, 37.

_____. "Pluggers War on Payola." *Billboard*, October 29, 1949, pp. 3, 13, 47.

_____. "Pubbers Put the Payola Finger on Peatman and Himber Sheets." *Billboard*, December 24, 1949, p. 17.

_____. "R and B Jockeys Ride Payola." *Billboard*, January 13, 1951, pp. 1, 13, 40.

"What Makes Howard Spin." *Time*, April 29, 1957, p. 50.

"Whiteman Audition for Song Pluggers Weekly." *Variety*, October 27, 1931, p. 61.

"Who's on the Tape that WAIT Aired About Deejays-on-the-Take?" *Variety*, November 18, 1959, p. 60.

"Widespread Payola Hurting Disk Jockey Shows, Arnold Warns Programmers' Clinic." *Billboard*, February 4, 1950, pp. 4, 47.

"With the Music Men." *Variety*, August 15, 1919, p. 10.

"With the Music Men." *Variety*, March 12, 1920, p. 23.

Witmark, Isidore. *From Ragtime to Swingtime*. New York: Da Capo, 1976.

"WNEW Jocks Answer the Big 'Have You Ever?'" *Billboard*, November 16, 1959, p. 16.

"Worst Payola Towns." *Variety*, August 8, 1951, p. 41.

"WOW Bandleader Offers BMI Plugs on NBC for $10-15 to Cover Cost of 'Arrangements.'" *Variety*, November 12, 1941, p. 45.

"Writer Sues Freddy Martin for 167G on Song Plug Pact." *Variety*, February 28, 1945, p. 39.

Index